Mrs. Shirley Rogachesky
9517 254th Terrace
O'Brien, FL 32071

JESUS, PETER & THE KEYS

JESUS, PETER & THE KEYS

A Scriptural Handbook on the Papacy

Scott Butler
Norman Dahlgren
David Hess

PUBLISHING COMPANY
P.O Box 42028 Santa Barbara, CA 93140-2028
(800) 647-9882 • (805) 957-4893 • Fax: (805) 957-1631

Nihil Obstat

I have concluded that the materials presented in this work are free from doctrinal or moral errors.

Bernadeane Carr, STL
Censor Librorum
September 17, 1996

Imprimatur

In accord with the 1993 CIC 827, permission to publish this work is hereby granted.

+ Robert H. Brom
Bishop of San Diego
September 18, 1996

Library of Congress Number # 96-70129

Published by:
Queenship Publishing
P.O. Box 42028
Santa Barbara, CA 93140-2028
(800) 647-9882 • (805) 957-4893 • Fax: (805) 957-1631

Printed in the United States of America

ISBN: 1-882972-54-6

The Catholic Answer

15 EAST 26 STREET
BAYONNE, NEW JERSEY 07002

Decades ago, T.S. Eliot declared, "In my beginning is my end."

In scholarly, professional and ecumenically sensitive manner, our authors examine the scriptural basis for the Petrine office, that ministry which Pope Paul VI frankly admitted was *the* major stumbling block to the reunion of all Christians. But like the Pontiff, these men also regard it as *the* essential basis for any true unity grounded in the saving plan and will of Christ for His Church.

Like Eliot returning to the sources, they help all – those in full communion with the See of Rome and those who are not — to re-discover the scriptural foundations of the papacy. For this service, they deserve an open hearing – and a grateful one.

Rev. Peter M.J. Stravinskas, Ph.D., S.T.D.
Editor, *The Catholic Answer*

UNISA

Fakulteit Teologie en
Godsdienswetenskap
DEPARTMENT OF CHURCH HISTORY

Faculty of Theology and
Religious Studies

22 October 1996

Ecumenical dialogue calls for continuous re-reading of the common Christian Tradition. Anyone who dares to call him/herself a "catholic" Christian is duty-bound to return again and again to the sources. *Jesus Peter and the Keys* is a significant contribution to this on-going task. The authors call on us to reconsider once again the biblical foundations of the Petrine Ministry exercised by the Bishop of Rome. The wide range of scriptural passages brought forward for examination, together with the collection of patristic texts provided by the authors, makes this work an indispensable tool in the ecumenical dialog on papal primacy. Utilising contemporary Protestant and Orthodox as well as Catholic theological sources, the authors build a case which cannot be ignored. A reunited Christendom is one which by historical and theological necessity includes the Successor of Peter at its centre. The authors have made a significant contribution in showing why this is so.

Father Chrysostom Frank
Orthodox priest, Associate professor and Deputy Head of the Department of Church History, Faculty of Theology, University of South Africa (Pretoria, South Africa)

TABLE OF CONTENTS

FOREWORD

This book is an excellent resource for anyone who wants to explain the Catholic doctrine on St. Peter and the Papacy. The authors' arguments for the Papacy are especially excellent aids for ecumenical dialogue. The most amazing feat of these researchers is the discovery of such a large number of Protestant Scripture scholars whose exegesis of key biblical texts about St. Peter coincides with the Catholic interpretations of the centuries. This collection of a wide array of Protestant and Catholic scholars on the role of St. Peter will open avenues of common dialogue and shared experience in place of past rancor. The Patristic texts also push the conversation forward in a positive way. The book offers the reflections of Catholic, Protestant and Orthodox witnesses to the early Christian texts and their influence on a better understanding of the office of St. Peter and his successors. Reading this book will increase understanding in an area of faith that still divides Christians because it shows the beliefs about St. Peter which are common to these three traditions. May God bring much fruit from it.

Fr. Mitchell Pacwa, S.J.
University of Dallas

INTRODUCTION

Christ our Lord, when he prayed on the last night of his earthly life, asked the heavenly Father to make his disciples one as he and the Father were one (John 17:22). When we contemplate our Lord's humanity so in evidence that night, we can almost feel the pain of his heart, at once human and divine, as he knew that divisions and dissensions would arise within the family of God. Still, he prayed for a unity that would be deep and lasting, a oneness in which all his disciples would share in the trinitarian life.

Jesus was not a wishful thinker. He knew that unity would be hard to achieve, impossible in fact for human beings saddled with sinful tendencies. So, along with his prayer he gave his apostles his peace (John 14:27), that *shalom*, that sense of total well-being that draws men inexorably to something greater than themselves. He established a church which would be his instrument for bringing salvation to the world. And he gave his Church apostles, official delegates who would carry on his work of redemption by doing greater works than he could do (John 14:12). In short, our Lord not only prayed for unity, he provided for it.

How did Jesus provide unity for his Church? Down through the ages, Christians have given a variety of answers to that question. One prominent theologian once suggested that the problem of differing and conflicting visions of the Church is rooted in the New Testament itself. And undoubtedly, the New Testament does not give us a picture of the Church as a monolithic entity. Paul's metaphor of the Church as a body stresses her diversity and multifaceted character. Yet that same image emphasizes the integrated and communal nature of the Church. The Church, though many, is still one.

One of the thorniest problems confronting Christians today is to understand how Jesus provided for that unity and the most difficult aspect of that question is the role that the Bishop of Rome, the Pope, plays in fulfilling Christ's will. In the midst of the many theological arguments and analyses that have been offered down through history, the basic data upon which any clear understanding of the Petrine doctrine must rest has sometimes been obscured. In this volume, the authors have sought to present a wide range of evidence from the Bible and the Church Fathers that supports the traditional and magisterial teaching of the Catholic Church. In-depth exegetical and theological analysis is not to be found here nor have the authors sought to draw many conclusions. The strength of their work is to present the data that must be taken into account by anyone who seeks to be faithful to the Scriptures and the history of Christian theology.

It is important to be clear on what the Petrine doctrine does and does not claim if the nature of Papacy in Catholic theology is to be understood. In my judgment, the Catholic doctrine of the Papacy rests on the Church's understanding of herself and the incarnation of our Lord. The truths of the incarnation give rise to the nature of the Church and these both in turn naturally lead to the Petrine doctrine. The logical sequence of doctrines is: INCARNATION—> CHURCH—> PAPACY. In such a short compass it is impossible to explain even a minor part of any of these doctrines but St. Paul has thankfully given us summary statements in his letters which capsulize these truths. One such summary is Galatians 4:4:

> But when the fullness of time came, God sent forth his Son, having come from a woman, placed under the law that He might redeem those under the law so we could receive the right of adoption.

Here Paul testifies to the unthinkable, the union of the divine and human natures in the Son of God. Though planned from all eternity, the act of taking on human nature required the voluntary co-operation of the second person of the Trinity. The plan of redemption involved an irreversible commitment to join to his eternal nature a human nature that suffered from all the wants, limitations and pain of mankind. The author of Hebrews tells us that Jesus was without sin (Heb 4:15), not to protect his divinity from accusation, but to show how he innocently suffered the effects of sin that were not of his own doing. His suffering encompassed all the sins and sufferings of the world, an act of sacrifice that could only be explained by his being at once fully human and fully divine. That self-sacrifice also grew out of the heart of the shepherd, a prominent theme in the fourth gospel.

St. John stresses that Christ the shepherd laid down his life willingly (10:11) so that he might make the sheep his very own. But Christ as shepherd also teaches his people the truth for he was sent to be the light of the world (1:8; 8:12). As truth-bearer and shepherd, Christ has gained a name to be honored above every name (Phil 2:9-10), a name that excels the angels' honors (Heb 1:4), a position of unparalleled authority (see Rev 2:26, 27; Mat 28:18). As head of the Church he guards his faithful ones against all the powers of darkness arrayed against the Church (Eph 1:20-22; Col 1:17-19). In short, Christ is the Lord of his Church. From these truths it follows that Christ is the infallible God-man. He can no more err than he can cease to be either God or man.

What was true of Christ can be said of Christ's Church. The Church, both human and divine, lives the sacrificial life of Christ in the world to bring the nations redemption. The human side of the Church does not need much elaboration since it is self-evident to any observer. The sins and failings of the members of the Church, both clergy and lay, are all too obvious. The Church has a human dimension, not only because of her sinfulness, but because her humanity is the instrument of redeeming humanity outside the Church. Just as Christ took on a human nature to save the world, the Church has to be human to enter empathetically into the sufferings of humanity. The Church is also divine because the divine Christ indwells the Church with his love and care. The outward body is animated by the inner presence of God, or, as the Church Fathers often said, the Holy Spirit is the soul of the Church. Wherever the Spirit of

God resides, there is a temple of God (cf. I Cor 3:16; 6:19). So the Lord who unites humanity and divinity in his own person continues to unite humanity and divinity in his mystical body.

That same Lord shepherds the Church with his ministry of teaching through his appointed representatives. St. Peter lays out the structure of the Church for the presbyters who are undershepherds of Christ (cf. I Pet 5:1-4), claiming that though there are many human undershepherds, there is only one original shepherd, Christ himself. Because human shepherds carry on Christ's ministry of teaching and care, they are endowed with an appropriate authority, not one derived from the Church but from Christ himself through the Church's ordination. From God's presence in the Church and the divine authority given to her, the Church possesses a primacy of honor in the hearts and minds of the faithful. The faithful are to honor the Church just as they would honor Christ himself. The Church rightfully exercises jurisdiction over the lives of the faithful, not in a dictatorial fashion, but as an expression of Christ's pastoral care. This explains how Paul and other scriptural authors can call for obedience to the appointed leaders of the Church.

If these things are true, then it suggests that the Church possesses an infallibility communicated by Christ the infallible one. The notion of infallibility stems from belief in Christ's divine presence in the Church. It is interesting that nowhere does the New Testament tell us that Christ left us an infallible book, one of the facts that has made many in the more liberal wings of Protestantism give up the notion of infallibility altogether. Those Protestants who affirm biblical infallibility must do so as a theological conclusion (*theolegoumenon*), not as an indubitable teaching of a biblical text. The New Testament, however, does affirm that the Church is "the pillar and foundation of the truth." (I Tim 3:15). The Catholic Church affirms the Bible to be infallible but that is because the Scriptures are the writings of the Church, divinely inspired by the Holy Spirit. Recognizing the New Testament to be the writings of the Church in her apostolic infancy raises the question of what the infallible Christ taught the Church through those writers who transmitted his teaching. Christians have always looked to the four gospels as special windows on our Lord's life and teaching. And

Matthew's gospel holds a preeminent place in that sacred quartet because it treats matters of ecclesiastical structure and authority in a manner that none of the other three do. It comes as no surprise then to find the issue of Petrine primacy arising out of the exegesis of Matthean texts.

Matthew 16:13-19 is one of the most crucial texts that bears on the biblical foundations of the Petrine doctrine and its exegesis shapes both the endorsement and the rejection of the Papacy. Since the Reformation in the sixteenth century, Protestant and Catholic exegetes have largely embraced polemical uses of this text to counter their opponents' claims. Here the authors have shown an increasing willingness on the part of evangelical Protestant scholars to recognize aspects of the traditional Catholic Exegesis, preeminently the recognition of Peter as the Rock on whom Christ founded the Church. They also cull quotations from the Church Fathers which show that the identification of Peter as the Rock was pervasive, if not universal, in the early centuries of Christianity.

They also marshal evidence to show that the power entrusted to Peter was not only a primacy of honor but of jurisdiction, founded on our Lord's words in verse 19 about the keys of the kingdom. This evidence is important because it is sometimes thought that the notion of Roman primacy developed only in later centuries. Certainly, the most explicit articulation of papal primacy was only stated later—for example by Boniface VIII in his famous bull *Unam Sanctam* (1205)—but belief in the primacy of the Roman See was by no means theologically novel, not even in the first few centuries of Christianity. The same can be said of papal infallibility. Even though this doctrine had to await full definition in Vatican I (1869-70), the belief in papal infallibility flowed naturally from belief in the infallibility of the Church. Just as Boniface argued that the uniqueness and sovereignty of Christ had to be expressed through *one* human head of the Church, so the infallibility of Christ had to be communicated to and through his Church, the visible head of which is the Universal Pastor, the Holy Father.

Such reasoning illumines the characteristically Catholic way of thinking about the Church. The Church is not an institution established by divine fiat or an arbitrary decision on the part of Jesus to provide for his dejected followers who would need some human company and comfort. The Church is an inevitable outgrowth and consequence of Christ himself, or—to use the imagery common among the Fathers—the Church was born from the water and blood that flowed from our Lord's side on the cross of Calvary. Since there is only one Christ, there can be only one Church with only one visible human head, says the Petrine doctrine.

Perhaps the greater challenge to Petrine primacy comes not from western Protestantism but from Eastern Orthodoxy, a fact that may underlie Pope John Paul's special burden to reconcile the eastern churches to Rome. Like Protestants, eastern Christians may find some objections to papal primacy based on Scripture but the witness of the Eastern Fathers and the seven ecumenical councils of the ancient Church provide much more of the basis for their objections. Eastern theologians have argued that there can be no doctrinal development of the kind Rome claims because the Church is divided. The doctrinal definitions of the first seven ecumenical councils were done by a united Church which no longer exists according to the Orthodox view. Consequently, the ecumenical councils in the West from the eighth through the twenty-first (Vatican II) have no authority in the Eastern Church. On the other side, the Catholic Church claims that the Church has never been divided although some sees of the East have cut themselves off from the center of unity, the Roman See. When this difference over the nature of unity is examined from many standpoints, it turns out to have profound implications. The question that must be honestly faced remains: is the Church divided or not? And the answer to that question depends on whether unity comes via consensus or by union with one center of unity. In my judgment, most eastern theology operates on a principle of consensus expressed in the Vincentian canon. This rule says that the content of faith is guided by what is believed everywhere, always and by all (*ubique, semper, et ab omnibus*) in the Church. Thus, in eastern Christianity, the ecumenical councils are infallible because they represent the whole Church and also because they were widely accepted by the same Church over a period of time. This method of determining the content of faith also guided the Western Church—Vincent of Lérins was after all a western monk—but the universal acceptance of a dogma was seen as a confirmation of a revealed truth already defined by an authoritative body because it is in communion with Rome. So this difference presents the inevitable question: is communion with the Roman See and its bishop necessary for doctrinal definition and legitimacy? Eastern Orthodoxy and Catholicism hold in common that Scripture and apostolic tradition as expressed in the Church Fathers will be the ground on which an answer will be founded. The authors here have cited many patristic witnesses in favor of the Catholic position.

Readers of this volume may find themselves agreeing with and cheering the authors for their work while others may be dismayed or even angered by what appears to be exclusive claims for the Papacy. But none should be in doubt about what the authors attempt. Theirs is not an attempt to defend the mistakes or sinful behavior of past holders of Peter's chair. Nor is their goal to counter every argument, theological or otherwise, offered in the past against the Papacy. One can think of Martin Luther's characterization of the Papacy as an institution of Satan or of the Puritans' belief that the Beast of the Apocalypse was the Roman Catholic Church. Although the spiritual descendants of these figures rarely embrace those beliefs today, considerable doubts still exist about the biblical legitimacy of that institution. It is those doubts that the authors have sought to dispel, not by extensive argument but by an impressive collection of data and commentary. No matter one's church affiliation, no matter one's theological predilections, no matter one's attitudes toward the Catholic Church, the biblical texts and the patristic witnesses adduced here in support of the Papacy must be honestly faced and explained. The authors' merit lies in placing the data before us in such an unmistakable fashion.

Will these biblical and patristic data for apostolic succession and papal primacy lead to a greater unity among Christians? Will they achieve the oneness for which Jesus prayed on the last night of his earthly life? Whatever the obstacles that remain, we can be sure that true unity will not be achieved without them. The approach to ecumenism that relies on seeking the lowest common denominator among Christian churches is happily dead. The only hope for unity is a return to the biblical and patristic foundations of the Church, a twofold basis that will lead to a renewed sense of the richness of the Christian heritage.

Kenneth J. Howell, Ph.D.
Reformed Theological Seminary (1984-85, 1988-94)
University of Indiana (1994-present)

PREFACE

There exist within the pages of the Bible remarkable passages that support the doctrinal statements of the Catholic Church. In this Scriptural handbook, we have arranged the material for spiritual meditation, fruitful discussion, and apologetic enlightenment. We hope that our readers will think about the questions and answers as we present them, and may pray that the Holy Spirit will illuminate and guide them.

This is not meant to be an exhaustive exegetical or hermeneutical treatment of texts. It is an *apologetical* meditation on the teachings of the Catholic Church, from a biblical perspective. We believe that the essential teachings of the Catholic Church today are also the teachings of Scripture and of the earliest Christians.

Interestingly, we have found that certain Protestant theologians, including Martin Luther and John Calvin, support traditional Catholic beliefs, while some Catholic scholars support the Church's critics. In any case, it is imperative that Catholics know the biblical underpinnings of their faith, and that Protestants and Eastern Orthodox know about other (and more cogent) ways to interpret certain key Scripture passages. Catholics are Bible-believing Christians, but many others are not acquainted with this fact.

The question always arises: *Whose* interpretation is correct? The authors of this book concur with Paul's imperative: "All scripture [is] given by inspiration of God, and [is] profitable for doctrine, for reproof, for correction, for instruction in righteousness (II Timothy 3:16)." Furthermore, since St. Paul in I Timothy 3:15 states that the Church of the living God is "the pillar and ground of the truth," we must rely on Christ's Church to aid us in determining the proper interpretation of Scripture. Those who doubt or dislike our presentation of the Church's interpretation of Scripture should nonetheless find it a profitable challenge to articulate something more plausible.

We have used the King James Version of the Bible because it is familiar to many of our separated brethren. What may not be familiar is that the original King James Version included the so-called "additional" Catholic books (the Deuterocanonical texts) until 1644. Originally, Protestants were familiar with the Septuagint form of the Old Testament, which all early Christians used religiously, including St. Jerome, who defended it in his work, "The Apology Against the Books of Rufinus" (trans. Joseph N. Hritzu, *Saint Jerome—Dogmatic and Polemical Works*, in Roy Joseph Deferrari, ed., *The Fathers of the Church*, vol. 53, (Washington, DC: Catholic University, 1965), 47 *et seq*). We therefore make use of the traditional canon.

We trust that most of you will enjoy this book. We pray that you will all become fools for Christ, and that you will develop the hearts and souls of little children in approaching Him in his Word.

Scott Butler, Norman Dahlgren, & David Hess

ACKNOWLEDGEMENTS

Many individuals have tirelessly given their time and expertise to review and critique various parts of the manuscript of this handbook during various phases of its production: Fr. Ronald Tacelli, S.J., Miss Bernadeane Carr (who also translated for us a few key quotations), Fr. Peter Stravinskas, Mr. Joseph Gallegos, Mr. Gregg Krehbiel, Fr. Mitchell Pacwa, S.J., Fr. Thomas Thompson, Deacon Lawrence Michaels, Fr. Charles Fuld, Dr. James Shelton, Dr. Kenneth Howell, Fr. William Most, and Mr. Robert Sungenis, who also inspires us with his commanding knowledge of the Bible and biblical Greek.

Dr. Scott Hahn's testimony gave us the impetus to research more into the biblical roots of the Papacy. Dr. Jacob Neusner was most helpful in our research of certain Rabbinic sources. William Hall, Anthony Harvell and Markel Tumlin, librarians at Copley Library, University of San Diego, and Lydia Fitch of the Chula Vista Public Library, were of assistance in obtaining hard-to-find sources for many of our quotations, as were the librarians at Westminster Theological Seminary, in Escondido and Philadelphia. We thank John Collorafi for his translations of Latin and Greek original texts that were unavailable in English.

We express our thanks to those who suggested we use standard quotation conventions. We chose, rather, to mark quotes so as not to confuse our sources with the referenced primary sources.

PART ONE

ST. PETER AND THE CHURCH

JESUS, PETER AND THE KEYS

CHAPTER I

PETER IN MATTHEW 16:18

References to Peter's prominence and teaching authority among the disciples and to his successors' position in the Church revolve around Peter's place in Scripture, the special role that Christ Jesus laid out for Peter, and in the way in which the Church received Peter and his successors in authority. Moreover, all the Apostles and their successors, the bishops, are intimately connected with this concept called the Papacy.

This handbook shall present various questions designed to elicit thinking on the particular subject being examined, from words and phrases to history to etymology to Greek grammar. First, we shall consider questions regarding the prominence of Peter among all of the Apostles.

The Preeminence of Peter

1. How prominent in the New Testament is Peter compared with the other Apostles? Catholic scholar Michael Winter, formerly lecturer in fundamental theology at St. John's Seminary, Wonersh, United Kingdom, analyzed Peter from a mathematical perspective:

    "A statistical analysis of the Gospels and the Acts shows that among the Twelve the name of Peter occurs no less than 195 times, whereas the rest of the Apostles can muster only 130 nominations. This proportion is further enhanced by the fact that the Apostle who comes next in prominence is St. John, with only 29 references to his name." Michael M. Winter, *Saint Peter and the Popes*, (Baltimore: Helicon, 1960), 1.

Garrigou-Lagrange, the French theologian, "has concluded that the Greek word *protos* (or Latin *primus*) in Matthew 10:2 unequivocally states Peter's primacy, declaring that the word *protos* in its context means 'primary first', and that Peter, out of all the Apostles, was first in the eyes of Christ. See further explanation in his *Evangile Selon Saint Matthieu*, Paris, 1927), 195." Arthur Ide, "An Apology for the Petrine Doctrine" (M.A. thesis, University of Northern Iowa, 1968), 9. Lesser mentioned disciples are, for example, James the Greater (24 times), Judas Iscariot (23 times), and Philip (6 times). Also, there is support from another Catholic source:

> "Wherever the Apostles are enumerated in the Gospels, St. Peter is invariably named first. St. Matthew expressly calls him 'the first' (x. 2), the same Greek word (*protos*) being rendered 'chief' in chap. xx. 27, and other passages. Mr. Allies remarks: 'Now, that second and third do not follow, shows that "first" is not a numeral here, but designates rank and pre-eminence. Thus in heathen authors this word "first" by itself indicates the more excellent in its kind: thus in the Septuagint occur, "first friend of the king," "first of the singers," "the first priest," i.e., the chief priest (Nehem. xii. 46; 2 Chron. xxvi. 20). So our Lord: "Whichever among you will be first" (Matt. xx. 27); "Bring forth the first robe" (Luke xv. 22); and St. Paul: "Sinners, of whom I am the first," i.e., chief (1 Tim. i. 15). Thus "the first of the island" (Acts xxviii. 7), means the chief magistrate; and "first" generally, in Latin phraseology, the superior or prince.' *St. Peter, His Name and Office*, p. 95, 2d. edit." Charles F. B. Allnatt, ed., *Cathedra Petri—The Titles and Prerogatives of St. Peter*, (London: Burns & Oates, 1879), 47.

Peter's role in the Gospels is outlined as follows: i) Peter and Andrew are the first disciples whom Jesus calls (Mark 1:16; Matthew 4:18); ii) Jesus permitted no one except Peter and the sons of Zebedee to follow him into the house of the ruler of the synagogue. (Mark 5:37); iii) Peter plays a major role in the miraculous catch of fish in his net (Luke 5:1); iv) Peter's faith allows him to walk on the sea toward Jesus (Matthew 14:28); v) Peter is the one who proposes to the transfigured Jesus that the Apostles erect tents for Jesus, Elijah and Moses (Mark 9:2-5).

Peter is the one in various situations who relates to Jesus what is on the minds of all the disciples: i) asking how many times should one forgive a brother (Matthew 18:21); ii) telling Jesus that they have left everything to follow him (Luke 12:41; Mark 10:28 and parallels); iii) it occurs in one gospel where all the disciples ask the question while in the parallel passage of the other gospel it is only Peter who asks (Mark 7:17 compared with Matthew 15:15; Matthew 21:20 compared with Mark 11:21); iv) Peter promises to be loyal to the Master (Mark 14:29); v) Peter and John are directed by Jesus to prepare the passover (Luke 22:8); vi) Peter is regarded by outsiders as a special representative of the group of disciples (Matthew 17:24); vii) Peter is given first place among all the disciples of Jesus, with the list in Matthew emphasizing that Peter is first (Mark 3:16; Matthew 10:2; Luke 6:14; Acts 1:13); viii) Peter and those with him are used to designate the group of disciples (Mark 1:36; Luke 9:32; Luke 8:45); ix) The word of the angel spoke, telling the women at the tomb to go and tell the disciples and Peter that Jesus goes before them to Galilee (Mark 16:7); x) Peter speaks for all of the disciples (Mark 11:21); xi) Peter and the Beloved Disciple run to the tomb, and even though the Beloved Disciple reaches the tomb ahead of Peter, he defers to Peter to enter the tomb first (John 20:4); xii) among the disciples, Christ first appears to Peter after the resurrection (Luke 24:34; I Corinthians 15:5).

The late John Meyendorff, who was dean and professor of church history and patristics at St. Vladimir's Seminary in New York, stated the historical Eastern Orthodox theological stance toward Peter as follows:

> "Peter is the *coryphaeus* of the apostolic choir; he is the first disciple of Christ and speaks always on behalf of all. It is true that other apostles, John, James and Paul, are also

called *coryphaei* and 'primates,' but Peter alone is the 'rock of the Church.' His primacy has, therefore, not only a personal character, but bears an ecclesiological significance." J. Meyendorff, A. Schmemann, N. Afanassieff, and N. Koulomzine, *The Primacy of Peter*, (Aylesbury, Bucks, UK: The Faith Press, 1973), 14.

The preeminence of Peter in the New Testament reflects God's purpose in calling Peter. As God had called others at significant times in the history of his people, so also he called Peter, the fisherman named Simon. As Simon's name was changed, he became Christ's preeminent player in salvation history. How prominent God made Peter will be explored in various questions concerning Peter, his authority, and his successors.

Change in Name—Change in Mission

Putting Peter in perspective requires viewing the typology present in the Old Testament as fulfilled in the New Testament. For example, Jesus is the new Adam; Mary is the new Eve. The Old Testament is replete with characterizations of our Lord in various ways and with various names. Christ as "Lord" appears in various passages in the Old Testament. Nebuchadnezzar sees one like the Son of God in the fiery furnace (Daniel 3:25). In a similar manner, God designates certain of his followers to assume new duties in the kingdom of God, for which he assigns them new names. Abram's name was changed to "Abraham"; Jacob became "Israel"; Simon became "Peter." Observe the development of the concept.

> *Genesis* 17:5 Neither shall thy name any more be called Abram, but thy name shall be Abraham; for a father of many nations have I made thee.

2. What did God do for Abram? He changed his name.

3. What was the purpose of God's act? By changing Abram's name, there was a change in his function, role, and mission:

from shepherd to founder of the Jewish nation. In Hebrew, Abram means "exalted father," and Abraham is rendered as "chief of the multitude."

> *Genesis* 32:28 And he said, Thy name shall be called no more Jacob, but Israel: for as a prince hast thou power with God and with men, and hast prevailed. (Compare Genesis 35:10.)

4. What is the significance of Jacob's name change? Here God calls Jacob to be the founder of the twelve tribes of Israel, the foundation of genealogy by *Israel* (Heb. "who prevails with God").

5. From whom does Jesus trace his lineage? From Abraham through Jacob. See Matthew 1:1 (from Abraham); Luke 3:23 (from Adam).

> *Psalms* 18:2 The LORD [is] my rock, and my fortress, and my deliverer; my God, my strength, in whom I will trust; my buckler, and the horn of my salvation, [and] my high tower.
> 18:31 For who [is] God save the LORD? or who [is] a rock save our God?
> 18:46 The LORD liveth; and blessed [be] my rock; and let the God of my salvation be exalted.

6. Who is the rock of Psalms 18:2; 18:31; and 18:46? God. See Deuteronomy 32:4; cf. Psalm 31:3-4, and Isaiah 30:29.

7. What is the Hebrew word for rock? *Sur.*

Just as we find meaning in the importance of designating one as the "rock" in one sense or another, we may also look to the metaphorical parallels set forth in Scripture. Parallelism pervades the Hebrew Scriptures: a preliminary phrase is repeated a second time in a strong metaphorical sense. Each phrase lies in juxtaposition with and reinforces the imagery of the other. For example, consider the following passage from Isaiah:

> *Isaiah* 51:1 Hearken to me, ye that follow after righteousness, ye that seek the LORD: look unto the rock [whence] ye are hewn, and to the hole of the pit [whence] ye are digged.
> 51:2 Look unto Abraham your father, and unto Sarah [that] bare you: for I called him alone, and blessed him, and increased him.

All of you who seek the Lord, look unto the rock. All of you who seek the Lord, look unto the man whom God names as the "rock," the recipient of the metaphorical rendering. "Look unto" is repeated before each of the phrases in order that no doubt may be entertained as to who is the metaphorical rock.

8. Who is the rock of Isaiah 51:1? Abraham. The Hebrew word used in this instance is *Sur*, as

> "'When God looked on Abraham, who was to appear, he said: Behold I have found a rock on which I can build and base the world. Therefore he called Abraham a rock.'. . . [T]he earliest parts of *Jalqut*, a compilation by Simeon Kara (12th century) of Midrash fragments, are from the 5th century! Actually, the earliest of half a dozen other Talmudic texts describing Abraham as rock, mentioned by Strack and Billerbeck, are from the middle of the second century A.D." Midrash Jalqut (1, 766), as cited in S. L. Jaki, *And On This Rock*, 2nd ed., (Manassas, VA: Trinity, 1987), 89.

Strack and Billerbeck, two great Jewish scholars, are certainly not partisans of any Christian sect. They are just making the point that Jewish rabbinical writings identify Abraham to be the rock in Isaiah 51:1-2. Also refer to the Protestant commentary by George Buttrick (George Arthur Buttrick and others, eds., *The Interpreter's Bible*, (New York: Abingdon, 1951), 452), wherein there is reference to Strack and Billerbeck quoting one midrash in which God dug down into the morass and found a rock, Abraham, on which to build his building, Israel.

Certain Protestant scholars accord Abraham the dignity of being designated rock:

> "Abraham is spoken of as 'the Rock from which you were hewn.' (Is. 51:1)" D. Guthrie and others, *The New Bible Commentary*, (Grand Rapids, MI: Eerdmans, 1953) [reprinted by Inter-Varsity Press], 837.

9. Does the status of Abraham as rock deny or diminish in any way the status of God as rock? No. God's making Abraham "Rock" (Heb. *sur*) did not, and could not, usurp his own position as "Rock." This is so because Abraham's status and authority is conferred by, and derives from, the One who has full and ultimate authority. God and Abraham are not in competition; their positions are complementary. God the creator is "Rock" [*sur*] in an ultimate sense; Abraham is made "Rock" [*sur*] of Israel by God.

In one rabbinic source, Abraham is described as "a rock upon whom I can found a world." *Yalkut Shimoni*, i, 766, in B. C. Butler, *The Church and Infallibility*, (New York: Sheed & Ward, 1954), 113.

David H. Stern, a Messianic Jewish scholar, buttresses Butler's view in quoting from the same source:

> "The word 'petra' appears as a loanword in Hebrew in a most interesting context. *Yalkut Shim'oni*, an anthology of *midrashim* on the Hebrew Bible from the Middle Ages, has in it this passage:
>
>> "'When the Holy One wanted to create the world he passed over the generations of Enoch and the Flood; but when he saw Abraham who was to arise, he said, "Behold, I have found a rock (*petra*) on which I can build and establish the world." Therefore he called Abraham a rock, as it is said (Isaiah 51:1), "Look to the rock from which you were hewn." (Yalkut 766 on Numbers 23:9, quoting an earlier source, Tanchuma B, Yelamdenu)'

"We can only speculate on whether this homily was known in Yeshua's day." David H. Stern, *Jewish New Testament Commentary*, (Clarksville, MD: Jewish New Testament Publications, 1992), 54.

I Corinthians 3:11 For other foundation [*themelion*] can no man lay than that is laid, which is Jesus Christ.

10. Who is the foundation in I Corinthians 3:11? Jesus Christ.

I Corinthians 10:3 And did all eat the same spiritual meat;
10:4 And did all drink the same spiritual drink: for they drank of that spiritual Rock [*petras*] that followed them: and that Rock [*petra*] was Christ.

11. In I Corinthians 10:4, who is the rock? Jesus Christ.

Ephesians 2:19 Now therefore ye are no more strangers and foreigners, but fellowcitizens with the saints, and of the household of God;
2:20 And are built upon the foundation [*themelio*] of the apostles and prophets, Jesus Christ himself being the chief corner [stone];

12. Who is the chief cornerstone of Ephesians 2:20? Jesus Christ, the chief part of the foundation of the Apostles and prophets.

13. Who forms the foundation upon which the household is built? The Apostles and prophets.

14. Does this passage take away from Christ as foundation? No. See Luke 10:16; Matthew 10:40.

> *Revelation* 21:14 And the wall of the city had twelve foundations [*themelious*], and in them the names of the twelve apostles of the Lamb.

15. On whom is Christ building the foundations in Revelation 21:14? The Apostles. The apostolic foundation of the Church consists of the original twelve Apostles (Peter, James, John, Andrew, Philip, Thomas, Bartholomew, Matthew, James of Alpheas, Simon the Zealot, Jude Thaddeus, and Judas Iscariot); less Judas Iscariot, who committed suicide after betraying Jesus; and Matthias, the successor to Judas Iscariot selected by the remaining eleven, according to divine lot, after the ascension of Jesus Christ into heaven.

16. Is Paul an apostle? Yes, according to I Corinthians 1:1.

> *I Corinthians* 1:1 Paul, an apostle of Jesus Christ by the will of God, and Timothy our brother, unto the church of God which is at Corinth, with all the saints which are in all Achaia:

17. Is Paul one of the original twelve apostles? No, according to the list of the disciples set forth in Acts 1:13, 26.

> *John* 1:41 He first findeth his own brother Simon, and saith unto him, We have found the Messias, which is, being interpreted, the Christ.
> 1:42 And he brought him to Jesus. And when Jesus beheld him, he said, Thou art Simon the son of Jona: thou shalt be called Cephas.

The Apostle Simon's name was changed to Peter in Matthew 16:18. In the first chapter of the Gospel of John, Jesus addresses Simon and says that he shall be called "Cephas." The full significance of this name change will unfold as we delve into the meanings of these words "Peter" and "Cephas." An early indication that Peter's role in the New Testament will be somehow different devolves from Jesus changing Simon's name to Peter, a significance not lost on the early Church.

18. What is Christ prophesying regarding Simon in John 1:42? That Simon (Greek *Simon*; from Heb. *simon* meaning "God has heard") will become Cephas [Eng. transliteration of the Gr. *Kephas*; from Aramaic word *kepha* meaning "rock"]. Interpreting this passage in the context of it prophetic utterance, one Catholic commentator has written:

> "'You shall be called Cephas': naming something is the same as taking possession of the thing named (cf. Gen 17:5; 22:28 [*sic*]; 32:28; Is 62:2). Thus, for example, Adam when he was made lord of creation, gave names to created things (Gen 2:20). 'Cephas' is the Greek transcription of an Aramaic word meaning stone, rock: therefore, St John, writing in Greek, has to explain the meaning of the word Jesus used. Cephas was not a proper name, but our Lord put it on Peter to indicate his role as his vicar, which he will later on reveal (Mt 16:16-18): Simon was destined to be the stone, the rock, of the Church." Jose Maria Casciaro and others, eds., *The Navarre Bible: The Gospel of Saint John*, (Dublin: Four Courts Press, 1992), 57.

Certain linguistic aspects of John 1:41-42 are detailed later. In the Appendix of this handbook is an investigation of Aramaic as the original written language of the book of Matthew.

The Rock of Matthew 16:18

> *Matthew* 16:13 When Jesus came into the coasts of Caesarea Philippi, he asked his disciples, saying, Whom do men say that I the Son of man am? [Cf. Daniel 7:13.]
> 16:14 And they said, Some [say that thou art] John the Baptist: some, Elias; and others, Jeremias, or one of the prophets.
> 16:15 He saith unto them, But whom say ye that I am?

> 16:16 And Simon Peter answered and said, Thou art the Christ, the Son of the living God. [Peter recognized Jesus as priest, prophet and king. Contrast, John 1:49, wherein Nathaniel recognized Jesus as king only.]
>
> 16:17 And Jesus answered and said unto him, Blessed art thou, Simon Bar-jona: for flesh and blood hath not revealed [it] unto thee, but my Father which is in heaven.
>
> 16:18 And I say also unto thee, That thou art Peter [*sur, kepha, petros*], and upon this rock [*sur, kepha, petra*] I will build my church; and the gates of hell shall not prevail against it. [Cf. Daniel 7:13-14; II Samuel 7:11-14.]
>
> 16:19 And I will give unto thee the keys of the kingdom of heaven: and whatsoever thou shalt bind on earth shall be bound in heaven: and whatsoever thou shalt loose on earth shall be loosed in heaven.

Jesus often chose a physical setting for making significant statements in his ministry, as evidenced by the Sermon on the Mount, Jacob's Well in Samaria, Mt. Horeb for the Transfiguration, and Jerusalem.

19 Where were Jesus and the Apostles when Jesus asked his disciples who he was? They were in the neighborhood of Caesarea Philippi,

> "the area of the headwaters of the Jordan, the sacred river that stopped flowing so that the ark [of the covenant] could be carried dry-shod into the promised land. . . . Standing at a distance, Jesus and the Twelve must have been impressed by the massive wall of rock rising over the source of the Jordan. Here was a sacred river taking its origin through an opening in a massive wall of rock, an opening which could evoke the wide-open jaws of death - both spiritual and physical death. Against this backdrop Jesus spoke to Simon: 'You are Rock and on this rock I will build my church, and the jaws of death shall not prevail against it.' To echo such words called for a wall of rock." S. L. Jaki, *And On This Rock*, 2nd ed., (Manassas, VA: Trinity, 1987), 78-79.

This massive outcropping at Caesarea Philippi is approximately 200 feet by 500 feet in dimensions.

A Protestant commentary comes to much the same conclusion regarding the whereabouts and significance of the rock of Matthew 16:18-19:

> "An Aram. fragment to Test. Levi 2:3-5 found at Qumran may give an astonishing complex of parallels to this passage and even to its connection with the country around Caesarea Philippi [Matthew 16:](13), on the slopes of Mt. Hermon and at the sources of the river Jordan, since this area played a role in the Jewish apocalypticism as a place of revelation and as a meeting-place for the upper and lower world [Matthew 16:] 18-19." Matthew Black and H. H. Rowley, eds., *Peake's Commentary on the Bible*, (London: Thomas Nelson, 1972), 787.

20. Who is the rock? Peter = *Kepha* = Rock. The position of the words in the sentence points to Peter as the Rock, just as he is the one who is entrusted with the keys to the kingdom. Also, there are philological reasons for concluding that Simon Peter is the rock.

As William Hendriksen (Th.D. Princeton) the renowned Reformed Protestant theologian, Professor of New Testament Literature at Calvin Seminary and member of the Christian Reformed Church, has written:

> "The meaning is, 'You are Peter, that is Rock, and upon this rock, that is, on you, Peter, I will build my church.' Our Lord, speaking Aramaic, probably said, 'And I say to you, you are *Kepha*,' and on this *kepha* I will build my church.' Jesus, then, is promising Peter that he is going to build his church on him! I accept this view." William Hendriksen, *New Testament Commentary: Exposition of the Gospel According to Matthew*, (Grand Rapids, MI: Baker, 1973), 647.

John Meyendorff, Orthodox theologian, in his chapter entitled, "St. Peter in Byzantine Theology," has written the following:

"The words of Jesus on the road to Caesarea Philippi—'On this rock I will build my Church'—are bound to the confession of Peter. The Church exists in history because man believes in Christ, the Son of God; without this faith, there can be no Church. Peter was the first to confess this faith, and has thus become the 'head of theologians,' to use an expression of the Office [or, Liturgy of the Hours] of June 29; he has received the messianic title of the 'Rock,' a title which in biblical language belongs to the Messiah himself." J. Meyendorff, A. Schmemann, N. Afanassieff, and N. Koulomzine, *The Primacy of Peter*, (Aylesbury, Bucks, UK: The Faith Press, 1973), 14.

"This negative statement [concerning Peter's powers, according to Orthodox/Byzantine theology], however, does not sufficiently explain all that the Bible means by the messianic image of the 'Petra' or the Rock, an image which Christ applies to Peter alone." J. Meyendorff, A. Schmemann, N. Afanassieff, and N. Koulomzine, *The Primacy of Peter*, (Aylesbury, Bucks, UK: The Faith Press, 1973), 28.

"The Byzantine authors consider that the words of Christ to Peter (Matt. 16:18) possess a final and eternal significance. Peter is a mortal man, but the Church 'against which the gates of hell cannot prevail,' remains eternally founded on Peter." J. Meyendorff, A. Schmemann, N. Afanassieff, and N. Koulomzine, *The Primacy of Peter*, (Aylesbury, Bucks, UK: The Faith Press, 1973), 14.

Veselin Kesich, Serbian Orthodox professor emeritus of New Testament at St. Vladimir's Seminary, stated:

"Jesus told Simon that a weak, mortal man, 'flesh and blood,' could not perceive who he was. For this insight the disciple needed a special revelation by God. He conferred upon Simon Bar-Jonah the title Peter, and promised that he would build his church upon him. 'You are Peter (*Petros*), and on this rock (*petra*) I will build my church (*mou ten ekklesian*).' These words are spoken in Aramaic, in which Cephas stands both for *Petros* and *petra*." Veselin Kesich, "Peter's Primacy in the New Testament and the Early Tradition," in John Meyendorff, ed., *The Primacy of Peter*, (Crestwood, NY: St. Vladimir's Seminary Press, 1992), 47-48.

Beginning with the end of Vatican Council II, the Catholic Church has reached out in a variety of ecumenical forms to various other Christian communities. Representatives of the Bishops' Committee for Ecumenical and Interreligious Affairs of the National Conference of Catholic Bishops "have met in dialogue with representatives of other churches since the 1960s, for discussion of a wide variety of subjects related to the quest for unity among Christians." (Felician Foy, ed., *1991 Catholic Almanac*, (Huntington, IN: Our Sunday Visitor, 1990), 282.

One of the most fruitful ecumenical dialogues has occurred between Lutherans and Catholics (the "Lutheran-Catholic dialogue"). Lutheran and Catholic theologians have met over 50 times to cover a variety of subjects separating them, including Scripture and tradition, the role of Mary, and the role of Peter in the New Testament. This handbook contains several quotes from the latter dialogue on Peter, one of which addresses the meaning of the rock:

> "On that level, precisely because of the Aramaic identity of *Kepha/kepha*, there can be no doubt that the rock on which the church was to be built was Peter." Raymond E. Brown, Karl P. Donfried, and John Reumann, eds., *Peter in the New Testament*, (Minneapolis, MN: Augsburg; New York: Paulist: 1973), 92.

Gerhard Maier, author of *The End of the Historical Critical Method* (1977), and leading conservative evangelical Lutheran theologian, has written:

> "Nowadays a broad consensus has emerged which - in accordance with the words of the text - applies the promise to Peter as a person. On this point liberal (H. J. Holtzmann, E. Schweiger) and conservative (Cullmann, Flew) theologians agree, as well as representatives of Roman Catholic Exege-

sis." Gerhard Maier, "The Church in the Gospel of Matthew: hermeneutical Analysis of the Current Debate," trans. Harold H. P. Dressler, in D. A. Carson, ed., *Biblical Interpretation and Church Text and Context*, (Flemington Markets, NSW: Paternoster Press, 1984), 58.

"With all due respect to the Reformers, we must admit that the promises in Matt 16:18 ff. is directed to Peter, and not to a Peter-like faith. The argument about the primacy of the Pope must be pursued from the right basis, not from the wrong basis. The point at which this argument should focus is that of vicarius Petri or vicarius Christi. That is, the real question is whether the unique historical commission of Peter demands or even allows the idea of successors to Peter. Gerhard Maier, "The Church in the Gospel of Matthew: hermeneutical Analysis of the Current Debate," trans. Harold H. P. Dressler, in D. A. Carson, ed., *Biblical Interpretation and Church Text and Context*, (Flemington Markets, NSW: Paternoster Press, 1984), 60.

"In Aramaic 'Peter' and Rock are the same word; in Greek (here), they are cognate terms that were used interchangeably by this period. For the idea of a person as the foundation on which something is built, cf Isaiah 51:1-2; Ephesians 2:20 (the promise is made to Peter because Peter was the one who confessed Jesus v16). Craig S. Keener, *The IVP Bible Background Commentary New Testament*, (Downer's Grove, IL: Intervarsity Press, 1993), 90.

From many American Protestant theologians, the analysis is surprisingly similar. D. A. Carson, Professor of New Testament at Trinity Evangelical Seminary, author of *The Expositor's Bible Commentary* on Matthew, writing from a Baptist perspective, says:

"Although it is true that *petros* and *petra* can mean 'stone' and 'rock' respectively in earlier Greek, the distinction is largely confined to poetry. Moreover the underlying Aramaic is in this case unquestionable; and most probably *kepha* was used in both clauses ('you are *kepha*' and 'on this *kepha*'), since the word was used both for a name and for a 'rock.' The Peshitta (written in Syriac, a language cognate with Aramaic) makes no distinction between the words in the two clauses. The Greek makes the distinction between *petros* and *petra* simply because it is trying to preserve the pun, and in Greek the feminine *petra* could not very well serve as a masculine name." Frank E. Gaebelein, ed., *The Expositor's Bible Commentary: Volume 8 (Matthew, Mark, Luke)*, (Grand Rapids, MI: Zondervan, 1984), 368 [additional editors include Walter C. Kaiser, Jr. of Trinity Divinity School; Bruce K. Waltke of Regent College; James Montgomery Boice, Pastor of Tenth Presbyterian Church, Philadelphia, Pennsylvania; and Merrill C. Tenney of Wheaton College].

The *NIV Bible Commentary*, although it labels as extreme what may be traditional Catholic teaching, provides:

"The word Peter *petros*, meaning "rock," (Gk 4377) is masculine, and in Jesus' follow-up statement he uses the feminine word *petra* (Gk 4376). On the basis of this change, many have attempted to avoid identifying Peter as the rock on which Jesus builds his church yet if it were not for Protestant reactions against extremes of Roman Catholic interpretations, it is doubtful whether many would have taken "rock" to be anything or anyone other than Peter." Donald A. Carson III, *Matthew*, in Kenneth L. Barker and John Kohlenberger, eds., *Zondervan NIV Bible Commentary—New Testament*, vol. 2, (Grand Rapids, MI: Zondervan, 1994), 78.

Analysis of the Language in Matthew 16:18

In English, one says "Thou art *Peter*, and upon this *rock*." But in Aramaic, it is "Thou art *Kepha*, and upon this *kepha*." And, in French, it is, "Tu es Pierre et sur cette pierre." ["Thou art *Pierre*, and upon this *pierre*."] In French, the feminine *pierre* is retained as the masculine personal name, as it would be in Aramaic. Such an analysis of the use of language in Matthew 16:18 has led many scholars to support Peter as the rock.

Protestant scholars have shown this in commentaries on John 1:42 and Matthew 16:18:

"'That thou art Peter'—At his first calling, this new name was announced to him as an honour afterwards to be conferred on him (John 1:43 [*sic*]). Now he gets it [in Matthew 16:18], with an explanation of what it was meant to convey. 'And upon this rock'—As 'Peter' and 'Rock' are one word in the dialect familiarly spoken by our Lord—the Aramaic or Syro-Chaldaic, which was the mother tongue of the country—this exalted play upon the word can be fully seen only in languages which have one word for both. Even in the Greek it is imperfectly represented. In French, as Webster and Wilkinson remark, it is perfect, Pierre-pierre." Robert Jamieson, Andrew Robert Fausset, and David Brown, *One Volume Commentary*, (Grand Rapids, MI: Associated Publishers, n.d. [197?]), 47-48.

The German Protestant scholar, John Peter Lange, wrote eloquently of the use of the Aramaic as paralleled in other Middle Eastern languages:

"The Saviour, no doubt, used in both clauses the Aramaic word *kepha* (hence the Greek *Kephas* applied to Simon, John i.42; comp. 1 Cor. i.12; iii.22; ix.5; Gal. ii.9), which means rock and is used both as a proper and a common noun. Hence the old Syriac translation of the N.T. renders the passage in question thus: 'Anath-her Kipha, v'all hode Kipha.' The Arabic translation has *alsachra* in both cases. The proper translation then would be: 'Thou art Rock, and upon this rock,' etc." John Peter Lange, trans. Philip Schaff, *Lange's Commentary on the Holy Scriptures: The Gospel According to Matthew*, vol. 8, (Grand Rapids, MI: Zondervan, 1976), 293.

"But the main answer here is that our Lord undoubtedly spoke Aramaic, which has no known means of making such a distinction [between feminine *petra* and masculine *petros* in Greek]. The Peshitta (Western Aramaic) renders, 'Thou are *kipho*, and on this *kipho*.' The Eastern Aramaic, spoken in Palestine in the time of Christ, must necessarily have said in like manner, 'Thou are *kepha*, and on this *kepha*.' (Comp. Buxtorf.) Beza called attention to the fact that it is so likewise in French: 'Thou art *Pierre*, and on this *pierre*'; and

Nicholson suggests that we could say, 'Thou art *Piers* (old English for Peter), and on this *pier*.'" John A. Broadus, *Commentary on the Gospel of Matthew*, (Valley Forge, PA: Judson Press, 1886), 355-356.

In order to form a personal name for a man in the Greek language from the Aramaic, one would have to change the feminine name for rock, *petra*, into a masculine personal name for rock, or *petros*. In the original Aramaic, there would be no need for a change. In Spanish, one needs to change *piedra* into *pedro* (which has no direct meaning in Spanish) in order to form the masculine name for "rock." Thus, it would be "Thou art *Pedro*, and upon this *piedra*." As in Italian, "Thou art *Pietro*, and upon this *pietra*." There is a change of the feminine noun to the masculine personal name.

Analysis of the Greek Words Lithos and Petros Relative to Matthew

Some who are unconvinced of the proposition that *petros* and *petra* mean the same thing should consider that there is another common Greek word that simply means "stone." It is the word *lithos*. "Had Matthew wanted to say no more than that Peter was a stone in contrast with Jesus the Rock, the more common word would have been *lithos* ("stone" of almost any size)." Frank E. Gaebelein, ed., *The Expositor's Bible Commentary: Volume 8 (Matthew, Mark, Luke)*, (Grand Rapids, MI: Zondervan, 1984), 368 [additional editors include Walter C. Kaiser, Jr. of Trinity Divinity School; Bruce K. Waltke of Regent College; James Montgomery Boice, Pastor of Tenth Presbyterian Church, Philadelphia, Pennsylvania; and Merrill C. Tenney of Wheaton College].

Analysis of the Greek Words *Petros* and *Petra*

John Broadus, writing in 1886 from a Baptist perspective, wrote on the illusory distinction between *petros* and *petra*:

"Many insist on the distinction between the two Greek words, thou art *Petros* and on this *petra*, holding that if the rock had meant Peter, either *petros* or *petra* would have been used both times, and that *petros* signifies a separate stone or fragment broken off, while *petra* is the massive rock. But this distinction is almost entirely confined to poetry, the common prose word instead of *petros* being *lithos*; nor is the distinction uniformly observed." John A. Broadus, *Commentary on the Gospel of Matthew*, (Valley Forge, PA: Judson Press, 1886), 355.

Broadus went on to scotch the thought that because Rabbinic commentators had used *petros* and *petra* in their writings, they somehow gave weight to the idea that Jesus distinguished the two words when speaking to Peter:

"Edersh. finds the words *petros* and *petra* borrowed in the late Rabbinical language, and thinks that Jesus, while speaking Aramaic, may have borrowed those Greek words here. But this is grossly improbable, and the suggestion looks like a desperate expedient; nor has he shown that the late Rabbis themselves make the supposed distinction between the two words." John A. Broadus, *Commentary on the Gospel of Matthew*, (Valley Forge, PA: Judson Press, 1886), 356.

The above analysis of the Greek in Matthew 16 represents over one hundred years of Protestant understanding of Peter as the rock of Matthew 16:18—hardly a recent anomaly but the objective result of intensive study.

While not conceding that Peter was the rock to whom Jesus spoke in Matthew 16, the reformer John Calvin nevertheless wrote, "I grant that in Greek Peter (*Petros*) and stone (*petra*) mean the same thing, save that the first word is Attic [from the ancient classical Greek dialect of the Attica region], the second from the common tongue." John Calvin, *Calvin's New Testament Commentaries—The Harmony of the Gospels Matthew, Mark, and Luke*, vol. 2, trans. T. H. L. Parker, ed. David W. Torrance and Thomas F. Torrance, (Grand Rapids, MI: Eerdmans, 1972), 188.

Robert A. Sungenis, a Catholic convert and apologist, is a longtime student of the Bible and biblical Greek, with a graduate degree from Westminster Seminary. His analysis of the Greek text, together with other passages, leads to the strong textual conclusion that *petros* and *petra* are interchangeable terms meaning rock:

"One of the more salient errors pointed out by these sources [Oscar Cullmann and Herman Ridderbos] is the Protestant claim that the original Greek of Matthew 16:18 made a lexical distinction between Peter (Greek: *petros*) and rock (Greek: *petra*). *Petros* was understood to be a small stone or pebble, while petra was understood to be a huge, immovable rock, or rocky cliff. Conclusion: Peter [i.e., *petros*] could not be the rock [i.e., *petra*] to which Jesus referred, since it is obvious that a small stone is not a huge, immovable rock. In discovering more about Greek etymology, however, Protestant scholars learned that *petros* and *petra* are actually interchangeable terms. Though desiring to complete the pun and convey assonance, the Gospel writer was simply limited by the fact that since Peter is a masculine name, it must be designated by a masculine Greek noun (i.e., *petros*), whereas *petra* is a feminine noun. . . .

"Even though Greek may not have been the original language in which Matthew penned his Gospel, it can be shown from the scriptural usage of Greek that *petra* does not refer exclusively to a huge rock. It also can refer to a stone or small rock. For example, in Romans 9:33 and 1 Peter 2:8, the Greek word *lithos* (a small stone) is coupled with *petra* in the imagery of making a man stumble and fall. The verse in the Old Testament from which this is taken is Isaiah 8:14: 'See, I lay in Zion a stone that causes men to stumble, and a rock that makes them fall.' The image is of a man walking on his way and stumbling over a stone or small rock so that he falls to the ground. It is not the picture of a big boulder appearing in his way or coming down from the sky and crushing him under its weight. Paul only refers to stumbling in Romans 9:32, and one cannot stumble and fall over a *petra* if it is a huge, massive rock." Robert A. Sungenis, "Will the Real Rock Please Stand Up!," *The Catholic Answer* 9:2 (May/June 1995): 50-51.

Analysis of the Greek Text of Matthew 16:18

James B. Shelton, Associate Professor in the School of Theology and Missions of Oral Roberts University (Tulsa, Oklahoma), addresses the Greek of Matthew 16:18, stating:

> "Our Lord's reference to Simon as Peter (*Petros*) in Matthew 16:18 has suffered partisan interpretation. Some interpreters with reformational and revisionist agendas have made much of the difference in Greek between the words Peter (*Petros*, masculine) and 'this rock' (*tautei tei petra*, demonstrative + definite article + feminine form, which is the usual gender of *petra*). They see *petra* as referring to the confession of the messiahship of Jesus, or the corporate faith of Jesus' followers, rather than to the person of Peter.
>
> "When using both the masculine and feminine forms of the word, however, Matthew is *not* trying to distance Peter, *Petros*, from 'this rock,' *petra*. Rather, the evangelist changes the genders simply because Simon, a male, is given a masculine form of the feminine noun for his new name.
>
> "Furthermore, the whole passage contains semitic structures. In Aramaic the word for both Peter's name and the rock would be identical, *Kepha' . . . kepha'.*
>
> "Finally, the force of the context calls for a direct identification between Peter(*Petros*) and the rock (*petra*). The case for petrine hegemony among the apostles must be seriously considered and not summarily dismissed by sectarian eisegesis." James B. Shelton, letter to authors, 21 October 1994, 1.

Taking the tack of scrutinizing the grammar and sequence of Greek phrasing in Matthew 16:18, while drawing upon other New Testament passages, Robert A. Sungenis writes:

> "It is important to note here that Jesus chooses the phrase *epi tautee tee petra* ('upon this rock') rather than more ambiguous phrasing such as *epi tee petra* ('upon the rock') or *epi petra* ('upon a rock'). Using the definite or indefinite article would seem to point to someone other than Peter,

whereas the demonstrative adjective *tautee* ('this') is more likely to specify someone in the immediate grammatical proximity to the accompanying noun 'rock.' The only other rock-like imagery that is illustrated in the immediate proximity is *Petros* ('Peter') which is a proper name meaning 'rock' (cf., John 1:42). Only in reference to Peter as the rock can the intended demonstrative force of *tautee tee* ('this') be satisfied.

"The Greek word *tautee* can also serve as a demonstrative pronoun if it does not have a noun following. In this instance, the rendering could have been, 'you are Peter and upon this (*tautee*) I will build my church.' Here we see that the demonstrative pronoun would naturally refer back to the nearest referent, Peter, (a rock), upon which Jesus would build the church. In light of this possible usage, the addition of 'rock' may just reinforce that *tautee*, as a demonstrative adjective, is denoting a connection between 'Peter' and 'rock.'

"The implied demonstrative force of *tautee tee* in reference to Peter is also noted in the way various English translations often render this Greek phrase. For example, the King James Bible translates the dative case of the phrase as, 'the same' and 'this same,' respectively, in 1 Cor. 7:20 ['Let every man abide in *the same* calling in which he was called'] and 2 Cor. 9:4 ['we should not be ashamed in *this same* confident boasting'], respectively. The accusative case is translated as 'the same' in Acts 13:33; 2 Cor. 8:6, 9:5. Similarly, the NASB [New American Standard Bible] translates the phrase as 'this very' in Luke 12:20 ['*This very* night your soul is required of you'] and Acts 27:23 ['For *this very* night there stood by me an angel'], as does the NIV [New International Version] and NEB [New English Bible] for the former. These translations do not require the use of 'very' or 'same' to specify the demonstrative quality, but the force of the qualifier is implied. Since Greek demonstrative adjectives like *tautee* assume the predicate position, this may serve, in some instances, to intensify its adjectival quality. If we were to use the same implied force in Matthew 16:18 the verse could be understood as, 'you are Peter and upon this very rock I will build my church." Robert A. Sungenis, letter to authors, 7 November 1995, 2.

From the original Greek, translated in light of other similar passages, it is even more possible to render Matthew 16:18 as emphatically referring to Peter as the rock upon which the Church of Christ would be built.

A Protestant grammatical argument sometimes made in trying to interpret Matthew 16:18 away from the traditional Christian interpretation centers on the "person" to whom statements are addressed; that is, Peter is addressed in the second person but the rock is referred to in the third person, thereby making for different referents. Robert Sungenis has a response:

> "The first thing we must point out is that on strict grammatical grounds nouns do not have person, only pronouns have person. The pronouns, 'I,' 'you,' and 'he' are first, second and third person, respectively. Nouns, on the other hand, have number, gender and case but not person. Hence, it is not correct to say that 'rock,' which MacKenzie and Gerstner have claimed is a 'third person' noun, cannot be matched up with the second person pronoun 'you' from the phrase 'you are Peter' in Matthew 16:18. One cannot claim a disjunction between 'you' and 'rock' based on person since technically speaking no such comparison is grammatically legitimate. Although one could possibly advance the argument that nouns have an inherent third person, this would not prohibit the coupling between 'you' and 'rock.' If MacKenzie's and Gerstner's argument were true, then they would also have to argue that 'I' and 'church' in Jesus' statement, 'I will build my church' could not be linked with one another since the former is in the first person and the latter would be a third person. One can plainly see that this would be a fallacious line of argumentation. In regard to Peter, Jesus could have said either 'you are Peter' or 'you are rock' in which the second person 'you' is directly identified by either of the nouns following." Robert A. Sungenis, letter to authors, 7 November 1995, 2-3.

There is thus strong evidence in the Greek language that Peter is the rock upon which the Church of Christ will be built.

Use of the Aramaic Word Kepha in the Greek New Testament

Even if Greek were the only language in which all of the New Testament were written, there is definite evidence in the Greek New Testament that Aramaic was the language spoken in Israel in the time of Jesus. There are many Aramaic words and phrases that became part of the Greek New Testament, some of which have already been cited. One of the most striking is the reference to Peter as "Cephas," which is a transliteration of the Aramaic word *kepha*:

> "PETER (Gr. *Petros*). Simon Peter, the most prominent of Jesus' twelve disciples. Peter's original name was Simon (Aram. *sim'on*, represented in Greek by *Simon* and *Symeon*). Jesus gave him the Aramaic name *kepha* "rock" (Matt. 16:18); Luke 6:14 par.; John 1:42), which is in Greek both transliterated (*Kephas*; Eng. Cephas) and translated (*Petros*)." Allen C. Myers, ed., *The Eerdmans Bible Dictionary*, (Grand Rapids, MI: Eerdmans, 1987), 818.

There are six Scripture references to Peter as Cephas (the anglicized spelling of *kepha*): John 1:42; I Corinthians 1:12, 3:22, 9:5, 15:5; and Galatians 2:9.

From the Gospel of John, the following passage quite capably demonstrates that Aramaic was the original tongue in which Jesus spoke to Peter, keeping in mind that *kepha* means "rock":

> *John* 1:41 He first findeth his own brother Simon, and saith unto him, We have found the Messias [*Christos*], which is, being interpreted, the Christ.
>
> 1:42 And he brought him to Jesus. And when Jesus beheld him, he said, Thou art Simon the son of Jona: thou shalt be called Cephas [*Kephas*], which is by interpretation, [*Petros*] A stone [properly, rock].

21. What linguistic usage in John 1:42 indicates that Jesus was using Cephas to be equivalent to Peter as rock, but not as stone? In John 1:41 the Aramaic *messias* is interpreted to mean the Greek *christos*. Likewise, in the next verse, John 1:42, in a par-

allel way to the previous verse, the Aramaic *kepha* or *kephas* (anglicized as "Cephas") is translated into the Greek as *petros* (anglicized as Peter in English Bible versions). The parallel use of Aramaic and Greek in the two verses leads one logically to the translation: *kephas* = *petros* = "rock." That *petros* may have meant stone, or even little stone in Greek at some other point in time is not apparent or relevant in the definitional usage of Aramaic and Greek in the foregoing two verses of John's Gospel.

> "Understanding that Jesus spoke [to Peter] in Aramaic (e.g., he called him Cephas, which is [anglicized] Aramaic, in John 1:42) and that Matthew was originally written in Aramaic as well, if Jesus had intended to characterize Peter as a "little stone" as opposed to a massive rock in John 1:42 or Matthew 16:18, there were perfectly adequate Aramaic words which could signify such a diminution. For example, *evna* in Aramaic means 'little stone.'" Robert A. Sungenis, "Will the Real Rock Please Stand Up?," letter to authors, June 1994, 4.

Simon is the First Man Called "Peter"

22. Was Peter used as a man's name in Palestine prior to Jesus renaming Simon? No.

Archaeological, philological and historical evidence all point to the naming of Simon as "Peter" by Jesus as the first instance of the use of "rock" as a man's name. See B. Bivin, "Queries and Comments," *Biblical Archaeology Review* 19:3 (May/June 1993): 19. Jesus Christ, God, had given a person, Simon, a new function or position under the New Covenant of God with his people. It was not a man's given name before Jesus used it as such.

> "*Rock* (Aram. *Kepha*). This is not a name, but an appellation and a play on words. There is no evidence of Peter or Kephas as a name before Christian times. On building on a rock, or from a rock, cf. Isa li 1ff.; Matt vii 24f. *Peter* as *Rock* will be the foundation of the future community (cf. *I*

will build). Jesus, not quoting the OT, here uses Aramaic, not Hebrew, and so uses the only Aramaic word which would serve his purpose." W. F. Albright, and C. S. Mann, *The Anchor Bible: Matthew*, (Garden City, NY: Doubleday, 1971), 195. (See also John 1:42 below and following notes.)

Furthermore, evidence of the use of the Aramaic word *kepha* as a man's name prior to Jesus renaming Simon would make the wordplay of Matthew 16:18 much stronger, according to Joseph A. Fitzmyer:

> "Indeed, this lack of attestation of *kp'* [transliterated Aramaic spelling] as a proper name has been seen as one of the major difficulties in viewing the occurrence of *Petros* and *petra* in Matt 16:18 as a reflection of an Aramaic wordplay. . . . The existence of it [*kepha*] as a proper name at least makes more plausible the suggestion that a wordplay in Aramaic was involved." Joseph A. Fitzmyer, *To Advance the Gospel*, (New York: Crossroad, 1981), 115, 118.

There is one instance existing (from a non-Palestinian source) in which there is an Aramaic use of the word *kp'*, or *kepha*:

> "Though the text in which it appears had been known since 1953, when it was first published, it has scarcely been noticed; as far as I know, it has not been introduced into the discussion of the *Kephas/Petros* problem. However, *kp'* does occur as a proper name in an Aramaic text from the Elephantine (BMAP 8:10) dated to the eighth year of Darius the King (= Darius II, 424-402 B.C.), hence to 416 B.C. The name is found in a list of witnesses to a document in which a certain Zakkur gives or transfers a slave, named Yedaniah, to a certain Uriah. Nine lines of the document spell out the details of the transfer, and the last three give the name of the witnesses, the first of which runs as follows:

> "10 *shdy' bgw trmlky br qlqln, snksr br sbty; shd qb br kp'*.

> "Witnesses hereto (are): Atarmalki, son of QLQLN; Sinkishir, son of Shabbetai; witness: Aqab, son of Kepha." Joseph A. Fitzmyer, *To Advance the Gospel*, (New York: Crossroad, 1981), 116.

The conclusion that Fitzmyer draws is that there is evidence of at least one use of the Aramaic word *Kepha* (unless the reference is to an Egyptian proper name, as some might suggest) as a proper name prior to the time of Christ. Fitzmyer's research stifles a line of argument that would conform exegetical study to a particular line of bias. A play on words in the Aramaic whereby Simon's name is changed to *Kephas* definitely makes him the rock on which the Church would be founded. Equally compelling is the line of argument whereby Simon is transformed by Christ from a mere disciple into a uniquely ordered new role, or office, requiring the new name of *Kephas*, the Rock on which the Church would be built. The new name, in either of the two aforementioned circumstances, indicates a unique role for Peter and his successors in the plan of salvation, and any argument to the contrary flies in the face of the Aramaic and the Greek.

Prominent Protestants Comment on Peter as the Rock

The old Protestant argument went like this: since *petros* purportedly means "little stone" in Greek, it could not conceivably signify the rock upon which Jesus said he would build his Church; therefore, Peter could not be the rock. It was Jesus Christ or Peter's confession of faith in Jesus (as the "Christ, the Son of the Living God") which was the Rock, not Peter himself.

23. Is there now dissent among prominent Protestant theologians regarding Peter being the rock of Matthew 16:18? No.

We have now reviewed dozens of prominent Protestant biblical commentaries relative to the meaning of Peter and rock in Matthew 16:18. All of them agree with the Catholic interpretation that Peter is the rock upon which Jesus will build his Church.

A representative sampling of the Protestant commentaries that support the Catholic teaching that Peter is the rock of Matthew 16:18 now follow.

J. Knox Chamblin, a Reformed theologian and New Testament Professor at Reformed Theological Seminary (member of the Presbyterian Church), comes to the following conclusion, after analyzing the Greek alone, regarding Peter as the rock:

"By the words 'this rock' Jesus means not himself, nor his teaching, nor God the Father, nor Peter's confession, but Peter himself. The phrase is immediately preceded by a direct and emphatic reference to Peter. As Jesus identifies himself as the Builder, the rock on which he builds is most naturally understood as someone (or something) other than Jesus himself. The demonstrative *this*, whether denoting what is physically close to Jesus or what is literally close in Matthew, more naturally refers to Peter (v. 18) than to the more remote confession (v. 16). The link between the clauses of verse 18 is made yet stronger by the play on words, 'You are Peter (Gk. *Petros*), and on this rock (Gk. *petra*) I will build my church.' As an apostle, Peter utters the confession of verse 16; as a confessor he receives the designation *this rock* from Jesus." J. Knox Chamblin, "Matthew," in Walter A. Elwell, ed., *Evangelical Commentary on the Bible*, (Grand Rapids, MI: Baker, 1989, 742.

Henry Alford, the Anglican Dean of Canterbury Cathedral, draws the inescapable conclusion that:

"The name Peter (not now first given, but prophetically bestowed by our Lord on his first interview with Simon (John i.42), or Cephas, signifying a rock, the termination being only altered from *Petra* to *Petros* to suit the masculine appellation, denotes the personal position of this Apostle in the building of the Church of Christ." Henry Alford, *The New Testament for English Readers*, vol. 1, (Grand Rapids, MI: Baker, 1983), 119.

Gerhard Kittel's theological dictionary (composed of ten volumes) analyzes the Greek text of Matthew 16:18 as follows:

"The obvious pun which has made its way into the Gk. text as well suggests a material identity between *petra* and *Petros*, the more so as it is impossible to differentiate strictly between the meanings of the two words. On the other hand, only the fairly assured Aramaic original of the saying enables us to assert with confidence the formal and material identity between *petra* and *Petros*: *petra = kepha = Petros*.

. . . If, then, Mt. 16:18 forces us to assume a formal and material identity between *petra* and *Petros*, this shows how fully the apostolate, and in it to a special degree the position of Peter, belongs to and is essentially enclosed within, the revelation of Christ. *Petros* himself is this *petra*, not just his faith or his confession. . . . In a way which transcends the Rabb. view of Abraham, Peter is brought into this picture of Abraham as the cosmic rock. He takes the place of Abraham, but he does so as the foundation of Israel *kata pneuma*, the community of the new covenant which Christ builds on the rock Peter (*oikodomeo*, V, 139, 3ff.; *ekklesia*, III, 518-526)." Gerhard Friedrich, ed., and Geoffrey W. Bromley, trans. and ed., *Theological Dictionary of the New Testament*, vol. VI, (Grand Rapids, MI: Eerdmans, 1968), 98-99.

"But what does Jesus mean when He says: 'On this rock I will build my church"? The idea of the Reformers that He is referring to the faith of Peter is quite inconceivable in view of the probably different setting of the story, 105, 38 ff. for there is no reference here to the faith of Peter. Rather, the parallelism of 'thou art Rock' and 'on this rock I will build' shows that the second rock can only be the same as the first. It is thus evident that Jesus is referring to Peter, to whom he has given the name Rock. He appoints Peter, the impulsive, enthusiastic, but not persevering man in the circle, to be the foundation of His *ecclesia*. To this extent Roman Catholic Exegesis is right and all Protestant attempts to evade this interpretation are to be rejected." Gerhard Friedrich, ed., and Geoffrey W. Bromley, trans. and ed., *Theological Dictionary of the New Testament*, vol. 6, (Grand Rapids, MI: Eerdmans, 1968), 108.

Craig L. Blomberg, Professor of New Testament at Denver Seminary, from a Baptist perspective declares:

"Acknowledging Jesus as The Christ illustrates the appropriateness of Simon's nickname "Peter" (*Petros* = rock). This is not the first time Simon has been called Peter (cf. John 1:42 [wherein he is called Cephas]), but it is certainly the most famous. Jesus' declaration, "You are Peter," parallels Peter's confession, 'You are the Christ,' as if to say, 'Since you can tell me who I am, I will tell you who you are.' The expression 'this rock' almost certainly refers to Peter, following immediately after his name, just as the words following 'the Christ' in v. 16 applied to Jesus. The play on words in the Greek between Peter's name (*Petros*) and the word 'rock' (*petra*) makes sense only if Peter is the rock and if Jesus is about to explain the significance of this identification." Craig L. Blomberg, *The New American Commentary: Matthew*, vol. 22, (Nashville: Broadman, 1992), 251-252.

In a publication of Beacon Hill Press (the publishing arm of the Church of the Nazarene), there is this description of Peter as the rock of Matthew 16:18:

"The foundation of the messianic community will be Peter, the rock, who is recipient of the revelation and maker of the confession (cf. Eph. 2:20). The significant leadership role of Peter is a matter of sober history. . . . [T]he plain sense of the whole statement of Jesus would seem to accord best with the view that the rock on which Jesus builds His Church is Peter." William E. McCumber, "Matthew," in William M. Greathouse and Willard H. Taylor, eds., *Beacon Bible Expositions*, vol. 1, (Kansas City, MO: Beacon Hill, 1975), 125.

From M. Eugene Boring, a Disciple of Christ teaching at Texas Christian University, writing for the Abingdon Press of the United Methodist Church, comes an interpretation of parallelism in Matthew 16:

"On the basis of Isa. 51:1,2 (cf. Matt. 3:9) some scholars have seen Peter as here paralleled to Abraham; just as Abram stood at the beginning of the people of God, has his name changed, and was called a rock, so also Peter stands at the beginning of the new people of God and receives the Abrahamic name rock to signify this." M. Eugene Boring, "Matthew," in Pheme Perkins and others, eds., *The New Interpreter's Bible*. vol. 8, (Nashville, TN: Abingdon Press, 1995), 345.

"'You are Rock, and on this Rock I will build my church.' Peter is here pictured as the foundation of the church." M.

Eugene Boring, "Matthew," in Pheme Perkins and others, eds., *The New Interpreter's Bible*. vol. 8, (Nashville, TN: Abingdon Press, 1995), 345.

Dr. John Broadus (1886), a Reformed Baptist Bible scholar, reminds us that Peter is the rock:

> "As Peter means rock, the natural interpretation is that 'upon this rock' means *upon thee*. No other explanation would probably at the present day be attempted. . . . But there is a play upon words, understand as you may. It is an even more far-fetched and harsh play upon words if we understand the rock to be Christ; and a very feeble and almost unmeaning play upon words if the rock is Peter's confession." John A. Broadus, *Commentary on the Gospel of Matthew*, (Valley Forge, PA: Judson Press, 1886), 355.

> "Let it be observed that Jesus could not here mean himself by the rock, consistently with the image, because he is the builder. To say, 'I will build,' would be a very confused image. The suggestion of some expositors that in saying 'thou art Peter, and on this rock' he pointed at himself, involves an artificiality which to some minds is repulsive." John A. Broadus, *Commentary on the Gospel of Matthew*, (Valley Forge, PA: Judson Press, 1886), 356.

Albert Barnes, a conservative 19th century evangelical Presbyterian theologian, wrote the following comments on Peter's expression of faith:

> "The meaning of this phrase may be thus expressed: 'Thou, in saying that I am the Son of God, hast called me by a name expressive of my true character. I, also, have given to thee a name expressive of your character. I have called you Peter, a rock, denoting firmness, solidity, stability, and your confession has shown that the name is appropriate. I see that you are worthy of the name, and will be a distinguished support of my religion.'" Albert Barnes, *Notes on the New Testament*, Robert Frew, ed., (Grand Rapids, MI: Baker, 1973), 170.

"Another interpretation is, that the word *rock* refers to Peter himself. This is the obvious meaning of the passage. . . . 'Thou art a rock. Thou hast shown thyself firm, and fit for the work of laying the foundation of the church. Upon thee will I build it. Thou shalt be highly honoured; thou shalt be first in making known the gospel to both Jews and Gentiles.'" Albert Barnes, *Notes on the New Testament*, Robert Frew, ed., (Grand Rapids, MI: Baker, 1973), 170.

Suzanne de Dietrich, a Presbyterian theologian, writes:

"The play on words in [Matthew 16] verse 18 indicates the Aramaic origin of the passage. The new name contains a promise. 'Simon,' the fluctuating, impulsive disciple, will, by the grace of God, be the 'rock' on which God will build the new community." Suzanne de Dietrich, *The Layman's Bible Commentary: Matthew*, vol. 16, trans. Donald G. Miller, (Atlanta: John Knox Press, 1961), 93.

David Hill (writing as a Presbyterian minister and Senior Lecturer in the Department of Biblical Studies, University of Sheffield, England) aptly described Peter as the rock:

"*On this rock I will build my church*: the word-play goes back to Aramaic tradition. It is on Peter himself, the confessor of his Messiahship, that Jesus will build the Church. The disciple becomes, as it were, the foundation stone of the community. Attempts to interpret the 'rock' as something other than Peter in person (e.g., his faith, the truth revealed to him) are due to Protestant bias, and introduce to the statement a degree of subtlety which is highly unlikely." David Hill, "The Gospel of Matthew," in Ronald E. Clements and Matthew Black, eds., *The New Century Bible Commentary*, (London: Marshall, Morgan & Scott, 1972), 261.

Another Protestant commentary edited by D. Guthrie, Lecturer in New Testament at London Bible College, reiterates the point:

"Some interpreters have therefore referred to Jesus as rock here, but the context is against this. Nor is it likely that Peter's faith or Peter's confession is meant. It is undoubtedly Peter himself who is to be the Rock, but Peter confessing, faithful and obedient." D. Guthrie and others, *The New Bible Commentary*, (Grand Rapids, MI: Eerdmans, 1953) [reprinted by Inter-Varsity Press], 837.

A natural conclusion is that of Davies and Allison:

> "The most natural interpretation [of Matthew 16:18] is that of the Roman Catholic tradition: the rock is Peter. The word-play, and the whole structure of the passage, demands that this verse is every bit as much Jesus' declaration about Peter as verse 16 was Peter's declaration about Jesus." W. D. Davies and Dale C. Allison, *A Critical and Exegetical Commentary on the Gospel according to Saint Matthew*, vol. 11, in J. A. Emerton, C. E. B. Cranfield, and G. N. Stanton, eds., *The International Critical Commentary*, (Edinburgh: Clark, 1991), 627. (J. A. Emerton is Fellow of St. John's College, Regius Professor of Hebrew in the University of Cambridge, and Honorary Canon of St. George's Cathedral, Jerusalem; C. E. B. Cranfield is Professor Emeritus at the University of Durham; and G. N. Stanton is Professor of New Testament Studies in King's College, University of London.)

As Herman Ridderbos, Professor of New Testament at the Theological School of the Reformed Churches of the Netherlands, Kampen (member of the Dutch Reformed Church), in analyzing the Greek text alone states:

> "It is well known that the Greek word (*petra*) translated 'rock' here is different from the proper name Peter. The slight difference between them has no special importance, however. The most likely explanation for the change from *petros* ('Peter') to *petra* is that *petra* was the normal word for 'rock.' Because the feminine ending of this noun made it unsuitable as a man's name, however, Simon was not called *petra* but *petros*. The word *petros* was not an exact synonym of *petra*; it literally meant 'stone'. Jesus therefore had to switch to the word *petra* when He turned from Peter's name to what it meant for the Church. There is no good reason to think that

Jesus switched from *petros* to *petra* to show that He was not speaking of the man Peter but of his confession as the foundation of the Church. The words 'on this rock [*petra*]' indeed refer to Peter. Because of the revelation that he had received and the confession that it motivated in him, Peter was appointed by Jesus to lay the foundation of the future church." Herman N. Ridderbos, *Bible Student's Commentary: Matthew*, (Grand Rapids, MI: Zondervan, 1987), 303.

The Anglican R. T. France, who does not interpret the passages in Matthew in the same manner as the Catholic Church, nevertheless follows the line of reasoning that Peter is the rock in Matthew 16:18:

"The feminine word for rock, *petra*, is necessarily changed to the masculine *petros* (stone) to give a man's name, but the word-play is unmistakable (and in Aramaic would be even more so, as the same form *kepha* would occur in both places). . . . The word-play, and the whole structure of the passage, demands that this verse is every bit as much Jesus' declaration about Peter as v. 16 was Peter's declaration about Jesus. Of course it is on the basis of Peter's confession that Jesus declares his role as the church's foundation, but it is to Peter, not to his confession, that the rock metaphor is applied. And it is, of course, a matter of historic fact that Peter was the acknowledged leader of the group of disciples, and of the developing church in its early years." R. T. France, *The Gospel According to Matthew*, (Grand Rapids, MI: Eerdmans, 1985), 254.

Donald A. Hagner, of Fuller Theological Seminary, recounts the situation succinctly:

"The natural reading of the passage [Matthew 16:18], despite the necessary shift from *Petros* to *petra* required by the word play in the Greek (but not the Aramaic, where the same word *kepha* occurs in both places), is that it is Peter who is the rock upon which the church is to be built (thus rightly Morris, France, Carson, Blomberg, Cullmann [*Peter*, 207], Davies-Allison; so too the interconfessional volume by Brown, Donfried, and Reumann [*Peter in the NT*, 92]). The frequent attempts that have been made, largely in the past, to deny this in favor of the view that the confession itself is the rock (e.g., most recently Caragounis) seem to be largely motivated by Protestant prejudice against a passage that is used by the Roman Catholics to justify the papacy." Donald A. Hagner, *Matthew 14-28*, in David A. Hubbard and others, eds., *Word Biblical Commentary*, vol. 33b, (Dallas: Word Books, 1995), 470.

JESUS, PETER AND THE KEYS

CHAPTER II

PETER AND THE KEYS

The Keys of the Kingdom of Heaven are given to Peter

Peter, the rock on which the Church will be built, also will be given the keys of the kingdom of heaven. Many writers and humorists have pictured St. Peter at the gates of heaven admitting, or not admitting, certain souls through the pearly gates, based on the degree of faithful obedience to the Word of God on earth exhibited by the entrants. Scripture portrays the holder of the keys to the kingdom of God in a more complete way.

As the steward of Jesus Christ on earth, St. Peter is the first of many who will govern the Church of Christ from the Chair of St. Peter. The keys are symbolic of the sovereign's power and authority as they are entrusted to his prime minister for a period of time to act for the sovereign in fulfilling the sovereign's wishes. The sovereign, or king, never relinquishes his authority during this period of delegation. At the end of the period of delegation, the king reassumes his total command and authority over the kingdom. Jesus Christ, while still retaining his sovereignty, entrusted the keys to the kingdom of heaven to Peter (and his successors) on earth until the end of time. One finds the scriptural basis for this delegation of authority in the Gospel of Matthew.

Matthew 16:19 And I will give unto thee the keys of the kingdom of heaven: and whatsoever thou shalt bind on earth shall be bound in heaven: and whatsoever thou shalt loose on earth shall be loosed in heaven.

16:20 Then charged he his disciples that they should tell no man that he was Jesus the Christ.

24. Christ's use of language regarding the keys is deliberately reminiscent of whose writings? The prophet Isaiah.

Isaiah 22:15 Thus saith the Lord GOD of hosts, Go, get thee unto this treasurer, [even] unto Shebna, which [is] over the house, [and say],

22:16 What hast thou here? and whom hast thou here, that thou hast hewed thee out a sepulchre here, [as] he that heweth him out a sepulchre on high, [and] that graveth an habitation for himself in a rock?

22:17 Behold, the LORD will carry thee away with a mighty captivity, and will surely cover thee.

22:18 He will surely violently turn and toss thee [like] a ball into a large country: there shalt thou die, and there the chariots of thy glory [shall be] the shame of thy lord's house.

22:19 And I will drive thee from thy station, and from thy state shall he pull thee down.

22:20 And it shall come to pass in that day, that I will call my servant Eliakim the son of Hilkiah:

22:21 And I will clothe him with thy robe, and strengthen him with thy girdle, and I will commit thy government into his hand: and he shall be a father to the inhabitants of Jerusalem, and to the house of Judah.

22:22 And the key of the house of David will I lay upon his shoulder; so he shall open, and none shall shut; and he shall shut, and none shall open.

22:23 And I will fasten him [as] a nail in a sure place; and he shall be for a glorious throne to his father's house.

22:24 And they shall hang upon him all the glory of his father's house, the offspring and the issue, all vessels of small quantity, from the vessels of cups, even to all the vessels of flagons.

22:25 In that day, saith the LORD of hosts, shall the nail that is fastened in the sure place be removed, and be cut down, and fall; and the burden that [was] upon it shall be cut off: for the LORD hath spoken [it].

Messrs. Albright (Professor Emeritus in the Oriental Seminary of Johns Hopkins University, internationally regarded as the "dean of biblical studies") and Mann, two respected biblical scholars, have concluded that Isaiah 22:15 *et seq.* is certainly intimately connected with Matthew 16:19, as follows:

> "Isaiah xxii 15 ff. undoubtedly lies behind this [Matthew 16:19] saying. *The keys* are the symbol of authority, and Roland de Vaux (*Ancient Israel*, tr. by John McHugh [New York: McGraw-Hill, 1961], 129 ff.) rightly sees here the same authority as that vested in the vizier, the master of the house, the chamberlain of the royal household in ancient Israel. Eliakim is described as having the same authority in Isaiah; . . . and Jotham as regent is also described as 'over the household' (II Kings xv 5)." W. F. Albright and C. S. Mann, *The Anchor Bible: Matthew*, (Garden City, NY: Doubleday, 1971), 196.

The late F. F. Bruce, former teacher of New Testament Biblical Exegesis at the University of Manchester (member of the Plymouth Brethren movement) has also written of the keys in Isaiah:

> "And what about the 'keys of the kingdom'? The keys of a royal or noble establishment were entrusted to the chief steward or majordomo; he carried them on his shoulder in earlier times, and there they served as a badge of the authority entrusted to him. About 700 B.C. an oracle from God announced that this authority in the royal palace in Jerusalem was to be conferred on a man called Eliakim: . . . (Isaiah 22:22). So in the new community which Jesus was about to build, Peter would be, so to speak, chief steward." F. F. Bruce, *The Hard Sayings of Jesus*, (Downers Grove, IL: Intervarsity, 1983), 143-144.

Interpreting the keys in Isaiah 22:22, John Calvin, one of the Protestant Reformers, had the following commentary to make:

"The keys of the house are delivered to those who are appointed to be stewards, that they may have the full power of opening and shutting according to their own pleasure. By 'the house of David' is meant 'the royal house.' This mode of expression was customary among the people, because it had been promised to David that his kingdom would be forever. (2 Samuel vii. 13; Psalm cxxxii. 11, 12.) That is the reason why the kingdom was commonly called 'the house of David.'

"*The key* is put in the singular number for *keys*. Though 'keys' are usually carried in the hands, yet he says that they are laid on the shoulders, because he is describing an important charge. Yet nothing more is meant than that the charge and the whole government of the house are committed to him, that he may regulate everything according to his pleasure; and we know that the delivering of keys is commonly regarded as a token of possession.

"Some commentators have viewed this passage as referring to Christ, but improperly; for the Prophet draws a comparison between two men, Shebna and Eliakim. Shebna shall be deprived of his office, and Eliakim shall succeed him. What has this to do with Christ? For Eliakim was not a type of Christ, and the Prophet does not here describe any hidden mystery, but borrows a comparison from the ordinary practice of men, as if the keys were delivered to one who has been appointed to be steward, as has been already said. For the same reason Christ calls the office of teaching the word, (Matt. xvi. 19,) 'the keys of the kingdom of heaven;' so that it is idle and foolish to spend much time in endeavouring to find a hidden reason, when the matter is plain, and needs no ingenuity. The reason is, that ministers, by the preaching of the word, open the entrance into heaven, and lead to Christ, who alone is 'the way.' (John xiv. 6.) By *the keys*, therefore, he means here the government of the king's house, because the principal charge of it would be delivered to Eliakim at the proper time." John Calvin, *Commentary on the Book of the Prophet Isaiah*, vol. 2, trans. William Pringle, (Grand Rapids, MI: Eerdmans, 1948), 136-137.

The United Methodist publication of *The New Interpreter's Bible* extends the thought of Calvin (in the above interpretation of Isaiah 22) to give the position of Peter a special teaching authority in the Church through the conferral of the keys:

> "The 'kingdom of heaven' is represented by authoritative teaching, the promulgation of authoritative Halakha that lets heaven's power rule in earthly things . . . Peter's role as holder of the keys is fulfilled now, on earth, as chief teacher of the church." M. Eugene Boring, "Matthew," in Pheme Perkins and others, eds., *The New Interpreter's Bible*. vol. 8, (Nashville, TN: Abingdon Press, 1995), 346.

> "The keeper of the keys has authority within the house as administrator and teacher (cf. Isa. 22:20-25, which may have influenced Matthew here). The language of binding and loosing is rabbinic terminology for authoritative teaching, for having the authority to interpret the Torah and apply it to particular cases, declaring what is permitted and what is not permitted. Jesus, who has taught with authority (7:29) and has given his authority to his disciples (10:1,8) here gives his primary disciple the authority to teach in his name." M. Eugene Boring, "Matthew," in Pheme Perkins and others, eds., *The New Interpreter's Bible*. vol. 8, (Nashville, TN: Abingdon Press, 1995), 346.

Intervarsity Press has produced a commentary analyzing Isaiah 22:22 and its relationship to Matthew 16:19, as follows:

> "The image of keys (plural) perhaps suggests not so much the porter, who controls admission to the house, as the steward, who regulates its administration (Is 22:22, in conjunction with 22:15). The issue then is not that of admission to the church (which is not what the kingdom of heaven means; see pp. 45-47) but an authority derived from a 'delegation of God's sovereignty." Craig S. Keener, *The IVP Bible Background Commentary New Testament*, (Downer's Grove, IL: Intervarsity Press, 1993), 256.

> "The keeper of the keys was one of the most important roles a household servant could hold (Mark 13:32-34). A higher

official held the keys in a royal kingdom (Is 22:22) and in God's house, the temple." Craig S. Keener, *The IVP Bible Background Commentary New Testament*, (Downer's Grove, IL: Intervarsity Press, 1993), 90.

Based on comparing Matthew 16:19 with Isaiah 22:22, a similar conclusion is drawn:

"The keys of the kingdom of heaven: the phrase [from Matthew 16:19] is almost certainly based on Is. 22:22 where Shebna the steward is displaced by Eliakim and his authority transferred to him." D. Guthrie and others, *The New Bible Commentary*, (Grand Rapids, MI: Eerdmans, 1953) [reprinted by Inter-Varsity Press], 837.

Other descriptions of the office of steward are found in the Old Testament, as follows:

II Kings 15:5 And the LORD smote the king, so that he was a leper unto the day of his death, and dwelt in a several house. And Jotham the king's son [was] over the house, judging the people of the land.

Genesis 41:39 And Pharaoh said unto Joseph, Forasmuch as God hath shewed thee all this, [there is] none so discreet and wise as thou [art]:
41:40 Thou shalt be over my house, and according unto thy word shall all my people be ruled: only in the throne will I be greater than thou.

The words regarding the steward of the house have equivalents in other Near Eastern languages:

"The exact semantic equivalent in Assyrian and Babylonian is *sha pan ekalli* and in Egyptian *mr pr*. They were high officials, but their authority seems to have been restricted to the administration of the royal palace: they were the king's stewards or majordomos. In Israel the powers of the master of the palace were far more extensive and the similarity between his functions and those of the Egyptian vizier is even more important than the verbal resemblances. This vizier used to report every morning to the Pharaoh and receive his instructions. He saw to the opening of the 'gates of the royal house', that is, of the various offices of the palace, and then the official day began. All the affairs of the land passed through his hands, all important documents received his seal, all the officials were under his orders. He really governed in the Pharaoh's name and acted for him in his absence. This is obviously the dignity which Joseph exercised, according to Genesis. He had no one above him except the Pharaoh, and he was appointed over the whole land of Egypt; he held the royal seal (Genesis 41:40-44), and to describe his dignity the Bible says that the Pharaoh 'put him in charge of his house'; he made him, in fact, his master of the palace (Genesis 41:40; 45:8).

"The master of the palace had similar functions at the court of Judah. Announcing the promotion of Elyaqim, Isaiah 22:22 says: 'I lay the key of the house of David upon his shoulder; if he opens, none will shut; if he shuts, none will open.'

"The Egyptian vizier's instructions are described in a very similar fashion. Every morning 'the vizier will send someone to open the gates of the king's house, to admit those who have to enter, and to send out those who have to go out.' One is reminded of the Lord's words to Peter, the Vizier of the Kingdom of Heaven (Matthew 16:19). Like the Egyptian vizier, the master of the palace was the highest official in the state: his name comes first in the list of 2 Kings 18:18; he alone appears with the king in 1 Kings 18:3; and Yotham bears this title when he acts as regent of the kingdom (2 Kings 15:5), as the vizier did in the absence of the Pharaoh." Roland de Vaux, *Ancient Israel*, trans. John McHugh (New York: McGraw-Hill, 1961), 130.

Matthew Henry, a Protestant theologian (member of the Puritan Reformed movement), writing in the 18th century, described the connection between opening/shutting and binding/loosing in the context of Joseph as vizier over Pharaoh's house (Genesis 41:39-40):

> "It is the power to bind and loose, that is (following the metaphor of the keys), to shut and open. Joseph, who was lord of Pharaoh's house, and steward of the stores, had power to bind. . . .[Psalm 105:21-22]." Matthew Henry, *Matthew Henry's Commentary: Matthew to John*, vol. 5, (McLean, VA: MacDonald, n.d. [originally published 1721]).

The Lutheran-Catholic dialogue has explored various theological points of similarity and difference between them over a period of several years after Vatican II. On the subject of the Papacy as it relates to Isaiah 22, the following was written:

> "The prime minister, more literally 'major-domo,' was the man called in Hebrew 'the one who is over the house,' a term borrowed from the Egyptian designation of the chief palace functionary. The bureaucracy of the Hebrew monarchy was adopted from Egyptian models. See R. de Vaux, *Ancient Israel* (New York: McGraw-Hill, 1961), pp. 129-32." Raymond E. Brown, Karl P. Donfried, and John Reumann, eds., *Peter in the New Testament*, (Minneapolis, MN: Augsburg; New York: Paulist: 1973), 96.

25. Who is the overseer of the house, and what was his authority? In Isaiah 22, Shebna acted as the overseer (chamberlain or prime minister) for King Hezekiah. In Genesis 41, Joseph acted for Pharaoh over his house and empire as overseer, and probably had the title of "vizier." In Egypt, the vizier was the highest ranking officer in the realm, other than the pharaoh, and acted for the pharaoh during his absence, as regent, i.e., in place of the king.

26. What is another way of expressing the full or unlimited authority of the overseer? Plenary authority.

The following quote is from a Protestant commentary regarding the plenary authority of the keys:

> "The keys of the kingdom would be committed to the chief steward in the royal household and with them goes plenary authority. In Isa. 22:22 the key of the house of David is promised to Eliakim. According to Paul, Jesus is the only foundation (I Cor. 3:11), and in Rev. 1:18; 3:7, Jesus possesses the key of David and the keys of death and Hades. But in this passage [Matthew 16:19] Peter is made the foundation (cf. Eph. 2:20, where the Christian apostles and prophets are the foundation and Christ is the cornerstone) and holds the keys." George Buttrick and others, eds., *The Interpreter's Bible*, (New York: Abingdon, 1951), 453.

The Power to Bind and to Loose

In Isaiah 22:16-19, Shebna is being informed that the Lord God and King Hezekiah have lost confidence in Shebna, and that he shall be replaced with another. It required the Lord's own authority to remove Shebna, the vizier of the king.

> *Isaiah* 22:16 What hast thou here? and whom hast thou here, that thou hast hewed thee out a sepulchre here, [as] he that heweth him out a sepulchre on high, [and] that graveth an habitation for himself in a rock?
> 22:17 Behold, the LORD will carry thee away with a mighty captivity, and will surely cover thee.
> 22:18 He will surely violently turn and toss thee [like] a ball into a large country: there shalt thou die, and there the chariots of thy glory [shall be] the shame of thy lord's house.
> 22:19 And I will drive thee from thy station [office], and from thy state shall he pull thee down.

27. What is the normal position and authority of the prime minister? In England, the King or Queen was the ruler of the realm, and the Prime Minister was the ruler of the government of the realm, under whom were the various ministers of the departments of government.

28. From what is Shebna being removed in Isaiah 22? From his office or station as chamberlain to the king, as the master of the palace of King Hezekiah. In verse 17, this action is presented as the work and will of the Lord.

Isaiah 22:20 And it shall come to pass in that day, that I will call my servant Eliakim the son of Hilkiah:

29. In Isaiah 22:20, who will be replacing Shebna? Eliakim, the son of Hilkiah. The king is Hezekiah during this period of time. The dynasty begun by King David is being continued by King Hezekiah, who is the 14th king of Judah. He faced many difficulties during his reign, being pressured by the Egyptians to the south, and the Assyrians from the northeast.

30. Did the king rule alone? No. Several ministers under him ruled for him in various capacities, and the chief among these was akin to the position of vizier in Egypt or the prime (first) minister in England.

31. When was David's kingdom set up? The house of David, or David's kingdom, was established in the 11th century B.C., or approximately 1010-970 B.C. Allen C. Myers, ed., *The Eerdmans Bible Dictionary*, (Grand Rapids, MI: Eerdmans, 1987), 262.

32. When was Isaiah written? Chapters 1-39 are ascribed to Isaiah, circa 8th century B.C. [Allen C. Myers, ed., *The Eerdmans Bible Dictionary*, (Grand Rapids, MI: Eerdmans, 1987), 531], or approximately 740-680 B.C.

33. How long, then, had the keys passed down in succession? For 300-400 years.

Isaiah 22:21 And I will clothe him with thy robe, and strengthen him with thy girdle, and I will commit thy government into his hand: and he shall be a father to the inhabitants of Jerusalem, and to the house of Judah.

22:22 And the key of the house of David will I lay upon his shoulder; so he shall open, and none shall shut; and he shall shut, and none shall open.

34. How are the keys being passed down? Through the successors of the chief palace administrator of the House of Judah. There shall be successive generations of palace administrators.

"In Isaiah 22:22 Eliakim is given the key of the house of David and fills the role of palace administrator for King Hezekiah. In Isaiah 36:3 he is designated literally as the person 'over the house' (Hebrew: *al habayith*). The *house* refers to the residence of the king, otherwise known as the king's palace. . . . As specified in Isaiah 22:22 the palace administrator was a very prestigious and responsible position since what he 'opens no one can shut, and what he closes no one can open.' Isaiah 22:22 also gives an indication as to the origin of this office by the phrasing, 'the house of David.' We would assume from such language that the position of palace administrator would have been a perpetual office beginning with David. This is almost the case. The first recording of the office of palace administrator is in I Kings 4:6 in which Ahishar is given the identical title as Eliakim, namely, the person 'over the house.' It would appear that Ahishar would have had the same prerogatives of 'opening' and 'shutting' that Eliakim had. This office actually began under the reign of King Solomon, the king after David. Other specific mentionings of this office are found in I Kings 16:9 (Arza under King Elah) and I Kings 18:3 (Obadiah under King Ahab). . . . Unlike the Old Testament kings, however, Jesus remains the only king of the Church. Before he left, Jesus designated a 'palace administrator' or 'chief of staff' to rule the affairs of his house, the Church. His name was Peter. Significantly, Peter is given the keys to bind and loose even as Eliakim was given the key to open and shut. Peter's successors, even as Ahishar had successors stretching throughout the history of Israel, would assume the same ruling prerogatives throughout the duration of the Church. All of these New Testament 'palace adminis-

trators,' i.e., popes, would be under one king, that is, Jesus."
Robert A. Sungenis, "The Palace Administrator," letter to
authors, June 1994.

During the reign of King David there was no palace administrator
mentioned, even though David inhabited a palace (cf. II Samuel
11:2). Father de Vaux proffers an answer to the problem:

> "It seems, however, that the master of the palace only
> gradually came to be the first minister, and perhaps in the
> early days of the monarchy he was only the steward of the
> palace and of the royal estate. This would account for his
> title and for the fact that he is not named among David's
> senior officials, and does not head the list of Solomon's civil
> servants. Under David and Solomon the secretary and the
> king's herald were the immediate representatives of the king:
> there was no place for a vizier.
>
> "In Is 22:15 Shebna, the master of the palace, is called
> the *soken*. . . the *skn* (in alphabetical script) or the *shakin
> mati* (in Akkadian) was an official at Ugarit, apparently the
> highest in the land; this corresponds to the position held in
> Judah by Shebna, *soken* and master of the palace." Roland
> de Vaux, *Ancient Israel*, vol. 1, trans. John McHugh (New
> York: McGraw-Hill, 1961), 130-131.

Following the Keys to Peter and Christ

> *Isaiah* 22:23 And I will fasten him [as] a nail in a
> sure place; and he shall be for a glorious throne to his
> father's house.
>
> 22:24 And they shall hang upon him all the glory
> of his father's house, the offspring and the issue, all
> vessels of small quantity, from the vessels of cups,
> even to all the vessels of flagons.
>
> 22:25 In that day, saith the LORD of hosts, shall
> the nail that is fastened in the sure place be removed,
> and be cut down, and fall; and the burden that [was]
> upon it shall be cut off: for the LORD hath spoken [it].

35. Does Eliakim, the new palace administrator, in Isaiah 22:23,
have a throne of honor granted to him? Yes.

36. According to Isaiah 22:24, is succession being implied? The earmarks of succession are there. The palace masters assisted the kings of the House of Judah, in a line of succession parallel to the kings. The "burden" of this office will be cut off at some time in the future (Isaiah 22:25).

37. What two roles are in this line of succession? The roles of the king and his prime minister rule in parallel lines of succession, one passed on from generation to generation through offspring and issue, the other through appointment.

38. What is the parallel between Eliakim and Peter? Oscar Cullmann, a Lutheran biblical scholar, makes the connection between Isaiah 22:22 and Matthew 16:19:

> "In Matthew 16:19 it is presupposed that Christ is the master of the house, who has the keys to the Kingdom of Heaven, with which to open to those who come in. Just as in Isaiah 22:22 the Lord lays the keys of the house of David on the shoulders of his servant Eliakim, so Jesus commits to Peter the keys of his house, the Kingdom of Heaven, and thereby installs him as administrator of the house." Oscar Cullmann, *Peter: Disciple, Apostle, Martyr*, trans. Floyd V. Filson, (Philadelphia: Westminster, 1953), 203.

39. Who are descendants of the house of Judah? King David (Genesis 49:10, Micah 5:2), and his lineage, including King Hezekiah, and the Messiah.

Before Christ, the Messianic role of King Hezekiah is to be found in Jewish tradition, beginning in Isaiah. The scriptural sources for the Messianic role of the lineage of King David are fairly clear (cf. II Samuel 7:13-14). These sources do not refer specifically to King Hezekiah. The Messianic role of King Hezekiah is fleshed out in Jewish commentaries. From Scripture and Talmud, David Stern and Jacob Neusner have culled key quotations and have written:

"See 2 Kings 20:8 (in which King Hezekiah is raised up from terminal illness to go up to the Temple on the third day)." David H. Stern, *Jewish New Testament Commentary*, (Clarksville, MD: Jewish New Testament Publications, 1992), 486.

"And as he [Rabbi Yohannan ben Zakkai, one of the foremost first century Pharisaic leaders upon the fall of Jerusalem,] breathed his last, he said, 'Clear the house of vessels which can receive corpse-uncleanness, and prepare a throne for Hezekiah, king of Judah, who cometh.'" Jacob Neusner, *First-Century Judaism in Crisis*, (Nashville: Abingdon Press, 1975), 200.

"King Hezekiah is identified in Jewish literature with the Messiah." David H. Stern, *Jewish New Testament Commentary*, (Clarksville, MD: Jewish New Testament Publications, 1992), 11.

The messianic king of Isaiah 33:17-22 (and Isaiah 22) would be variously identified with King Hezekiah and the Lord God (cf. Reginald C. Fuller, Leonard Johnston, and Conleth Kearns, eds., *A New Catholic Commentary on Holy Scripture*, (Nashville: Thomas Nelson, 1969), 32; Confraternity of Christian Doctrine, *The New American Bible* (Giant Print Edition), fn. [Isaiah] 33:17, (Huntington, IN: Our Sunday Visitor, 1988), 1350). The key role of King Hezekiah's new chief steward, Eliakim, foreshadows and underscores the key role that Peter will play as the chief steward of Jesus the Messiah under the New Covenant, according to Matthew 16:18-19.

40. Who is also in the lineage of the House of Judah, along with King David and King Hezekiah? Jesus Christ, according to the genealogy of Matthew 1.

Opening/Shutting and Binding/Loosing in Isaiah and Matthew

One Jewish interpreter of Torah who involved the concept of binding and loosing in his daily prayers was Nehunya (or, "Nechonya"), a respected first-century rabbi (circa 70 A.D.).

"Nehunya Ben Ha-Kanah (second half of first century), *tanna*. Nehunya was highly regarded by Johanan b. Zakkai, who was apparently his teacher. . . . He was a native of Emmaus in Judea and is therefore referred to as Nehunya b. ha-Kanah of Emmaus by the *Tanhuma* (Deut. to 26:13) which cites a halakhic discussion between him and Joshua b. Hahaniah." *Encyclopaedia Judaica*, 1971 ed., s.v. "Nehunya ben ha-Kanah."

A Catholic Christian writer has quoted him in regard to binding and loosing in the context of Matthew 16:19:

"'Whatsoever thou shalt bind.' In these words Jesus was conferring on Peter in a special and unique way power which was conferred on the Apostles as a body on another occasion. He was simply *using the language of the day* [emphasis added]. Everybody knew what it meant. The Rabbis were said to bind when they forbade something and to loose when they permitted it. We know of a Rabbi called Nechonya [or, "Nehunya"] who lived about the year 70. He always put the following prayer before his lessons: 'May it please thee, O Yahweh, my God and God of my Fathers, that we may not declare impure what is pure and pure what is impure; that we may not bind what is loosed nor loose what is bound.'" Francis J. Ripley, *The Pope: Vicar of Jesus Christ*, (Dublin: Catholic Truth Society, 1965), 9. Cf. *Encyclopaedia Judaica*, 1971 ed., s.v. "Nehunya ben ha-Kanah [wherein reference is made to 'TJ, Ber. 4:2, 7d; cf. Ber. 28b for variant readings' related to Nehunya's prayers on entering the house of study]."

Peter is the Vicar (Prime Minister) of Christ on earth, the one who opens and shuts, binds and looses. Cf. S. T. Lachs, *A Rabbinic Commentary on the New Testament: The Gospels of Matthew, Mark, and Luke*, (Hoboken, NJ: Ktav, 1987), 256 [the respected Jewish scholar who comments on Isaiah 22:22 and Matthew 16:19 thus: "The authority of Peter is to be over the Church, and this authority is represented by the keys."]

Isaiah 22:22 And the key of the house of David will I lay upon his shoulder; so he shall open, and none shall shut; and he shall shut, and none shall open.

Matthew 16:19 And I will give unto thee the keys of the kingdom of heaven: and whatsoever thou shalt bind on earth shall be bound in heaven: and whatsoever thou shalt loose on earth shall be loosed in heaven.

Oscar Cullmann develops the significance of the terms "bind" and "loose":

"What do the expressions 'bind' and 'loose' signify? According to Rabbinical usage two explanations are equally possible: 'prohibit' and 'permit,' that is, 'establish rules'; or 'put under the ban' and 'acquit.'" Oscar Cullmann, *Peter: Disciple, Apostle, Martyr*, trans. Floyd V. Filson, (Philadelphia: Westminster, 1953), 204-205.

In analyzing "bind" and "loose," the Protestant scholar R. T. France (formerly teacher of New Testament in the University of Nigeria; formerly Librarian and Warden at Tyndale House, Cambridge; formerly Vice President and Senior Lecturer at London Bible College; and currently Principal of Wycliffe Hall, Oxford, concludes:

"These terms [binding and loosing] thus refer to a teaching function, and more specifically one of making halakhic pronouncements [i.e., relative to laws not written down in the Jewish Scriptures but based on an oral interpretation of them] which are to be 'binding' on the people of God. In that case Peter's 'power of the keys' declared in [Matthew] 16:19 is not so much that of the doorkeeper, who decides who may or may not be admitted to the kingdom of heaven, but that of the steward (as in Is. 22:22, generally regarded as the Old Testament background to the metaphor of keys here), whose keys of office enable him to regulate the affairs of the household." R. T. France, *Matthew: Evangelist and Teacher*, (Grand Rapids, MI: Zondervan, 1989), 247.

Ralph Earle, Th.D., then Professor of New Testament, Nazarene Theological Seminary, Kansas City, Missouri, comments on binding and loosing in the *Beacon Bible Commentary*, from the perspective of the Church of the Nazarene:

> "Even more striking [than the keys] is Jesus' statement that whatever Peter bound on earth would be bound in heaven, and whatever he loosed on earth would be loosed in heaven. What is meant by *bind* and *loose*? M'Neile explains: '"Bind" and "loose" appear to represent the Aramaic . . . technical terms for the verdict of a teacher of the Law who, on the strength of his expert knowledge of the oral tradition, declared some action or thing "bound" i.e. forbidden, or "loosed" i.e. permitted.' In other words, Peter would give decisions, based on the teachings of Jesus, which would be *bound in heaven*; that is, honored by God." Ralph Earle, "Matthew," in A. F. Harper and others, eds., *Beacon Bible Commentary*, vol. 6, (Kansas City, MO: Beacon Hill, 1964), 156.

Intervarsity Press, in its commentary, states:

> "That authority is exercised in binding and loosing, which were technical terms for the pronouncement of rabbis on what was and was not permitted (to bind was to forbid, to loose to permit). This verse [Matthew 16:19] therefore probably refers primarily to a legislative authority in the church." Craig S. Keener, *The IVP Bible Background Commentary New Testament*, (Downer's Grove, IL: Intervarsity Press, 1993), 90.

Albright, a Protestant scholar, defines "bind" as follows:

> "*bind*. The role of Peter as steward of the Kingdom is further explained as being the exercise of administrative authority, as was the case of the OT chamberlain who held the 'keys.' The clauses *on earth*, *in heaven*, have reference to the permanent character of the steward's work. Peter's initiative is well illustrated by the admission of a Gentile

to the community in Acts x-xi, under the guidance of the spirit - an event which the historian considered as meriting a great deal of attention in his work." W. F. Albright and C. S. Mann, *The Anchor Bible: Matthew*, (Garden City, NY: Doubleday, 1971), 197.

The early writers and fathers of the Church looked to Peter and his successors as having the power and authority of the keys of the Kingdom of Heaven. An example from Tertullian (ca. 200 A.D.) follows:

"Was anything hidden from Peter, who was called the Rock whereon the Church was to be built; who obtained the keys of the kingdom of heaven, and the power of loosing and of binding in heaven and on earth?" Tertullian, *De Praescript Haeret* n. 22, p. 209, in Colin Lindsay, *The Evidence for the Papacy*, (London: Longmans, 1870), 19.

Additional quotations are in Part Two of this book.

St. John Cassian [c. 362-435], whose feast day is July 23 in the Western Church and February 29 in the Eastern Church, writes strongly in defense of the Papacy having the power of the keys:

"O Peter, Prince of the Apostles, it is just that you should teach us, since you were yourself taught by the Lord; and also that you should open to us the gate of which you have received the key. Keep out all those who are undermining the heavenly House; turn away those who are trying to enter through false caverns and unlawful gates since it is certain that no one can enter in at the gate of the kingdom except the one unto whom the key, placed by you in the churches, shall open it." Michael Malone, *The Apostolic Digest*, (Irving, TX: Sacred Heart, 1987), 243-244.

St. Bede the Venerable, a Father of the Church [c. 673-735 A.D.], wrote:

"Blessed Peter so received the keys of the kingdom and the supremacy of judicial power, that all who believe throughout the world may understand that whosoever shall cut themselves off in any way . . . cannot enter the kingdom of Heaven . . . Peter received the keys to Heaven as a sign to all the children of the Church, so that if they separate from the one faith which he teaches, they give up all hope of being acquitted of their guilt and of entering the eternal portals . . . And I say unto you that Peter is the doorkeeper whom I will not contradict, but I will obey his decrees in everything, lest when I come to the gates of the kingdom of Heaven there should be no one to open them, since he will be my adversary who is proven to have possession of the keys." Michael Malone, *The Apostolic Digest*, (Irving, TX: Sacred Heart, 1987), 243.

The Ultimate Authority of the Keys of the Kingdom of Heaven

> *Revelation* 3:7 And to the angel of the church in Philadelphia write; These things saith he that is holy, he that is true, he that hath the key of David, he that openeth, and no man shutteth; and shutteth, and no man openeth;

41. Who, specifically, holds the key to the house of David in Revelation 3:7? Jesus Christ.

42. Who, specifically, has the power to open and shut in Revelation 3:7? Jesus Christ.

> *Revelation* 1:17 And when I saw him, I fell at his feet as dead. And he laid his right hand upon me, saying unto me, Fear not; I am the first and the last:
> 1:18 I [am] he that liveth, and was dead; and, behold, I am alive for evermore, Amen; and have the keys of hell and of death.

43. According to Revelation 1:17-18, who under the New Covenant holds the keys? The Alpha and the Omega (the first and the last), the Almighty, Christ the King.

The passage in Revelation 1:18 indicates that the keys of hell and death are different from the keys of the Kingdom of God held by Peter (see Revelation 3:7; Matthew 16:19). On the other hand, the power of binding and loosing inherent in Peter's keys is exercised in excommunicating non-adherents from the People of God (the Church) on earth; and this action may have eternal ramifications in determining whether one enters through the gates of hell or death hereafter. In any event, the Lord Jesus Christ ultimately holds the authority of all keys and has delegated a certain authority of these keys to Peter on earth. A king never relinquishes his authority to hold the keys, but he may delegate his authority to whomever he pleases. They then both hold the authority of the keys, one by right, the other by delegation.

"Materially, then, the keys of the kingdom of God are not different from the key of David. This is confirmed by the fact that in Mt. 16:19, as in Rev. 3:7, Jesus is the One who controls them. But in what sense is the power of the keys given to Peter? . . .

"There are numerous instances to show that in biblical and later Jewish usage handing over the keys implies full authorisation. He who has the keys has full authority. Thus, when Eliakim is given the keys of the palace he is appointed the royal steward (Is. 22:22, cf. 15). When Jesus is said to hold the keys of death and Hades (Rev. 1:18) or the key of David (3:7), this means that He is, not the doorkeeper, but the Lord of the world of the dead and the palace of God. . .

"Hence handing over the keys implies appointment to full authority. He who has the keys has on the one side control, e.g., over the council chamber or treasury, cf. Mt. 13:52, and on the other the power to allow or forbid entry, cf. Rev. 3:7.

"Mt. 23:13 ['ye shut up the kingdom of heaven against men'] leads us a step further. This passage is particularly important for an understanding of Mt. 16:19 because it is the only one in the NT which presupposes an image not found elsewhere, namely, that of the keys of the kingdom (royal dominion) of God. Mt. 23:13 shows us that the scribes of the time of Jesus claimed to possess the power of the keys in respect of this kingdom. They exercised this by declaring the will of God in Holy Scripture in the form of preaching, teaching and judging. Thereby they opened up for the congregation a way into this kingdom, . . . As Lord of the Messianic community He thus transferred the keys of God's royal dominion . . . to Peter." J. Jeremias, "Kleis," in Gerhard Kittel, ed., and Geoffrey W. Bromley, trans. and ed., *Theological Dictionary of the New Testament*, vol. 3, (Grand Rapids, MI: Eerdmans, 1968), 749-750.

The Church recognizes that Jesus Christ is the chief holder of the keys of death and Sheol (Revelation 1:18) and the key of David (Revelation 3:7), just as she realizes that Jesus Christ is the chief Shepherd of the Church. The keys that Peter has entrusted to him (Matthew 16:19), he must relinquish when Christ visibly returns at the end of time (Revelation 3:7).

Moreover, in John 21:15-17 Jesus makes Peter the shepherd of the flock until the Lord returns (cf. I Peter 5:4), but Christ never relinquishes his authority over (or ownership of) the flock, as he says, "Feed *my* lambs. . . Tend *my* sheep. . . Feed *my* sheep." Jesus speaks possessively and with authority. Peter accedes.

44. To whom did Jesus Christ delegate stewardship of the keys of the kingdom of heaven before leaving this earth? To Peter, according to Matthew 16:19. Christ is the primary holder of the keys that he delegates to Peter. The contents of Matthew 16:19 and Revelation 3:7 are not mutually exclusive. There is not a handing-off of the keys. While Christ has delegated the keys to Peter, Christ still holds the keys as a king holds the authority of the keys that he has delegated to his chief steward or regent. Peter is the rock that is exercising Christ's authority in holding the keys of the kingdom, standing as Christ's regent or vicar: one delegated to head the visible Church until the end of time.

Peter's Power to Bind and Loose as the Human Holder of the Keys

45. What did Martin Luther, one of the early leaders of the Protestant Reformation, say about the keys? In 1530, nine years after his excommunication in 1521, Luther wrote a tract entitled "The Keys." Although he overlooks Christ's primary possession of the keys, even in heaven, Luther does underline Peter's true authority, as the holder of the keys:

> "So we stand there and with open mouth stare heavenward and invent still other keys. Yet Christ says very clearly in Matt. 16:19 that he will give the keys to Peter. He does not say he has two kinds of keys, but he gives to Peter the keys he himself has and no others. It is as if he were saying: Why are you staring heavenward in search of the keys? Do you not understand I gave them to Peter? They are indeed the keys of heaven, but they are not found in heaven. I left them on earth. Don't look for them in heaven or anywhere else except in Peter's mouth where I have placed them. Peter's mouth is my mouth, and his tongue is my key case. His office is my office, his binding and loosing are my binding and loosing." Martin Luther, "The Keys," in Conrad Bergendoff, ed., trans. Earl Beyer and Conrad Bergendoff, *Luther's Works*, vol. 40, Philadelphia: Fortress, 1958), 365-366.

Making the connection between the relevant passages of Isaiah 22 and Revelation 3, Allen Willoughby writes:

> "He who held the keys would have power within it, power to admit, power to exclude. In Rev. 3 this power is held by Christ Himself: 'he that hath the key of David, that openeth and none shall shut, and that shutteth and none shall open.' The words are modelled on Is. 22, and express supreme authority. To hold the keys is to have absolute right, which can be contested by none. . . . To 'bind' and to 'loose' in Jewish legal terminology are equivalent to 'forbid' and 'allow,' to 'declare forbidden' and to 'declare allowed.'" C. Allen Willoughby, *The International Critical Commentary: St. Matthew*, (Edinburgh: T. & T. Clark, 1977), 177.

While the keys of David are held alone by the king in Revelation 3, the king's keys simultaneously belong to the king and are held by his steward in Isaiah 22.

The Delegation of the Keys to Peter

From an analysis of the language in Matthew 16:19, one can determine that Peter was the first to hold the keys of Christ. He held them singularly, not jointly with the rest of the Apostles:

> *Matthew* 16:19 And I will give unto thee [*soi* = singular you] the keys of the kingdom of heaven: and whatsoever thou shalt bind [*deses* = singular you] on earth shall be bound [*estai dedemenon* = shall be, having been bound] in heaven: and whatsoever thou shalt loose [*luses* = singular you] on earth shall be loosed [*estai lelumenon* = shall be, having been loosed] in heaven.

46. To whom does Jesus Christ promise stewardship of the keys to the kingdom of heaven? To Peter.

47. Does stewardship of the keys apply to a singular or plural "you" in Matthew 16:19? To a singular "you," i.e., to Peter. *Soi* is the singular dative form of "you" in Greek, and the verb forms of bind and loose are in the singular form also.

48. As this promise concerning the keys is made singularly and solely to Peter, are the other Apostles granted stewardship of the keys of the kingdom of heaven? No.

> "That Peter is given these privileges in an exclusive realm is demonstrated by the use of the Greek singular throughout the passage. The 'you' in the phrases, 'I [will] give *you* the keys,' '*you* shall bind,' and '*you* shall loose' are Greek singulars, referring to one man, namely Peter. In Matthew 18:18, the plural of 'you' is used when Jesus is addressing all the apostles, but in Matthew 16:19 he is only addressing Peter. Peter is the only one of the apostles who is given the

keys of the kingdom. These keys are directly related to the power of binding and loosing of which Peter is given a singular prerogative not given to any other apostle. Hence, heaven will confirm the singular decrees [on faith and morals] of Peter and keep him from error, independent of the other apostles." Robert A. Sungenis, "The Precedent for Infallibility," letter to authors, November 1993, 5.

Peter and the Other Apostles' Powers of Binding and Loosing

Jesus addresses the Apostles, including Peter, to set forth their powers over the brethren on earth and the way in which they should proceed in the event of certain occurrences:

> *Matthew* 18:15 Moreover if thy brother shall trespass against thee, go and tell him his fault between thee and him alone: if he shall hear thee, thou hast gained thy brother.
> 18:16 But if he will not hear [thee, then] take with thee one or two more, that in the mouth of two or three witnesses every word may be established.
> 18:17 And if he shall neglect to hear them, tell [it] unto the church: but if he neglect to hear the church, let him be unto thee as an heathen man and a publican.
> 18:18 Verily I say unto you [*humin* = plural you], Whatsoever ye [plural you] shall bind [*deseste*] on earth shall be bound [*estai dedemena* = shall be, being bound] in heaven: and whatsoever ye [plural you] shall loose [*lusete*] on earth shall be loosed [*estai lelumena* = shall be, being loosed] in heaven.
> 18:19 Again I say unto you [*humin* = plural you], That if two of you shall agree on earth as touching any thing that they shall ask, it shall be done for them of my Father which is in heaven.

David Stern looks at Matthew 18:18 from the point of view of the Messianic Jewish Christian:

> "Contrary to most Christian interpreters, I take the *p'shat* ('plain sense') of this passage [Matthew 18] to be dealing

with making legal judgments and *halakhah* [i.e., relative to laws not written down in the Jewish Scriptures but based on an oral interpretation of them], not prayer.

"The words rendered 'prohibit' and 'permit' (v.18) are, literally, 'bind' and 'loose.' these terms were used in the first century Judaism to mean 'prohibit' and 'permit,' as is clear from the article, 'Binding and Loosing,' in the *Jewish Encyclopedia*, 3:125:

> "'Binding and Loosing (Hebrew *asar ve-hittar* . . . Rabbinical term for "forbidding and permitting.". . .'
>
> "'The power of binding and loosing was always claimed by the Pharisees. Under Queen Alexandra the Pharisees, says Josephus (*Wars of the Jews* 1:5:2), "became the administrators of all public affairs so as to be empowered to banish and readmit whom they pleased, as well as to loose and to bind." . . . The various schools had the power "to bind and to loose"; that is, to forbid and to permit (Talmud: Ta'anit 12a). This power and authority, vested in the rabbinical body of each age or in the Sanhedrin, received its ratification and final sanction from the celestial court of justice (Sifra, Emor, ix; Talmud: Makkot 23b).'
>
> "'In this sense Jesus, when appointing his disciples to be his successors, used the familiar formula (Matt. 16:19, 18:18). By these words he virtually invested them with the same authority as that which he found belonging to the scribes and Pharisees who "bind heavy burdens and lay them on men's shoulders, but will not move them with one of their fingers"; that is, "loose them," as they have the power to do (Matthew 23:2-4).'" David H. Stern, *Jewish New Testament Commentary*, (Clarksville, MD: Jewish New Testament Publications, 1992), 56-57.

49. According to rabbinical sources, what do "bind" and "loose" mean?

> "In rabbinical language to 'bind' and to 'loose' is to declare certain actions forbidden or permitted; e.g., *Terumoth* 5:4: 'If one seah of unclean Heave-offering falls into a hundred

seahs of clean, the School of Shammai bind [forbid] the entire lot, but the School of Hillel loose [permit] it.' Thus Peter's decisions regarding the O.T. law (e.g., Acts 10:44-48) will be ratified in heaven." George Arthur Buttrick and others, eds., *The Interpreter's Bible*, (New York: Abingdon, 1951), 453.

50. What power do all the Apostles (including Peter) together possess that Peter singularly possesses? The power to bind and to loose, according to Matthew 18:18 and 16:19.

The ecumenical Vatican Council II describes the relationship between Peter and the other Apostles in this manner:

"The order of bishops, which succeeds to the college of apostles and gives this apostolic body continued existence, is also the subject of supreme and full power over the Universal Church, provided we understand this body together with its head the Roman Pontiff and never without this head. This power can be exercised only with the consent of the Roman Pontiff. For our Lord placed Simon alone as the rock and the bearer of the keys of the Church, and made him shepherd of the whole flock; it is evident, however, that the power of binding and loosing, which was given to Peter, was granted also to the college of apostles, joined with their head." *Lumen Gentium* (Constitution on the Church, Para. 22, November 21, 1964), (Washington, DC: United States Catholic Conference, n.d.), 24.

51. Is the apostolic collective power to bind and to loose included in the power of the keys? Yes, the power of the keys includes the power of binding and loosing granted to the steward of Christ on earth (Matthew 16:19), and to the Apostles (and their successors) in communion with Peter (cf. Matthew 18:18). The keys signify the singular office of Christ's vicar on earth. The power of the keys is the wider responsibility for the pastoral care of the Church, which requires binding and loosing; the keys are not a component of binding and loosing. Binding and loosing (whether forbidding/permitting, or forgiving/retaining) are the jurisdictional power of the keys, which includes ap-

pointing others to office, teaching doctrine, and other governing duties allocated to the Vicar of Christ and the Apostles.

> "The power to 'bind and loose' connotes the authority to absolve sins, to pronounce doctrinal judgements, and to make disciplinary decisions in the Church. Jesus entrusted this authority to the Church through the ministry of the apostles and in particular though the ministry of Peter, the only one to whom he specifically entrusted the keys of the kingdom." *Catechism of the Catholic Church*, Par. 553, (London: Geoffrey Chapman—Libreria Editrice Vaticana, 1994), 125.

52. Is there anything to distinguish the power of the keys granted to Peter alone from the powers of binding and loosing granted to the college of Apostles? Peter possesses the keys himself, while the college of Apostles (and later bishops and cardinals) share in the authority of the keys by virtue of union with Peter.

The keys are delegated from Christ to Peter, to exercise the power of binding and loosing in its fullness and its entirety, when necessary, alone in his own right as Christ's vicar. The power of the keys, the power of binding and loosing, is delegated directly by Christ to the other Apostles (cf. John 20:21-23), but their exercise of the power of the keys can be carried out properly only in communion with Peter.

Cardinal Cajetan, who responded for the Catholic faithful against Martin Luther during the Reformation, interpreted the relevant passages of Matthew as follows:

> "In the words we have been treating Matthew the evangelist relates that Our Lord promised Peter four things, the last two of which (the power to bind and to loose) he also conferred upon the other apostles. But the first two remain proper to Peter: 'On this rock I will build my Church,' and 'I will give you the keys of the kingdom of heaven [Matthew 16:18f]. Jared Wicks, ed. and trans., *Cajetan Responds* (Washington, DC: Catholic University, 1978), 110.

53. In Matthew 18:18, is the power of binding and loosing given to the Apostles in the singular or the plural form? In the plural form. The Greek word for the plural "you" is *humin*.

54. Do all of the Apostles have the power to bind and to loose? Yes. The power of the Apostles (and their successors the bishops) to bind and loose cooperates with, and in its exercise is dependent upon, the power of the keys given to Peter and his successors. From the standpoint of the Church, the relationship of Pope and Bishops in communion with one another is described as follows:

> "But the college or body of bishops has no authority unless it is understood together with the Roman Pontiff, the successor of Peter as its head. The pope's power of primacy over all, both pastors and faithful, remains whole and intact. In virtue of this office, that is as Vicar of Christ and pastor of the whole Church, the Roman Pontiff has full, supreme and universal power over the Church. And he is always free to exercise this power. The order of bishops, which succeeds to the college of apostles and gives this apostolic body continued existence, is also the subject of supreme full power over the Universal Church, provided we understand this body together with its head the Roman Pontiff and never without this head. This power can be exercised only with the consent of the Roman Pontiff. For our Lord placed Simon alone as the rock and the bearer of the keys of the Church and made him shepherd of the whole flock; it is evident, however, that the power of binding and loosing, which was given to Peter, was granted also to the college of apostles, joined with their head. *Lumen Gentium* (Constitution on the Church, Para. 22, November 21, 1964), (Washington, DC: United States Catholic Conference, n.d.), 24.

> "'The power which they [the bishops] exercise personally in the name of Christ, is proper, ordinary and immediate, although its exercise is ultimately controlled by the supreme authority of the Church [*Lumen Gentium* 27].' But the bishops should not be thought of as vicars of the Pope. His ordinary and immediate authority over the whole Church does

not annul, but on the contrary confirms and defends that of the bishops. Their authority must be exercised in communion with the whole Church under the guidance of the Pope." *Catechism of the Catholic Church*, Par. 895, (London: Geoffrey Chapman—Libreria Editrice Vaticana, 1994), 207-208.

55. But, who has the supreme authority, and what represents it? Peter has the supreme authority in holding the keys of the kingdom of heaven. He holds individually and personally the power that all the Apostles hold in common (binding and loosing). He can exercise his authority and use this power alone, because Jesus has given the keys to Peter singularly in Matthew 16:19, while the exercise of the power is given to the Apostles in the plural sense by dependence on Peter in Matthew 18:18.

The Absence of the Keys in Matthew 18:18 and John 20:23

While the Apostles' binding and loosing are conditional upon communion with Peter, Peter was given individual singular authority apart from the rest of the Apostles to bind and to loose. The keys are the symbol of the authority that he and his successors have received from Jesus Christ to be the Vicars of Christ on earth.

56. What possible reasons are there that the keys to the kingdom of heaven are absent from passages other than Matthew 16:19, where one might expect to find them?

> "Jesus entrusted a specific authority to Peter: 'I will give you the keys of the kingdom of heaven, and whatever you bind on earth shall be bound in heaven, and whatever you loose on earth shall be loosed in heaven.' The 'power of the keys' designates authority to govern the house of God, which is the Church. Jesus, the Good Shepherd, confirmed this mandate after his Resurrection: 'Feed my sheep.' The power to 'bind and loose' connotes the authority to absolve sins, to pronounce doctrinal judgements, and to make disciplinary decisions in the Church. Jesus entrusted this authority

to the Church through the ministry of the apostles and in particular through the ministry of Peter, the only one to whom he specifically entrusted the keys of the kingdom." *Catechism of the Catholic Church*, Par. 553, (London: Geoffrey Chapman—Libreria Editrice Vaticana, 1994), 125.

"It is of considerable importance in other contexts, when the disciplinary affairs of the community are being discussed (cf. [Matthew] xviii 18; John xx 23) the symbol of the *keys* is absent, since the sayings apply in those instances to a wider circle. In John xx 23 the words are used of pardon, and in that context the Greek words *luein* and *kratein* derive from a secondary interpretation of Isaiah's Hebrew." W. F. Albright and C. S. Mann, *The Anchor Bible: Matthew*, (Garden City, NY: Doubleday, 1971), 196.

Matthew 18:18 Verily I say unto you, Whatsoever ye shall bind on earth shall be bound in heaven: and whatsoever ye shall loose on earth shall be loosed in heaven.

John 20:23 Whose soever sins ye remit, they are remitted unto them; [and] whose soever [sins] ye retain, they are retained.

From the Messianic Jewish perspective of David Stern, the Church, through her hierarchy, has continued the powers of binding and loosing:

"'a very different, non-Jewish interpretation, equating binding and loosing with remitting and retaining sins (Yn 20:23), was adopted by Tertullian and all the church fathers, thus investing the head of the Christian Church with the power to forgive sins, referred to on the basis of Mt 16:18 as the 'key power of the Church.'" David H. Stern, *Jewish New Testament Commentary*, (Clarksville, MD: Jewish New Testament Publications, 1992), 57.

Different Concepts of Church in Matthew 16:18 and 18:17

57. How do the concepts of "church" differ between Matthew 16:18 and Matthew 18:15-17? Matthew 16:18 refers to the Universal Church, and Matthew 18:15-17 describes a situation in the local community.

The Lutheran-Catholic dialogue investigating the role of Peter in the New Testament stated:

> "In Matt 16:18, when Jesus speaks of building *his* church, certainly 'church' cannot be interpreted to refer simply to the local Matthean community, in isolation from the other Christian communities. (A universalistic outlook in Matthew is attested in 28:18-19 where the disciples are commissioned to go forth to make disciples of all nations and baptize them.) But Matthew also knows of *ekklesia* applied to the local community (18:17). It is interesting that the binding/loosing power given to the disciples (18:18) is mentioned in the context of the latter, while the binding/loosing power given to Peter is mentioned in the context of the former." Raymond E. Brown, Karl P. Donfried, and John Reumann, eds., *Peter in the New Testament*, (Minneapolis, MN: Augsburg; New York: Paulist: 1973), 100.

> "As the word [*ekklesia*] is used in Matthew it has two slightly different meanings. In 16.18 the Universal Church is in view, in 18.18 the local assembly (cf. the apparent fluctuation in Acts and the Pauline epistles)." W. D. Davies and Dale C. Allison, *A Critical and Exegetical Commentary on the Gospel according to Saint Matthew*, vol. 11, in J. A. Emerton, C. E. B. Cranfield, and G. N. Stanton, eds., *The International Critical Commentary*, (Edinburgh: Clark, 1991), 629.

The Power of the Keys as Ordained Authority

In the context of Matthew 18:15-18, Jesus speaks to the twelve Apostles and describes a situation where an unrepentant sinner is brought before the local ecclesial community, whose leadership then exercises their authority of binding and loosing on the sinner in need of repentance.

58. According to Matthew 18:17-18, do all Christians, as believers, have the power to bind and to loose? In the context of Matthew 18:17, the Church exercises this power. More specifically, the Apostles (church leaders) in Matthew 18:18 are "ye" (the "disciples") who are given this power (cf. Matthew 10:1-2, where "disciples" are specifically recounted as the twelve disciples (Apostles); and, unlike Luke, Matthew ordinarily denotes Jesus' inner group of twelve as simply "disciples," seldom calling them the Twelve, but clearly distinguishing them from the crowd, and names those to be present at his last Passover (Matthew 26:17-19) as the "disciples").

This power given by Jesus Christ to the Apostles is to bind and to loose and is given only to the ordained, not to laymen. The Anchor Bible Dictionary describes the power thus:

> "By conferring the power to bind and loose upon church leadership, Jesus authorizes it to interpret the Scriptures and establish norms for Christian behavior, the Christian *halakah*. Some authors (e.g., Bornkamm and E. Schweizer) would make a distinction between the meaning of the expression in Matt 16:19 and its meaning in 18:18, interpreting the former as a *teaching* authority and the latter as a *disciplinary* authority.
>
> "On the other hand, binding and loosing are often interpreted as the power to ban members from the community and to readmit them. Sometimes this notion is combined with the disciples' authority to establish a Christian *halakah*. Thus church leadership has both the authority to determine forbidden and permitted conduct and to exclude members from the congregation." David Noel Freedman and others, eds., *The Anchor Bible Dictionary*, vol. 1, (New York: Doubleday, 1992), 743-744.

> "'Binding and loosing' is used in rabbinical speech in the sense of the authentic interpretation of the Law, and means according to this, the judgment as to the permissibility or otherwise of an action. Further, it means the exclusion from the community by the imposition of a ban, or the re-accep-

tance by the removal of a ban. As sin is the ground for the exclusion, the power to forgive sins is included in the power of binding and loosing." Ludwig Ott, *Fundamentals of Catholic Dogma*, 4th ed. (1960), (Rockford, IL: TAN, 1974), 418.

The Ramifications of Peter's Power of Binding and Loosing

This handbook has developed the concept of the power and authority of the keys and of binding and loosing given to Peter as "the symbol of authority (Albright and Mann)," "the office of teaching the word (Calvin)," the "delegation of God's sovereignty (IVP Bible Commentary)," "the master of the house (de Vaux)," "plenary authority (Interpreter's Bible)," authority to "establish rules (Cullmann)," "making halakhic pronouncements (France)," making "decisions based on the teachings of Christ (Earle)," "legislative authority in the Church (IVP Bible Commentary)," and "power to admit, power to exclude (Willoughby)." The Christian symbols and power of the keys and of binding and loosing naturally lead one to conclude that the Church, through her teaching leaders, has full authority to prescribe doctrine on matters of faith and morals.

Matthew 16:19 And I will give unto thee the keys of the kingdom of heaven: and whatsoever thou shalt bind on earth shall be bound in heaven: and whatsoever thou shalt loose on earth shall be loosed in heaven.

59. What do binding and loosing deal with, specifically? They deal with the authority to prescribe: a) the doctrines of faith, such as the Trinity, the two natures of Christ, the divinity of the Holy Spirit, the Eucharist and the other sacraments; and b) the doctrines of morality, such as the serious sin of abortion as the killing of innocent human life.

The prime minister of Christ is given the authority to speak for Christ in matters of faith and morals.

Robert Sungenis, describing the dynamic interplay between Matthew 16:16-17 and 16:18-19, has come to the following conclusion regarding the development of faith and morals:

"Regarding your [the reader's] contention that Matthew 16:18-19 only deals with moral issues, I don't think the context of the passage bears that out. As I said above [regarding Matthew 16:16-17], the binding and loosing are prefaced by a discussion on who Jesus really is. In other words, there is a Christological issue at the forefront, not a moral issue. Granted, Matthew 18:15-19 incorporates the moral dimension within the binding and loosing, but you cannot isolate this passage from Matthew 16:18-19. In fact, the *faith* issue in Matthew 16:13-17 and *moral* issue in Matthew 18:15-17 express precisely the Catholic position of infallibility in the areas of faith and morals. Further, the New Testament does not make a distinction between faith and morals in regards to making decisions for the benefit of the church. They are so intertwined as to be inseparable, and separating them would cripple the church." Robert A. Sungenis, letter to Greg Krehbiel, 22 September 1994, 3.

Faith and morals are the essence of life in Christ. In the ecumenical Vatican Council II, the Church defined such matters in which the bishops and the pope are empowered to act:

"Bishops, teaching in communion with the Roman Pontiff, are to be respected by all as witnesses to divine and Catholic truth. In matters of faith and morals the bishops speak in the name of Christ and the faithful are to accept their teaching and adhere to it with a religious assent. This religious submission of mind and will must be shown in a special way to the authentic magisterium of the Roman Pontiff, even when he is not speaking ex cathedra; that is, it must be shown in such a way that his supreme magisterium is acknowledged with reverence, the judgments made by him are sincerely adhered to, according to his manifest mind and will. His mind and will in the matter may be known either from the character of the documents, from his frequent repetition of the same doctrine, or from his manner of speaking." *Lumen Gentium* (Constitution on the Church, Para. 25, November 21, 1964), (Washington, DC: United States Catholic Conference, n.d.), 27.

From the Lutheran-Catholic dialogue, another perspective on binding and loosing follows:

> "What else might this broader power of the keys include? It might include one or more of the following: baptismal discipline; post-baptismal or penitential discipline; excommunication; exclusion from the Eucharist; the communication or refusal of knowledge; legislative powers; and the power of governing." Raymond E. Brown, Karl P. Donfried, and John Reumann, eds., *Peter in the New Testament*, (Minneapolis, MN: Augsburg; New York: Paulist: 1973), 97.

The Role of Binding and Loosing in the Post-Apostolic Era

That Peter received dynamic power in the keys is conceded by most biblical scholars. A question that remains is whether Peter's successors received the same power and authority as Peter did. Some say that Matthew 16:18-19 contains no language that would lead them to believe that successive "rocks" were intended after Peter's death. This conclusion begs the question: Why would Jesus bother himself to invest Peter with the tremendous role of founding the Church, giving him the keys of regental authority, and then allowing the Church to flounder without a leader upon Peter's departure? As Jesus truly appointed Peter to steer the Body of Christ after his Ascension, logically there must be earthly leaders of the Church of Christ after Peter's departure. Scripture, through Sacred Tradition and history, leads to the conclusion that papal and apostolic succession is a living reality.

60. In what sense do Peter and his successors make decisions regarding faith and morals? They make heavenly decisions.

> "The Greek phrasing in Matthew 16:19: 'whatever you bind on earth shall be bound in heaven' offers decisive support for the doctrine of infallibility. Though there is some discussion among scholars whether the Greek periphrastic future perfect should carry perfect force, i.e., the future perfect would be translated 'shall having been bound' as op-

posed to the future 'shall be bound' (cf. Hebrews 6:13 ff. where the future perfect is understood as a future), the dynamic relationship that Jesus sets up between heaven and earth is remarkable. The future tense shows that a binding occurs in heaven either prior to or simultaneous with the binding performed on earth. In addition, the Greek verb is in the passive voice which indicates that heaven is *receiving* the binding, not initiating it. How does all this prove infallibility? Simply by the fact that since God cannot lie, he cannot validate or dispense any decision in faith or morals that is in error. When the Church makes a binding or loosing decision it must be inerrant otherwise God would not be able to issue an error-free binding or loosing in heaven. How does the Church form its inerrant judgments? God must intrude into the consciousness of the Pope so that no errors are made in dogmatic proclamations. Only then can heaven reciprocate and certify the binding or loosing of the Church." Robert A. Sungenis, "The Precedent for Infallibility," letter to authors, November 1993, 5.

"'Shall be bound' and 'shall be loosed' are literally future perfects ('shall have been bound' and 'shall have been loosed'), and as the future perfect sounds as stilted in Greek as in English, the tense is apparently deliberate. In that case it is not that heaven will ratify Peter's independent decisions, but that Peter will pass on decisions that have already been made in heaven." R. T. France, *The Gospel According to Matthew: An Introduction and Commentary*, (Grand Rapids, MI: Eerdmans, 1989), 257.

Peter's power of binding and loosing is continued by his successors, who recognize the power of succession:

"'In the same sense in the second epistle of Clement to James II ("Clementine Homilies [purported]," Introduction), Peter is represented as having appointed Clement as his successor, saying: "I communicate to him the power of binding and loosing so that, with respect to everything which he shall ordain in the earth, it shall be decreed in the heavens: for he shall bind what ought to be bound and loose what ought to be loosed as knowing the rule of the church.""" David H. Stern, *Jewish New Testament Commentary*, (Clarksville, MD: Jewish New Testament Publications, 1992), 57.

Cullmann further describes the power of binding and loosing set forth in Matthew 16:19:

"Just as this saying concerning the keys of the Kingdom of Heaven connects directly with the one that deals with the 'building' of the *ekklesia* and with the gates of the realm of the dead, so also the words concerning 'binding' and 'loosing' must be understood in connection with what precedes. This must be considered first of all in regard to the way the expressions 'on earth' and 'in heaven' correspond. These expressions are to be understood first of all not in a spatial but in a temporal sense. What Peter does for the *ekklesia* is effective for the coming Kingdom of Heaven. Here again it is seen how close is the connection between the Messianic present and the future, between the already realized fulfillment and the consummation yet to come." Oscar Cullmann, *Peter: Disciple, Apostle, Martyr*, trans. Floyd V. Filson, (Philadelphia: Westminster, 1953), 204.

Martin Luther stated that Peter had the power to bind and loose:

"His office is my office, his binding and loosing are my binding and loosing. His keys are my keys, and I have no others, nor do I know of any others. What they bind that is bound, what they loose is free, just as if there were no other to bind or to loose in heaven or on earth. If there are any other keys in heaven, on earth, or in hell, they do not concern me. I know nothing of them. Whatever they might bind or loose is not my affair. Therefore, don't concern yourself about it either, and don't be led astray. I pay attention only to what my Peter binds and looses. I rely on that, and you should do likewise. In so doing you are already bound and loosed as far as I am concerned. For Peter binds and looses in heaven, and nobody else. This is the right way of thinking and speaking of the keys." Martin Luther, "The Keys," in Conrad

Bergendoff, ed., *Luther's Works*, vol. 40, trans. Earl Beyer and Conrad Bergendoff Philadelphia: Fortress, 1958), 366.

61. In the process of "binding and loosing" by Peter, who preserves Peter from making errors as he makes decisions regarding faith and morals? God, the Holy Spirit.

In quoting from the Orthodox scholar Alexis Stawrowsky's *Essai de la théologie irenique: l'Orthodoxie et Catholicisme* (Madrid, 1966), James Likoudis has sifted some fertile ground for dialogue and reconciliation with Eastern Orthodoxy on this most important issue of primacy, succession and infallibility of the Pope of Rome (in this handbook referred to as the "Pope"):

> "Asserting that the 'Church proclaimed by the Fathers of Vatican II in its general traits is the same Church which Orthodoxy confesses,' the author gives his judgment on the Roman Primacy:
>
> > "'. . . it is impossible to deny that from the first day of the existence of the Roman See, the Bishops of Rome have constantly reaffirmed its primacy and proclaimed that it was founded not on any pretended ecclesiastical right or on conciliar decrees but on specific texts of Scripture. That is why it is truly difficult, and even simply impossible, to reasonably affirm that the doctrine on the supremacy of the Pope in the Church is a "novelty" or "innovation," or as numerous Orthodox polemicists have declared in following Protestant theories in this matter, that the growth of the Pope's primacy is due exclusively to the False Isidorian Decretals [p. 194]...'
> >
> > "'Infallibility is conferred uniquely by the Holy Spirit who acts in many ways in the Church. And, certainly, one of the forms of that infallibility was the confession of Peter which was revealed to him 'not by flesh and blood.' If one admits the doctrine on the primacy of the Roman Pontiff in the Church, there is no difficulty in recognizing that in certain determined circumstances,

precisely in his quality as the First Bishop, a special assistance of the Holy Spirit is given to him to define the
sense of such or such doctrine involving faith and morals contained in Divine Revelation and in the common
teaching of the Church. And in these cases it is not possible to say that the Pope has the power of inventing
'new dogmas,' for he remains always bound by Divine
Revelation and can never act against Holy Scripture,
Holy Tradition, or the teaching of Ecumenical Councils
and the holy Fathers of the Church [p. 240].'" James
Likoudis, *Ending the Byzantine Greek Schism*, (New
Rochelle, NY: Catholics United for the Faith, 1992), 92.

Robert Sungenis clarifies the prerogative of the Church regarding infallibility:

"In what areas does the Church have the prerogative of infallibility? Those dealing with salvation, that is, those areas
the Church has defined as 'faith and morals.' And by what
right has the Church to define infallibility in this way? By
the mere fact that Jesus said to Peter, '*whatsoever* you bind.
. .' The term 'whatsoever' indicates that the Church has the
prerogative, under direct guidance of the Holy Spirit, to dog-
matize any soteriological truth it sees as beneficial for the
Church. This does not mean that infallibility is a new doctrine. It was practiced throughout the Church as the history
of the Councils and Papal decrees testify. The dogma of infallibility, so defined in 1870 in the papal decree called *Pastor Aeternus*, was confined to matters of faith and morals
since that is the specific area of divine truth that has been
passed down from the apostolic tradition of the Church."
Robert A. Sungenis, letter to authors, 21 January 1995, 1.

SUMMARY REMARKS REGARDING
MATTHEW 16:18-19

62. What five important points can be drawn from Matthew 16:18-
19? Christ reveals that: (i) Simon shall be called Peter, the rock;
(ii) Christ shall found his Church on Peter; (iii) none shall ever
prevail against the Church; (iv) Christ gives to Peter alone,

above all apostles, the keys to the Kingdom of Heaven; and (v) Christ gives to Peter acting alone (but also to the other Apostles acting locally and in concert with Peter) the power of binding and loosing on earth what is bound and loosed in heaven.

63. In Matthew 16:18-19, if Jesus Christ says that he will delegate to Peter, as Rock, the keys of the kingdom of heaven (i.e., Christ's kingly authority) in order to build Christ's Church, against which the gates of hell would not prevail, what would Christ be if he did not keep his word? A liar.

64. Do Catholics take Jesus at his word in Matthew 16:18-19? Yes.

"Many Protestant scholars who have admitted that the rock of Matthew 16:18-19 is referring to Peter have not been able to surmount the difficulty of succession, (i.e., that Peter was the first pope to be followed by an unbroken succession of popes). Logic would dictate, however, that if Jesus were going to take the trouble to set up an office for Peter, (i.e., giving him the keys of the kingdom), that this office would continue for the life of the church. If not, what would be the sense in establishing such a high-ranking office if Jesus had no intention of seeing it last beyond Peter's death? It would be the most anticlimactic event in the life of Jesus and the history of the church, not to mention a complete shutdown of the Old Testament precedent of dynastic succession. Imagine the framers of the U.S. Constitution creating the office of president and electing George Washington as its first official, all the while musing that the office would be dissolved after Washington's death! That would be an absurd proposition. Were the framers of the Constitution smarter than Jesus? Certainly not. They were emulating what had been passed down since the dawn of history—that a single individual takes the reins of power but hands them over to his successor upon his vacancy from the office." Robert A. Sungenis, letter to authors, June 1994, 5.

CHAPTER III

PETER'S AUTHORITY IN THE NEW TESTAMENT CHURCH

Peter's Authority in the Early Church

65. Is Peter individually given the roles of priest, prophet and king? Yes. In Matthew 16:17, Peter is given the role of prophet as he proclaims Jesus as the Christ, which was revealed to him by the Father (in Matthew 11:27). In Matthew 16:18 Peter is made the rock upon which the Church would be built, and in John 21:15-17 Peter is called the shepherd of the lambs and the sheep, being given the kingly role transferred to him by Christ. In Matthew 16:19 Peter is given the keys of kingly authority held by his sovereign, Jesus Christ.

66. Who takes the lead in calling for the selection of a replacement for Judas Iscariot? Peter. After Jesus Christ's ascension into heaven, Peter's first act was to initiate the selection of a new Apostle to replace Judas Iscariot, who betrayed Jesus:

> *Acts* 1:15 And in those days Peter stood up in the midst of the disciples, and said, (the number of names together were about an hundred and twenty,)

1:16 Men and brethren, this scripture must needs have been fulfilled, which the Holy Ghost by the mouth of David spake before concerning Judas, which was guide to them that took Jesus.

"S. Peter here assumes, as a matter of right, the function of Chief governor, and Chief Pastor of the Church. A vacancy occurs in the apostolic body, through the treason and death of Judas. He then, apparently without previous concert with his co-apostles, directs, not *suggests*, as some say, but directs, or rather *commands*, another to be ordained in his place; and he further states authoritatively, from what class of men a successor must be chosen, limiting thereby their choice; 'wherefore of these men which have companied with us all the time that the Lord Jesus went in and out among us . . . must one be ordained,' &c. From the above nothing can be clearer than the nature of that office S. Peter assumed on this occasion, namely, that of the Ruler, the Governor, and Chief Pastor of the Church." Colin Lindsay, *The Evidence for the Papacy*, (London: Longmans, Green, 1870), 8-9.

Acts 1:20 For it is written in the book of Psalms, Let his habitation be desolate, and let no man dwell therein [Psalms 69:25]: and his bishoprick [*episkopee*] let another take [Psalms 109:8].

1:21 Wherefore of these men which have companied with us all the time that the Lord Jesus went in and out among us,

1:22 Beginning from the baptism of John, unto that same day that he was taken up from us, must one be ordained to be a witness with us of his resurrection.

1:23 And they appointed two, Joseph called Barsabas, who was surnamed Justus, and Matthias.

1:24 And they prayed, and said, Thou, Lord, which knowest the hearts of all [men], shew whether of these two thou hast chosen,

1:25 That he may take part of this ministry and apostleship, from which Judas by transgression fell, that he might go to his own place.

1:26 And they gave forth their lots; and the lot fell upon Matthias; and he was numbered with the eleven apostles.

67. When Judas died, who was selected to take his place? Matthias.

68. What role did Matthias take? He was given the role of Apostle (ambassador of Christ) that Judas Iscariot had occupied, and he also occupied in the community the office of *episkopoi*, meaning overseer. Besides being ambassadors of Christ, the Apostles also were overseers (later bishops), acting as shepherds, of the flock.

69. Who were Apostles besides the twelve? Matthias (Acts 1:26); Paul (Galatians 1:1; Titus 1:1); and Barnabas (Acts 14:14). One might also conclude that Paul and Barnabas were bishops of the Church as a result of their "looking after" the brothers of the community in Acts 15:36:

> *Acts* 15:36 And some days after Paul said unto Barnabas, Let us go again and visit [*episkepsometha* = look after, oversee] our brethren in every city where we have preached the word of the Lord, [and see] how they do. [translated not as "visit" but as "look after" in Jay P. Green, Sr., ed. and trans., *The Interlinear Hebrew-Greek-English Bible One Volume Carrying Edition*, (London: Trinitarian, 1981), 839.]

70. Who are the successors to the Apostles? The Bishops, who are to function as the Apostles did before them:

> "That divine mission, entrusted by Christ to the apostles, will last until the end of the world, since the Gospel they are to teach is for all time the source of all life for the Church.

And for this reason the apostles, appointed as rulers in this society, took care to appoint successors.

"For they not only had helpers in their ministry, but also, in order that the mission assigned to them might continue after their death, they passed on to their immediate coopera- tors, as it were, in the form of a testament, the duty of con- firming and finishing the work begun by themselves, recom- mending to them that they attend to the whole flock in which the Holy Spirit placed them to shepherd the Church of God. They therefore appointed such men, and gave them the order that, when they should have died, other approved men would take up their ministry. Among those various ministries which, according to tradition, were exercised in the Church from the earliest times, the chief place belongs to the office of those who, appointed to the episcopate, by a succession running from the beginning, are passers-on of the apostolic seed. Thus, as St. Irenaeus testifies, through those who were appointed bishops by the apostles, and through their successors down to our own time, the apostolic tradition is manifested and preserved." *Lumen Gentium* (Constitution on the Church, Para. 20, November 21, 1964), (Washington, DC: United States Catholic Conference, n.d.), 21-22.

71. Who were appointed as bishops by the Apostle Paul? Timothy (II Timothy 1:16) and Titus (Titus 1:5).

72. What type of organization is being revealed in the New Testa- ment, particularly in Acts? A hierarchical, episcopal organiza- tion. See Numbers 27:12-23 for an Old Testament model, in which Eleazer, in the presence of Moses, lays hands on Joshua as the successor to Moses.

73. How is the Catholic Church set up? In a hierarchical, episco- pal way, in which deacons, priests, bishops, and pope all work together as spiritual servants of the laity.

74. What role does Peter have, according to the Book of the Acts of the Apostles? The chief leader of the Church. Consider the following significant events in the new Church's life in which Peter was the primary figure:

Acts 1:15	(Shortly after the ascension of Jesus into heaven, Peter takes charge of the community and conducts the selection of Matthias as the first successor Apostle.)
Acts 2:14	(At Pentecost, the birthday of the Church, Peter is the first to proclaim the gospel of the resurrection of Jesus of Nazareth.)
Acts 3:1-12	(The first public miracle is worked through Peter.)
Acts 4:8-12	(Peter publicly professes the Church's faith before the Sanhedrin.)
Acts 5:1-5	(Peter exercises church discipline on the congregation in the case of Ananias and his wife Sapphira.)
Acts 5:3-10	(Peter's ecclesial pronouncements).
Acts 5:15	(Insomuch that they brought forth the sick into the streets, and laid [them] on beds and couches, that at the least the shadow of Peter passing by might overshadow some of them.)
Acts 8:14-15	(Peter's visit to Samaria).
Acts 8:20-24	(Simon Magus experiences that Peter makes the decisions for the disciples.)
Acts 10:1-48	(Peter baptizes the first pagans into the Church—Cornelius and his family.)
Acts 11:18	(When they heard these things, they held their peace, and glorified God, saying, Then hath God also to the Gentiles granted repentance unto life. [Peter's pronouncement regarding his vision of Gentile converts is accepted.])

I Peter 5:1 The elders [*presbuterous*] which are among you I exhort, who am also an elder [*presbuteros*], and a witness of the sufferings of Christ, and also a partaker of the glory that shall be revealed:

5:2 Feed the flock of God which is among you, taking the oversight thereof, not by constraint, but willingly; not for filthy lucre, but of a ready mind;

> 5:3 Neither as being lords over God's heritage, but being ensamples to the flock.
>
> 5:4 When the chief Shepherd shall appear, ye shall receive a crown of glory that fadeth not away.

Peter refers to himself in I Peter 5:1 as a fellow "presbyter." From this passage, some might want to diminish the status of Peter as Christ's regent on earth; however, from the Lutheran-Catholic dialogue there is an explanation:

> "In 5:1 the author of I Peter, addressing himself to the presbyters (elders) of the communities of Asia Minor, assumes the title of 'fellow presbyter' or 'co-presbyter.' We should not be deceived by this modest stance as if the author were presenting himself as their equal. He has already identified his authority as apostolic (1:1); and so the use of 'fellow presbyter' is a polite stratagem of benevolence, somewhat as when a modern bishop of a diocese addresses his 'fellow priests.'" Raymond E. Brown, Karl P. Donfried, and John Reumann, eds., *Peter in the New Testament*, (Minneapolis, MN: Augsburg; New York: Paulist: 1973), 152.

From very early in the history of the Church, Popes have also referred to themselves individually as "*servum servorum Dei* (servant of the servants of God)." This designation retains the emphasis of Christ—to serve the People of God. Pope St. Gregory the Great (590-604 A.D.) used the phrase extensively, although he was not the first:

> "The designation, however, had been used by others before him, as by Pope Damasus [366-384] (*Ep. IV. ad Stephanum et Africae Episcopos*), and Augustine (*Ep. ad Vitalem* [427]). Gregory may have been the first to use it habitually." Philip Schaff and Henry Wace, eds., *Nicene and Post-Nicene Fathers*, vol. 12—*Leo the Great, Gregory the Great*, 2nd series, (n.p.: Christian Literature, 1895; repr., Peabody, MA: Hendrickson, 1994), 73.

Besides serving the flock, Scripture also stresses leadership. In Matthew 20:26-28 (and in Luke 22:26-27), Christian leadership took the form of hierarchy: Christ's dedicated followers are servants of our Lord Jesus Christ, just as Christ was the servant of his disciples and of others. Contextually, this passage in Matthew (and in Luke) controverts neither the kingship of Christ nor the hierarchical "chief" authority that his Apostles or their successors possess:

> *Matthew* 20:26 But it shall not be so among you: but whosoever will be great among you, let him be your minister;
> 20:27 And whosoever will be chief among you, let him be your servant:
> 20:28 Even as the Son of man came not to be ministered unto, but to minister, and to give his life a ransom for many.
> *Luke* 22:26 But ye [shall] not [be] so: but he that is greatest among you, let him be as the younger; and he that is chief, as he that doth serve.
> 22:27 For whether [is] greater, he that sitteth at meat, or he that serveth? [is] not he that sitteth at meat? but I am among you as he that serveth.

To serve and to lead is the dual requirement of the Apostles and of their successors.

In modern times, the Church (as set forth in the Lutheran-Catholic dialogue) recognizes the various hierarchical roles that the Petrine officeholder performs:

> "Since the pope is related to the church and to the churches under various titles, namely, bishop of the Catholic church, bishop of the 'Italian' see of Rome, primate of Italy, patriarch of the West, he does not relate to the plurality of churches in the same manner. Though the Petrine function is a ministry to the whole church, the occupant of the Roman see does not always act in terms of that papal function. He can also act as primate of Italy or bishop of the 'Italian' city of Rome, or as patriarch of the West." Kilian McDonnell, "Papal Primacy: Development, Centralization, and Chang-

ing Styles," in Paul C. Empie and T. Austin Murphy, *Papal
Primacy and the Universal Church—Lutherans and Catholics in Dialogue V*, (Minneapolis: Augsburg, 1974), 186-187.

The Pope is also called "vicar," that is, one who is authorized
to act for Christ on earth as his deputy or regent. Some of the first
references to the Petrine officeholder as the "Vicar of Christ" come
from the Eastern Church. Canon XXXIX of *The Arabic Canons of
the Council of Nicaea [325 A.D.]* refers to Peter "as he who is the
Vicar of Christ our Lord over all peoples and over the whole Christian Church" (Philip Schaff and Henry Wace, eds., *Nicene and Post-
Nicene Fathers*, vol. 14—*The Seven Ecumenical Councils*, 2nd
series, (New York: Charles Scribner's Sons, 1900; repr., Peabody,
MA: Hendrickson, 1994), 48). St. Ephraem, the great Syriac Father of the Church (ca. 306-373), wrote: "Then Peter deservedly
received the Vicariate (of Christ) over His people" (*in Sermone de
Martyrio. SS. Appl. Petri et Pauli*, in S. Herbert Scott, *The Eastern
Churches and the Papacy*, (London: Sheed & Ward, 1928), 62).
Even the "front rank" Nestorian theologian Elias, Bishop of Anbara
(ca. 420-450 A.D.), remarked of Peter: "Christ the true Rock, had
to return to heaven, and he established his vicar on Earth, and named
him the Rock of the Edifice" (S. Herbert Scott, *The Eastern
Churches and the Papacy*, (London: Sheed & Ward, 1928), 175).
In the West, St. Ambrose (ca. 390 A.D.), wrote of the Pope as vicar:

> "'Lovest thou me? [John 21:15]' For he [Peter] about whom
> there is a doubt is questioned, but the Lord is not in doubt,
> and he was asking the question, not in order to get information, but in order to teach him whom he was leaving for us,
> as a vicar of his love, seeing that he was to be raised into
> heaven." Ambrose, *Expositio in Lucam*, Book 10 (*Patr. Lat.*
> 15, 1848), in E. Giles, ed., *Documents Illustrating Papal
> Authority—A.D. 96-454*, (London: S.P.C.K., 1952), 144.

The Pope of Rome is called by various names that indicate the
roles of his office as regent of Christ on earth. While varied in
emphasis, all designations of the Pope reflect the call that Christ
made to Peter: serve and lead—feed and tend.

The Role of the Bishops in the Hierarchy of the Church

Acts 20:28 Take heed therefore unto yourselves, and to all the flock, over the which the Holy Ghost hath made you overseers [*episkopous*], to feed the church of God, which he hath purchased with his own blood.

75. Who are the "overseers" being addressed in Acts 20:28? Presbyters (see Acts 20:17). However, the role of oversight that is theirs in this passage would in the near future become clearly the role of the one called "bishop," or *episkopos*.

76. How do we know this? The English word "bishop" derives from the Greek word *episkopos*, meaning "overseer," from which also derives the English words "episcopal" and "episcopacy."

Consider the scriptural pronouncement regarding the position of Jesus Christ, who later bequeathed his authority to the Apostles on earth:

I Peter 2:25 For ye were as sheep going astray; but are now returned unto the Shepherd and Bishop [*episkopos*] of your souls.

77. What was the degree of hierarchy in the early Church? It was threefold (bishop, presbyter (or priest), and deacon), according to St. Ignatius of Antioch, who wrote his *Letter to the Smyrnaeans*, circa 110 A.D., describing the hierarchy as follows:

"You must all follow the bishop as Jesus Christ follows the Father, and the presbytery [priests] as you would the Apostles. Reverence the deacons as you would the command of God. Let no one do anything of concern to the Church without the bishop. Let that be considered a valid Eucharist which is celebrated by the bishops, or by one whom he appoints. Wherever the bishop appears, let the people be there; just as wherever Jesus Christ is, there is the Catholic Church." W. A. Jurgens, ed., *The Faith of the Early Fathers*, vol. 1, (Collegeville, MN: Liturgical, 1970), 25.

It should be noted that the English word "priest" derives "ultimately from Latin *presbyter* (*-biter*), adopted from Greek *presbuteros.*" *The Oxford English Dictionary*, 2nd ed. (1989), vol. 12, s.v. "priest." One will find an explanation of the etymology of this word under question 190.

From his *Letter to the Trallians*, Ignatius reiterates the function of the hierarchy:

> "[2, 1] Your obedience to your bishop, as though he were Jesus Christ, shows me plainly enough that yours is no worldly manner of life, but that of Jesus Christ Himself, who gave His life for us that faith in His death might save you from death. [2] At the same time, however, essential as it is that you should never act independently of the bishop— as evidently you do not—you must also be no less submissive to your clergy, and regard them as apostles of Jesus Christ our Hope, in whom we shall one day be found, if our lives are lived in Him. [3] The deacons too, who serve the mysteries of Jesus Christ, must be men universally approved in every way; since they are not mere dispensers of meat and drink, but servants of the church of God, and therefore under obligation to guard themselves against any slur or imputation as strictly as they would against fire itself.
>
> "[3, 1] Equally, it is for the rest of you to hold the deacons in as great respect as Jesus Christ; just as you should also look on the bishop as a type of the Father, and the clergy as the Apostolic circle forming His council; for without these three orders no church has any right to the name. [2] I am sure these are your own feelings too, for I have had with me, and still have, an example of your affection in the person of your bishop himself, whose grave demeanor is a notable lesson in itself, and whose very gentleness is power. I cannot doubt that even the heathen have a respect for him. I am measuring my words here, out of love for you, for I could well write more forcibly on his behalf, if it were not that as a condemned prisoner I have not thought myself entitled to use the peremptory tone of an Apostle." *Early Christian Writings—The Apostolic Fathers*, trans. Maxwell Staniforth, (New York: Dorset Press, 1968), 95-96.

In his *Letter to the Magnesians*, St. Ignatius continues:

> "[6,1] Take care to do all things in harmony with God, with the bishop residing in the place of God and with the presbyters in the place of the council of the Apostles, and with the deacons, who are most dear to me, entrusted with the business of Jesus Christ, who was with the Father from the beginning and is at last made manifest." W. A. Jurgens, ed., *The Faith of the Early Fathers*, vol. 1, (Collegeville, MN: Liturgical, 1970), 19.

> "[13,1] Take care, therefore, to be confirmed in the decrees of the Lord and of the Apostles, in order that in everything you do, you may prosper in body and in soul, in faith and in love, in Son and in Father and in Spirit, in beginning and in end, together with your most reverend bishop; and with that fittingly woven spiritual crown, the presbytery; and with the deacons, men of God. Be subject to the bishop and to one another, as Jesus Christ was subject to the Father, and the Apostles were subject to Christ and to the Father; so that there may be unity in both body and in spirit." W. A. Jurgens, ed., *The Faith of the Early Fathers*, vol. 1, (Collegeville, MN: Liturgical, 1970), 20.

Peter's Role in the Council of Jerusalem

78. How often does Peter appear in the story of the founding of the Church? Peter's name appears 53 times in the first 12 chapters of Acts. Peter is the leader of the Church.

To support this view, Orthodox scholar Nicholas Koulomzine in his "Peter's Place in the Early Church" says:

> "For Peter's actions after the Ascension give us a means to discover the real meaning of the words that Christ had spoken to him. Jerusalem is the place where Peter stands forth, in the Pentecostal Church and surrounded by the Twelve (he is never dissociated from them in the Gospels); here he first showed that he could be a Rock, Rock of the Church, as Christ called him when He said, 'Thou art Peter, and on this rock I will build my Church ' (Matt. 16:18). At Jerusalem, again, Peter was to show a faith that did not fail, and

acted out Christ's promise, 'Thou then, when thou hast turned again, stablish thy brethren' (Luke 22:32). And, still at Jerusalem, Peter became the Shepherd of the Church and carried out Christ's injunction, 'Feed my lambs, feed my sheep' (John 21:15-17).

"The Gospel of the Church of Jerusalem, St. Matthew's, is furthermore the Gospel which underlines Peter's primacy, and places him apart in the list of the Twelve (Matt. 10:2); quoting the solemn word of the Christ, 'Thou art Peter, and on this rock I will build my Church' (Matt. 16:18)." J. Meyendorff, A. Schmemann, N. Afanassieff, and N. Koulomzine, *The Primacy of Peter*, (Aylesbury, Bucks, UK: The Faith Press, 1973), 134.

Acts 15:6 And the apostles and elders came together for to consider of this matter.

15:7 And when there had been much disputing, Peter rose up, and said unto them, Men [and] brethren, ye know how that a good while ago God made choice among us, that the Gentiles by my mouth should hear the word of the gospel, and believe.

79. Where did the Apostles and elders come together? Jerusalem. Read Acts 15:1-5.

80. In what form did the Apostles and elders come together? They came together in the prototype ecumenical council of the Church.

"Thus, the Council of Jerusalem displays the same features as the later ecumenical councils in the history of the Church: a) it is a meeting of the rulers of the entire Church, not of the ministers of one particular place; b) it promulgates rules which have binding force for all Christians; c) the content of its decrees deals with faith and morals; d) its decisions are recorded in a written document—a formal proclamation to the whole Church; e) Peter presides over the assembly.

"According to the [Latin Rite's] Code of Canon Law (can. 338-341) ecumenical councils are assemblies—summoned and presided over by the Pope—of bishops and some others endowed with jurisdiction; decisions of these councils do not oblige unless they are confirmed and promulgated by the Pope." Jose Maria Casciaro and others, eds., *The Navarre Bible—The Acts of the Apostles*, (Dublin: Four Courts Press, 1992), 161.

"This college [or body of bishops], insofar as it is composed of many, expresses the variety and universality of the People of God, but insofar as it is assembled under one head, it expresses the unity of the flock of Christ. In it, the bishops, faithfully recognizing the primacy and pre-eminence of their head, exercise their own authority for the good of their own faithful, and indeed of the whole Church, the Holy Spirit supporting its organic structure and harmony with moderation. The supreme power in the Universal Church, which this college enjoys, is exercised in a solemn way in an ecumenical council. A council is never ecumenical unless it is confirmed or at least accepted as such by the successor of Peter; and it is [the] prerogative of the Roman Pontiff to convoke these councils, to preside over them and to confirm them. This same collegiate power can be exercised together with the pope by the bishops living in all parts of the world, provided that the head of the college calls them to collegiate action, or at least approves of or freely accepts the united action of the scattered bishops, so that it is thereby made a collegiate act." *Lumen Gentium* (Constitution on the Church, Para. 22, November 21, 1964), (Washington, DC: United States Catholic Conference, n.d.), 24.

81. In what year did this first council take place? It is set in about 48 or 49 A.D.

82. During the initial phase of the council, what happens? There is much discussion and debate. See Acts 15:6-7.

83. In the second phase, after the discussion and debate, who speaks authoritatively for the council? Peter. See Acts 15:7-11. Tertullian and St. Chrysostom support the Catholic interpretation of Peter's effect on the council at Jerusalem:

"Tertullian [ca. 214 A.D.] has, of course, seen that Peter speaks last, after the discussion is over (Acts xv.7), as St. Chrysostom points out: 'He first permits the question to be moved in the Church, and then speaks' (on Acts *in loco.*; Oxf. trans. pp. 446, 447)." Dom John Chapman, *Bishop Gore and the Catholic Claims*, (New York: Longmans, 1905), 50.

84. In Acts 15:7-11, what truth does Peter proclaim? That the Gentiles would now be welcomed into the Church by the action of the Holy Spirit. See also Acts 10:24-43 (Peter's vision).

"S. Peter had received the Keys of the kingdom of heaven, and, consequently, he alone could open heaven to the Gentiles. Accordingly, Cornelius was directed to send men to Joppa to invite S. Peter to visit him. While they were on their way, the Lord made known to S. Peter his will respecting the Gentiles, and directed him to go down to Caesarea, 'doubting nothing.' S. Peter obeyed, heard what Cornelius had to say, and after witnessing the miraculous descent of the Holy Ghost upon the Gentiles, 'commanded them to be baptized in the name of the Lord.' This was the exercise of the Supreme use of the Keys, of which he was the Custodian, and this too without any previous consultation with his brother Apostles. S. Peter acted here in his capacity as our Lord's Viceregent, on whom He built His Church, and to whom He had intrusted the Keys of the kingdom of heaven. There is no passage in the New Testament which exhibits S. Peter's supremacy in the Church more fully than this." Colin Lindsay, *The Evidence for the Papacy*, (London: Longmans, Green, 1870), 10.

Acts 15:12 Then all the multitude kept silence [*esigese*], and gave audience to Barnabas and Paul, declaring what miracles and wonders God had wrought among the Gentiles by them.

85. Why does the assembly fall silent before Paul and Barnabas speak? Because it is contemplating the momentous words that Peter had just spoken:

"A careful examination of the position of St. Peter indicates which of the two [he or St. James] had the superior authority, thereby elucidating the principal matter under discussion. It is his speech which decides the course of action to be adopted, and when he gives his reasons he makes it clear that the course has been indicated by God *to him*. This speech does not require the approval of the assembly, but rather it puts an end to the discussion." Michael M. Winter, *Saint Peter and the Popes*, (Baltimore: Helicon, 1960), 32.

Then, the third phase of the Council begins, as Barnabas and Paul speak.

86. What do Barnabas and Paul relate to the Council in Acts 15:12? They substantiate Peter's pronouncement by telling all of God's miracles and wonders performed among the Gentiles in spreading the Gospel.

The late F. F. Bruce, Emeritus Professor at the University of Manchester, wrote:

"During the silence which followed Peter's appeal, Barnabas and Paul (who are named naturally in this order in a Jerusalem setting) added further evidence which could only support Peter's argument. But Barnabas and Paul spoke as witnesses, not as consultants or as participants in the debate, and in Jerusalem their words could carry nothing like the weight that Peter's did." F. F. Bruce, *The Book of Acts*, (Grand Rapids, MI: Eerdmans, 1988), 291.

A second silence occurs after Paul and Barnabas had spoken, as the assembly contemplated their testimony in support of Peter's proclamations regarding the Gentiles:

Acts 15:13 And after they had held their peace [Gr. *sigesai* = fallen silent], James answered, saying, Men [and] brethren, hearken unto me:

There are two uses of the Greek word *sigao* (meaning to be silent) in Acts 15:12-13. In recognizing the placement of these silences, one is struck by the reverence that the assembly shows for Peter and then for the testimony of Paul and Barnabas in support of Peter. Some may argue that the first silence is for Paul and Barnabas and that the second silence is for James, but this begs the question as to how the words are related to their subject matter in the Greek language. Mr. Robert Sungenis writes:

> "In Acts 15:12-13, Luke uses two forms of the Greek verb *sigao*, which means 'be silent.' Both are in the aorist tense and thus refer to an action in the past that was completed. The first usage in verse 12 refers to the silence caused in the assembly by the previous speaker, namely, Peter. The verse, literally translated, would read, 'And was silent all the multitude. . . .' This past tense usage shows that the multitude was silent when Peter was speaking and remained so when Paul and Barnabas start[ed] speaking. The second use of *sigao* in verse 13 is an infinitive aorist. It is preceded by an accusative preposition and the infamous Greek article which would be translated as: 'after they had become silent' or more colloquially, 'after they had finished speaking.' Since Paul and Barnabas were the ones who were previously speaking, then the second use of *sigao* refers only to them. In other words, when Paul and Barnabas were 'finished speaking,' James began speaking. The passage gives us the normal events occurring when single individuals speak in turn to an assembly. According to the aorist usage of *sigao* in verse 12, the initial silence occurs when Peter begins speaking in verse 7. That silence continues in verse 13 as Paul and Barnabas begin to speak, and continues further when James begins to speak in verse 14. According to the meaning of the second aorist, the silence is not caused by James. He is only the recipient of the silence occurring before him at the completion of the speech by Paul and Barnabas."
> Robert A. Sungenis, letter to authors, January 13, 1995, 2.

From St. Jerome there is the following regarding the Council of Jerusalem:

"When there had been much disputing, Peter rose up, with his wonted readiness, and said, 'Men and brethren . . . we shall be saved even as they.' And to his opinion the apostle James and all the elders together gave consent.

These quotations should not be tedious to the reader, but useful both to him and to me, as proving that, even before the apostle Paul, Peter had come to know that the law was not to be in force after the gospel was given; nay more, that *Peter was the prime mover in issuing the decree* by which this was affirmed. Moreover Peter was of so great authority that Paul has recorded in his epistle 'Then after three years I went up to Jerusalem to see Peter'. . . . proving that he would not have had confidence in his preaching of the gospel if he had not been confirmed by the consent of Peter and those who were with him. . . . No one can doubt, therefore, that the *apostle Peter was himself the author of that rule* which he is accused of breaking [ca. 404 A.D.]." Jerome, *Ep[istle] 112, to Augustine (P.L. 33-255; M.D. 6.284)*, in E. Giles, ed., *Documents Illustrating Papal Authority—A.D. 96-454*, (London: S.P.C.K., 1952), 160.

James Supports Peter

Acts 15:13 And after they had held their peace, James answered [*apekrithe*], saying, Men [and] brethren, hearken unto me:

15:14 Simeon hath declared [*exegesato*] how God at the first did visit the Gentiles, to take out of them a people for his name.

87. Who then rises to speak after Paul and Barnabas? James, who answered and was not declaring a point.

"There is nothing in this account which witnesses against S. Peter; on the contrary what little is said confirms the position he is alleged to have held, for he first delivered judgment, and the cause was virtually concluded; for all accepted his judgment as final. S. James did but echo what S. Peter said, and supported it by reference to the prophecies." Colin Lindsay, *The Evidence for the Papacy*, (London: Longmans, Green, 1870), 11.

88. Who is James? He is the Bishop of Jerusalem.

89. What are the first words out of James' mouth? "Men [and] brethren, hearken unto me: Simeon [Peter] hath [has] declared [*exegesato*]. . . ."

Regarding "hearken unto me [listen to me]," Robert Sungenis analyzes the Greek phrasing:

> "In an effort to make James, as opposed to Peter, stand out as the primary decision maker at the Council of Jerusalem in Acts 15, some Protestant apologists have seized on the statement given by James in verse 14, 'Men and brethren, hear me.' The inference is made that because the words 'hear me' are in the Greek imperative mood (the mood used to issue commands), that James is issuing an ecclesiastical dictate to the rest of the assembly which denotes the supreme authority he held as the bishop of Jerusalem, even over Peter who was also present. The net effect of elevating James' command is to make it appear that Peter, who also spoke at the assembly, had no fundamental authority at this point and that James was the undisputed and final decision maker. Such conclusions are totally without warrant.
>
> "The Greek word translated as 'hear me' in Acts 15:14 is *akouoo* which is used hundreds of times in the New Testament. For example, the same word is used in two verses prior in Acts 15:12 in the Greek indicative mood and translated as 'and heard [*akouoo*] Barnabas and Paul.' It is a word that, in itself, does not connote authority. Placing *akouoo* in the Greek imperative mood in Acts 15:14 can simply be understood as a request for those gathered to give their undivided attention to what will subsequently be spoken. the use of the imperative mood can be made strong or weak depending upon the context in which it is placed, but the use of the imperative does not necessarily denote any official authority of the one using the mood. the imperative mood of *akouoo* can be used for ANY desire of one person seeking the attention of another. It can be used, for example, in a simple request such as, 'Listen, did you hear that noise?' Or, it can be used in a stronger context such as: 'Listen, do

not do that again.' It can even be used of a subordinate who issues a request to a superior such as: 'Listen, sir, to how I will do your bidding.' These different senses of the imperative mood are used throughout the New Testament (e.g., Acts 22:1 ('fathers, listen to my defense'); James 2:5 ('hear me, my beloved brothers'); Matt. 15:10 ('hear and understand'). Again, these uses do not necessarily mean that the speaker is vested with authority over the person or group he is addressing; rather, it can be as simple as requesting their attention to the things he wishes to tell them. hence, James' use of the imperative mood in Acts 15:14 does not necessarily mean that James is speaking from a supreme authoritative position; rather, it is the perfectly normal means of speech one would employ to summon the attention of his hearers." Robert A. Sungenis, "James's Use of the Imperative Mood in Acts 15:14," letter to authors, 28 July 1995, 1.

The word *exegesato* also occurs in John 1:18, wherein the Son declares the Father. The use of this same word could be significant. It could mean: as Jesus declares the Father to the world, Peter declares Jesus (and therefore also the Father) to the world.

John 1:18 No man hath seen God at any time; the only begotten Son, which is in the bosom of the Father, he hath declared [*exegesato*] [him].

The Church has constantly believed and taught that Peter speaks, or declares, Christ's truth to all the faithful through Peter's successors. At the Fourth General Council (Chalcedon in 451 A.D.), after Pope St. Leo's letter was read to them, the Eastern and Western bishops cried out: "This is the faith of the fathers, this is the faith of the Apostles. So we all believe, thus the orthodox believe. Anathema to him who does not thus believe. *Peter has spoken thus through Leo.* So taught the Apostles" [emphasis added]. Philip Schaff and Henry Wace, eds., *Nicene and Post-Nicene Fathers*, vol. 14—*The Seven Ecumenical Councils*, 2nd series, (New York: Charles Scribner's Sons, 1900; repr., Peabody, MA: Hendrickson, 1994), 259.

The Eastern and Western Fathers repeat similar words in declaring to the Roman emperor the results of the Sixth General Council (III Constantinople in 680 A.D.): "Peter spoke through Agatho." Philip Schaff and Henry Wace, eds., *Nicene and Post-Nicene Fathers*, vol. 14—*The Seven Ecumenical Councils*, 2nd series, (New York: Charles Scribner's Sons, 1900; repr., Peabody, MA: Hendrickson, 1994), 348. Further, in its reply to Pope St. Agatho's letter, the Council declared: "We acknowledge that this letter was divinely written (*perscriptas*) as by the Chief of the Apostles, and through it we have cast out the heretical sect of many errors. . . ." (Philip Schaff and Henry Wace, eds., *Nicene and Post-Nicene Fathers*, vol. 14—*The Seven Ecumenical Councils*, 2nd series, (New York: Charles Scribner's Sons, 1900; repr., Peabody, MA: Hendrickson, 1994), 349). The words that St. Peter and his successors spoke (declared) continued to be followed throughout Christendom during its 2000-year history. The Catholic faithful have always borne witness to the Bishop of Rome as the authoritative voice for Christ.

Significantly, Pope St. Agatho ("Peter spoke through Agatho") was a Greek himself, as were many Bishops of Rome, even during times of strain between the Eastern and Western Churches (e.g., before and after the Monophysite schism of 484-519 begun by the excommunication of Patriarch Acacius of Constantinople):

"It is suitable, at this juncture, to continue the list [of Greek and African Popes of Rome]. . . .

Pope	Year	Nationality
Zosimus	417	Greek of Mesuras
Gelasius I	498	African
John IV	640	Dalmatian
Theodore	642	Greek of Levantine Colony at Rome
Agatho	678	Greek Sicilian
John V	685	Syrian. Antioch
Conon	687	Thracian? Greek.
Sergius I	687	Syrian. Palermo
John VI	701	Greek
John VII	705	Greek. Calabria

Sisinnius	708	Greek
Constantine	708	Syrian
Gregory III	731	Syrian
Zachary	741	Greek. Calabria"

S. Herbert Scott, *The Eastern Churches and the Papacy*, (London: Sheed & Ward, 1928), 366.

Acts 15:16 After this I will return, and will build again the tabernacle of David, which is fallen down; and I will build again the ruins thereof, and I will set it up:

15:17 That the residue of men might seek after the Lord, and all the Gentiles, upon whom my name is called, saith the Lord, who doeth all these things.

15:18 Known unto God are all his works from the beginning of the world.

90. From what Old Testament prophet does James quote in these passages? Amos, in Amos 9:11-12.

91. Why is he quoting these verses from Amos? James accepted the truth of what Peter has proclaimed, and he is supporting Peter's declaration with what the prophet Amos had said long before.

92. In Acts 15:16-18, does James himself place any conditions on Gentile converts? No, he is declaring scriptural support from Amos for welcoming them into the fold. Conditions come later.

Acts 15:19 Wherefore my sentence is [*ego krino* = I give my voice, or opinion], that we trouble not them, which from among the Gentiles are turned to God:

93. What language indicates that the opinion of James is not a pronouncement of the council? Verse 19: "my sentence".

"The actual words used, 'And so I give my voice' (*Ego krino*) (v.19), do not actually favor the view that he [James] was summing up, or deciding the matter on his own authority. Elsewhere in Acts [13:46, 16:15, 26:8] the same verb *krino* is used to denote the expression of an opinion and could better be expressed by the phrase 'in my opinion', or 'as for me.'" Michael M. Winter, *Saint Peter and the Popes*, (Baltimore: Helicon, 1960), 32.

"The speech of St. James is of a different character [from that of St. Peter]. He acquiesces to what St. Peter had said, although it seems to have been against his personal inclinations, and then puts forward a practical suggestion for the sake of harmony." Michael M. Winter, *Saint Peter and the Popes*, (Baltimore: Helicon, 1960), 33.

Robert Sungenis, in studying the Greek of Acts 15:19, in context with other New Testament passages, has determined:

"The Greek phrase *ego krino* in Acts 15:19 which James uses to introduce his contribution to the discussion at the Council of Jerusalem should not be absolutized to represent a dogmatic or unilateral proclamation on James' part. The Greek word *krino* has an extensive semantic range, including such strong determinations as God's judgment on various entities (cf. Rom. 2:16; 3:6; 2 Tim. 4:1), but at the other extreme it refers merely to one's opinion on a subject without positive proof or absolute fact (cf. Rom. 14:5; 1 Cor. 7:37). In the passage in question, James' use of the phrase is closer to the opinion side of the semantic range. the emphatic *ego* ('I') shows that James is prefacing his remarks by an indication to his own feelings on the issue. There are only two other uses of *ego krino* in the New Testament. In John 8:15 the phrase 'I judge not . . .' is in a context which is speaking about forming opinions about men merely from external standards that have no basis in fact. Jesus teaches that one is to exclude himself from such false opinions. In the second usage in John 12:47 Jesus excludes himself from forming a judgment about someone, the emphasis being that he cannot do such without corroboration. According to *A Translator's Handbook on the Acts of the Apostles*, scholars

Newman and Nida state that the words *ego krino* naturally mean 'It is my opinion' ([London:] United Bible Societies, 1972). This understanding was followed by such translators as Goodspeed [and Smith, *The Short Bible*, Chicago: University of Chicago Press] , Moffatt [*The New Testament*, New York: Harper] and the TEV [Today's English Version]. The Lutheran scholar Lenski [*The Interpretation of the Acts of the Apostles*, Minneapolis: Augsburg] paraphrases the phrase to be, 'I for my part judge,' noting that James is posing a question to the members of the assembly rather than an emphatic declaration of fact. We also find that the church father Irenaeus inserts the idiomatic Greek phrase *to kat' eme* ('as much as in me is') after *ego* to show that it is James' opinion rather than a dogmatic declaration (Irenaeus, *Against Heresies*, ch. 7, no. 14). This phrase (*to kat' eme*) is used by Paul in Romans 1:15 to say the same. The fact that James' contribution must first be accepted by the rest of the council shows that it was not a unilateral decision on James' part but a worthy recommendation. If it was anything more than a recommendation, there certainly is no precedent set for James in the New Testament to be the definitive determiner of truth on such issues." Robert A. Sungenis, letter to authors, 16 March 1995, 2.

G. Campbell Morgan, a prominent Protestant theologian, makes the following point regarding James:

"It has been pointed out that the pronoun 'I,' 'I decide,' is emphatic in the Greek. An emphatic pronoun depends after all upon the tone and emphasis. The emphatic 'I' must be interpreted in harmony with the rest of the New Testament and the Bible. It is absurd to believe that James at this moment gave his personal opinion as the final word, from which there could be no appeal. . . . The very emphasis on the 'I' shows that he was only expressing a personal conviction. G. Campbell Morgan, *The Acts of the Apostles*, (Tarrytown, NY: Revell, 1924), 362-363.

Thus, James gives his opinion as to what reasonable conditions the assembly should place on Gentile converts, not that such converts should become Jews first. James believes "that we should not trouble them which from among the Gentiles are turned to God." From his perspective James apparently does not believe that the Noachide laws are a stumbling block to Gentile converts. See Herbert G. May and Bruce M. Metzger, eds., *The New Oxford Annotated Bible, with Apocrypha*, Revised Standard Version, (New York: Oxford, 1977), 1340-1341.

Welcoming Gentiles into the Church
—The Noachide Laws

> *Acts* 15:20 But that we write unto them, that they abstain from pollutions of idols, and [from] fornication [*porneias*], and [from] things strangled, and [from] blood.

94. Does James seek to place conditions on the acceptance of the Gentles into the Christian community? Yes. James fully accepted Peter's pronouncement that Gentiles would henceforth be accepted into the Church. James also suggests implementing certain pastoral regulations for maintaining harmony between Jewish and Gentile Christians. He naturally chose those regulations applicable to all humanity, according to the covenant of God with Noah after the flood: that they should stay away from sacrificial offerings to idols (and from eating the meat sacrificed to idols); that they do not engage in *porneias* (variously translated as fornication, adultery, incest, or sexual immorality); and that they do not eat bloody, unkosher meats.

> "Noachide Laws. Seven key rules of morality which, in the rabbinic view, are the duty of all mankind to obey as the descendants of a common ancestor. Traditionally imposed on Noah, these Noachide (or 'Noachian') Laws preceded the Torah and the *Halakhah*—the legal system meant only for the Jewish people. According to Maimonides, acceptance—on the basis of the Bible—of the seven universal precepts means that any such righteous Gentile is numbered with 'the pious ones among the nations of the world (*Haside Ummotha-olam*) deserving a share in the world to come' (*Tosef. Sanh.* 13.2). Noachide Laws: (1) civil justice [the

duty to establish a legal system]; (2) the prohibition of blasphemy [which includes the bearing of false witness]; (3) the abandonment of idolatry; (4) the prohibition of incest [including adultery and other sexual offenses]; (5) the prohibition of murder; (6) also that of theft; (7) the law against eating flesh ['a limb'] cut from a living animal [i.e., cruelty in any shape or form] (*TB Sanh.* 56a).

"Christians and Muslims are regarded by most halakhic authorities as non-idolaters and as having accepted the Noachide Laws." *The Encyclopedia of Judaism*, 1989 ed., s.v. "Noachide Laws."

"Let us press further, therefore, into this question of the four regulations. Originally such regulations were part of the Israelite law governing the behavior of the foreigner (*ger*) resident in Israel. The Gentile residents had to abstain from these impurities so that Israelites could associate with them without contamination (Lev 17:8-12; 18:6ff.)." Raymond E. Brown, Karl P. Donfried, and John Reumann, eds., *Peter in the New Testament*, (Minneapolis, MN: Augsburg; New York: Paulist: 1973), 51-52 [from the Lutheran-Catholic dialogue on the primacy of Peter].

95. What is the effect of the conditions that James has suggested? Essentially, these conditions would put Gentile Christians under certain of the Noachide laws binding on all the world, according to Jewish tradition. (Even today, the Christian community upholds the universal moral law, as originally given to Moses on Mt. Sinai.) James follows Jewish tradition in the manner in which a Jew would accept Gentiles into social association. James was not opposing Peter; he was rather explaining and expanding on what Peter had stated regarding Gentile converts. James was speaking within the context of Jewish tradition. The rules of the Noachide covenant conditions are:

"The Babylonian Talmud (*Sanh.* 56a; cf. Pseudo-Phocylides *Sentences*) cites seven more 'Noachian laws' that were to be binding upon all people: they were to recognize government, avoid blasphemy and idolatry, refrain from adultery, refrain from bloodshed, resist robbery, and abstain from

eating any flesh cut from a living animal. God then signified his promise, sealing the covenant with a rainbow (Gen.
9:8-17)." Allen C. Myers, ed., *The Eerdmans Bible Dictionary*, (Grand Rapids, MI: Eerdmans, 1987), 766.

Or, translated another way:

"Gentiles . . . have a share in the world to come, provided
they observe the seven moral laws revealed to Noah [The
seven laws of Noah prohibited (1) blasphemy, (2) theft, (3)
idolatry, (4) murder, (5) incest, (6) eating flesh from a living animal; also, (7) courts of justice were to be established.]"
Abraham E. Millgram, *Jewish Worship*, (Philadelphia: Jewish Publication Society, 1971), 401, 623.

For all converts to Judaism today, there remains a series of
queries, one of which is described as follows:

"she [or he] will then be asked why she [or he] seeks a place
in Judaism, with all its burdens and travails, when as a Christian she [or he] is only required to observe the seven
Noachide laws to be assured a place in the kingdom of
Heaven." Chaim Bermant, *The Walled Garden: The Saga
of Jewish Family Life and Tradition*, (New York: Macmillan,
1975), 231; cf. Lillian Freudmann, "Paul Undermined Torah," *Bible Review* 9:4 (August 1993): 6.

In the context of Acts and of the Noachide Laws, James is
revealing that he saw the world through Jewish eyes. He was merely
trying to bring Gentiles into Christianity the best way he knew—
according to his Jewish sense of what was proper for Gentile-Jew-
ish harmony. He was not necessarily trying to make Gentile converts become Jews before they could become part of the Body of
Christ. Rather, Gentile converts would naturally be expected to
conform to Noah's covenant laws, which were expected to be followed by all just men. This was a pastoral thought on the part of
James, reflecting his Jewish background.

96. Why did James not set forth all of the Noachide laws?

The Lutheran-Catholic dialogue discusses the regulations for Gentile converts given at the Council of Jerusalem and a very practical reason for them:

> "James set forth only a few regulations to be observed by the Gentile Christians, seemingly lest they scandalize the followers of Moses who lived alongside of them (15:21)." Raymond E. Brown, Karl P. Donfried, and John Reumann, eds., *Peter in the New Testament*, (Minneapolis, MN: Augsburg; New York: Paulist: 1973), 50.

David Stern disccusses the issue of the Noachide laws with broader implications for the emerging universalitstic religion:

> "The four prohibitions [of Acts 15:20] are a variant of the Noachide laws, presented in the Talmud as what God has required of all mankind since the days of Noah (i.e., before 'Jew' and 'Gentile' were defined):
> "'Our rabbis taught, "The sons of Noah were given seven commandments: practicing justice and abstaining from blasphemy, idolatry, adultery, bloodshed, robbery and eating flesh torn from a live animal." Rabbi Chananyah ben-Gamli'el said, "Also not to drink blood taken from a live animal."' (*Sanhedrin* 56a)
> "There follows the scriptural basis for these [Noachide] laws in the form of a *midrash* on Genesis 2:16. Thus Judaism is not only a particularistic national religion specifying God's requirements for Jews but also a universalistic religion that states what God demands of non-Jews as well. Possibly the Jerusalem Council based its prohibitions on this tradition, although its four requirements neither state nor imply anything about practicing justice or eschewing robbery. On the other hand, the council may have specified only minimum requirements, with the expectation that other moral attributes would be acquired later, possibly as a result of Gentiles' attending synagogue services and learning there the Jewish moral tradition (v.21&N)." David H. Stern, *Jewish New Testament Commentary*, (Clarksville, MD: Jewish New Testament Publications, 1992), 278.

Alternatively, one may speculate that James referred to all of the Noachide laws in a shorthand fashion, as Christ had done when referring to the Ten Commandments in Matthew 19:16-20 by not naming them all. In Acts 15:20 James specified the disciplinary parts of the covenant (not eating meat sacrificed to idols, not marrying within certain degrees, not eating unkosher foods). The more universal moral aspects of the covenant were implied.

> *Acts* 15:21 For Moses of old time hath in every city them that preach him, being read in the synagogues every sabbath day.
> 15:22 Then pleased it the apostles and elders, with the whole church, to send chosen men of their own company to Antioch with Paul and Barnabas; [namely], Judas surnamed Barsabas, and Silas, chief men among the brethren:
> 15:23 And they wrote [letters] by them after this manner; The apostles and elders and brethren [send] greeting unto the brethren which are of the Gentiles in Antioch and Syria and Cilicia:

> *Acts* 15:28 For it seemed good to the Holy Ghost, and to us [the council and Peter], to lay upon you no greater burden than these necessary things;
> 15:29 That ye abstain from meats offered to idols, and from blood, and from things strangled, and from fornication: from which if ye keep yourselves, ye shall do well. Fare ye well.

97. How do we know that James was not trying to usurp Peter's position of primal authority? The letter of the council was written in the names of all the Apostles and elders, rather than in James's name alone. Paul too abides by this letter:

> *Acts* 21:25 As touching the Gentiles which believe, we have written [and] concluded that they observe no such thing, save only that they keep themselves from [things] offered to idols, and from blood, and from strangled, and from fornication.

98. What is suggested in the conclusion of the letter (Acts 15:23-29) sent by the Apostles, elders and brethren to certain Gentile converts? That Gentile Christian converts would do well to abstain from certain acts that are contrary to Jewish law in order to fellowship with them. This would be the Jewish sense of how the Noachide laws were to be observed, even until to-day. In the letter promulgated by the Council of Jerusalem, those were the rules most appropriate for engendering peace between Gentile and Jewish converts to Christianity.

99. What can we conclude from the decisions of the Council of Jerusalem? That the Gentiles would be encouraged to enter the community of Jesus Christ via the Holy Spirit and baptism, without conditions, except as to certain rules originally placed on all men under God's covenant with Noah.

Certain of the disciplinary parts of the Noachide laws, being pastoral in nature for the good of the community, eventually ceased being a part of Church discipline and were no longer in evidence by the end of the first century A.D. Christ would enlighten the truth of Noah's covenant as he did the truth of the Mosaic covenant. The guide is Christ. The universal natural "moral law [like Mosaic law] finds its fullness and unity in Christ. Jesus is in person the way of perfection." (*Catechism of the Catholic Church*, Par. 1953, (London: Geoffrey Chapman—Libreria Editrice Vaticana, 1994), 423). The Noachide covenant, informed by Christ's law of love, still stands:

> "The covenant with Noah remains in force during the times of the Gentiles, until the universal proclamation of the Gospel [Cf. Gen 9:16; Lk 21:24; *Dei Verbum* 3]." *Catechism of the Catholic Church*, Par. 58, (London: Geoffrey Chapman—Libreria Editrice Vaticana, 1994), 20.

Paul's Teaching Ten Years After the Council of Jerusalem

100. Did the early Christian community follow the precepts set forth by the Council of Jerusalem? Yes. Paul would recog-

nize the disciplines put forth by the Council as pastoral, not absolute, norms. Paul associates sinfulness with violating the proscriptive provisions of Acts 15:20 relative to eating meat offered to idols as follows:

> *I Corinthians* 8:4 As concerning therefore the eating of those things that are offered in sacrifice unto idols, we know that an idol [is] nothing in the world, and that [there is] none other God but one.
> 8:9 But take heed lest by any means this liberty of yours become a stumblingblock to them that are weak.
> 8:10 For if any man see thee which hast knowledge sit at meat in the idol's temple, shall not the conscience of him which is weak be emboldened to eat those things which are offered to idols;
> 8:11 And through thy knowledge shall the weak brother perish, for whom Christ died?
> 8:12 But when ye sin so against the brethren, and wound their weak conscience, ye sin against Christ.
> 8:13 Wherefore, if meat make my brother to offend, I will eat no flesh while the world standeth, lest I make my brother to offend.

"The Corinthians' second question concerns meat that has been sacrificed to idols; in this area they were exhibiting a disordered sense of liberation that Paul here tries to rectify. . . . Essentially Paul urges them to take a communitarian rather than an individualistic view of their Christian freedom. Many decisions that they consider pertinent only to their private relationship with God have, in fact, social consequences." Confraternity of Christian Doctrine, *The New American Bible* (Giant Print Edition), fn. [I Corinthians] 8:1-11, (Huntington, IN: Our Sunday Visitor, 1988), 2028.

Refer also to the context of communitarian freedom in other passages such as I Corinthians 10:23-31; Colossians 2:20-22; Galatians 2:11-21.

101. When is Paul writing to the Corinthians? Within ten years after the Council of Jerusalem, or about 56-57 A.D., after

much missionary activity had greatly increased the number of Gentiles in the Church.

102. Did Paul submit to the Council's pastoral decisions regarding their apparent concern for the Noachide covenant? Yes, but as more and more Gentiles came into the Church, and the Church was evangelized farther and farther away from Jerusalem and the Jewish community, there were other pastoral needs not directly addressed at the Council of Jerusalem. The enunciations of James (confirmed in the letters drafted in the Council) were originally made in order to apply the pastoral decisions of the Council to the question of harmony between Jews and Gentiles, so as not to cause scandal to the brethren. As a Jewish scholar, Paul could accept the decisions of the Council and still recognize true freedom in Christ. An exception to the general pastoral disciplines, based on the facts and circumstances encountered by the believer, could alleviate rigid interpretations. For example, in eating with unbelievers, such practices could be set aside unless there was cause for scandal to the Jewish Christian believer (cf. I Corinthians 10:25-30).

Paul's own common sense and spiritual inclination is to go to the Gentiles. Paul, though, waits for the confirmation of his apostolate from Peter and the other bishops in unity with Peter at the Council of Jerusalem.

103. Why did Paul implore the Corinthians to retain their freedom as Christians? In light of I Corinthians 8:10-13, Paul taught that eating meat (often the best) that was sacrificed to idols becomes an occasion of sin only if the eating of the meat connected with idolatrous sacrifice could cause another to misinterpret Christian freedom, mistaking it for idolatrous practice. The better course of action is not to eat the meat if it is known to come from a sacrifice to idols, if someone might be scandalized. The message is clear: do not cause scandal and do not cause another Christian to stumble in his walk with the Lord, even if one is free to do something. Read the counsel in I Corinthians 10:23-31.

Peter Teaches Paul

> *Galatians* 1:18 Then after three years I [Paul] went up to Jerusalem to see [*historesai*] Peter, and abode with him fifteen days.
> 1:19 But other of the apostles saw [*heiden*] I none, save James the Lord's brother.

104. Would Paul consider the meeting with Peter important because of Peter's role as the leader of all Christians? Yes. Paul unashamedly went to Jerusalem to meet with St. Peter, and probably learn from him, for a period of fifteen days, thereby evidencing his submission to Peter's authority.

"Why does S. Paul mention this event [Gal 1:18-19], if there was no important reason for so doing? Did he recognise by this visit S. Peter's office as the Chief Shepherd, to whom he was under the necessity of showing respect, if nothing more? Else why did he see none of the other Apostles save S. James? And why did he see S. James? Surely because he was the Bishop of Jerusalem and 'the Lord's Brother,' to whom honour was due. S. Chrysostom believes that S. Paul's visit to S. Peter was in order to recognise his Headship. (See *Extract*, No. 73, Pt. II.)" Colin Lindsay, *The Evidence for the Papacy*, (London: Longmans, Green, 1870), 9.

105. Whom did Paul go up to Jerusalem to visit for fifteen days? Peter.

106. Whom did Paul also encounter in Jerusalem? James.

107. Why would Paul have spent the fifteen days with Peter rather than with James? Peter is the head of the Church, as well as being the Apostle to the Jews. Any Pope of the Catholic Church is the leader of the whole Church; at the same time, he is the Bishop of Rome, in which capacity he ministers to the needs of Christians in Rome.

Language Analysis of the Greek Word *Historesai* in Galatians 1:18

108. Is there anything significant about using the Greek word *historesai* rather than *heiden* to describe Paul's visit with Peter? Yes. It is a much stronger word of visiting for the purpose of examination and of obtaining knowledge of the person himself.

"In verse 18 Paul explains that he went up to Jerusalem to visit Peter. The verb used is *historesai* which in this case can be best understood if we begin with its cognate noun form *histor*. The *histor* in ancient Greece functioned as examiner and arbiter in legal matters. He was learned in the law and skilled in examining witnesses. He knew how to ask the right questions of people who were being examined in order to ascertain the truth in matters of dispute. The truth he was after was not philosophical truth in some abstract metaphysical sense, but rather the kind of truth that can issue in practical wisdom. In the final analysis the *histor* would be called upon to make a judgment. The *histor* was a judge." William R. Farmer and Roch Kereszty, *Peter and Paul in the Church of Rome*, (New York: Paulist, 1990), 30.

"The verb *historesai* can mean to inquire into or about a thing, or to inquire about a person. Or it can also mean to 'examine' or to 'observe.' Such a questioner or observer would then become 'one who is informed' about something, or 'one who knows.'

In the case at hand the verb is used with the accusative of person, so that it can mean to 'inquire of' or 'to ask.' One can inquire of an oracle." William R. Farmer and Roch Kereszty, *Peter and Paul in the Church of Rome*, (New York: Paulist, 1990), 30-31.

"The most complete study of *historesai* as used by Paul has been made by G. D. Kilpatrick. Kilpatrick takes into consideration the Latin, Coptic and Syriac versions, all of which understand *historesai* in the sense of 'to see.' He notes, however, that later commentators were not content with this interpretation. Chrysostom perceived that *historesai* must mean more than 'see.' He makes a distinction between *heiden* (to see) and *historesai* and explicitly notes that Paul does not write: *heiden Petron*, but *historesai Petron*." William R. Farmer and Roch Kereszty, *Peter and Paul in the Church of Rome*, (New York: Paulist, 1990), 31.

St. John Chrysostom (ca. 395), a Greek-speaking priest and preacher at Antioch from A.D. 381-398, and Bishop of Constantinople from A.D. 398-404, interprets the meaning *historesai* of Galatians 1:18 as follows:

"And the only object of this journey was to visit Peter, thus he pays due respect to the Apostles, and esteems himself not only not their better but not their equal. Which is plain from this journey, for Paul was induced to visit Peter by the same feeling from which many of our brethren sojourn with holy men: or rather by a humbler feeling for they do so for their own benefit, but this blessed man, not for his own instruction or correction, but merely for the sake of beholding and honoring Peter by his presence. He says, 'to visit Peter,' he does not say to see (*hidein*,) but to visit and survey, (*historesai*,) a word which those who seek to become acquainted with great and splendid cities, apply to themselves. Worthy of such trouble did he consider the very sight of Peter; . . ." Philip Schaff, ed., *The Nicene and Post-Nicene Fathers of the Christian Church*, vol. XIII, *Saint Chrysostom: Homilies on Galatians*, trans. Gross Alexander, (repr., Grand Rapids: Eerdmans; Edinburgh: T. & T. Clark, 1991), 12-13.

Farmer and Kereszty continue, relating Paul's visit to "information" gathering:

"On the basis of Liddell and Scott's article which Kilpatrick regards as probably the best guide we have, but also taking into account other lexicographical aids, he concludes that '*historesai Kephan*' at Galatians 1:18 is to be taken as meaning 'to get information from Cephas.'" William R. Farmer and Roch Kereszty, *Peter and Paul in the Church of Rome*, (New York: Paulist, 1990), 31-32.

"and since Paul seeks information from Peter and not from James, with whom he also had some contact, Kilpatrick asks: 'Is there any information that one had to give him that the other could not provide?' In answer he writes: 'St. Peter had been an eyewitness and disciple of Jesus. St. James could not claim to be a comparable informant about the teaching and the ministry.' In conclusion Kilpatrick writes: 'We know then of one kind of information for which St. Paul would go to St. Peter rather than St. James, information about Jesus' teaching and ministry.'" William R. Farmer and Roch Kereszty, *Peter and Paul in the Church of Rome*, (New York: Paulist, 1990), 32.

"Paul is not forensically diminishing his authority by 'making inquiry' of Peter. On the contrary, his use of *historesai* in this context conceptually places Peter in the dock. Paul is the *histor*. Peter is the one being cross-examined. What is at issue is the truth in a whole range of practical matters which Paul wants to discuss with Peter." William R. Farmer and Roch Kereszty, *Peter and Paul in the Church of Rome*, (New York: Paulist, 1990), 36.

109. What was accomplished when Paul spent fifteen days in Jerusalem conferring with Peter? We will never know for sure. Paul may have examined Peter in great detail concerning the Christian faith.

"We will never know how they spent those days together in Jerusalem. The point is that two weeks for important leaders, not to say the two persons who eventually emerged as the two leading apostles of the church, is a considerable length of time for a visit. Seldom do great leaders have the luxury of such schedules.

"Two weeks provided ample time for both Peter and Paul to discuss whatever was uppermost in their minds, including such topics, we must presume, as the Lord's supper and other matters bearing upon the preaching of the gospel, including the resurrection."

"And when we realize the full range of meanings that Paul's readers could rightfully associate with his use of

historesai in this context, presuming that he was careful in
his choice of language, we must be open to understanding
Paul as saying that he went to Jerusalem to question, examine and observe, to the end that he would leave informed
and ready to report to others on the results of his inquiry."

"Peter was Paul's host throughout the two-week period. As Peter's guest Paul was being afforded an unparalleled opportunity to gain an inside view of Peter's life and
manners. To remain with Peter for two weeks would, of
necessity, have afforded them the opportunity to share table
fellowship, and it is altogether likely that they observed the
Lord's supper together in accordance with the words of institution which are preserved for us in I Corinthians 11:23-
26 sometime during that two week period." William R.
Farmer and Roch Kereszty, *Peter and Paul in the Church of
Rome*, (New York: Paulist, 1990), 38-39.

The Pillars of the Church Teach in Galatians 2:9-10

Galatians 2:9 And when James, Cephas, and John,
who seemed to be pillars, perceived the grace that
was given unto me, they gave to me and Barnabas
the right hands of fellowship; that we [should go] unto
the heathen, and they unto the circumcision.

110 Who were the acknowledged pillars of the faith in Galatians
2:9? James, Cephas [Peter], and John. In other passages Peter's
name is listed first in recounting the names of the Apostles.
Explanations of this singular instance are:

"There is only one place in the New Testament where St.
Peter's name is not standing in the place of honour and that
is in Galatians 2:7 [2:9]. 'Those who were reputed to be the
main support of the church, James and Cephas and John. . .
.' This order of names seemed so unnatural to the fathers
that it was rewritten as 'Peter and James and John' by
Marcion, Irenaeus, Tertullian, Origen, Gregory of Nyssa,
Jerome, Ambrose, Ephraim and Augustine. The same rear-
rangement is to be found in several of the oldest manuscripts
of the Epistle." Michael M. Winter, *Saint Peter and the
Popes*, (Baltimore: Helicon, 1960), 37.

Additionally:

> "The Epistles of St. Paul appear in sharp contrast with this
> arrangement of Apostolic names. In the First Epistle to the
> Corinthians he gives them in the order Paul, Apollos, Cephas,
> Christ [I Cor. 1:12; 3:22]. It appears that St. Peter has been
> relegated to the last place, but St. John Chrysostom [*Homi-*
> *lies on I Cor., No. 3, M.P.G.*, vol. 61, col. 24] declared that
> the list was written in order of ascending dignity. The same
> pattern is to be found later in this Epistle (9:4-6), where the
> persons are: the other apostles, the Lord's brethren, and
> Cephas. Chrysostom's theory of ascending dignity is per-
> haps even clearer in this case [*Homilies on I Cor., No. 21,*
> *M.P.G.*, vol. 61, col. 172]." Michael M. Winter, *Saint Peter*
> *and the Popes*, (Baltimore: Helicon, 1960), 37.

> "There is *only one* place in Holy Scripture where St.
> Peter is not named first in rank: 'James and Cephas and
> John, who are accounted pillars, gave to me and to Barnabas
> the right hand of fellowship' (Gal. ii. 9). Against the cardi-
> nal doctrines of Christianity objections may be made from
> isolated passages, in spite of other conclusive proofs. But
> the few passages have to be interpreted in accordance with
> the many. Here we have a single instance against more than
> two dozen which are clear: thus the Protestant argument
> from this passage that St. Paul did not admit any primacy in
> St. Peter falls to the ground.
> "There was some reason for this order. Probably James
> was the first of the three seen by St. Paul, and John the last.
> What is most noticeable is that to the Fathers this order of
> names was so unnatural that Irenaeus, Tertullian, Gregory
> of Nyssa, Jerome, Ambrose, Augustine, are found to quote
> St. Paul as saying 'Peter and James and John'! This reading
> is also found in the uncial MSS. [manuscripts] D [Codex
> Bezae, 5th century], E [Codex Laudianus, 6th century], F
> [Codex Brixianus, 6th century], G [Codex Boernerianus,
> 9th century]." Dom John Chapman, *Bishop Gore and the*
> *Catholic Claims*, (New York: Longmans, 1905), 46-47.

111. How do we know that Paul and Barnabas were in agreement
    with the other Apostles as to their teaching of Christian doc-

trine? They were given the right hand of fellowship, evidencing that there was consensus that they would teach the Gospel of Jesus Christ to the Gentiles.

"Some think that the actual 'minutes' of the meeting are here quoted [Gal 2:7-9]. Paul's apostleship to the Gentiles (1, 16) is recognized alongside that of Peter to the Jews. Morever, the right to proclaim the gospel without requiring circumcision and the Jewish law is sealed by a handshake." Confraternity of Christian Doctrine, *The New American Bible* (Giant Print Edition), fn. [Galatians] 2:7-9, (Huntington, IN: Our Sunday Visitor, 1988), 2064.

Galatians 2:10 Only [they would] that we should remember the poor; the same which I also was forward to do.

112. What mandate did the pillars of the Church give to Paul and Barnabas? They were told to be mindful of the poor. Paul acceded to the idea of organizing a collection of alms among the Gentile communities for the poor Christians in Jerusalem.

CHAPTER IV

STRUCTURE AND AUTHORITY IN THE CHURCH

The Role of the Shepherd

> *John* 10:11 I am the good shepherd: the good shepherd giveth his life for the sheep.
> 10:14 I am the good shepherd, and know my [sheep], and am known of mine.
> 10:16 And other sheep I have, which are not of this fold: them also I must bring, and they shall hear my voice; and there shall be one fold, and one shepherd.

113. Who is the good shepherd in John 10:11,14? Jesus Christ.

114. What is God's plan in John 10:16? That there should be one flock and one shepherd.

In recent times, Vatican II stated the provision this way:

> "This Sacred Council, following closely in the footsteps of the First Vatican Council, with that Council teaches and declares that Jesus Christ, the eternal Shepherd, established His holy Church, having sent forth the apostles as He Himself had been sent by the Father; and He willed that their

successors, namely the bishops, should be shepherds in His Church even to the consummation of the world. And in order that the episcopate itself might be one and undivided, He placed Blessed Peter over the other apostles, and instituted in him a permanent and visible source and foundation of unity of faith and communion." *Lumen Gentium* (Constitution on the Church, Para. 18, November 21, 1964), (Washington, DC: United States Catholic Conference, n.d.), 20.

115. Before he left the earth and ascended to his father in heaven, did Jesus appoint another visible shepherd to succeed him in guiding the flock? Yes, Simon the Rock.

> *John* 21:2 There were together Simon Peter, and Thomas called Didymus, and Nathanael of Cana in Galilee, and the [sons] of Zebedee, and two other of his disciples.

All of these had gathered to fish together. Later, they saw the resurrected Lord Jesus on the shore cooking; Peter waded ashore from the boat to join him; and they all ate together (John 21:3-14). To Peter, a question remains:

> *John* 21:15 So when they had dined, Jesus saith to Simon Peter, {Simon, [son] of Jonas, lovest thou me more than these?} He saith unto him, Yea, Lord; thou knowest that I love thee.

So, before the Lord commands Peter to shepherd his flock, he first must get Peter's assent and commitment to serve the Lord and the People of God. To that end, the Lord singularly asks Simon Peter: "Do you love me more than these?" Peter responds affirmatively, "Yes, Lord; you know that I love you."

> "The singular here [spoken to Peter] is even further accentuated when Christ says: 'Lovest thou Me *more than these*?' When Our Lord said this there were present Nathaniel, James, and John, with Thomas and two other disciples [John 21:2].

It is therefore St. Peter, as distinct from these other Apostles, who is to feed the lambs and sheep of Christ." St. George Kieran Hyland, "The Papal Supremacy During the First Three Centuries," *The Irish Ecclesiastical Record* (July 1908), 194.

Looking at the text of John 21:15-17, one is immediately struck by varying usages of certain Greek words:

> *John* 21:15 So when they had dined, Jesus saith to Simon Peter, Simon, [son] of Jonas, lovest thou me more than these? He saith unto him, Yea, Lord; thou knowest that I love thee. He saith unto him, Feed [Gr. *boskein* = feed] my lambs.
>
> 21:16 He saith to him again the second time, Simon, [son] of Jonas, lovest thou me? He saith unto him, Yea, Lord; thou knowest that I love thee. He saith unto him, Feed [Gr. *poimainein* = tend] my sheep.
>
> 21:17 He saith unto him the third time, Simon, [son] of Jonas, lovest thou me? Peter was grieved because he said unto him the third time, Lovest thou me? And he said unto him, Lord, thou knowest all things; thou knowest that I love thee. Jesus saith unto him, Feed [Gr. *boskein* = feed] my sheep.

"Anyone who overheard that conversation [in John 21:15-17] at the time would have found nothing strange about Our Lord's use of the metaphor of the shepherd. Profane and sacred writers used it to indicate the functions of teaching and governing. Homer, the first Greek poet, author of the Iliad and the Odyssey, who is said to have lived before 700 B.C., referred to kings as to 'shepherds of the people.' Hesychius, the grammarian of Alexandria, who probably lived in the fifth century A.D., wrote a Greek dictionary in which he said that 'shepherd' means the same as 'king.' There are many examples in Scripture. God said to David: 'Thou shalt feed my people, Israel, and thou shalt be prince over Israel' (2 [Samuel] 5:2). This is an example of the Hebrew way of speaking in which the second phrase repeats the meaning of the first in a different metaphor. It is called Hebrew parallelism. Again: 'Behold the Lord shall come with strength; and his arm shall rule . . . he shall feed his flock like a shepherd' (Isaias 40:9-11)." Francis J. Ripley, *The Pope: Vicar of Jesus Christ*, (Dublin: Catholic Truth Society, 1965), 9-10.

Consider several scriptural references to "shepherd" and "ruler" in the Old and New Testaments, set forth below:

Numbers 27:17 Which may go out before them, and which may go in before them, and which may lead them out, and which may bring them in; that the congregation of the LORD be not as sheep which have no shepherd.

II Samuel 5:2 Also in time past, when Saul was king over us, thou wast he that leddest out and broughtest in Israel: and the LORD said to thee, Thou shalt feed my people Israel, and thou shalt be a captain over Israel.

Isaiah 40:9 O Zion, that bringest good tidings, get thee up into the high mountain; O Jerusalem, that bringest good tidings, lift up thy voice with strength; lift [it] up, be not afraid; say unto the cities of Judah, Behold your God!
40:10 Behold, the Lord GOD will come with strong [hand], and his arm shall rule for him: behold, his reward [is] with him, and his work before him.
40:11 He shall feed his flock like a shepherd: he shall gather the lambs with his arm, and carry [them] in his bosom, [and] shall gently lead those that are with young.

Jeremiah 31:10 Hear the word of the LORD, O ye nations, and declare [it] in the isles afar off, and say, He that scattered Israel will gather him, and keep him, as a shepherd [doth] his flock.

Ezekiel 34:23 And I will set up one shepherd over them, and he shall feed them, [even] my servant David; he shall feed them, and he shall be their shepherd.

34:24 And I the LORD will be their God, and my servant David a prince among them; I the LORD have spoken [it].

Micah 5:2 But thou, Beth-lehem Ephratah, [though] thou be little among the thousands of Judah, [yet] out of thee shall he come forth unto me [that is] to be ruler in Israel; whose goings forth [have been] from of old, from everlasting.

Zechariah 10:2 For the idols have spoken vanity, and the diviners have seen a lie, and have told false dreams; they comfort in vain: therefore they went their way as a flock, they were troubled, because [there was] no shepherd.

Revelation 2:27 And he shall rule them with a rod of iron; as the vessels of a potter shall they be broken to shivers: even as I received of my Father.

Revelation 17:17 For God hath put in their hearts to fulfil his will, and to agree, and give their kingdom unto the beast, until the words of God shall be fulfilled.

Revelation 19:15 And out of his mouth goeth a sharp sword, that with it he should smite the nations: and he shall rule them with a rod of iron: and he treadeth the winepress of the fierceness and wrath of Almighty God.

Revelation 12:5 And she brought forth a man child, who was to rule all nations with a rod of iron: and her child was caught up unto God, and [to] his throne.

"All these references make it clear that when Christ is called the 'Good Shepherd' He is really invoked as Christ the King. The significance of the two metaphors is the same throughout Scripture. The shepherd is the king and the king is the shepherd. So when Jesus bestowed the office of being the shepherd of His whole flock on St. Peter he was really giving him kingly supremacy, a power not only of honour but of jurisdiction." Francis J. Ripley, *The Pope: Vicar of Jesus Christ*, (Dublin: Catholic Truth Society, 1965), 10-11.

116. Whom did Christ appoint to be the shepherd of the New Covenant flock? Peter, according to John 21. Christ commanded Peter to feed and to tend the Lord's flock of sheep and lambs. This flock will be under Peter's (and his successors') care until Christ's glorious return. Then, Jesus, the chief Shepherd (cf. I Peter 5:4), again will take sole charge of his flock at the end of time.

Oscar Cullmann, a Lutheran scholar, summarizes Peter's office as shepherd of the flock:

> "We still must consider the wording of the commission as it is formulated in John 21:16 ff.: 'Feed my sheep.' It has rightly been pointed out that the Damascus Document discovered in 1910, which in connection with the recent manuscript discoveries in Palestine takes on particular importance, speaks of the leader of the fellowship as the 'shepherd of the flock.' His duty is to proclaim the word, explain the Scripture, and exercise community discipline (ch. 13:9)." Oscar Cullmann, *Peter: Disciple, Apostle, Martyr*, trans. Floyd V. Filson, (Philadelphia: Westminster, 1953), 63-64.

To reiterate that Peter is given a special commission as the particular one who is to feed and to tend the Lord's flock, one should consider:

> "Not the least important expression used in St. John's text is the pronoun *my*. 'Feed *My* lambs, feed *My* lambs, feed *My* sheep.' Our Lord did not say feed *these* lambs, nor *those* lambs. He said *My* lambs, to show that they are and remain His. He does not dismiss them from Himself when He confides them to Peter; He does not abdicate His office of pas-

tor when He appoints a Vicar; He makes him co-pastor with Him and in Him. All the lambs and sheep of Christ are Peter's also. No one in the whole flock, no disciple of Christ, can claim exemption from the jurisdiction of Peter. Nor can any number of lambs and sheep in counsel or consort set themselves in opposition to this authority. In the words of the Divine Master there is no limitation to the pastor's rule: it is identical with that of the Good Shepherd Himself." St. George Kieran Hyland, "The Papal Supremacy During the First Three Centuries," *The Irish Ecclesiastical Record* (July 1908), 193.

The flock always belongs to Christ. The Lord relinquishes neither his authority as chief shepherd nor as holder of the keys of the kingdom of heaven (cf. I Peter 5:4; Revelation 1:18, 3:7). Yet, Peter is the one who is commissioned to serve and to lead the Lord's visible flock until the Lord Jesus Christ returns.

117. What are the three specific commands that Christ gives to Peter? "Feed my lambs." (21:15); "Feed [tend] my sheep." (21:16); and "Feed my sheep." (21:17).

"In John 21:15-17 there are three sets of word exchanges that set the stage for Peter's ascent to the primacy of the Church. First, there is the change from 'lambs' (Greek: *arnia*) to 'sheep' (Greek: *probatia*)." Robert A. Sungenis, "John 21:15-17," letter to authors, June 1994.

☙ ☙ ☙

There are none in the Church but sheep and lambs to be tended and fed. St. Ambrose (ca. 385 A.D.) wrote of the sheep as the more perfect, implying the lambs as the less perfect of the flock:

"Him whom, as He is about to be raised to heaven, He was leaving to us, as it were, the Vicar of His love. For thus you have it: 'Simon, son of John, lovest thou Me? . . . Feed My sheep. . . . Because he alone out of all makes this profession (of love), he is preferred before all. . . . And now he is not ordered, as at first, to 'feed His lambs,' . . . but 'His sheep,' that the more perfect [Peter] might govern the more perfect [sheep]." (*In Lucam*, lib. x. p. 1848, tom. ii.), in Charles F. B. Allnatt, ed., *Cathedra Petri—The Titles and Prerogatives of St. Peter*, (London: Burns & Oates, 1879), 41-42.

Some writers even have treated the symbolism of sheep and lambs as a way to distinguish between clergy and laity. St. Eucherius, Bishop of Lyons (ca. 440), thus wrote:

"First He committed to him [Peter] the lambs, then the sheep; because He constituted him not only shepherd, but the shepherd of shepherds. Therefore, Peter feeds the lambs, he feeds also the sheep; he feeds the offspring, he feeds also the mothers; he rules both subjects and prelates. He is the shepherd, therefore, of all, because, besides lambs and sheep, there is nothing in the Church." (*Serm. de Natal. SS. Apost. Petri et Pauli*), in Charles F. B. Allnatt, ed., *Cathedra Petri— The Titles and Prerogatives of St. Peter*, (London: Burns & Oates, 1879), 45-46.

Continuing his analysis, Mr. Sungenis writes:

"Second, there is the change from friendly love (Greek: *phileo*) to profound love (Greek: *agape*). Though Jesus . . . [two times] uses *agape* inquiring of Peter [and *phileo* once], Peter uses *phileo*, the more shallow of the two, in each of his three responses to Jesus. Perhaps after the experience of denying Jesus three times, Peter is timid about using the higher form of love that Jesus wishes to elicit from him. When Peter is strengthened by the Comforter [Holy Spirit] he will again be able to use *agape* when speaking about his Christian faith (I and II Peter). Third, there is the change from 'feed' (Greek: *boske*) to 'shepherd' (Greek: *poimaine*). Peter is told to 'feed' the lambs, but both 'shepherd' and 'feed' the sheep. Of the two, *poimaine* is the more technical and comprehensive of the two. It is used of 'ruling' in other texts, (e.g., Matthew 2:6; Revelation 2:27; 12:5; 19:15), whereas *boske* refers only to feeding. In each one of these three word exchanges there is a movement from weaker to stronger. The weaker words, *arnia*, *phileo*, and *boske* are replaced by the stronger words, *probatia*, *agape*, and *poimaine*. The progression from weaker to stronger helps to show, in a preliminary way, the parameters and requirements for the ministry that Peter will soon undertake. Under the divine assistance that he will eventually receive from the Holy Spirit, Peter will inaugurate his rule over the clergy and laity that, in turn, will be followed by his successors. At Pentecost, Peter received the complete installment of this divine assistance; the book of Acts subsequently recording his profound and unquestioned leadership in the Church (Acts 1:15; 2:14,38; 3:6,12; 4:8; 5:3f,15,29; 8:20; 9:32f; 10:1f; 11:1f; 12:1f; 15:7). Robert A. Sungenis, "John 21:15-17," letter to authors, June 1994.

A more detailed analysis of the use of the Greek word *poimanao* in John 21:16 follows:

"The Greek word *poimanao*, which is used in John 21:16 when Jesus directs Peter to 'shepherd' the sheep, has a linguistic range which includes the aspects of 'feeding,' 'tending,' and 'ruling.' This semantic range is shown both in the traditional role of a shepherd who both feeds and guides his flock, as well as the New Testament and Septuagint usage of the word in various contexts. The verbal form *poimanao* is used 11 times in the New Testament in which only one reference, perhaps two, refer exclusively to 'feeding' (Jude 12, possibly 1 Cor. 9:7). The other nine references show either an exclusive meaning of 'ruling' (Rev. 2:27; 12:5; 19:15) or a combination of both nourishing and ruling (Matt. 2:6; Luke 17:7; Acts 20:28; 1 Peter 5:2; Rev. 7:17).

"The same semantic range is true in the use of *poimanao* in the Septuagint. The Septuagint uses the verbal form approximately 50 times. All of the usages of *poimanao* are from the Hebrew word *raah*. Similar to *poimanao*, the word *raah* can refer to 'feeding' (Genesis 30:31), 'tending' (Ex. 3:1; 1 Sam. 16:11), or 'ruling' (Psalm 2:9). Since our interest lies in the 'ruling' dimension of this word for the understanding of Jesus' use of the Greek counterpart *poimanao* in addressing the responsibilities of Peter in John 21:16, it is necessary to observe how this word was understood in context. The Septuagint shows a frequent use of *poimanao* exclusively with reference to ruling. Psalm 2:9, for example, not only denotes the rule of God but the context shows it is a rather austere ruling. For this reason some translations render the passage, 'he shall break them with a rod of iron' rather than 'he shall rule them with a rod of iron.' The former translation is appropriate since the latter half of the passage from the Hebrew is translated: 'like a potters vessel you shall smash them.' Understanding the common Hebrew poetic style, the Septuagint uses *poimanao* for the Hebrew *raah* ('break') and matches it with *suntribo* for the Hebrew *naphats* ('smash'). The word *suntribo*, used frequently in the LXX [Septuagint], refers exclusively to some type of destruction (cf. Gen. 19:9; Ex. 9:25, *et al.*). In addition, the Hebrew word *raah*, from which the translation *poimanao* is used by the LXX in Psalm 2:9, is a simple Qal imperfect tense. The use of the Qal tense shows that the word normally means 'to rule' since Hebrew could use other verbal forms such as the Hif'il, or Hitpa'el to make the same word more intensive. Hence, *raah* does not need to be intensified to connote 'ruling' or 'breaking' since that is its normal Qal meaning.

"The exegetical significance of such strong usages of these words in Psalm 2:9 becomes apparent when we see the passage is quoted directly in the New Testament in Revelation 2:27 as the measure of Christ's reign over the once rebellious nations. In Revelation 19:15, the part of Psalm 2:9 concerning the 'ruling with a rod of iron' is quoted but instead of including the smashing of the potters vessel, the apostle John follows with: 'and he treads the wine press of the fierce wrath of God, the Almighty.' Here, 'ruling with the rod' has its strongest connotation as it is coupled with God's ultimate wrath. This widens the possible meaning of *poimanao* to include not only a 'ruling' but a total subjugation with harsh punishment.

"Other uses of *poimanao* in regards to 'ruling' in the Septuagint are 2 Samuel 5:2 ('You shall shepherd (*poimanao*) my people Israel and you shall be a leader over Israel.'). Here again *poimanao* is coupled with a 'leader which connotes ruling. Similar couplings can be seen in 1 Chronicles 11:2, 17:6; Psalm 78:72; Isaiah 40:10; Ezek. 34:23.

"Other interesting and informative uses of *poimanao* in the LXX include Jeremiah 3:15: 'I will give you shepherds and they will feed you with knowledge and understanding.' Though in this instance *poimanao* refers only to feeding, it is a spiritual feeding that is in view. The spiritual feeding is what Jesus has envisioned for Peter in John 21:16 as he will become the leader and strengthener of the entire Church, as will his papal successors.

"Another usage occurs in Micah 7:14 in the rendering: 'Pasture (*poimanao*) your people with your rod.' Some translations replace the word 'rod' with 'scepter' (although it is the same Hebrew word for 'rod' used in Psalm 2:9 seen above). In either case the meaning is plain. 'Pasturing' or 'shepherding,' (the Greek *poimanao* or the Hebrew *raah*) of necessity, includes the concept of 'ruling.'

"In conclusion, Jesus' use of the word *poimanao* in regards to the future, sole responsibilities of Peter in the New Testament church cannot be denied in John 21:16. According to the general meaning *poimanao*, Peter was to rule over all the church with the authority vested in him by Jesus, as well as be the primary source of spiritual nourishment (truth) for the church with the guidance promised by the Holy Spirit." Robert A. Sungenis, "The Use of the Greek *Poimanao* in John 21:16," letter to authors, 2 June 1995, 1-2.

Veselin Kesich reviews the Greek words *boskein* and *poimainein* from the Eastern Orthodox perspective:

"In the last scene of John's gospel we have an interchange between Jesus and Peter (Jn 21:15-17). This is a truly Petrine passage. Three times Jesus asks Peter, 'Do you love Me?'; and three times Peter answers that he loves the Lord. After each response the Risen Christ commissions Peter to feed (*boskein*) and tend (*poimainein*) his, i.e., Christ's, flock. Clearly, after the resurrection, Peter is reestablished and given the role of shepherd. The verb *poimainein* conveys more than *boskein*. In a figurative sense, *poimainein* points to the duties and responsibilities of church leaders—protecting, governing, leading, and caring for the people under their charge. *Boskein*, on the other hand, points to the shepherd's activities of feeding or tending." Veselin Kesich, "Peter's Primacy in the New Testament and the Early Tradition," in John Meyendorff, ed., *The Primacy of Peter*, (Crestwood, NY: St. Vladimir's Seminary Press, 1992), 43.

The Lutheran-Catholic dialogue further defines the shepherd (bolstered by a statement of Philo [20 B.C.? - 40 A.D.?], a historian living at the time of Jesus) as follows:

> "The commands in John 21:15-17 use two Greek verbs for "feed" in the sequence: *boskein, poimainein, boskein* . . . *poimainein* covers a somewhat broader field of meaning, for it describes not only feeding the flock, but also guarding and guiding them; equivalently it can mean 'to rule, govern.' (II Sam 7:7; Ps 2:9; Matt 2:6). Note the distinction in Philo [20 B.C.? - 40 A.D.?], *Quod deterius* VIII 25: 'Those who feed [*boskein*] supply nourishment . . . but those who tend [*poimainein*] have the powers of rulers and governors." Raymond E. Brown, Karl P. Donfried, and John Reumann, eds., *Peter in the New Testament*, (Minneapolis, MN: Augsburg; New York: Paulist: 1973), 142-143.

118. When Christ commanded Peter to feed and to tend his lambs and sheep in John 21:15, what is the deeper reality of what Christ asks of Peter? Christ is asking Peter to feed the People of God, who are lambs in the Kingdom of God.

119. In John 21:16, what is the significance of the word *poimainein* (found in the original Greek)? *Poimainein* means more than feed; it means to guide, to tend, to protect the sheep, who also represent a portion of the of Christ's flock. Peter's role is to rule, to lead, to govern. The word *poimainein* is more than feed. Peter is to tend to the Apostles and the rest of the Christian flock. Juxtaposing various words with slightly different meanings in this passage assist in understanding Peter's authority as the ruler, the vizier, the governor of all, including the shepherds of the Church.

120. What is John 21:17 saying regarding Peter? Peter is to shepherd by teaching, by feeding the flock with spiritual truth. After giving Peter universal jurisdiction over the whole Church in John 21:16, Jesus made sure that Peter realized that he himself was to be the shepherd who was to feed (teach) and shepherd (govern) the flock. The Greek word *boskein* (feed) is used in John 21:15.

Repeating the mandate three times has significance in custom and in the interpretation of various authors.

> "P. Gaechter, 'Das dreifache 'Weide meine Lammer,'' *Zeitschrift fur Katholische Theologie* 69 (1947), pp. 328-44, considers the threefold character of the command separately from the threefold question. He cites the ancient Near Eastern legal custom of saying something three times before witnesses in order to solemnize it or make it legal, e.g., in a contract conferring rights. However, a threefold repetition automatically has an air of solemnity without the suggestion of such a legal parallel." Raymond E. Brown, Karl P. Donfried, and John Reumann, eds., *Peter in the New Testament*, (Minneapolis, MN: Augsburg; New York: Paulist: 1973), 142.

Therefore, Peter, the feeder of the lambs and sheep, was being treated as the official shepherd of Christ's flock:

> "The primacy was conferred when Christ, after His Resurrection, gave the mandate to Peter after the latter's threefold assurance of His love: 'Feed my lambs! . . . Feed my lambs! . . . Feed my sheep!' (John 21, 15-17) [Douay-Rheims Version]. Here, as in Mt. 16, 18 et seq., the words are directed solely and immediately to Peter. The 'lambs' and the 'sheep' designate Christ's whole flock, that is, the whole Church (cf. John 10). 'Feed' in ancient and biblical language means, in its application to human beings, rule or govern (cf. Acts 20, 28). By Christ's thrice-repeated mandate, Peter obtained, not re-appointment to the Apostolic office—he did not lose this through his denial—but the supreme power of government over the Church. After the ascension of Our Lord, the Primacy devolved on Peter, and was exercised by him." Ludwig Ott, *Fundamentals of Catholic Dogma*, 4th ed. (1960), (Rockford, IL: TAN, 1974), 281.

121. What is the deeper significance of Christ's affirmation of Peter being three-fold? It was to strengthen Peter after his threefold denial of our Lord, preparing him to take the reins of

leadership in the Church of Christ. Jesus strengthens Peter after his three-fold denial of our Lord outside the high priest's house after Jesus had been arrested.

Arnobius Junior (ca. 440 A.D.), a priest or bishop of Gaul, wrote:

> "Behold, that succour is given to a penitent Apostle, who is the Bishop of bishops, and a greater rank is restored to him now weeping than was taken from him when he 'denied.' That I may prove this, I show that no other Apostle received the name of Shepherd. For the Lord Jesus alone said, 'I am the Good Shepherd;' and again, 'My sheep,' He says, 'Follow Me.' This holy name, therefore, and the power of the same name, He, after the resurrection, conceded to the penitent Peter; and the Denied bestowed on him who denied Him this power which he alone had; that he might be proved not only to have recovered what he had lost, but also to have acquired even much more by being penitent than he had lost by denying." (*Com. in Ps.* cxxxviii. tom. viii. *Bib. Max. Pat.* p. 320), in Charles F. B. Allnatt, ed., *Cathedra Petri—The Titles and Prerogatives of St. Peter*, (London: Burns & Oates, 1879), 46.

Previously, Cyril of Alexandria (ca. 424 A.D.) set forth the conditions of the three-fold denial by Peter, together with his confirmation as the leader of the flock:

> "For the wondrous Peter, overcome by uncontrollable fear, denied the Lord three times. Christ heals the error done, and demands in various ways the threefold confession. . . . For although all the holy disciples alike fled . . . still Peter's fault in the threefold denial was in addition, special and peculiar to himself. Therefore by the threefold confession of blessed Peter, the fault of triple denial was done away. Further by the Lord's saying 'Feed my lambs,' we must understand a renewal as it were of the apostleship already given to him, washing away the intervening disgrace of his fall, and the littleness of human infirmity." *Commentary on John's Gospel, Book 12*, in J. P. Migne, ed., *Patrologiae*

Cursus Completus: Series Graeca, (Paris, 1866), 74:749 in
E. Giles, *Documents Illustrating Papal Authority A.D. 96-454*, (London: SPCK, 1952), 258.

A complementary interpretation is that Jesus affirmed Peter in a threefold way to reiterate the threefold mandate that Christ had given to Peter in Matthew 16:17-19.

> "The primacy was promised on the occasion of the solemn confession of the Messiahship in the house of Caesarea Philippi (Mt. 16:17-19): 'Blessed art thou, Simon Barjona: because flesh and blood hath not revealed it to thee, but my Father who is in heaven. And I say to thee: [i] That thou are Peter (= Cephas); and upon this rock I will build my Church. And the gates of hell shall not prevail against it [unity and strength]. [ii] And I will give to thee the keys of the Kingdom of Heaven [power and dominion]. [iii] And whatsoever thou shalt bind upon earth, it shall be bound also in Heaven: and whatsoever thou shalt loose on earth, it shall be loosed also in heaven [jurisdiction, teaching, and interpretation].' These words are addressed solely and immediately to Peter. In them Christ Promises to confer on him a threefold supreme power in the new religious community (*ekklesia*) which He is to found." Ludwig Ott, *Fundamentals of Catholic Dogma*, 4th ed. (1960), (Rockford, IL: TAN, 1974), 280.

One could also view Jesus (in John 21:15-17) as testing and confirming Peter's faithful utterances, not his denials:

> "Much stress is laid upon the circumstance that several of the Fathers say, that our Lord was merely testing S. Peter's fidelity [John 21:15-17]; for, as he had three times denied Him, so he was three times to confess his love and attachment to Him. But this does not in the least degree touch the question at issue. It has always been the custom of God to try His servants before calling them to any great work. Abraham was tried, and found faithful. Blessed Mary's faith was tried, and she believed. The Apostles were tried, when Christ said to them, 'Whom say ye that I am?' S. Peter alone answered, whom He had predestined to become the Rock,

and to receive the Keys. And now our Lord, just before His departure, intending to complete His work of organizing the Church, and of appointing one in His place as Chief Shepherd, tried S. Peter's love; and after each confession of his love, delivered to his special care the lambs and sheep of the Church." Colin Lindsay, *The Evidence for the Papacy*, (London: Longmans, Green, 1870), 6.

122. When do most contemporary biblical scholars believe the Gospel of John was written? Although scholars assign widely varying dates for writing the Gospel of John, generally the dates 80-95 A.D. are within the range of plausibility for most authors. For another perspective, see J. A. T. Robinson, *Redating the New Testament*, (Philadelphia: Westminster, 1976) [wherein Robinson believes that all twenty-seven books of the New Testament were written prior to the destruction of the Temple in 70 A.D.]

123. When did Peter die? Between 64-70 A.D. Therefore, Peter had already died when John wrote the Gospel proclaiming that Peter had been named as the pastor of the flock of Jesus' disciples.

124. Why does John find it significant to make Peter the shepherd of the flock, after Peter had already died? Because the truth is that Jesus Christ wanted to establish the Petrine office to guide the Church until the second coming of Christ at the end of time. The Fathers of the Church upheld the shepherding role of Peter (see Part Two, Chapter VIII, for further references).

The Unity of the Church

Christ left the Church with a leader-servant and a plea for unity. The Church was to be one. Jesus, at the Last Supper, prayed to his Holy Father for this unity:

John 17:19 And for their sakes I sanctify myself, that they also might be sanctified through the truth.

17:20 Neither pray I for these alone, but for them also which shall believe on me through their word;

17:21 That they all may be one; as thou, Father, [art] in me, and I in thee, that they also may be one in us: that the world may believe that thou hast sent me.

17:22 And the glory which thou gavest me I have given them; that they may be one, even as we are one:

17:23 I in them, and thou in me, that they may be made perfect in one; and that the world may know that thou hast sent me, and hast loved them, as thou hast loved me.

John 17:11 And now I am no more in the world, but these are in the world, and I come to thee. Holy Father, keep through thine own name those whom thou hast given me, that they may be one, as we [are].

Christians must ask themselves whether Jesus' extended prayer in John 17 for visible unity ("these are in the world . . . that they may be one, as we are") only addressed a unified Church during the times of the Apostles, and not later. Early Church history demonstrates the struggle for visible unity in the Body of Christ throughout time. Popes and Councils sought to preserve Church unity.

St. Paul sought to reiterate and reinforce the unity for which Christ himself prayed at the last supper as he ministered to potential divisions within the Corinthian community:

I Corinthians 1:10 Now I beseech you, brethren, by the name of our Lord Jesus Christ, that ye all speak the same thing, and that there be no divisions among you; but that ye be perfectly joined together in the same mind and in the same judgment.

St. Paul's plea for unity of speech, mind and judgment speaks to a certain unity of faith and practice, teaching and doctrine, that unites the Body of Christ. Paul's Letter to the Ephesians eloquently describes the essence of our oneness in Christ:

> *Ephesians* 4:4 [There is] one body, and one Spirit, even as ye are called in one hope of your calling;
> 4:5 One Lord [governance], one faith, one baptism [worship],
> 4:6 One God and Father of all, who [is] above all, and through all, and in you all.

Jesus' prayer for unity to our Holy Father in heaven at the end of the Last Supper in the Upper Room would be answered throughout the end times with growth in visible unity in the Church of Jesus Christ. It is difficult, if not impossible, to believe that Jesus' prayer would not be answered with lasting impact.

125. How many churches did Jesus Christ establish? One, Holy, Catholic, and Apostolic Church. Our faith cries for unity, even as Jesus Christ prayed, "that they may be one."

Orthodox scholar Alexander Schmemann, in "The Idea of Primacy in Orthodox Ecclesiology," states:

> "The important point here is for us to see that in the light of this doctrine [of universal organic Church unity] the need for and the reality of a universal head, i.e. the Bishop of Rome, can no longer be termed an exaggeration. It becomes not only acceptable but necessary. If the Church is a universal organism, she must have at her head a universal bishop as the focus of her unity and the organ of supreme power. The idea, popular in Orthodox apologetics, that the Church can have no visible head, because Christ is her *invisible* head, is theological nonsense." J. Meyendorff, A. Schmemann, N. Afanassieff, and N. Koulomzine, *The Primacy of Peter*, (Aylesbury, Bucks, UK: The Faith Press, 1973), 36.

In the early Church, there was no argument as to the primal authority of Peter as the ministering head of the Church. Even the Eastern Orthodox Church, which split from Rome in 1054, never questioned the unifying authority of the Pope until centuries after the schism.

"As Father [John] Meyendorff writes in his *The Orthodox Church*:

'Curiously enough, the ecclesiological problem was never posed as a real issue in the medieval debate between Constantinople and Rome. . . . only in 1204 . . . after the sack of Constantinople did Byzantine theologians begin to discuss seriously the origin of the power which the popes claimed to have.'"

James Likoudis, *Ending the Byzantine Greek Schism*, (New Rochelle, NY: Catholics United for the Faith, 1992), 73, citing John Meyendorff, *The Orthodox Church* (New York: Pantheon Books, 1962), 209.

To refute Church unity, some would may argue that the Catholic Church has always been a "Roman" Church, with the Eastern Church being distinctly different from the Church that calls herself universal. On the contrary, the early Church was an "Eastern" Church in the very real sense that many of her "Roman" pontiffs came from the East:

"It would be profitable if historical writers more frequently drew attention to the significance of the fact that numerous sons of the East sat on the papal throne. Something more will be said of this point later. Meanwhile I would remark that apart from S. Peter, nine of the popes of this first period are 'Easterns':

Pope	Date	Nationality
Evaristus	100	Greek
Telesphorus	127	Greek
Hyginus	139	Athenian
Anicetus	157	Syrian of Emesa

Eleutherius	177	Greek of Nicopolis
Anterus	235	Greek
Sixtus II	257	Greek (Athenian)
Caius	288	Dalmatian
Eusebius	310	Greek of Calabria

Victor (193) and Melchiades (311) are Africans.

"The witnesses who have been adduced as to the position of Rome in these first three centuries, are all members of Eastern Churches. Not one of them attributes the authority of the Bishop of Rome to the fact that Rome is the capital of the Empire. Such a basis could not bear the superstructure. They speak of the Apostles Peter and Paul; of their martyrdom at Rome. Not one of them speaks of the presence of an emperor. The rights which the Bishops of Rome claim and exercise are no grants of an emperor. That fantastic assertion which is sometimes made is seen to be manifestly baseless." S. Herbert Scott, *The Eastern Churches and the Papacy*, (London: Sheed & Ward, 1928), 69-70.

Original Roman ministerial hegemony over the Church sprang from the blood of her two great martyrs Peter and Paul, who died at Rome, not from Roman political power. Later, even as the capital of the Roman Empire was transferred to Constantinople in 330 A.D., the Church maintained her seat of authority at Rome.

126. Under the ecumenical Roman Pontiff, how many distinct divisions of the Catholic Church are there? According to the *Annuario Pontificio* there are essentially seven (7) liturgical rites within the Catholic Church of the West and twenty-two (22) distinct churches within the Catholic Church of the East using (entirely or in modified form) six (6) principal liturgical rites, which are set forth as follows:

| Latin Rite: | Roman (Latin), Ambrosian (Milanese), Gallican (Celtic), Mozarabic (Toledo), Lyonnais, and Braga. [Regarding Anglican converts and an Anglo-Catholic |

"rite": "Parishes may be set up, and the form of Mass and of the sacraments retains some elements of traditional Anglican usage found in the Prayer Book." Peter M. J. Stravinskas, ed., *Our Sunday Visitor's Catholic Encyclopedia*, (Huntington, IN: Our Sunday Visitor, 1991), 71.]

Alexandrian Rite: Copts and Ethiopians.

Antiochene Rite: Malankarese (Syro-Malankarese), Maronites, and Syrians.

Armenian Rite: Armenians.

Byzantine Rite: Albanians, Bulgarians, Byelorussians (White Russians), Georgians, Greeks, Hungarians, Italo-Albanians, Melkites (Greek Catholics-Melkites), Romanians, Russians, Ruthenians (Carpatho-Russians), Slovaks, Ukrainians (Galician Ruthenians), and Yugoslavs (Serbs and Croatians).

Chaldean Rite: Chaldeans and Syro-Malabarese.

Felician Foy, ed., *1991 Catholic Almanac*, (Huntington, IN: Our Sunday Visitor, 1990), 210, 265-267. See also Thomas A. Baima, "Papal Claims: Beyond the Misconceptions," *Touchstone* 5.2 (1992): 35.

Facets of this universality of the Catholic Church are also reflected in the various titles that the Pope bears:

"His Holiness the Pope is the Bishop of Rome, the Vicar of Jesus Christ, the successor of St. Peter, Prince of the Apostles, the Supreme Pontiff who has the primacy of jurisdiction and not merely of honor over the Universal Church, the Patriarch of the West, the Primate of Italy, the Archbishop and Metropolitan of the Roman Province, the Sovereign of the

State of Vatican City, Servant of the Servants of God."
Felician Foy, ed., *1991 Catholic Almanac*, (Huntington, IN:
Our Sunday Visitor, 1990), 143.

The Eastern Orthodox Church's position regarding the concept of universal organic Church unity has been aptly stated by
Alexander Schmemann:

> "We must simply admit that if the categories of organism
> and organic unity are to be applied primarily to the Church
> universal as the sum of all its component parts (i.e. local
> churches), then the one, supreme, and universal power as
> well as its bearer become a self-evident necessity because
> this unique visible organism must have a unique visible head.
> Thus the efforts of Roman Catholic theologians to justify
> Roman primacy not by mere historical contingencies but
> by divine institution appear as logical. Within universal
> ecclesiology primacy is of necessity *power* and, by the same
> necessity, a divinely instituted power; we have all this in a
> consistent form in the Roman Catholic doctrine of the
> Church." J. Meyendorff, A. Schmemann, N. Afanassieff,
> and N. Koulomzine, *The Primacy of Peter*, (Aylesbury,
> Bucks, UK: The Faith Press, 1973), 36.

Even Photius, from an earlier era of the Eastern Church (before the final break in 1054 A.D.), upheld the authority of the Pope
at Rome:

> "Moreover, the Patriarch Photius [who died in communion
> with Rome, but is considered by our Orthodox brethren as
> one of their forefathers], himself, clearly acknowledged the
> Roman See's primacy of jurisdiction. In Photius' Greek
> version of the letter of Pope John VIII to the Emperor read
> in the Acts of the Council of 879-80, the Pope's words were
> recorded with no objection.
>
> "'One can ask from what master you have learned to
> act in that way? First of all, certainly from the coryphaeus
> of the Apostles, Peter, whom the Lord had constituted head

of all churches when he said [to him]: 'Feed my sheep.' (John 21:17). Not only [from Him] but also from the holy synods and constitutions. And also from the holy and orthodox decrees and constitutions of the fathers, as it is testified by your divine and pious letters.'" James Likoudis, *Ending the Byzantine Greek Schism*, (New Rochelle, NY: Catholics United for the Faith, 1992), 79.

John Meyendorff, Orthodox scholar, reiterates this point:

"Thus, for Photius, as for the later Byzantine theologians, the polemical argument artificially opposing Peter to his confession did not exist. By confessing his faith in the Divinity of the Saviour, Peter became the Rock of the Church. The Council of 879-80, which followed the reconciliation between Photius and John VIII, went even so far as to proclaim: 'The Lord placed him at the head of all Churches, saying . . . "Feed my sheep."'" J. Meyendorff, A. Schmemann, N. Afanassieff, and N. Koulomzine, *The Primacy of Peter*, (Aylesbury, Bucks, UK: The Faith Press, 1973), 12.

Jesus is calling the visible Universal Church of Christ to become one, as He had so prayed to his Holy Father at the Last Supper. Poignantly, the last words of Pope John XXIII to the bishops assembled around his death bed were, "*ut unum sint*," meaning in Latin, "that they may be one." (*New York Times*, 4 June 1963, 1)

The Delegation of Covenant Authority

> *Revelation* 3:21 To him that overcometh will I grant to sit with me in my throne, even as I also overcame, and am set down with my Father in his throne.

127. Who sits on the throne in Revelation 3:21? Jesus Christ.

> *Matthew* 19:28 And Jesus said unto them, Verily I say unto you, That ye which have followed me, in the regeneration when the Son of man shall sit in the throne of his glory, ye also shall sit upon twelve thrones, judging the twelve tribes of Israel.

128. Who is the king in Matthew 19:28? Jesus Christ.

129. To whom does Jesus Christ entrust his kingly authority in the New Testament? To the Apostles.

130. In Matthew 19:28, does Jesus give kingly authority to all Christians, or to the Apostles? To the Apostles.

♣ ♣ ♣

Luke 22:24 And there was also a strife among them, which of them should be accounted the greatest.

22:25 And he said unto them, The kings of the Gentiles exercise lordship over them; and they that exercise authority upon them are called benefactors.

22:26 But ye [shall] not [be] so: but he that is greatest among you, let him be as the younger; and he that is chief, as he that doth serve.

22:27 For whether [is] greater, he that sitteth at meat, or he that serveth? [is] not he that sitteth at meat? but I am among you [*humon*, plural "you"] as he that serveth.

22:28 Ye [*humeis*, plural "you"] are they which have continued with me in my temptations.

22:29 And I appoint unto you [*humin*, plural "you"] a kingdom, as my Father hath appointed unto me;

22:30 That ye may eat and drink at my table in my kingdom, and sit on thrones judging the twelve tribes of Israel.

131. What is the context of Luke 22:24-30? At the Last Supper in the Upper Room in Jerusalem, the Apostles began to argue among themselves as to who would be the greatest in the kingdom that the Lord Jesus Christ rules.

132. Who are those who eat and sup with Jesus Christ? All twelve Apostles (Luke 22:14).

133. Who are to judge the twelve tribes of Israel? The Apostles (Luke 22:30).

134. How many of the Apostles are to judge the twelve tribes? Twelve.

> *Luke* 22:31 And the Lord said, Simon, Simon, behold, Satan hath desired [to have] you [*humas*, plural "you"], that he may sift [you] [*siniasai*, plural "you"] as wheat:

135. In Luke 22:31, whom does Satan desire to sift as wheat? All twelve of the apostles. The Lord speaks to Simon Peter, but addresses the rest also. The Greek words meaning "you" in this verse are plural in number and form, and are used two times: "Satan hath desired to have *you*, that he may sift *you* as wheat."

The Lord, in the next verse, speaks to Peter solely:

> *Luke* 22:32 But I have prayed for thee [*sou*, singular "you"], that thy [*sou*, singular "your"] faith fail not: and when thou [*su*, singular "you"] art converted, strengthen thy [*sou*, singular "your"] brethren.

136 In Luke 22:32, of the twelve Apostles, whom does the Lord Jesus Christ uniquely pick to lead the rest? Simon Peter.

137. In Luke 22:32, is the "you" plural or singular? The Greek words meaning "you" in this verse are singular in number and form, and they are used four times. They are directed at Peter alone: "Simon, Simon, behold." (Luke 22:31).

138. What assurance does he give to Peter in Luke 22:32? That he has prayed for Peter that *his* (i.e., Peter's own) faith may not fail.

139. Does this mean that Peter's faith will not fail? Yes, it does; it is guaranteed by Jesus Christ. Otherwise, Jesus' prayer would have been in vain. God will see to it that Peter's faith will not

fail when he acts in the role of Christ's vicar after the ascension; just as Christ will see to it that the gates of hell will not prevail against the Church. Reread Matthew 16:18.

140. What is Christ safeguarding in his assurance to Peter that his faith may not fail? Peter's appointment to the holy office is most important to Christ at this point in time. Christ has delegated the fulness of his teaching authority to his prime minister (or vizier, or vicar), just as the Lord commanded in Isaiah 22:22. Jesus assures that Peter's faith will not fail.

Strengthening the People of God is what Peter is called to do after his appointment and conversion:

> *Luke* 22:32 But I have prayed for thee, that thy faith fail not: and when thou art converted, strengthen thy brethren.

141. Once Peter has converted, or turned back, what is he called to do? Jesus calls Peter to "strengthen" (i.e., brace, correct, reinforce, energize, revitalize, enhance, fortify) his fellow Apostles, who are the first bishops of the Church. No fellow Apostle, and none in the rest of the community, is called to strengthen St. Peter; Christ does that personally. Luke 22:32 gives Peter ministerial, hierarchical charge over his bishops as a direct grace-filled command from Jesus "when thou art converted."

> "It is important to notice the real force of this word 'Strengthen.' The verb *sterixo* is almost always used in the New Testament in connection with the gifts of grace. 'For I long to see you, that I may impart unto you some spiritual gift, to the end ye may be established,' *sterixthesai* (Rom. i. 11): in the same manner as regards S. Timothy, who was sent to the Thessalonians to establish or confirm (*sterixai*) their faith. (I Thess. iii. 2.) It is used also for grace received

direct from Christ, as in Rom. xvi. 25; 2 Thess. ii. 17; and iii. 3. The verb *sterixo* signifies to prop, to support, to make fixed or firm. The commission then given to S. Peter, as Head of the viceroys of God's kingdom, was to perform the function of confirming, or fixing immovably the faith of his brethren, the Apostles; imparting to them that gift or grace of Strength, which he (S. Peter), as the Rock appointed by God, received from Him (the true Rock) for that end. For which purpose Christ said to S. Peter, 'I have prayed for thee, that thy faith fail not.' By S. Peter's immovable faith he was to be the prop, support, and the sustainer of his brethren, the Apostles." Colin Lindsay, *The Evidence for the Papacy*, (London: Longmans, Green, 1870), 6.

The role of Peter in strengthening his brothers is clearly evidenced in the early Church, as set forth in the Acts of the Apostles:

> *Acts* 9:32 And it came to pass, as Peter passed throughout all [quarters], he came down also to the saints which dwelt at Lydda.
> 9:33 And there he found a certain man named Aeneas, which had kept his bed eight years, and was sick of the palsy.
> 9:34 And Peter said unto him, Aeneas, Jesus Christ maketh thee whole: arise, and make thy bed. And he arose immediately.
> 9:35 And all that dwelt at Lydda and Saron saw him, and turned to the Lord.

142. What did Peter do for the brethren? He strengthened them in faith with his presence, his words, and his deeds just as the Apostles, in turn, strengthened others.

In another vein, consider a passage from the Gospel of Matthew which refers to Peter's stewardship for the Lord Jesus, his master:

Matthew 17:24 And when they were come to Capernaum, they that received tribute [money] came to Peter, and said, Doth not your [plural "your"] master pay tribute?

17:25 He saith, Yes. And when he was come into the house, Jesus prevented him, saying, What thinkest thou, Simon? of whom do the kings of the earth take custom or tribute? of their own children, or of strangers?

17:26 Peter saith unto him, Of strangers. Jesus saith unto him, Then are the children free.

17:27 Notwithstanding, lest we should offend them, go thou to the sea, and cast an hook, and take up the fish that first cometh up; and when thou hast opened his mouth, thou shalt find a piece of money: that take, and give unto them for me and thee.

Regarding the covenant authority delegated to Peter, the late Colin Lindsay, a former Anglican clergyman who had converted to Catholicism, analyzed Matthew 17:24-27 as follows:

"There are three points to be noticed here, (1) The tax-gatherers recognised S. Peter as our Lord's steward or agent, and they accost him, saying, 'Doth not your Master pay tribute?' (2) Our Lord directed S. Peter to extract a stater [coin] out of the fish's mouth; and added (3) 'That take and give unto them for Me and thee.' Why 'Me and thee,' and not also the other Apostles, who were with Him? or if they did not lodge with Him, then the position of S. Peter is stronger in relations to our Lord, still more intimate, inasmuch as he of all the rest was selected to be nearest His Person. 'Me and thee,' then, identifies the two, the Master and the Chief Servant; the Householder and the Steward; the Principal and His Delegate. Origen has some remarkable observations on this passage. 'Jesus having assigned a reason for paying the tribute-money, sends Peter to draw out with the hook a fish, in the mouth of which he declares a stater would be found, to be given for Himself and Peter. It seems, therefore, to me, that they, considering this to be the greatest honour to Peter on the part of Jesus, as judging him greater than the rest of the disciples . . . wished to ascertain clearly that which they fancied; and they accordingly inquired, in order to learn from Jesus whether, as they suspected, He had separated Peter as greater than they; and they at the same time, hoped to know the cause of Peter's having been preferred before the rest.' (T.iii. *Comment. in Matt.* Tom. xiii. n. 14, pp. 588, 589.) Whether Origen's reasoning is sound may be a question, but the point in his comment, so far as our subject is concerned, appears to be this, viz., that it was believed that our Lord intended by this incident to show, how exalted was to be S. Peter's position in the household of God. Doubtless the 'We,' and 'Me and thee' express relationship of the very closest and most intimate nature, implying that S. Peter held a position next to the very Person of his Lord." Colin Lindsay, *The Evidence for the Papacy*, (London: Longmans, Green, 1870), 7.

St. John Chrysostom supports the significance of the tribute money relative to the honor accorded Peter:

"St. Chrysostom also calls attention to the episode of the tribute money (Matt. xvii [24]). Christ, he says, had to pay the didrachma as being a first-born son, and 'as Peter seemed to be the first of the disciples,' the collectors came to him for information. When our Lord by a miracle pays for Peter as well as Himself, 'Do you see' cries the commentator 'the excellence of the honour?'" Dom John Chapman, *Studies on the Early Church*, (Port Washington, NY: Kennikat Press, 1928), 85.

In another passage, after knowing that Peter was later chosen to lead the Apostles and the Church, one can glean intimations of being chosen by Jesus:

Luke 5:1 And it came to pass, that, as the people pressed upon him to hear the word of God, he stood by the lake of Gennesaret,
5:2 And saw two ships standing by the lake: but the fishermen were gone out of them, and were washing [their] nets.

5:3 And he entered into one of the ships, which was Simon's, and prayed him that he would thrust out a little from the land. And he sat down, and taught the people out of the ship.

5:4 Now when he had left speaking, he said unto Simon, Launch out into the deep, and let down your nets for a draught.

5:5 And Simon answering said unto him, Master, we have toiled all the night, and have taken nothing: nevertheless at thy word I will let down the net.

5:6 And when they had this done, they inclosed a great multitude of fishes: and their net brake.

5:7 And they beckoned unto [their] partners, which were in the other ship, that they should come and help them. And they came, and filled both the ships, so that they began to sink.

5:8 When Simon Peter saw [it], he fell down at Jesus' knees, saying, Depart from me; for I am a sinful man, O Lord.

5:9 For he was astonished, and all that were with him, at the draught of the fishes which they had taken:

5:10 And so [was] also James, and John, the sons of Zebedee, which were partners with Simon. And Jesus said unto Simon, Fear not; from henceforth thou shalt catch men.

"Nothing could be more pointed or more marked than our Lord's preference for S. Peter. Let us consider each point in order: (1) Christ entered 'one of the ships, which was Simon's (2) 'He sat down and taught the people out of (this) ship.' (3) When he had finished, he said, 'Launch out into the deep, and let down your nets for a draught.' (4) On a great multitude of fishes being taken, Simon summoned his partners to his help, and they came and filled both the ships, i.e. the second ship received of the overflow of S. Peter's. (5) S. Peter's astonishment was so great that he fell down and adored Christ; and (6) our Lord said, 'Fear not, from henceforth thou shalt catch men.' It seems impossible to avoid the inevitable conclusion that our Lord, by this incident, was pointing out S. Peter as the Head and Chief of His Church, for He teaches out of his ship, i.e. the Church; and, without reference to the others, directs him to let down his net for a draught of fishes (i.e. of men), the others, S. James and S. John, assisting as his partners; and He then informs S. Peter, in their presence, 'Henceforth *thou*' (not ye, but thou, Peter,) 'shalt catch men.' S. Ambrose thus observes on this incident, 'The ship is not agitated wherein prudence sails, where perfidy is not, where faith breathes. For how could that be agitated, over which he (Peter) presided, in whom is the foundation of the Church? . . . Though the rest are ordered to let down their nets, yet to Peter alone it is said, *Launch out into the deep*; that is, into the depth of disputations. . . . Into this deep of disputation the Church is led by Peter, so as to see thence rising again the Son of God, thence flowing the Holy Spirit. . . . They of the synagogue came to Peter's ship, that is, unto the Church.' (T.I., *Expos. in Luc.* l.iv.n.70,71,77, p. 1355,4.) Colin Lindsay, *The Evidence for the Papacy*, (London: Longmans, Green, 1870), 8.

Peter's Fall and the Covenantal Office

In light of the foregoing support for the appointment of Peter to lead and to strengthen the People of God in fulfillment of Christ's delegation of covenantal authority, one must nevertheless deal with Peter's threefold denial of our Lord:

> *Matthew* 26:34 Jesus said unto him, Verily I say unto thee, That this night, before the cock crow, thou shalt deny me thrice.

143. Even though Christ knew that Peter would deny him three times, and even though the beloved disciple John remained at the foot of the cross with Mary, why did Peter become the leader of the Church of Christ? Because the power and authority of God reside in those whom Christ wills. Christ created the best office for the man, not the best man for the office. It is the office, not the man, that is divine. The officeholder performs its prerogatives.

144. By Peter's denying Christ three times before the cock crows, does Jesus Christ take back his promises to Peter? No. Despite his denials, Peter is called to preach the gospel to all

people. It is not sinlessness (impeccability) that distinguishes the Vicar of Christ from the other Apostles, it is his infallibility as teacher in matters of faith and morals. The sinfulness of an individual Pope would not revoke the tremendous nature of the office in which he resides. One does not abolish the Presidency of the United States because of the personal sinfulness of the human being in that office.

Cardinal Cajetan challenged the idea that there was something odd about Peter's fall, considering the exalted position in which Jesus had placed him (cf. Matthew 16; Luke 22):

> "This [the fact of Peter's failure] does not therefore mean that each successor to Peter has to fall from love of Christ, since Our Lord's words do not entail the necessity of one's turning away, but point out the possibility of failing in love while continuing always in faith. If therefore one does fall, when he turns back he will strengthen his brethren. The text consequently affirms the indefectibility in faith gained by Christ's prayer for Peter and his successors. It obligated them to strengthening the brethren. It also shows a fall can occur, but it foretells conversions to follow. The adverb 'once' [Luke 22:32] suggests the latter, for just as conversion is foretold as happening 'once' and not always, the falling away is also suggested as coming at one time. For this to come true, it must not necessarily be that each successor fall away but it is enough—or even too much—that at some time a successor fall away from love of Christ." Jared Wicks, ed. and trans., *Cajetan Responds*, (Washington, DC: Catholic University, 1978), 128.

Even though Simon Peter would be the foundation of the Church and was called to strengthen his brethren (Luke 22:32) after Peter's fall, some might also look at Jesus rebuking Peter in Matthew 16:23 ("Get behind me Satan") as somehow snatching away from Peter what had been promised to him in Matthew 16:18-19. As Jesus said that he must go to Jerusalem, suffer, die and be raised on the third day (Matthew 16:21), the Apostles were baffled. Peter then brashly asserted that Jesus would not so fare, as he rebuked the Lord:

> *Matthew* 16:22 Then Peter took him, and began to rebuke him, saying, Be it far from thee, Lord: this shall not be unto thee.
> 16:23 But he turned, and said unto Peter, Get thee behind me, Satan: thou art an offence unto me: for thou savourest not the things that be of God, but those that be of men.

145. What did Peter do in Matthew 16:22-23? He tempted Christ not to fulfill his earthly mission to save the world from its original sin. Peter acted as an adversary, an opponent of what Christ knew he had to do. The mistake of Peter here was personal, but Peter certainly was not possessed by the evil one.

146. Is Jesus referring to Peter as the "evil one" in Matthew 16:22-23? No, he is rather rebuking Peter as one who is attempting, albeit unwittingly, to obstruct his mission. The Hebrew word *satan*, in this context, means adversary, opponent in war or before a tribunal. A satan is one who obstructs another's way. Whether the adversary is evil depends on the context of the passage. Cf. Numbers 22:22; I Samuel 1:6, 29:4; II Samuel 19:22; I Kings 5:4 and 11:14, 23, 25. Yet, the word satan generally has a negative connotation in the New Testament. Peter had lapsed from supernatural revelation (Matthew 16:16) into misperception (Matthew 16:22) after his regental appointment (Matthew 16:18-19).

The late F. F. Bruce, a leading Protestant theologian, former Rylands Professor of Biblical Criticism at the University of Manchester in England, describes the encounter this way:

> "And now, from the lips of Peter, Jesus heard what he recognised to be the same temptation again [as he had heard from Satan in the wilderness]. Peter, in effect, was trying to dissuade him from obeying his Father's will. Peter had

no idea that this was what he was doing; he was moved only by affectionate concern for his Master's well-being and did not like to hear him utter such ominous words: 'The Son of man must suffer many things and be rejected' (Mark 8:31). But he was, for the moment, playing the part of an adversary, however inadvertently, for as Jesus told him, 'you are not on the side of God, but of men' (Mark 8:33)." F. F. Bruce, *The Hard Sayings of Jesus*, (Downers Grove, IL: Intervarsity, 1983), 148.

147. By rebuking Peter, did Christ deny Peter his future office as the Vicar of Christ? No, because impeccability (incapability of sinning or wrongdoing) is not equivalent to infallibility, which represents Peter's error-free teaching authority and power here on earth, until Christ comes again to hold the keys solely by himself. Sinful popes do not destroy the continuing error-free teaching office of Peter.

Robert Sungenis writes:

"Some criticize the Catholic understanding of Matthew 16:18 by pointing out that since Peter is rebuked by Jesus in Matthew 16:23 for having suggested that Jesus not fulfill his mission to go to the cross, therefore, Peter is stripped of any semblance of prominence or infallibility among the apostles as Jesus addresses him with 'Get thee behind me Satan.' First, we must say that the Catholic Church does not define infallibility such that it includes the personal opinions of Peter, and by extension those of subsequent Popes or Bishops. Certainly Peter cannot be said to be teaching dogmatic Christian truth in his alternative suggestion to Jesus and thus this instance would certainly not fit under the rubric of infallibility as defined by the Catholic Church.

"Second, . . . since Peter did not have the specific knowledge of Jesus' ultimate mission, therefore he is not to be faulted for initially trying to prohibit Jesus from such a course of action nor can he be denied the later prerogative of infallibility. . . .

"We can also learn from this incident that, contrary to the Protestant view, it is not so much Peter's *faith* that is being emphasized surrounding his acknowledgement that Jesus is the Messiah. For at this point, all the apostles have faith in Jesus. What is different about Peter is the revelation he received from God, as Jesus makes clear in the statement, '. . . for this was not revealed to you by man but by my Father in heaven.' Consequently, it is the special knowledge given to him by the Father that sets him apart from the other apostles, not his faith, per se. Faith certainly overlaps and is perhaps the prerequisite of Peter's divine revelation but the former is made subordinate to the latter in this exchange. It is the revelation to Peter that becomes the basis for the Catholic understanding of papal infallibility for it is the Holy Spirit who 'reveals' truth to the Church and subsequently inhibits the introduction of dogmatic error by the same divine fiat to Peter's successors." Robert A. Sungenis, letter to authors, 7 November 1995, 3.

In 1871, John Henry Cardinal Newman, the great convert from the Anglican faith, has stated the case most eloquently:

"No pope can make evil good. No pope has any power over those moral principles which God has imprinted on our hearts and consciences . . . yet he is infallible for infallibility does not mean impeccability . . . in questions of right and wrong, there is nothing really strong in the whole world, nothing decisive and operative, but the voice of him to whom have been committed the Keys of the kingdom and the oversight of Christ's flock. That voice is now, as ever it has been a real authority, infallible when it teaches, prosperous when it commands, even taking the lead wisely and distinctly in its own province, adding certainty to what is probable and persuasion to what is certain. Before it speaks, the most saintly may mistake; and after it has spoken, the most gifted must obey." Derek Stanford and Muriel Spark, eds., *The Letters of John Henry* Newman (Baltimore: Newman Press, 1957), 236.

The Symbol of Teaching Authority under the Old Covenant

> *Deuteronomy* 17:8 If there arise a matter too hard for thee in judgment, between blood and blood, between plea and plea, and between stroke and stroke, [being] matters of controversy within thy gates: then shalt thou arise, and get thee up into the place which the LORD thy God shall choose;
>
> 17:9 And thou shalt come unto the priests the Levites, and unto the judge that shall be in those days, and inquire; and they shall show thee the sentence of judgment:
>
> 17:10 And thou shalt do according to the sentence, which they of that place which the LORD shall choose shall shew thee; and thou shalt observe to do according to all that they inform thee:
>
> 17:12 And the man that will do presumptuously, and will not hearken unto the priest that standeth to minister there before the LORD thy God, or unto the judge, even that man shall die: and thou shalt put away the evil from Israel.

148. In the Old Testament, is there an authoritative human voice to decide matters of doctrine and life? Yes.

149. Who held this authoritative voice? The Levitical priests, a select group.

150. What is the process involved in exercising this authority? a) In a matter of controversy, b) there shall be a forum for deciding the proper course of action, c) that shall show the truth of judgment, and d) decide on death or excommunication (Cf. Leviticus 7:22-27; Deuteronomy 19:3) for those who do not follow the authoritative voice. This is binding authority.

John 11:47 Then gathered the chief priests and the Pharisees a council, and said, What do we? for this man doeth many miracles.

11:48 If we let him thus alone, all [men] will believe on him: and the Romans shall come and take away both our place and nation.

11:49 And one of them, [named] Caiaphas, being the high priest that same year, said unto them, Ye know nothing at all,

11:50 Nor consider that it is expedient for us, that one man should die for the people, and that the whole nation perish not.

11:51 And this spake he not of himself: but being high priest that year, he prophesied that Jesus should die for that nation;

11:52 And not for that nation only, but that also he should gather together in one the children of God that were scattered abroad.

11:53 Then from that day forth they took counsel together for to put him to death.

151. Who is the high priest that headed the council of Pharisees? Caiaphas.

152. Under what authority does Caiaphas speak? He speaks not for himself, but for God, from his office as the authoritative spokesman for God in the seat of the high priest.

153. How is this proclaimed? By Caiaphas speaking prophetically as the oracle of God. Caiaphas does not understand what he is saying. God used Caiaphas as his instrument.

154. Is the authority of Caiaphas binding on the Sanhedrin? Apparently yes; from the day that Caiaphas spoke prophetically from Moses' seat, the chief priests and Pharisees formed a plot to put Jesus to death (John 11:53).

Sinful men of authority, such as Caiaphas, are used by God to teach authoritatively, not because of who they are but because of the office that they occupy. The symbol of this authority under the Old Covenant is Moses' seat:

> "*Kathedra Mouseos*, 'Moses' seat', represents the teaching office and does not necessarily allude to a particular magisterial chair in the synagogue or elsewhere. As the first verse of the Mishna tractate *Abote* indicates, the Jews understood that God's revelation, received by Moses, had been handed down from him in uninterrupted succession, through Joshua, the elders, the prophets and those of the great Sanhedrin (cf. Acts 15:21). The scribes and Pharisees participated in this authoritative tradition and as such their teaching deserved to be respected." Leopold Sabourin, *The Gospel According to St. Matthew*, vol. 1, (Bandra, India: Bombay St. Paul Society, 1982), 793.

> "Moses received the Torah from Sinai, and he delivered it to Joshua; and Joshua (delivered it) to the Elders; and the Elders (delivered it) to the Prophets; and the Prophets delivered it to the men of the Great Synagogue." W. O. E. Oesterley, trans., *The Sayings of the Jewish Fathers (Pirke Aboth)*, (New York: Macmillan, 1919), 1.

Besides the Moses' seat, other symbols of priestly authority included the keys to the temple, given back to God when the temple was destroyed:

> "All those texts which tell us how these keys were given back to God when the temple was destroyed indicate at least that the priestly possession of the keys of the temple was of great importance as a sign of authority as long as the temple was in existence. The oldest of these texts is probably 2 Apoc. Bar. 10:18, where we read how Baruch urges the priests (at the fall of the temple in 587 B.C.) to throw the keys of the temple up to heaven to God with the words, 'Guard your house yourself, because, behold, we have been found to be false stewards.' This text as well as Par. Jer. 4:4-5 and Pesiqta Rab. 26 give us a theological interpretation of the events of the year A.D. 70." Tord Forberg, "Peter—the High Priest of the new Covenant?," *The East Asia Journal of Theology* 4:1 (1986): 114.

The Mishna *Pirke Aboth* relates the truth of Jewish tradition. It is a long line in succession of authoritative Jewish teachers and leaders. Each was considered a man of authority because of the role, the position, that he occupied. A sinful man, such as Caiaphas, may still be used by God to teach authoritatively, not because of who he is but rather because of the office that he occupies according to God's will.

Moses' Seat and Teaching Authority under the New Covenant

155. Are there examples in the New Testament of Peter speaking prophetically in the manner of Caiaphas? Yes, for Peter, like Caiaphas, spoke prophetically in Matthew 16:16 ("You are the Messiah, the Son of the living God"). Jesus recognized that Peter had not spoken from his own knowledge, but prophetically from the knowledge given to him by God ("Flesh and blood has not revealed this to you, but my heavenly Father").

One could interpret Peter's speech as prophetic: that the Holy Spirit spoke through Peter in Matthew 16:16, as He would later speak through Peter after his trance in Acts 10. One could conclude that it was not simply Peter speaking, but the Holy Spirit speaking through Peter. In such instances, Peter could not err because God does not err.

Prophecy and infallibility are both charisms. Prophecy is transitory; it comes and goes as a gift according to God's purpose. Infallibility is a permanent gift of the Vicar of Christ for one who interprets God's truth under the inspiration of the Holy Spirit for as long as he occupies the office.

156. For Christians, what is the relationship between the New Testament/Covenant and the Old Testament? The New Testament explains, fulfills, and builds upon the Old Testament.

157. What is the relationship between Caiaphas under the Old Covenant and Peter under the New Covenant? Since Caiaphas, as the high priest, had the gift of binding teaching authority in his office as one speaking from Moses' seat, it stands to reason that this gift would be far surpassed when such an office passes to Peter under the New Covenant. This binding authority under the Old Covenant even foreshadows papal infallibility under the New Covenant:

> "The problem [of exemption from prophetic error] cries loudly for the Catholic solution of papal infallibility when one considers the case of a Moses, a David, and even of a Caiaphas, who at the same time and in the same person were both very fallible religious leaders and truly infallible prophets." Stanley L. Jaki, *The Keys of the Kingdom*, (Chicago: The Franciscan Herald, 1986), 204.

Cardinal Cajetan referred to Caiaphas speaking prophetically from Moses' seat in John 11:51 to foreshadow papal authority:

> "Jesus Christ has given testimony on these matters. Why should the faithful be astonished at such a great help given by divine grace to Christ's vicar on earth? Grace aided Caiaphas when he held pontifical office over the synagogue, as it was losing its rightful character and was persecuting Christ himself. By reason of his pontifical office he was given prophetic speech, as John the Evangelist bore witness. 'He did not say this on his own, but being high priest for that year, he prophesied that Jesus would die for the people' [John 11:51]. Why else did John teach and reveal this, if not to reveal the special divine assistance given one in pontifical office?" Jared Wicks, ed. and trans., *Cajetan Responds*, (Washington, DC: Catholic University, 1978), 139.

Cajetan used the above example from Scripture to respond to the anti-papal diatribes of Martin Luther, who had attacked the papacy based on his estimation of the low degree of personal holiness exhibited by the Popes of Rome.

When the scribes and Pharisees spoke from Moses' seat, Jesus judiciously separated their binding dogmatic authority from their lack of personal holiness:

> *Matthew* 23:1 Then spake Jesus to the multitude, and to his disciples,
> 23:2 Saying, The scribes and the Pharisees sit in Moses' seat [*kathedras*]:
> 23:3 All therefore whatsoever they bid you observe, [that] observe and do; but do not ye after their works: for they say, and do not.

158. Where is Moses' seat found in the Old Testament? It is apparently found nowhere in Scripture, but it is found in oral tradition and in written commentaries:

"The seat (Gr. *kathedra*) of Moshe. The Midrash Rabbah says:

"'They made for him [Moses] a *katedra* like that of the advocates, in which one sits and yet seems to be standing.' (Exodus Rabbah 43:4)

"*Pesikta diRav Kahana* 1:7 mentions the seat of Moses, and the editors of the English edition comment:

"'The particular place in the synagogue where the leaders used to sit was known metaphorically as the seat of Moses or as the throne of Torah, symbolizing the succession of teachers of Torah down through the ages.' (William G. Braude and Israel J. Kapstein, *Pesikta diRav Kahana*, Philadelphia: Jewish Publication Society of America, 1975, p. 17)

"A third-century C.E. 'Chair of Moses' from Korazin (11:21) is on display at the Israel Museum in Jerusalem; a photograph and description may be found in *Biblical Archeology Review* 13:5 (1987), pp. 32-35. According to the Hebrew University scholarly journal *Tarbitz I*, p. 145, they can also be found in Hamot, Tiberias and Delos (Greece).

"The *Torah*-teachers and *P'rushim* . . . sit in the seat of Moshe, exercising the power of 'the *cohen* or judge in the office at that time' (Deuteronomy 17:8-13), officially inter-preting the *Torah*." David H. Stern, *Jewish New Testament Commentary*, (Clarksville, MD: Jewish New Testament Publications, 1992), 67.

159. What is the Greek word for Moses' seat in Matthew 23:2? *Kathedras*, a physical example of which (from the 1st century A.D.) was found at Delos. See E. L. Sukenik, *Ancient Syna-gogues in Palestine and Greece* (London: OUP, 1934), 61.

160. In Matthew 23:1-3, to what does Jesus Christ morally bind the Apostles? To oral tradition, not simply to written tradition.

"These leaders [of Matthew 23:1-3] 'sit in Moses' seat.' E. L. Sukenik (*Ancient Synagogues in Palestine and Greece* [London: OUP, 1934], pp. 57-61) has shown that synagogues had a stone seat at the front where the authoritative teacher, usually a *grammateus* ('teacher of the law'), sat. Moreover, 'to sit on X's seat' often means 'to succeed X' (Exod. 11:5; 12:29; 1 Kings 1:35, 46; 2:12; 16:11; 2 Kings 15:12; Ps 132:12; cf. Jos. Antiq. VII, 353[xiv.5]; XVIII, 2[i.1]. This would imply that the 'teachers of the law' are Moses' legal successors, possessing all his authority—a view the scribes themselves held (M *Sanhedrin* 11:3; cf. Ecclus 45:15-17; M *Aboth* 1:1; M *Yebamoth* 2:4; 9:3).

"The astounding authority conceded 'the teachers of the law and the Pharisees' in [Matthew 23] v.2 becomes explicit in v.3. Even if the emphasis in v.3 falls at the end, where Jesus denounces the Jewish leaders' hypocrisy, the beginning of the verse gives them full authority in all they teach, even if they do not live up to it. *Panta hosa* ('everything') is a strong expression and cannot be limited to 'that teaching of the law that is in Jesus' view a faithful interpretation of it'; they cover *everything* the leaders teach, including the oral tradi-tion as well (Garland, pp. 48f.; contr Allen; Plummer; Schlatter; Stonehouse, *Witness of Matthew*, pp 196f.; and others). Nor does the test say their authority rests in their roles but not in their doctrine; on the contrary, v.3 affirms their doctrine but condemns their practice." D. A. Carson, "Matthew," in Frank E. Gaebelein, ed., *The Expositor's Bible Commentary: Volume 8 (Matthew, Mark, Luke)*, (Grand Rapids, MI: Zondervan, 1984), 471-472 [additional editors include Walter C. Kaiser, Jr. of Trinity Divinity School; Bruce K. Waltke of Regent College; James Montgomery Boice, Pastor of Tenth Presbyterian Church, Philadelphia, Pennsylvania; and Merrill C. Tenney of Wheaton College].

161. To what are Christians morally bound in Matthew 23:1-3? Christians are bound to the magisterial seat of Moses, which Christ passes singly to Peter and corporately to Peter and the Apostles acting together. The seat of authority and interpretation symbolically is in the seat of Moses, which was assumed by Jesus Christ and passed on to Peter and the Apostles until the end of time. Evidence exists that the Popes know of this potent symbol of authority.

During the Photian Schism (named for Photius, who displaced Ignatius as Patriarch of Constantinople), the prudent Pope St. Nicholas the Great (858-867) wrote to the Byzantine Emperor Michael of the Moses' seat and the authority that the Pope of Rome has:

> "You ought not to examine who the priests of God are, but what they say in the Name of the Lord. You have not to enquire into what the Vicars who sit on the throne of Peter are, but only what they endeavour to do for the reformation of the Churches and for your own salvation. You will not say indeed that they are inferior to the Scribes and Pharisees who sit on Moses' seat, but this is what the Lord said of them: 'All things that they shall say to you observe and do, but do not after their works [Mat 23:3].' Consider, therefore, this, O Emperor; if it was necessary to obey those who were seated upon the seat of Moses, ought not people with far stronger reason to obey those sitting on the seat of Peter?" S. Herbert Scott, *The Eastern Churches and the Papacy*, (London: Sheed & Ward, 1928), 325.

162. If a Pope morally does not live up to the standards of a Christian, what does Matthew 23:1-3 demand? Practice what the one occupying Moses' seat officially proclaims *ex cathedra*, not what he does personally. The Chief Rabbi in the Church is St. Peter and his papal successors.

Cardinal Cajetan shows the precedence for this principle in Scripture:

> "Although one failing to love and feed is unworthy of pastoral office and deserves to be deprived of it, he is not thereby deprived of office. Both testaments bear witness to this. In Ezechiel 34[:2-10], the evil shepherds were condemned for feeding themselves and not God's flock. Prophetic threats were made that God himself would deprive them of the shepherd's office, but they still remained shepherds. In Matthew 23[:2-3], Our Lord said, 'The scribes and Pharisees have sat on the seat of Moses; and so observe and do whatever they say to you, but do not act according to their deeds.'"
> Jared Wicks, ed. and trans., *Cajetan Responds*, (Washington, DC: Catholic University, 1978), 128.

As a matter of interest, even symbolic significance, Peter may be said to have "replaced" Caiaphas, by having "his" edifice built on top of the house of Caiaphas:

> "The church below Mount Zion, overlooking the ancient City of David, is the church of "St. Peter where the Cock Crowed" [St. Peter in Galli Cantu]. . . . Excavations beneath the property have uncovered what may have been the quarters of the high priest where Jesus was denied by Peter, mocked, scourged, and spent the night in prison. Crosses on the walls [of the unused cistern into which Jesus was probably lowered] indicate the early veneration of the site by pilgrims."
> Stephen Doyle, *The Pilgrim's New Guide to the Holy Land*, (Collegeville, MN: Liturgical Press, 1985), 61.

The Roles of Priest, Prophet, and King

> *Luke* 10:16 He that heareth you heareth me; and he that despiseth you despiseth me; and he that despiseth me despiseth him that sent me.
>
> 10:17 And the seventy returned again with joy, saying, Lord, even the devils are subject unto us through thy name.

163. Under the New Covenant, is Jesus Christ the new high priest? Yes. Read Hebrews 8:1-3.

164. By what authority do the disciples speak, according to Luke 10:16? Jesus Christ ("He that hears you hears me").

165. In listening to Jesus Christ, whom do they hear? God the Father.

166. In the context of Luke 10:16-17, to whom is Jesus speaking? The seventy-two disciples (or seventy disciples, according to other translations).

> *Matthew* 10:1 And when he had called unto [him] his twelve disciples, he gave them power [against] unclean spirits, to cast them out, and to heal all manner of sickness and all manner of disease.
>
> 10:2 Now the names of the twelve apostles are these; The first, Simon, who is called Peter, and Andrew his brother; James [the son] of Zebedee, and John his brother;
>
> 10:3 Philip, and Bartholomew; Thomas, and Matthew the publican; James [the son] of Alphaeus, and Lebbaeus, whose surname was Thaddaeus;
>
> 10:4 Simon the Canaanite, and Judas Iscariot, who also betrayed him.
>
> 10:5 These twelve Jesus sent forth, and commanded them, saying, Go not into the way of the Gentiles, and into [any] city of the Samaritans enter ye not:

167 In Matthew 10:1-5, to whom is Jesus speaking? He is speaking to the twelve Apostles, whom Jesus calls his twelve "disciples," according to Matthew.

John 13:20 Verily, verily, I say unto you, He that receiveth whomsoever I send receiveth me; and he that receiveth me receiveth him that sent me.

"Debates about the keys of the kingdom will go on forever unless Christians steep themselves not so much in reading the Bible as in the attitude invariably urged there, the attitude of loyal adherence to those who were sent to speak with authority. Such adherence was conjured up by Christ who said to the twelve after having washed their feet: 'I solemnly assure you, he who accepts anyone I send accepts me, and in accepting me accepts him who sent me.' (Jn 13:20)." Stanley L. Jaki, *The Keys of the Kingdom*, (Chicago: The Franciscan Herald, 1986), 169.

Matthew 10:40 He that receiveth you receiveth me, and he that receiveth me receiveth him that sent me.
10:41 He that receiveth a prophet in the name of a prophet shall receive a prophet's reward; and he that receiveth a righteous man in the name of a righteous man shall receive a righteous man's reward.

168. According to Matthew 10:40-41, are the Apostles' teachings important? Yes ("He who receives you receives me").

169. Why are their teachings important? Because they are teaching of Jesus Christ, whose teachings are from the Father himself.

170. By receiving the Apostles, whom are they receiving? They are receiving Jesus Christ himself and His Father.

171. When receiving Jesus Christ's teachings, whose teachings are they receiving? The Father's teachings.

172. By receiving the Apostles' teachings, what is received? The prophet's rewards are received.

173. Who is *the* prophet? Jesus Christ.

174. What role is transferred from Christ to the Apostles? Jesus has transferred the authority of his prophetic role to the Apostles in common, and we are called to obey these leaders according to Scripture:

> *Hebrews* 13:17 Obey them that have the rule over you, and submit yourselves: for they watch for your souls, as they that must give account, that they may do it with joy, and not with grief: for that [is] unprofitable for you.

175. What roles of Christ do the Apostles perform? According to Scripture, the roles are priest (Matthew 23:1-3), prophet (Matthew 10:40-41) and king (Matthew 19:28; Luke 22:28-30).

> "Christ delegated to the Apostles the mission which He, as man, received from the Father (John 20,21). Christ's mission embraces His three-fold office of Redeemer. He gave them the mandate to proclaim His Gospel through the whole world (Mt. 28,19; Mk. 16,15), endowed them with His authority (Luke 10,16; Mt. 10,40), promised them a wide power of binding and loosing (Mt. 18,18), and transferred to them the sacerdotal powers of baptism (Mt. 28,19), of celebrating the Eucharist (Luke 22,19), of forgiving sins. According to St. Paul's testimony, the Apostles considered themselves ... as 'ministers of Christ and dispensers of the mysteries of God' (I Cor. 4,1)." Ludwig Ott, *Fundamentals of Catholic Dogma*, 4th ed. (1960), (Rockford, IL: TAN, 1974), 277.

176. What authority does Jesus delegate to Peter and the Apostles? His roles of priest, prophet and king.

177. How is the prophetic teaching authority of the Church understood today? In the documents of Vatican II, the Church as a whole, and the successor bishops together with the Pope, may

proclaim God's truth infallibly in matters of belief, according to the following conditions:

"The holy people of God shares also in Christ's prophetic office; it spreads abroad a living witness to Him, especially by means of a life of faith and charity and by offering to God a sacrifice of praise, the tribute of lips which give praise to His name. The entire body of the faithful, anointed as they are by the Holy One, cannot err in matters of belief. They manifest this special property by means of the whole people's supernatural discernment in matters of faith when 'from the Bishops down to the last of the lay faithful' they show universal agreement in matters of faith and morals. That discernment in matters of faith is aroused and sustained by the Spirit of truth. It is exercised under the guidance of the sacred teaching authority, in faithful and respectful obedience to which the people of God accepts that which is not just the word of men but truly the word of God. Through it, the people of God adheres unwaveringly to the faith given once and for all to the saints, penetrates it more deeply with right thinking, and applies it more fully in its life." *Lumen Gentium* (Constitution on the Church, Para. 12, November 21, 1964), (Washington, DC: United States Catholic Conference, n.d.), 14.

"Although the individual bishops do not enjoy the prerogative of infallibility, they nevertheless proclaim Christ's doctrine infallibly whenever, even though dispersed through the world, but still maintaining the bond of communion among themselves and with the successor of Peter, and authentically teaching matters of faith and morals, they are in agreement on one position as definitively to be held. This is even more clearly verified when, gathered together in an ecumenical council, they are teachers and judges of faith and morals for the Universal Church, whose definitions must be adhered to with the submission of faith." *Lumen Gentium* (Constitution on the Church, Para. 25, November 21, 1964), (Washington, DC: United States Catholic Conference, n.d.), 27.

Matthew 18:18 Verily I say unto you, Whatsoever ye shall bind on earth shall be bound in heaven: and whatsoever ye shall loose on earth shall be loosed in heaven.

Robert Sungenis relates the concept of binding and loosing in the context of Matthew 18:15-18 to the concept of singular and corporate infallibility. Infallibility involves the Pope, or all of the bishops acting in concert with the Pope, teaching faith and morals:

> "Some may object that the formula of 'binding and loosing' should not infer infallibility since in Matthew 18:15-18 it is included in a context of church discipline, not morals, per se. It is granted that infallibility does not necessarily apply to all the juridical areas of the Church. This is especially true since Matthew 18:15-18 is in the context that includes the local church, not exclusively the Universal Church as in Matthew 16:18-19. However, consistent with the universal Church's infallibility in all areas of salvation, issues of Universal Church discipline which fall under the rubric of faith and morals must necessarily be infallible." Robert A. Sungenis, letter to authors, 21 January 1995, 1.

There is a logical necessity for the gift of infallibility if one considers the direct meaning of Christ's plea for Church unity under the inspiration of the Holy Spirit. To have true unity of thought and mind, there must be some arbiter of the truth or falsity of any philosophical or theological idea that arises. This arbiter of the truth of the matter needs to address any significant issue authoritatively and conclusively. The charism that would accompany this position, or office, necessarily demands finality according to very strict guidelines that are delimited by reason, revelation, and tradition. Prophecy involves a charism of the Holy Spirit that is inadequate to explain the ongoing necessity of an authoritative interpretive voice speaking for Christ. Peter and his successors, together with the bishops (on most occasions), have exercised the gift of infallibility judiciously, utilizing the symbols of authority inherited from those occupying Moses' seat.

JESUS, PETER AND THE KEYS

CHAPTER V

APOSTOLIC SUCCESSION AND INFALLIBILITY

The Visible Church and Her Leaders

The Lord Jesus Christ commissioned the Church as a visible shining light to the world until the end of time; the gates of hell would not prevail against her. He made the Church to exercise her ministry as a beacon to the world, a holy city, and a visible symbol and working sacramental presence of Christ in the world. The Church is the visible Body of Christ (cf. Acts 22:7):

> *Matthew* 5:14 Ye are the light of the world. A city that is set on an hill cannot be hid.
> 5:15 Neither do men light a candle, and put it under a bushel, but on a candlestick; and it giveth light unto all that are in the house.
> 5:16 Let your light so shine before men, that they may see your good works, and glorify your Father which is in heaven.
>
> *Matthew* 16:18 And I say also unto thee, That thou art Peter, and upon this rock I will build my church; and the gates of hell shall not prevail against it.

> *Matthew* 28:18 And Jesus came and spake unto them, saying, All power is given unto me in heaven and in earth.
>
> 28:19 Go ye therefore, and teach all nations, baptizing them in the name of the Father, and of the Son, and of the Holy Ghost:
>
> 28:20 Teaching them to observe all things whatsoever I have commanded you: and, lo, I am with you alway, [even] unto the end of the world. Amen.

> *Ephesians* 3:9 And to make all [men] see what [is] the fellowship of the mystery, which from the beginning of the world hath been hid in God, who created all things by Jesus Christ:
>
> 3:10 To the intent that now unto the principalities and powers in heavenly [places] might be known by the church the manifold wisdom of God,
>
> 3:11 According to the eternal purpose which he purposed in Christ Jesus our Lord:
>
> 3:12 In whom we have boldness and access with confidence by the faith of him.

178. How did Christ establish his visible Church on earth? Through Peter and the Twelve Apostles.

179. How long will the Church last? Until Christ visibly returns.

180. Which church is this? It is the Church of Christ led by Peter and his successors, together with the bishops in apostolic succession from the Apostles.

181. What do the gates of hell signify? All that may seek to destroy the Church of Christ—the Anti-Church, Anti-Christ.

In this context hell, transliterated as "hades" from the Greek, or "sheol" from the Hebrew, means the place of the dead. Gates of Hades would mean that which prevents escape from death but the gates of death are helpless against those with eternal life. Hell as a place of punishment (e.g., the hades of the rich man looking up to Lazarus in Luke 16:23) is a poor translation of Matthew 16:18, according to some scholars. However, another interpretation of the gates of hell is contained in the following vivid description of the battle between Church and the Anti-Church:

> "'Gates of hell,' by metonymy represents Satan and his legions as it were storming out of hell's gates in order to attack and destroy the church. What we have here is an oft-repeated promise of the victory of Christ's church over the forces of evil. See John 16:33; Rom. 16:20; Eph. 6:10-13; Rev. 12:13-16; 17:14; 20:7-10." William Hendriksen, *New Testament Commentary: Exposition of the Gospel According to Matthew*, (Grand Rapids, MI: Baker, 1973), 649.

Viewed another way, combining the two concepts above, one may portray the Church as a fortress keep in which those seeking eternal life find refuge from the forces of death, and against which Satan's legions seek to wrest control of eternal life from the believers holding onto the fortress. Were the walls of the Church to be breached, Satan would wreak havoc and death among the erstwhile believers. It is safe in the Church, the Body of Christ. Jesus has promised that the gates of hell would never prevail against the Church.

The Visible Church Perpetuated Until the End of Time

> *Matthew* 19:28 And Jesus said unto them, Verily I say unto you, That ye which have followed me, in the regeneration when the Son of man shall sit in the throne of his glory, ye also shall sit upon twelve thrones, judging the twelve tribes of Israel.

> *Luke* 22:28 Ye are they which have continued with me in my temptations.
> 22:29 And I appoint unto you a kingdom, as my Father hath appointed unto me;
> 22:30 That ye may eat and drink at my table in my kingdom, and sit on thrones judging the twelve tribes of Israel.
> 22:31 And the Lord said, Simon, Simon, behold, Satan hath desired [to have] you, that he may sift [you] as wheat:

22:32 But I have prayed for thee, that thy faith fail not: and when thou art converted, strengthen thy brethren.

J. Du Pont, in interpreting the above verses from Matthew 19 and Luke 22, linked the eschatological judgment (by the Apostles sitting on thrones judging the twelve tribes of Israel) with the function of the successors of the bishops (*episkopous*) in the earthly realm:

"Let us mention here an old explanation that a recent study has once again given force to (A. Feuillet, in 1949, and P. Benoit in *The Jerusalem Bible*, 1961): 'The twelve tribes of Israel designate the spiritual Israel, the Christian community, because the Twelve did not hesitate to link themselves with Jesus against the Israel of the flesh, they would reign with Him over the spiritual Israel. . . . And it is not necessary to limit this promise to life in this world: the apostles would govern - with Christ - the new world inaugurated by the Resurrection and Pentecost; they would begin to do so in this life, and they would continue to do so in the hereafter. Today still, St. Peter and St. Paul, all the apostles and, we might add, all those who through the course of the centuries have fulfilled the same function continue to reign over the Church." J. Du Pont, "Le logion des douze trones," [trans. Bernadeane Carr, S.T.L., 7/15/93], *Biblica* 45 (1962): 370.

"Death did not permit the Twelve to achieve an earthly mission, which has to be extended to the entire world. It is necessary, in effect, that the Scriptures be fulfilled which say that 'the Christ suffered, and having been raised the first from among the dead, he announced the light to the People (Jews) and the Nations (pagans).' (Acts 26:23) The Twelve thus would have 'continuers,' i.e., heirs of their responsibility to evangelize the earth. We must add: responsible in solidarity with the apostles. For they participate in a mission which pertains properly speaking to Christ. He is the one whom God charged to announce the light to the people and the Nations. Established at the time of the evangelization of Galilee, the principle of a collegial association in this mission was confirmed by the promise of a collegial association of the twelve at the last judgment. It would not be normal to suppose that the principle of collegial association was not to be maintained in the interval. Those who are supposed to pursue this earthly task of the apostles bear responsibility in solidarity with them.

"These reflections show quite clearly the concrete impact and validity of the logion of the thrones, at this time when the Catholic Church has endeavored to emphasize the doctrine of episcopal collegiality." J. Du Pont, "Le logion des douze trones," [trans. Bernadeane Carr, S.T.L., 7/15/93], *Biblica* 45 (1962), 389.

Matthew 28:18 And Jesus came and spake unto them, saying, All power is given unto me in heaven and in earth.

28:19 Go ye therefore, and teach all nations, baptizing them in the name of the Father, and of the Son, and of the Holy Ghost:

28:20 Teaching them to observe all things whatsoever I have commanded you: and, lo, I am with you alway, [even] unto the end of the world. Amen.

Ephesians 3:10 To the intent that now unto the principalities and powers in heavenly [places] might be known by the church the manifold wisdom of God,

3:11 According to the eternal purpose which he purposed in Christ Jesus our Lord:

3:12 In whom we have boldness and access with confidence by the faith of him.

182. Are the successors of Peter alluded to in the parables of Jesus? Yes.

"Along with all the direct indications in the New Testament that the succession of Peter was divinely mandated and practiced in the early church, there are more subtle inferences to the common understanding and practice of succession. In various parables of Jesus, for example, one will notice that there is a consistent theme which depicts the wealthy landowner who goes off on a long journey and leaves the care of his property to his trusted servant or servants (Matthew 25:14-30; 22:1-3; 21:33-41; 18:23-25; Luke 19:11-26; 20:9-19). Though in the spiritual lesson these parables are targeted toward convicting individuals of their God-given responsibilities, this particular aspect is not of interest here. Rather, with regard to the concept of succession our interest lies in the ancient motif utilized in these parables in which the sovereign places temporary control of his kingdom in the hands of a regent. The appearance of this motif highlights the common understanding in biblical times that positions of office and authority are not left vacant upon the temporary departure of the sovereign. According to historical documents, the regent to whom power is transferred assumes the full authority of the sovereign while he is away. If the regent is incapacitated for any reason, the authority is transferred to a vice-regent until the sovereign returns. Upon his arrival, the sovereign once again assumes power and begins making his own decisions to govern his kingdom, no the least of which is judging the performance and conduct of his regent or vice-regents. In some Old Testament applications of this motif, the regent rules alongside of but subordinate to the sovereign (cf., Genesis 41:41; Daniel 6:3), or, takes office upon the death of his predecessor (Deuteronomy 34:9; 2 Timothy 1:6-7; 2 Samuel 2:7; 1 Kings 2:15). Hence, the concept that Peter and his successors act as regents and/or vice-regents, respectively, assuming full and uncontestable authority over the kingdom of God (Matthew 16:19) until Christ, the Sovereign, returns, stems, in part, from a common understanding of the transfer of office and authority in ancient times and which was practiced immediately in the early centuries of the Church." Robert A. Sungenis, "The Succession Motif in the Landowner/Servant Parables," letter to authors, February 1994.

183. For how long will this visible apostolic succession last? Until the end of the world, just as Jesus promised his Apostles:

John 14:16 And I will pray the Father, and he shall give you another Comforter, that he may abide with you for ever;

14:17 [Even] the Spirit of truth; whom the world cannot receive, because it seeth him not, neither knoweth him: but ye know him; for he dwelleth with you, and shall be in you.

14:18 I will not leave you comfortless: I will come to you.

John 14:26 But the Comforter, [which is] the Holy Ghost, whom the Father will send in my name, he shall teach you all things, and bring all things to your remembrance, whatsoever I have said unto you.

John 16:12 I have yet many things to say unto you, but ye cannot bear them now.

16:13 Howbeit when he, the Spirit of truth, is come, he will guide you into all truth: for he shall not speak of himself; but whatsoever he shall hear, [that] shall he speak: and he will shew you things to come.

184. Who will preserve the Church and the successors of Peter and the Apostles from teaching error? The Holy Spirit.

"Whosoever, therefore, knowing that the Catholic Church was made necessary by Christ [for salvation], would refuse to enter it or to remain in it, could not be saved." *Lumen Gentium* (Constitution on the Church, Para. 14, November 21, 1964), (Washington, DC: United States Catholic Conference, n.d.), 16.

The Visible Church Confirmed in Apostolic Succession

185. Did the patriarchs and early writers of the visible Church of Jesus Christ preach apostolic succession as a fact? Yes. Consider the following excerpts from the early leaders of the Catholic Church.

Pope St. Clement, in his *Letter to the Corinthians* [ca. A.D. 80-98], aptly described apostolic succession:

"[42, 1] The Apostles received the gospel for us from the Lord Jesus Christ; and Jesus Christ was sent from God. [2] Christ, therefore, is from God, and the Apostles are from Christ. Both of these orderly arrangements, then, are by God's will. [4] Through countryside and city they preached; and they appointed their earliest converts, testing them by the spirit, to be the bishops and deacons of future believers. W. A. Jurgens, ed., *The Faith of the Early Fathers*, vol. 1, (Collegeville, MN: Liturgical, 1970), 10.

"[44, 1] Our Apostles knew through our Lord Jesus Christ that there would be strife for the office of bishop. [2] For this reason, therefore, having received perfect foreknowledge, they appointed those who have already been mentioned, and afterwards added the further provision that, if they should die, other approved men should succeed to their ministry." W. A. Jurgens, ed., *The Faith of the Early Fathers*, vol. 1, (Collegeville, MN: Liturgical, 1970), 10.

Ptolemaeus, the Valentinian, in substituting his concept of apostolic succession, attempts to impose a gnostic heretical view. Nevertheless, his *Letter to Flora* [ca. 160 A.D., in Epiphanius, *Pan. haer.* xxxiii. 3-7] reveals how well entrenched was the concept of apostolic succession in the middle of the second century A.D. As James McCue, in the Lutheran-Catholic dialogue, has written:

"Thus in all likelihood Ptolemaeus' *Letter to Flora* is the earliest extant work after *1 Clement* to make significant use of apostolic succession ideas, and it is the earliest (except perhaps for the Pastorals) to connect apostolic succession with the handing on of teaching. The relevant text runs as follows: 'For, if God permit, you will later learn about their origin and generation, when you are judged worthy of the apostolic tradition which we too have received by succession.' [Ptolemaeus uses certain comparative terms:] . . . *kai hemeis*—'we too'—indicates that Ptolemaeus is countering an already advanced orthodox claim that the orthodox doctrine goes back through succession to the apostles. Thus wherever the idea originated, it presumably existed in orthodox writers or bishops prior to Ptolemaeus." James F. McCue, "The Roman Primacy in the Apostolic Era—The

Beginnings Through Nicaea," in Paul C. Empie and T. Austin Murphy, *Papal Primacy and the Universal Church—Lutherans and Catholics in Dialogue V*, (Minneapolis: Augsburg, 1974), 57.

From a fragment of the *Memoirs* of St. Hegesippus [ca. A.D. 180], found in Eusebius's *History of the Church*:

> "[4, 22, 3] When I had come to Rome, I made a succession up to Anicetus, whose deacon was Eleutherus. And after Anicetus, Soter succeeded [him]; and after him Eleutherus. In each succession and in each city there is a continuance of that which is proclaimed by the Law, the Prophets, and the Lord." W. A. Jurgens, ed., *The Faith of the Early Fathers*, vol. 1, (Collegeville, MN: Liturgical, 1970), 80.

St. Irenaeus wrote the following text in *Against Heresies (Detection and Overthrow of the Gnosis [knowledge] Falsely So-Called)*, sometime between 180-199 A.D., regarding apostolic succession and the "preeminent authority" of the Church of Rome:

> "[3, 3, 1] It is possible, then, for everyone in every church, who may wish to know the truth, to contemplate the tradition of the Apostles which has been made known to us throughout the whole world. And we are in a position to enumerate those who were instituted bishops by the Apostles, and their successors to our own times: men who neither knew nor taught anything like what these heretics rave about. For if the Apostles had known hidden mysteries which they taught to the elite secretly and apart from the rest, they would have handed them down especially to those very ones [the bishops] to whom they were committing the self-same churches. For surely they wished all those and their successors to be perfect and without reproach to whom they handed on their authority." Irenaeus, in W. A. Jurgens, ed., *The Faith of the Early Fathers*, vol. 1, (Collegeville, MN: Liturgical, 1970), 89.

> "[3, 3, 2] That tradition derived from the apostles, of the very great, the very ancient, and universally known Church founded and organized at Rome by the two most glorious apostles, Peter and Paul; as also [by pointing out] the faith preached to

men, which comes down to our time by means of the successions of the bishops. For it is a matter of necessity that every
Church should agree with this Church, on account of its pre-
eminent authority, that is, the faithful everywhere, inasmuch
as the apostolical tradition has been preserved continuously
by those [faithful men] who exist everywhere.

"3. The blessed apostles, then, having founded and built
up the Church, committed into the hands of Linus, the office
of the episcopate. Of this Linus, Paul makes mention in the
Epistles to Timothy [II Timothy 4:21—'Do thy diligence to
come before winter. Eubulus greeteth thee, and Pudens, and
Linus, and Claudia, and all the brethren.']. To him succeeded
Anacletus; and after him, in the third place from the apostles,
Clement was allotted the bishopric. This man, as he had seen
the blessed apostles, and had been conversant with them,
might be said to have the preaching of the apostles still echo-
ing [in his ears], and their traditions before his eyes. [Cf.
Philippians 4:3—'And I [Paul] intreat thee also, true
yokefellow, help those women which laboured with me in
the gospel, with Clement also, and [with] other my
fellowlabourers, whose names [are] in the book of life.']"
Irenaeus, in Alexander Roberts and James Donaldson, eds.,
Ante-Nicene Fathers, vol. 1—*Apostolic Fathers, Justin
Martyr, Irenaeus*, (n.p.: Christian Literature Pub. Co., 1885;
repr., Peabody, MA: Hendrickson, 1994), 415-416.

"[3, 3, 4] Polycarp, however, was instructed not only by the
Apostles and conversed with many who had seen Christ,
but was also appointed bishop of the Church in Smyrna by
the Apostles in Asia. I saw him in my early youth; for he
tarried a long time, and when quite old he departed this life
in a glorious and most noble martyrdom. He always taught
those things which he had learned from the Apostles, and
which the Church had handed down, and which are true. To
these things the churches in Asia bear witness, as do also
the successors of Polycarp even to the present time."
Irenaeus, in W. A. Jurgens, ed., *The Faith of the Early Fathers*, vol. 1, (Collegeville, MN: Liturgical, 1970), 90.

"[4, 26, 2] It is necessary to obey those who are the presbyters in the Church, those who, as we have shown, have suc-

cession from the Apostles; those who have received, with the succession of the episcopate, the sure charism of truth according to the good pleasure of the Father. But the rest, who have no part in the primitive succession [of bishops] and assemble wheresoever they will, must be held in suspicion. Irenaeus, in W. A. Jurgens, ed., *The Faith of the Early Fathers*, vol. 1, (Collegeville, MN: Liturgical, 1970), 96.

"[4, 33, 8] The true *gnosis* [knowledge] is the doctrine of the Apostles, and the ancient organization of the Church throughout the whole world, and the manifestation of the body of Christ according to the succession of bishops, by which succession the bishops have handed down the Church which is found everywhere." Irenaeus, in W. A. Jurgens, ed., *The Faith of the Early Fathers*, vol. 1, (Collegeville, MN: Liturgical, 1970), 97.

"[5, 20, 1] For all these [heretics] are of much later date than are the bishops to whom the Apostles handed over the churches; and this fact I pointed out most carefully in the third book. It is of necessity, then, that these aforementioned heretics, because they are blind to the truth, walk in various and devious paths; and on this account the vestiges of their doctrine are scattered about without agreement or connection. The path of those, however, who belong to the Church, goes around the whole world; for it has the firm tradition of the Apostles, enabling us to see that the faith of all is one and the same." Irenaeus, in W. A. Jurgens, ed., *The Faith of the Early Fathers*, vol. 1, (Collegeville, MN: Liturgical, 1970), 101.

From Tertullian's *Demurrer Against the Heretics* (ca. 200 A.D.), the following defense of apostolic succession is obtained:

"[32, 1] Moreover, if there be any [heresies] bold enough to plant themselves in the midst of the apostolic age, so that they might seem to have been handed down by the Apostles because they were from the time of the Apostles, we can say to them: let them show the origins of their churches, let them unroll the order of their bishops, running down in succession from the beginning, so that their first bishops shall have for author and predecessor some one of the Apostles or of the apostolic men who continued steadfast with the Apostles. [2] For this is the way in which the apostolic churches transmit their lists: like the Church of the Smyrnaeans, which records that Polycarp was placed there by John; like the Church of the Romans where [Linus, then] Clement was ordained by Peter. [3] In just this same way the other churches display those whom they have as sprouts from the apostolic seed, having been established in the episcopate by the Apostles." W. A. Jurgens, ed., *The Faith of the Early Fathers*, vol. 1, (Collegeville, MN: Liturgical, 1970), 121.

Firmilian, Bishop of Caesarea in Cappadocia, wrote his *Letter to Cyprian*, sometime between 255-256 A.D. Although incorrectly denying heretical baptism, he upheld Apostolic succession, saying:

"[75, 16] But what is his error, and how great his blindness, who says the remission of sins can be given in the synagogues of the heretics, and who does not remain on the foundation of the one true Church which was founded upon the rock by Christ, can be learned from this, which Christ said to Peter alone: 'Whatever things you shall bind on earth shall be bound also in heaven; and whatever you loose on earth, they shall be loosed in heaven;' and by this, again in the Gospel, when Christ breathed upon the Apostles alone, saying to them: 'Receive the Holy Spirit: if you forgive any man his sins, they shall be forgiven; and if you retain any man's sins they shall be retained.' Therefore, the power of forgiving sins was given to the Apostles and to the churches [Church] which these men, sent by Christ, established; and to the bishops who succeeded them by being ordained in their place." W. A. Jurgens, ed., *The Faith of the Early Fathers*, vol. 1, (Collegeville, MN: Liturgical, 1970), 245.

St. Jerome wrote his *Letter to Heliodorus* between 374-379 A.D., recounting the successors of the Apostles as the ones having the power and authority to confect (consecrate) the Eucharist:

"[14, 8] Far be it from me to speak adversely of any of these clergy who, in succession from the Apostles, confect by their sacred word the Body of Christ and through whose efforts also it is that we are Christians." W. A. Jurgens, ed., *The Faith of the Early Fathers*, vol. 2, (Collegeville, MN: Liturgical, 1970), 183.

Pope St. Gregory I wrote his *Homilies on the Gospels* (inter 590-591), wherein he stated:

"[2, 26, 4] Certainly it is now the bishops who hold their [the Apostles'] place in the Church. They receive the authority of binding and of loosing, who have as their lot a degree of governing. It is a magnificent honor, but that honor carries with it a heavy burden." W. A. Jurgens, ed., *The Faith of the Early Fathers*, vol. 3, (Collegeville, MN: Liturgical, 1970), 323-324.

In the letters of Pope St. Gregory the Great there is a moving description of the valid manner in which the apostolic succession of bishops, under the authority of the Roman Pontiff, takes place. The Pope was writing to John, Subdeacon:

"Inasmuch as it is manifest that the Apostolic See, is, by the ordering of God, set over all Churches, there is, among our manifold cares, especial demand for our attention, when our decision is awaited with a view to the consecration of a bishop. Now on the death of Laurentius, bishop of the church of Mediolanum, the clergy reported to us that they had unanimously agreed in the election of our son Constantius, their deacon. But, their report not having been subscribed, it becomes necessary, that we may omit nothing in the way of caution, for thee to proceed to Genua (Genoa), supported by the authority of this order. And, inasmuch as there are many Milanese at present there under stress of barbarian ferocity, thou must call them together, and enquire into their wishes in common. And, if no diversity of opinion separates them from the unanimity of the election—that is to say, if thou ascertainest that the desire and consent of all continues in favour of our aforesaid son, Constantius,—then thou art to cause him to be consecrated by his own bishops, as ancient usage requires, with the assent of our authority, and the help of the Lord; to the end that through the observance of such custom both the Apostolic See may retain the power belonging to it, and at the same time may not diminish the rights which it has conceded to others." *Register of the Epistles of Saint Gregory the Great*, Book III, Epistle XXX, in Philip Schaff and Henry Wace, eds., *Nicene and Post-Nicene Fathers*, vol. 12—*Leo The Great, Gregory The Great*, 2nd series, (New York: Charles Scribner's Sons, 1900; repr., Peabody, MA: Hendrickson, 1994), 129-130.

186. Where did the early writers and fathers of the Church place Peter in apostolic succession as the Bishop of Rome and Vicar of Christ? Augustine strongly supported Peter, and his successors, as the Rock of the Christian Church. In *Letter 53 to Fortunatus* during the time of the Donatist heresy, he stated:

"For, if the order of succession of bishops [Popes] is to be considered, how much more surely, truly and safely do we number them from Peter, to whom, as representing the whole Church, the Lord said: 'Upon this rock I will build my church and the gates of hell shall not prevail against it.' For, to Peter succeeded Linus, to Linus Clement, to Clement Anacletus, to Anacletus Evaristus, to Evaristus Sixtus, to Sixtus Telephorus, to Telephorus Hyginus. . . . [Later scholarship has determined a somewhat different order of succession.]

"Even if in that succession of bishop [Popes] which comes down from Peter to Anastasius, now occupying the throne, there had happened to be a betrayer, there would still be no harm to the church and to innocent Christians, to whom the Lord, foreseeing it, said, of evil rulers: 'Whatsoever they say to you, . . . do, but according to their works, do ye not, for they say and do not.' [Matthew 23:3] Thus He made sure that a faithful hope, founded not on man but on the Lord, should never be scattered by the storm of sacrilegious schism, as those are scattered who read the names of churches in the holy books which the Apostles wrote, but they have not a single bishop in them." Roy J. Deferrari, ed., *The Fathers of the Church*, vol. 12, *Saint Augustine Letters*, Volume I (1-82), trans. Wilfrid Parsons, (New York: Fathers of the Church, Inc., 1951), 247.

Other early support for the apostolic line of Peter and his successors abounds. Herbert Cardinal Vaughn, Archbishop of Westminster, in his tenth lecture in a series delivered at Free Trade Hall, Manchester, England, in the autumn of 1895, set forth some of the early support for the role of Peter, and his successors, as the primate of the Church:

"1. *Tertullian* speaks of Peter apart from Paul as ordaining Clement. (*De Praescrip. Haer. xxxii.*) He also speaks of Peter baptising in the Tiber. (*De Bapt. 4.*)

"2. *Clement of Alexandria* speaks of Peter apart as proclaiming the word publicly at Rome. (*Euseb. He.E., VI., 14.*)

"3. *The Poem against Marcion* tells how 'Peter bade Linus take his place and sit on the chair whereon himself had sat.' (*III.*, 80.) The word chair (*cathedra*), in ecclesiastical language, always means episcopal throne; wherever the chair of Peter is spoken of, it means that he sat in the chair as bishop of the see.

"4. *Caius* (214) calls Pope Victor thirteenth bishop of Rome after Peter. (Euseb. *H.E.*, V., 28.)

"5. *Hippolytus* (225) counts Peter as first bishop of Rome. (*Dict. Christian Biog.*, I., 577.)

"6. *S. Cyprian* (250) speaks of 'the place of Peter' (*Ep. ad Anton.*), 'the of Peter.' (*Ep. ad Cornel.*)

"7. *Firmilian* (257) speaks of the 'succession of Peter' and 'the chair of Peter.' (*Ep. ad Cyp.*)

"8. *Eusebius* (314) says that Peter was twenty-five years bishop of Rome (*Chron. an. 44*), calls Linus first after Peter (*Chron. an. 66*) to obtain the episcopate (*H.E. III.*, 4), and Victor the thirteenth bishop of Rome after Peter (*H.E.V.*, 28).

"9. *The Council of Sardica* 'honours the memory of the Apostle Peter' by referring appeals to the head, i.e., to the See of Peter. (*Can. IV.*, and *Ep. ad. Julium.*)

"10. *S. Athanasius* calls Rome the Apostolic Throne. (*Hist. Arian. ad Monach*, 35.)

"11. *Pope Julius* speaks of the doctrines received by him from Peter. (*Apud Apol. Athanas.*, 35).

"12. *S. Optatus* says that the episcopal chair was first established by Peter, in which chair sat Peter himself. (*Schism. Donat. II.*, 2) 'Peter first filled that pre-eminent chair,' which 'is the first of the marks of the church.' (*Ib. II.*, 3.)

"13. *Pope Damasus* (370) speaks of the 'Apostolic chair' in which the 'holy Apostle sitting, taught his successors how to guide the helm of the Church.' (*Ep. ix., ad Synod, Orient. apud Theodoret, V.*, 10).

"14. *S.Ambroserose* speaks of 'Peter's chair' and the Roman church, where 'Peter, first of the apostles, first sat.' (*De Poenit. I.*, 7-32, *Exp. Symb. ad Initiand.*)

"15. *S. Jerome* speaks of the 'chair of Peter,' the 'Apostolic chair,' and states that S. Peter held the episcopal chair for twenty-five years at Rome. (*Epp. xv., CXXX.*, and *de Vir. Illust. I.*, 1.)

"16. *S. Augustine* tells us to number the bishops from the chair itself of Peter (in *Ps. contra Part. Donat.*). 'The chair of the Roman church in which Peter first sat.' (*Contra Lit. Petil.*)

"17. *Bachiarius* (420) speaks of 'the chair of Peter, i.e., the seat of faith.' (*De Fide* 2.)

"18. Pope Leo says 'the whole church acknowledges Peter in the See of Peter.' (*Serm. II.*, 2.)

"19. *The Legates at Ephesus* (431) declared it 'a matter doubtful to none that Peter lived and exercised judgment in his successors.'

"20. *S. Peter Chrysologus* (440) speaks of 'blessed Peter living and presiding in his own see.' (*Ep. ad Eutech.*)

"21. *Prosper of Acquitaine* (429) calls Rome 'the See of Peter.' (*Carm. de Ingratis.*)

"22. *The Canons of S. Patrick* (450) call Rome 'the Apostolic See,' 'the Chair of the Apostle Peter.' (Apud Moran, *Essays on Early Irish Church*, Dublin, 1864, Chap. II. and Appendix VI.)

"23. *Prudentius* (405) writes of 'the two princes of the Apostles, one the apostle of the Gentiles, the other holding the first chair.' (*Hymn II. in honor. S. Laurent, V.*, 459-64, *Galland VIII.*, 440.)

"24. *At the Council of Chalcedon* (451) the assembly cry out, 'Peter has spoken through Leo.' And the sentence pronounced by the legates was in the name of Leo, the Council, and S. Peter.

"25. *The Synodal Epistle* to the Pope calls the Pope 'the interpreter of Peter's voice.'

"26. *Theodosius* and *Valentinian*, Emperors (450), speak of 'the primacy of the apostolic See, made firm on account of the merits of Peter, chief of the corona of bishops.' (*Inter ep. Leon. I., Vol. XI.*, col. 637, Migne.)

"27. *The Bishops of Spain* (440) call the Pope 'the vicar of Peter.' (*Epist. ep. Terracon. Hilario.*)" Herbert Cardinal Vaughn, *Ten Lectures delivered in Free Trade Hall, Manchester*, (Manchester: John Heywood, Excelsior Printing and Bookbinding Works, 1896), 342-345.

For more quotations from the early Fathers and writers of the Church, refer to Part Two of this handbook.

The Role of Laying on Hands

John 13:20 Verily, verily, I say unto you, He that receiveth whomsoever I send receiveth me; and he that receiveth me receiveth him that sent me.

Acts 6:5 And the saying pleased the whole multitude: and they chose Stephen, a man full of faith and of the Holy Ghost, and Philip, and Prochorus, and Nicanor, and Timon, and Parmenas, and Nicholas a proselyte of Antioch:
6:6 Whom they set before the apostles: and when they had prayed, they laid [their] hands on them.

Acts 13:2 As they ministered to the Lord, and fasted, the Holy Ghost said, Separate me Barnabas and Saul for the work whereunto I have called them.
13:3 And when they had fasted and prayed, and laid [their] hands on them, they sent [them] away.

187. Where do the Apostles (and their successors) get the authority to lay hands on, or ordain, their successors? From God

himself, through those in apostolic succession. Paul recognizes his call from God by and through those in authority in the Church, the Body of Christ. Paul and Timothy are obedient to that call and to the measure of the Church's authority, which is superior to those who attempt to make apostolic claims but are outside the teaching and preaching authority of the Church.

Acts 13:1 Now there were in the church that was at Antioch certain prophets and teachers; as Barnabas, and Simeon that was called Niger, and Lucius of Cyrene, and Manaen, which had been brought up with Herod the tetrarch, and Saul.

13:2 As they ministered to the Lord, and fasted, the Holy Ghost said, Separate me Barnabas and Saul for the work whereunto I have called them.

13:3 And when they had fasted and prayed, and laid [their] hands on them, they sent [them] away.

II Corinthians 1:19 For the Son of God, Jesus Christ, who was preached among you by us, [even] by me [Paul] and Silvanus and Timotheus, was not yea and nay, but in him was yea.

1:21 Now he which stablisheth us with you in Christ, and hath anointed us, [is] God;

1:22 Who hath also sealed us, and given the earnest of the Spirit in our hearts.

II Corinthians 10:5 Casting down imaginations, and every high thing that exalteth itself against the knowledge of God, and bringing into captivity every thought to the obedience of Christ;

10:6 And having in a readiness to revenge all disobedience, when your obedience is fulfilled.

10:8 For though I should boast somewhat more of our authority, which the Lord hath given us [Paul and Timothy] for edification, and not for your destruction, I should not be ashamed:

10:12 For we dare not make ourselves of the number, or compare ourselves with some that commend themselves: but they measuring themselves by themselves, and comparing themselves among themselves, are not wise.

10:13 But we will not boast of things without [our] measure, but according to the measure of the rule which God hath distributed to us, a measure to reach even unto you.

10:17 But he that glorieth, let him glory in the Lord.

10:18 For not he that commendeth himself is approved, but whom the Lord commendeth.

11:2 For I am jealous over you with godly jealousy: for I have espoused you to one husband, that I may present [you as] a chaste virgin to Christ.

11:4 For if he that cometh preacheth another Jesus, whom we have not preached, or [if] ye receive another spirit, which ye have not received, or another gospel, which ye have not accepted, ye might well bear with [him].

11:13 For such [are] false apostles, deceitful workers, transforming themselves into the apostles of Christ.

11:14 And no marvel; for Satan himself is transformed into an angel of light.

11:15 Therefore [it is] no great thing if his ministers also be transformed as the ministers of righteousness; whose end shall be according to their works.

If you are not with Christ, you are against him. "And if a house be divided against itself, that house cannot stand." (Mark 3:25). And if you oppose his Apostles, and those in succession to them in the Church, you have not partaken of the fullness of light. Paul's commitment to Christ came directly from God. He was commissioned to preach the Gospel to the world when he was anointed by the Holy Spirit in the laying on of hands by the Church's apostles. Paul did not send himself to the Gentiles (Acts 13:2-3). Christ called Paul, and the community's leaders sent him, as they had been called and sent by God prior to Paul. Those who attempt to stand outside the teaching and anointing of this line of succession will sooner or later fall into error because they do not have the fullness of truth to guide them.

188. How are positions of leadership in the Church passed on? By the bishops laying hands on the individual being ordained or consecrated.

189. What is the Old Testament precedent for this action in passing the position, or office, from one individual to another under the auspices of the Church's hierarchy? When Moses had Eleazer lay hands on Joshua as Moses' successor among the Israelites:

> "Numbers 27:12-23 depicts Moses laying hands on Joshua to mark him as his successor. The act symbolizes transfer of power and authority. But it also reminds the audience that the hands of Moses parallel the rod as instruments to effect the power of God/Moses for the people. Laying hands on Joshua marks not simply a transfer of power and authority, but even more, a transfer of spirit that characterizes Moses, a recognition of divine presence, the defining quality of Moses as man of God, now passed to the successor. . . . In Joshua appears a new Moses, one shaped by tradition and experience as a disciple of the teacher, a new form of the ideal model." George W. Coats, *Moses: Heroic Man, Man of God*, (Sheffield, UK: Sheffield Academic Press, 1988), 191.

> *Acts* 14:23 And when they had ordained them elders [*presbuterous*] in every church, and had prayed with fasting, they commended them to the Lord, on whom they believed.

190. What is the Greek word meaning "elder"? *Presbuteros*, which one can also transliterate as *presbyteros*, from which Greek the Latin word *presbyter* is derived. In the English language, "presbyter" derives as follows:

> "adopted from late Latin *presbyter* (Tertullian), adaptation of Greek *presbuteros*, in New Testament an elder of the Jewish council or Sanhedrim [*sic*], an elder of the apostolic church; properly adjective "older, elder", comparative of *presbus* an old man. So. French *presbytre*.
> "The Vulgate regularly renders Greek *presbuteros, -oi* by *senior, seniores*, exc. in Acts xx. 17, xxii. 5, where it has

majores natu, and in Acts xiv. 23, xv. 2, I Timothy v. 17, 19, Titus i. 5, James v. 14, where the Greek is retained as *presbyter, -eri.* . . . The 16-17th English versions from the Greek, and the Revised, have uniformly *elder, -s*, in every instance. The Rhemish New Testament has *priest* wherever the Vulgate has *presbyter*; in other places regularly *auncients*; but, from I Peter onward (18 places) *senior, seniors.*

"Notwithstanding the prevalence of *senior* in the Vulgate, *presbyter* became the official name of the ecclesiastical order, when also the Com. Romanic *prester*, Old French and Provencal *prestre*, French *pretre*, Spanish and Catalan *preste*, Italian *prete*; . . . Old English *preost*, English *priest* (as an order in the Latin and Anglican churches): see PRIEST.]" *The Oxford English Dictionary*, 2nd ed. (1989), vol. 12, s.v. "presbyter."

191. What is the English word that is ultimately derived from the Greek word *presbuteros*? Priest.

The English word "priest" derives ultimately from the Greek word *presbuteros*. Over the years, certain attempts have been made to distinguish the meanings of the English words presbyter and priest, but in early English, Latin, and Greek usage, they were indistinguishable. One should not rule out that the elders of the early Church (in the first century A.D.) were those who confected the body and blood of Christ from the bread and wine offered in the sacrifice of the mass:

"What is particularly noteworthy is the fact that Ignatius ties the celebration of the Eucharist closely to ecclesiastical office. In the absence of the bishop or one of his deputies there is to be no Eucharist (*Smyrn.* 8:9)." David Noel Freedman and others, eds., *The Anchor Bible Dictionary*, vol. 4, (New York: Doubleday, 1992), 369.

The word "priest" derives from *presbuteros* and *presbyter* as follows:

"Etymologically *priest* represents Greek *presbuteros*, Latin *presbyter*, ELDER; but by A.D. 375 or earlier, and thus long before the Latin or Romantic word was taken into English, the Latin word *sacerdos*, originally, like Greek *hiereus*, applied to the sacrificing priests of the heathen deities, and also, in the translations of the Scriptures, to the Jewish priests, had come to be applied to the Christian ministers also, and thus to be a synonym of *presbyter*. In Old English, Latin *presbyter* was usually represented by *preost*; Latin *sacerdos*, applied to a heathen or Jewish priest, was usually rendered by *sacerd* (regularly so in Hexateuch, Psalms, and Gospels); sometimes, when applied to a Jewish or Christian priest, by *preost*, or more particularly *maesse-preost* (MASS-PRIEST). But, *preost, prest*, like Old French *prestre*, became the current word alike for *presbyter* and *sacerdos*, and thus an ambiguous term." *The Oxford English Dictionary*, 2nd ed. (1989), vol. 12, s.v. "priest."

Besides etymologically and historically, the amalgam of the two concepts of "elder" and "priest" may be scripturally traced as follows:

"We also see in the New Testament that the functions of the Old Testament elder—who served in the synagogue—have been fused with the functions of the Old Testament priest—who served in the temple.

"We can see the fusion of the two concepts in Romans 15:15-16. In the New International Version of this passage, we read: 'I have written you quite boldly on some points, as if to remind you of them again, because of the grace God gave me to be a minister of Christ Jesus to the Gentiles with the priestly duty of proclaiming the gospel of God, so that the Gentiles might become an offering acceptable to God, sanctified by the Holy Spirit. . . .

"A second passage revealing the fusion of the offices of Old Testament elder and Old Testament priest is Revelation 5:8, where we read: 'And when he had taken it, the four living creatures and the twenty-four elders fell down before the Lamb. Each one had a harp and they were holding golden bowls full of incense, which are the prayers of the saints.' Here we have the twenty-four heavenly elders (*presbyteroi*) depicted as offering incense to God in bowls, just as the Old Testament priests did with their own gold incense bowls (Numbers 7:84-86).

"It is especially important to note that this was a function only priests could perform, as indicated a few chapters later, in Numbers 16, which records the story of Korah's rebellion. This story concerns precisely the issue which is before us today: whether the fact that all believers are priests means that there is no ministerial priesthood. Korah said it does mean that [there is], and he gathered a rebellion gainst Moses and Aaron to usurp the priesthood from them:

"'You have gone too far, sons of Levi! . . . [I]s it too small a thing for you that the God of Israel has separated you from the congregation of Israel . . . would you seek the priesthood also? Therefore it is against the LORD that you and all your company have gathered together; what is Aaron that you murmur against him?' (Num. 16:1-11).

. . .

"Finally, we can see the fusion of the offices of elder and priest in the fact that the church is a combination of the Old Testament synagogue (where the teaching occurred) and the Old Testament temple (where the sacrifice occurred). The New Testament church incorporates both of these elements, with the liturgy of the Word (teaching) and the liturgy of the Eucharist (sacrifice), which has been the structure of Christian worship since the first century." James Akin, "The Office of the New Testament Priest," unpublished paper, 1995, 1, 2.

I Timothy 4:14 Neglect not the gift that is in thee, which was given thee by prophecy, with the laying on of the hands of the presbytery [priests].

192. How was the gift imparted to the recipient? By the laying on of hands of the presbytery, to signify the gift given by prophecy.

I Timothy 5:22 Lay hands suddenly on no man, neither be partaker of other men's sins: keep thyself pure.

193. Is the laying on of hands to be done impulsively? No. It is a serious matter, requiring great prayer and reflection. If not done reflectively, the person laying on hands could partake in another's sin.

> Titus 1:5 For this cause left I thee in Crete, that thou shouldest set in order the things that are wanting, and ordain elders in every city, as I had appointed thee:

194. Why did Paul leave Titus in Crete? To appoint presbyters in every town.

> II Timothy 1:6 Wherefore I put thee in remembrance that thou stir up the gift of God, which is in thee by the putting on of my hands.

195. What does the laying on of hands do here? It confers the gift of God in consecrating Timothy to his office as bishop.

> II Corinthians 1:21 Now he which stablisheth us with you in Christ, and hath anointed us, [is] God;

196. From whom does the anointing come? From God.

197. To whom is the gift given? To the bishops.

Choosing Successors to the Apostles

> Acts 1:20 For it is written in the book of Psalms, Let his habitation be desolate, and let no man dwell therein: and his bishoprick [episkopee] let another take.
> 1:21 Wherefore of these men which have companied with us all the time that the Lord Jesus went in and out among us,
> 1:22 Beginning from the baptism of John, unto that same day that he was taken up from us, must one be ordained [genesthai] to be a witness with us of his resurrection.

198. To what office will a successor to Judas Iscariot be ordained? To the office of Apostle, later called bishop. The bishops [Gr. *episkopoi*] were those who were given oversight of the Church. By the power of the Holy Spirit, another individual must be ordained [Gr. *genesthai*], or made, an official ambassador of Christ in the same way that Christ had ordained his first twelve disciples.

199. What Old Testament passages are being quoted in Acts 1:20 ("and his bishoprick let another take.")? Psalm 69:25, followed by Psalm 109:8.

> *Psalm* 69:25 Let their habitation be desolate; and let none dwell in their tents.

> *Psalm* 109:8 Let his days be few; and let another take his office [Gr. *episkopee*].

The Douay-Rheims Version translates the same passage as:

> *Psalm* 108[109]:8 May his days be few : and his bishopric [Gr. *episkopee*] let another take.

Considering this passage in light of others, and in light of the Greek language, Robert A. Sungenis develops the concept that it is the office that is being passed from one individual to another:

> "In Acts 1:20, Peter cites Psalm 69:25 and Psalm 109:8, respectively, regarding the succession of Judas' office of apostleship. Our initial interest in this citing stems from the fact that in order for Peter to comprehend the meaning and intention of these specific Psalms, he would have had to be enlightened by divine guidance as to their meaning. The Psalms themselves say nothing about the application to Judas or to the office of apostleship in general. It is only Peter's spiritually guided interpretation of these Psalms that leads to their application to the succession of Judas' apostleship. . . . This Petrine interpretation of Scripture lays down the precedent that would be followed later in the church wherein

Peter's successors would also exhibit a divine understanding and authoritative interpretation of Scriptural passages.

"In another light, the fact that Psalms 69:25 and 109:8 do not specifically mention Judas means that the passages contain general principles of succession independent of Judas or the apostleship. In context, the Psalmist is speaking of his many enemies, most likely those in places of high office and leadership, that he wishes God would banish and replace with others more faithful and qualified. The principle of succession was apparently a common practice and understanding during the Psalmist's lifetime; so strong, in fact, that New Testament interpreters such as Peter seize on its provisions to support the succession of the highest office in the New Testament Church. As obscure as these Psalms are on the surface as to their meaning, extent and applicability, a millennia later they are made strong enough to be used as a basis for succession for one of the most important offices in the New Testament." Robert A. Sungenis, "The Biblical Basis for Papal Succession," letter to authors, 22 May 1995, 1.

200. **How does the Church accomplish apostolic succession?** The Church, by and through its bishops, officially passes episcopal, or oversight, authority to successor bishops by way of laying hands on others to fill the office created for the Apostles by Christ. Robert Sungenis has determined the pointed significance of the office, not the officeholder:

"What is even more revealing about Acts 1:20 is the particular word used by Luke to designate the succession. Luke uses the Greek word *episkopee* which specifies the 'office' of the person in view rather than the person himself. This is why most translations will render the verse, 'And his office let another take,' rather than 'his apostleship let another take.' The word *episkopee* is used four times in the New Testament. Though twice the semantic range of the word allows it to refer to a mere 'visitation' (Luke 19:44; 1 Peter 2:21), the other two usages refer exclusively to an ecclesiastical office (Acts 1:20; 1 Timothy 3:1). In contrast, the Greek word used to designate the actual person rather than the office is *episkopos* which is used five times in the New

Testament (Acts 20:28; Phil. 1:1; 1 Tim. 3:2; Titus 1:7; 1 Peter 2:25).

"The fact that Acts 1:20 uses the Greek word for the 'office' rather than the 'person' shows that the succession of the office is of primary importance in Peter's interpretation of the Psalms. . . .

"The ramifications for the succession of office in Acts 1:20 is carried beyond the office of apostle to the office of bishop. This is seen in the only other usage of *episkopee* in reference to office in the New Testament. In 1 Timothy 3:1 Paul states that 'anyone desiring the office (*episkopee*) desires a good work.' We are aware that Paul is referring to the office of a bishop since in the next verse he uses the word *episkopos* to specify the person of a bishop ('A bishop then must be blameless. . .'). Here, the office of the bishop and the person of the bishop are mentioned within the same context showing that the two are distinct yet related. Hence, to the office of apostle in Acts 1:20 Paul adds the office of bishop in 1 Timothy 3:1, both of which are specified by the New Testament's only usage of the Greek word *episkopee* in reference to ecclesiastical office.

"The conclusion we can make from the above facts is this: the Greek word *episkopee*, not being specific to either apostle, bishop or any other title, refers only to the office in view. It is the office, in itself, which Peter interprets from Psalm 69:25 and 109:8 as being applicable to the situation at hand, namely, the succession of the office of the twelfth apostle. Therefore, since the same word *episkopee* is used in reference to the office of bishop in 1 Timothy 3:1, the same principle of succession of that office must hold since that is the way Peter first interpreted and used the word. A bishop who deceases must have the office filled by a successor. In effect, as Peter laid down the principle of Psalm 69:25 and 109:8 as applying to succession of office in the New Testament church, this means that these Psalms are not only applicable to the office of apostle but also to the office of bishop. Whatever title is in view, the office of that title will be succeeded due to the application of the principle established by Peter in his interpretation of the Psalms." Robert A. Sungenis, "The Biblical Basis for Papal Succession," letter to authors, 22 May 1995, 1-2.

201. How are the bishops to be followed? As if one were following God himself. St. Ignatius of Antioch described this quite
succinctly:

> "[8, 1] You must all follow the bishop as Jesus Christ fol-
> lows the Father, and the presbytery as you would the
> Apostles. Reverence the deacons as you would the com-
> mand of God. Let no one do anything of concern to the
> Church without the bishop. Let that be considered a valid
> Eucharist which is celebrated by the bishop, or by one whom
> he appoints. [2] Wherever the bishop appears, let the people
> be there; just as wherever Jesus Christ is, there is the Catho-
> lic Church." "Letter to the Smyrnaeans [ca. A.D. 110]," in
> W. A. Jurgens, ed., *The Faith of the Early Fathers*, vol. 1,
> (Collegeville, MN: Liturgical, 1970), 25.

> "[6, 1] Take care to do all things in harmony with God, with
> the bishop presiding in the place of God and with the presby-
> ters in the place of the council of the Apostles, and with the
> deacons, who are most dear to me, entrusted with the busi-
> ness of Jesus Christ, who was with the Father from the begin-
> ning and is at last made manifest." "Letter to the Magnesians
> [ca. A.D. 110]," in W. A. Jurgens, ed., *The Faith of the Early
> Fathers*, vol. 1, (Collegeville, MN: Liturgical, 1970), 19.

Acts 1:26 And they gave forth their lots; and the
lot fell upon Matthias; and he was numbered with the
eleven apostles.

202. Who was selected as the Apostle (later called bishop) to succeed Judas Iscariot? Matthias. He was chosen by God, through
the sacred lot, at Peter's insistence:

> "The precedent for obtaining error-free decisions from God
> starts way back into the history of Israel. Whether by de-
> tailed explanations through a prophet, by the simple 'yes or
> no' of the *Urim* and *Thummim* (also *ephod*), or vivid dreams
> (cf., 1 Samuel 28:6; 23:9-12; Numbers 27:21), Israel had
> access to God's infallible decisions in the difficult areas of

life. Similarly, in the New Testament the same sort of communication persists. In choosing the man to replace Judas, the eleven apostles pray, 'Lord . . . show us which of these two you have chosen.' God, knowing the hearts of all men, decided that the lot should fall to Matthias rather than Joseph (Acts 1:24-26)." Robert A. Sungenis, "The Precedent for Infallibility," letter to authors, November 1993.

203. Who chose lots to select Matthias? The Apostles as a body, at the direction of Peter. Even though Jesus himself had chosen an unworthy man as an apostle (i.e., Judas), this did not affect the succession of this office passed on by the Apostles, under the inspiration of the Holy Spirit, to Matthias.

Dynastic Succession and Apostolic Succession

> *Isaiah* 22:20 And it shall come to pass in that day, that I will call my servant Eliakim the son of Hilkiah:
> 22:21 And I will clothe him with thy robe, and strengthen him with thy girdle, and I will commit thy government into his hand: and he shall be a father to the inhabitants of Jerusalem, and to the house of Judah.
> 22:22 And the key of the house of David will I lay upon his shoulder; so he shall open, and none shall shut; and he shall shut, and none shall open.
> 22:23 And I will fasten him [as] a nail in a sure place; and he shall be for a glorious throne to his father's house.
> 22:24 And they shall hang upon him all the glory of his father's house, the offspring and the issue, all vessels of small quantity, from the vessels of cups, even to all the vessels of flagons.

204. Are the keys of the kingdom held or passed on, according to Isaiah 22? They are passed on, yet the sovereign, the king, always holds ultimate authority.

205. Who holds the keys under the New Covenant? Christ, who has delegated the authority of these keys to Peter for serving and ruling the Church on earth.

206. Is the authority passed on? Yes, just as the authority was passed on under the Old Covenant, with God retaining the ultimate authority of the keys. Refer to the explanation of Isaiah 22:15-25 earlier in this handbook.

A similar example of authority being passed on to successors occurs as Abraham founds God's people under the Old Covenant. Not only is he called the rock, but "Abraham was the first of a line of leaders of the sacred race, and as such did bequeath his leadership to Isaac and through him to Jacob." B. C. Butler, *The Church and Infallibility*, (New York: Sheed & Ward, 1954), 113.

The Lasting Effect of Peter's Apostolic Succession

207. What is the effect of Peter's apostolic succession? It places in the hands of the Popes of Rome responsibility and authority as the ones to teach and preserve unity in Christ.

"1. *S. Irenaeus* (170) speaks of the '*potentior principalitas* of the Roman Church, on account of which the churches of all parts must "convene" to her.'

"2. *S. Cyprian* called the Roman Church 'the chief or ruling church, whence the unity of the Priesthood has its source.' (*Ep. lv.*)

"3. *S. Optatus of Milevis* (368), propounding the marks of the Church, enumerates as first 'the possession of the Apostolic Chair of Peter, in which one chair unity is preserved by all. Nor did the other Apostles each contend for a distinct chair for himself, so that whoso should set another chair against that single chair should be at once a schismatic and a sinner—assuming sacrilegiously the keys of the Kingdom of Heaven; sacrilegiously fighting against the Chair of Peter, by his presumption and audacity. The possession of the chair is then the first mark of the Church possessed through Peter, and the first mark carries with it the angel of jurisdiction.' (*De Schism. II.*, 1-6.)

"4. *The Council of Milevis* recognised that the authority of the Pope was derived from Holy Scripture. (*Ep. Conc. Mil.*)

"5. *S. Ambrose* speaks of communion with the 'Catholic bishops' as synonymous with communion with the Roman Church (*De Excessu Fratris, no. 47*); and says that 'those have not Peter's inheritance who have not Peter's chair.' (*De Poenit. I.*, vii.) 'From the Roman church,' he says, 'the rights of venerable communion flow to all.' (*Ep. xi., ad Imp.* 4.)

"6. *S. Augustine* speaks of 'the Roman church in which the supremacy of the Apostolic See has always been in force.' (*Ep. xliii. ad Glor.*) 'This Apostolic SSeeee, through its succession of bishops, holds the summit of authority.' (*De Util., Cred. 35*) He also treats the Roman succession as an inseparable mark of the Catholic Church. (*Contra Epistl, Man. 5*)

"7. *S. Jerome* held that union with the chair of Peter was the one test of Catholicity (*Ep. xvi.*) and the one protection from strange doctrine. (*Ep. ad Demet. xcvii.*) The very name 'Roman' represented Catholicism in this father's writings. (*Adv. Rufin. i.*, 4)

"8. *S. Peter Chrysologus* says that 'B. Peter, who lives and presides in his own See, gives the true faith to those who seek it.' 'For we,' he goes on, 'in our solicitude for truth and faith, cannot, without the consent of the Roman church, hear causes of faith.' (*Ep. ad Eutych.*)"

Herbert Cardinal Vaughn, *Ten Lectures delivered in Free Trade Hall, Manchester*, (Manchester: John Heywood, Excelsior Printing and Bookbinding Works, 1896), 346-348.

"It is enough, with these passages before us, to observe that a Church, whence the unity of the priesthood, and the right of communion flow; fellowship with which constitutes one of the marks of the Church; by which the supremacy of the Apostolic See, and the summit of authority is held; to whom no heretical perfidy can have access; the name of which is a synonym for the Catholic Church, and conformity with which is a test of Catholicity, and a protection from false doctrines; in which S. Peter himself presides in the person of his successors; it is, I repeat, enough to say that a church described by the Fathers in terms like these, is not merely a *prima inter pares*; she can be nothing less than the centre of unity, of jurisdictional authority and infallible orthodoxy; such, in short, as the Roman church has ever claimed to be, the supreme ruler and infallible teacher of the world." Herbert Cardinal Vaughn, *Ten Lectures delivered in Free Trade Hall, Manchester*, (Manchester: John Heywood, Excelsior Printing and Bookbinding Works, 1896), 348.

The Russian Orthodox writer Bolotov summarizes:

"'By virtue of the primacy of Peter, the Bishop of Rome confirms the decision of councils, decides most often without councils, receives appeals from everywhere; from which Roman decision there is no appeal.' (Lektsii, t. iii, p. 303, quoted by d'Herbigny, *Op. cit.*, p. 22.)", in S. Herbert Scott, *The Eastern Churches and the Papacy*, (London: Sheed & Ward, 1928), 201.

Some say that even if Peter were the leader of the early Christian community, there is no evidence of successors to Peter, much less a plan for this eventuality. But why would Jesus take the trouble to set up Peter as the head of the Church in the first place, if there were to be no successors to Peter? Jesus set up an institution that will function until the end of time. Jesus did not set up a momentary or hypothetical apostolic arrangement to last only until the completion of the Canon of Scripture. It is most reasonable to believe that Christ foresaw successors to Peter and to the other Apostles. The Church is the Bark of Peter steering a course toward eternity with the successors of Peter at the helm. "Where Peter is, there is the Church. And where the Church, no death is there, but life eternal." Ambrose, *Commentaries on Twelve of David's Psalms* [40,30], in W. A. Jurgens, *The Faith of the Early Fathers*, vol. 2, (Collegeville, MN: The Liturgical Press, 1970), 150. Jesus created the leadership and succession of that leadership that would continue until the end of time.

Infallibility versus Impeccability

The Catholic Church teaches that Peter and his successors are infallible, i.e., incapable of error in matters of faith and morals under certain conditions. Some people misunderstand the Church to be teaching that St. Peter and his successors are impeccable, i.e., incapable of sin. This is not true. Every pope is a sinner in need of the Saviour, just as Peter was.

Nevertheless, it is useful to look at the passage most often used against the doctrine of papal infallibility—Galatians 2:1-17:

> *Galatians* 2:1 Then fourteen years after I went up again to Jerusalem with Barnabas, and took Titus with [me] also.
> 2:2 And I went up by revelation, and communicated unto them that gospel which I preach among the Gentiles, but privately to them which were of reputation, lest by any means I should run, or had run, in vain.

208. Whom did Paul take with him to Jerusalem? Titus and Barnabas.

209. What did Paul do when he was in Jerusalem? He presented to the leaders what he had been teaching to the Gentile community.

> *Galatians* 2:6 But of these who seemed to be somewhat, (whatsoever they [formerly] were, it maketh no matter to me: God accepteth no man's person:) for they who seemed [to be somewhat] in conference added nothing to me:

210. What is Paul speaking of in Galatians 2:6? That God impartially uses men for his purposes, notwithstanding their former life.

The Greek word *pote*, which is left out of many biblical translations, means "once" or "formerly." What they were formerly makes no difference to God. Paul acknowledges the apostolic status of the Apostles in the community and their former status as fisherman, tax collectors, or whatever.

The Conditions of Infallibility

There is an incident in Paul's Epistle to the Galatians in which Paul rebukes Peter to his face. Some have sought to diminish the teaching authority of Peter in matters of faith and morals because of this incident. The Scripture reads:

> *Galatians* 2:11 But when Peter was come to Antioch, I withstood him to the face, because he was to be blamed.
> 2:12 For before that certain came from James, he did eat with the Gentiles: but when they were come, he withdrew and separated himself, fearing them which were of the circumcision.
> 2:13 And the other Jews dissembled likewise with him; insomuch that Barnabas also was carried away with their dissimulation [*hupokrisei*].

211. Why did Paul withstand Peter to his face? For acting hypocritically, as Paul described it in Galatians 2:13. *Hupokrisei* is the Greek word for acting hypocritically, or "dissembling." Paul saw that Peter's actions were not in accord even with his vision to welcome the Gentiles into the Church (cf. Acts 10:1-48).

It appears that Peter was trying to accommodate both Jews and Gentiles in the Church. Paul wrote that Peter should have acted incontrovertibly for the Gentiles, certainly at mealtime. Peter had sinned, was blamed, and some might argue that by this incident he showed himself a truly fallible leader and teacher, one who certainly could not make "infallible" pronouncements.

212. Does the definition of "infallibility" exclude a Pope from making a mistake? No, anyone, including the Pope, can sin or commit errors in all sorts of matters, including personal conduct. The doctrine of infallibility rather states that when a successor of St. Peter speaks to the entire Church, either alone or with the bishops in the communion of the college of bishops or in a council, on doctrinal matters of faith and morals, he cannot err.

"With the approval of the sacred council [Vatican I], We teach and define that it is a dogma divinely revealed: that the Roman Pontiff, when he speaks *ex cathedra*, that is, when, in discharge of the office of pastor and teacher of all Christians, by virtue of his supreme Apostolic authority, he defines a doctrine regarding faith or morals to be held by the Universal Church, is, by the divine assistance promised to him in Blessed Peter, possesed of that infallibility with which the Divine Redeemer willed that his Church should be endowed in defining doctrine regarding faith or morals; and that, therefore, such definitions of the Roman Pontiff are of themselves, and not from the consent of the Church, irreformable." *Pastor Aeternus* (July 18, 1870), in Benedictine Monks of Solesmes, ed., *The Church*, trans. E. O'Gorman, (Boston: Daughters of St. Paul, 1980), 217,

"The double-negative [infallibility] has the precise meaning, 'the inability to err.' It is not conceptually equivalent to 'being correct.' One could be simply correct without being necessarily so. Infallibility in the absolute sense is predicable of God alone, but in the sense meant here, it is the result of the divine assistance." Peter M. J. Stravinskas, ed., *Our Sunday Visitor's Catholic Encyclopedia*, (Huntington, IN: Our Sunday Visitor, 1991), 510.

"The Pope's prerogative is with regard to defining doctrines that are explicitly and implicitly in the deposit of faith given by Christ in the keeping of His Church. It means not that the Pope is inspired or that he is immune from sin: it means that the Pope is divinely protected from contradicting, from denying and from changing the revelations of Christ. It means not that the Pope receives new revelations: it means that the Pope holds inviolate the truths revealed. It means not that the Pope invents new doctrines or that he cannot err in matters, economic, political, scientific or historical: it means that the Pope cannot admit doctrinal changes in religion. It means not that the Pope is given the power to dictate to Caesar, to depose rulers, to absolve persons from their obligations to the state: it means the Pope's infallible power lies exclusively within the sphere of faith and morals." David Goldstein, *What Say You?*, (St. Paul, MN: Radio Replies, 1945), 236.

"Giovanni Perrone, S.J., one of the influential theologians blamed by some nowadays for Vatican I, was therefore on most biblical grounds when he pointed out that Christians must adhere to the pope not because he is infallible; but since they must, on divine command [according to John 13:20], adhere to the pope, he has to be infallible." Stanley L. Jaki, *The Keys of the Kingdom*, (Chicago: The Franciscan Herald, 1986), 170.

213. Are the Popes in need of Jesus Christ as savior? Yes.

214 Why would the Popes need a savior? Because they are sinners, just like us.

Impeccability, the absence of or inability to sin, is not and never was a part of the definition of infallibility. Popes have made mistakes, have even been sinful. The late Hans Urs von Balthasar, a leading Catholic theologian, states the case succinctly:

"Certainly, this office [of Pope] was placed in the 'holy' center of the Church (hence the demand for a declaration of love from the first pope [cf. John 21:15-17]). From this center, however, it does not reach out only to the sinners who are displaced from it and thus 'eccentric'; it is not only *for* them but rather *with* them (it is Peter, who denied the Lord, who is given office), in such a way that the personal guilt of the officeholder does not vitally affect the indefectibility of the office. Peter is *simul*—though not in the same respect—*justus et peccator, fallibilis et infallibilis* (both righteous and sinner, fallible and infallible)." Hans Urs von Balthasar, *The Office of Peter and the Structure of the Church*, trans. Andrée Emery, (San Francisco, CA: Ignatius, 1986), 181.

"Obviously, Peter's successor is not 'impeccable', sinless; and so to avoid misunderstandings—particularly when it comes to translations into other languages—one should not speak of the 'infallibility of the pope' but '[the infallibility] of the Magisterium exercised by him.' . . . infallibility pertains to the concrete person. On the other hand, the charism is not given to the pope as a private person because as such he is by no means infallible. . . . Yet it would be too little (and again abstract) to grant infallibility, not to the person, but to the 'function'; rather it is a question of the public person who expressly represents the whole Church. But even to him (who is always the 'highest judge in matters of faith and morals'), infallibility is not granted as an inherent characteristic. It is strictly limited to the act by which, with the help of the Holy Spirit, he explicitly exercises the office of judge in matters concerning the whole Church." Hans Urs von Balthasar, *The Office of Peter and the Structure of the Church*, trans. Andrée Emery, (San Francisco, CA: Ignatius, 1986), 217-218.

215. What are the conditions of papal infallibility?

"And this is the infallibility which the Roman Pontiff, the head of the college of bishops, enjoys in virtue of his office, when, [1] as the supreme shepherd and teacher of all the faithful, who confirms his brethren in their faith, [2] by a definitive act [3] he proclaims a doctrine of faith or morals." *Lumen Gentium* (Constitution on the Church, Para. 25, November 21, 1964), (Washington, DC: United States Catholic Conference, n.d.), 27-28.

While Peter and his successors may be infallible in proclaiming doctrines regarding faith and morals, there is no assurance that Peter and his successors shall be free of sin. Paul recounts his exasperation with Peter:

> *Galatians* 2:14 But when I saw that they walked not uprightly according to the truth of the gospel, I said unto Peter before [them] all, If thou, being a Jew, livest after the manner of Gentiles, and not as do the Jews, why compellest thou the Gentiles to live as do the Jews?
> 2:15 We [who are] Jews by nature, and not sinners of the Gentiles,

The Lutheran-Catholic dialogue sheds a different light on Peter's actions in eating with the Judaizers, and Paul's severe reaction to them, analyzing Peter's actions by referring to other scripture besides Galatians:

> "We are describing this from Paul's point of view [under inspiration of the Holy Spirit] in Galatians. As we shall see, Acts 15 gives a different view of the procedures, according to which, *prima facie*, the Jerusalem authorities in the presence of Paul commanded an observance by the Gentile converts of certain Jewish regulations and thus adopted Peter's position at Antioch, not Paul's. We must face the possibility that what Paul saw as cowardice and failure to act according to principle was interpreted by Peter as intelligent compromise over non-essentials—a spirit not unlike that advocated by Paul (but applied by him in a very different way) in I Cor 8:9; 10:23-24; and Rom 14:1-15:3." Raymond E. Brown, Karl P. Donfried, and John Reumann, eds., *Peter in the New Testament*, (Minneapolis, MN: Augsburg; New York: Paulist: 1973), 30.

From the letter of the Council at Jerusalem, the following words are recorded:

> *Acts* 15:24 Forasmuch as we have heard, that certain which went out from us have troubled you with words, subverting your souls, saying, Ye must be circumcised, and keep the law: to whom we gave no such commandment:
>
> 15:25 It seemed good unto us, being assembled with one accord, to send chosen men unto you with our beloved Barnabas and Paul,
>
> 15:26 Men that have hazarded their lives for the name of our Lord Jesus Christ.
>
> 15:27 We have sent therefore Judas and Silas, who shall also tell you the same things by mouth.

216. In another context, aside from Paul's castigation of Peter in Galatians, what possible reasons could Paul have had for circumcising Timothy (Acts 16:3) in preparation for their mis-

sionary journey, in light of the decisions made at the Council of Jerusalem? According to Acts 16:3, Paul followed the Mosaic laws and circumcised a certain bishop, Timothy, the son of a Greek father and Jewish mother, in order to allow Timothy to minister among the Jews. Timothy was considered a Jew, inasmuch as his mother was Jewish, and therefore ought to have been circumcised, even though his family never did so during his youth. Paul insisted on it, however, seemingly in direct contradiction to his statements in Galatians 5:2, 6 (wherein he says that circumcision avails nothing) and in contravention to the pronouncements of the letter from the Council at Jerusalem. Paul circumcised Timothy for the sake of evangelization:

> *Acts* 16:3 Him [Timotheus] would Paul have to go forth with him; and took and circumcised him because of the Jews which were in those quarters: for they knew all that his father was a Greek.

> "'Paul had him circumcised': he did this in order that Timothy might be able to associate with the Jews and so perform a ministry among them. Paul did not object to the Jewish Christains' adherence to the law. But he insisted that the law could not be imposed on the Gentiles. Paul himself lived in accordance with the law, or as exempt from the law, according to particular cirumstances (see 1 Cor 9, 19-23)." Confraternity of Christian Doctrine, *The New American Bible* (Giant Print Edition), fn. [Acts] 16:3, (Huntington, IN: Our Sunday Visitor, 1988), 1972.

In light of Paul's actions, one might interpret Peter's in much the same way. According to the "particular circumstances" (see above) in the Pauline sense, Peter refused to eat with Gentile Christians and ate with the Judaizing Christians for what he perceived was the sake of pastoral care. The pastoral, non-dogmatic, decisions made at Jerusalem would be adapted over time.

Also, Paul underwent purification, following the ritual law, which to some makes Paul look as if he is giving into Jewish ritual laws for the sake of harmony. Peter may have done likewise. Paul, himself a Jew, obligingly carried out Jewish prescripts, as advised:

> *Acts* 21:24 Them take, and purify thyself with them, and be at charges with them, that they may shave [their] heads: and all may know that those things, whereof they were informed concerning thee, are nothing; but [that] thou thyself also walkest orderly, and keepest the law.
> 21:26 Then Paul took the men, and the next day purifying himself with them entered into the temple, to signify the accomplishment of the days of purification, until that an offering should be offered for every one of them.

217. Are Christians free to follow the moral law, as revealed to Moses on Mt. Sinai? Yes, the universal moral law, as set forth in the ten commandments, is fully valid for us as Christians, and Paul reiterates this many times throughout his writings.

218. Did Paul and Barnabas consistently live up to the Gospel? None can.

219. Why did Paul single out Peter for rebuke in Galatians 2:11? As the leader of the Church, Peter should have known better than to give in to the Judaizers' push to require Gentiles to conform to the whole law, signaled by Peter's refusal to eat with the Gentiles.

Paul had good grounds to believe that Peter had acted insincerely, even hypocritically. Is that a sin? Scripture says that Peter had separated himself from the Gentile converts and had apparently refused to eat with them, which makes his act direct and without equivocation. This shows a certain intent to ignore the truth to suit Peter's perception of what he should do. Perhaps Peter did not intend to transgress God's moral law, but had merely wanted to make the Judaizers feel "at home."

Peter, under the inspiration of the Holy Spirit, had previously enunciated the doctrine that the Gentiles did not have to become circumcised as Jews before they became baptized as Christians. In Galatians, Paul wants Peter to practice what he preaches and to be good, especially regarding the Gentiles. Paul, for the sake of evangelization, applies the discipline of the Church in a variety of ways to the following: procuring circumcision (Acts 16:3); eating unclean (unkosher) meat (I Corinthians 8:4); and submitting to the Jewish purification rites (Acts 21:24, 26). Yet, in Galatians Paul says (in agreement with Peter in Acts 15:11):

> *Galatians* 2:16 Knowing that a man is not justified by the works of the law, but by the faith of Jesus Christ, even we have believed in Jesus Christ, that we might be justified by the faith of Christ, and not by the works of the law: for by the works of the law shall no flesh be justified.
>
> 2:17 But if, while we seek to be justified by Christ, we ourselves also are found sinners, [is] therefore Christ the minister of sin? God forbid.

220. Are the Apostles in agreement regarding faith and morals? Yes. All knew what was required for obedience to the faith through the gospel of Christ Jesus.

221. What are the works of the law? Circumcision, dietary and sabbath ordinances, and the other rules included in the *mitzvot* (613 religious ritual, ceremonial, and moral laws of conduct according to which Jews are commanded to live). Christ came to fulfill the law. The ritual or ceremonial laws are now gone; it is the moral laws that are to be followed, as they are written on the heart of every believer.

222. Are Christians still commanded to live up to the moral laws, as set forth in the ten commandments? Yes, definitely.

Even as the sinfulness of a successor to St. Peter shows that he is not impeccable, Peter's successors are nonetheless infallible insofar as they make pronouncements on the truth of Christian faith and morals, truth that the Church has upheld for almost 2,000 years. Just because St. Peter was guilty of inconsistent behavior, as Paul described the scene under the inspiration of the Holy Spirit, Peter's sin does not detract from his undeniable leadership of the Church. Peter did not err doctrinally in any of his actions or statements set forth in Galatians. If he erred at all, he erred personally in his conduct.

We can conclude that whatever Peter's sin was, his sinfulness did not affect his position or office in the Church; he remained the leader of the universal community. He continued to hold the keys given to him by Christ (Matthew 16:19) until the authority of the keys was transferred to his successors in order to continue to build the Church (Matthew 16:19). The office of Peter was heavenly placed by the Lord Jesus Christ. The authority of the keys of this office cannot be humanly removed because of a Pope's sins. Peter is the model of this truth.

Guarding the Deposit of Faith

I Corinthians 4:1 Let a man so account of us, as of the ministers of Christ, and stewards of the mysteries of God.

I Timothy 6:20 O Timothy, keep that which is committed to thy trust, avoiding profane [and] vain babblings, and oppositions of science falsely so called:

II Timothy 1:13 Hold fast the form of sound words, which thou hast heard of me, in faith and love which is in Christ Jesus.

223. What should Timothy do with the office given to him? Timothy must guard the deposit of faith given to him by the Apostles. The faithful are obliged to obey this authority, in compliance with Scripture:

> *Hebrews* 13:17 Obey them that have the rule over you, and submit yourselves: for they watch for your souls, as they that must give account, that they may do it with joy, and not with grief: for that is unprofitable for you.

Timothy must pass on the deposit of faith to faithful men, who are likewise entrusted with teaching others the faith. An unbroken line of teaching authority is to be passed down by the bishops, in accordance with Scripture:

> *II Timothy* 2:1 Thou [Bishop Timothy] therefore, my son, be strong in the grace that is in Christ Jesus.
> 2:2 And the things that thou hast heard of me among many witnesses, the same commit thou to faithful men, who shall be able to teach others also.

St. Paul appears to be the first of four generations of apostolic succession indicated in II Timothy 2:1-2. Paul passes leadership to St. Timothy, who will, in turn, commit to other "faithful men" who will "teach others" as chosen teachers of the Gospel of Christ. While one could not say that these succeeding generations of chosen teachers were definitely bishops, one cannot assume that they were not bishops, either.

Jude's "Korah" Warning to the Church to Follow the Hierarchy

224. In Chapter 16 of Numbers, against whom were the people of Korah rebelling? The religious hierarchy established by Moses.

> *Numbers* 16:1 Now Korah, the son of Izhar, the son of Kohath, the son of Levi, and Dathan and Abiram, the sons of Eliab, and On, the son of Peleth, sons of Reuben, took [men]:
> 16:2 And they rose up before Moses, with certain of the children of Israel, two hundred and fifty princes of the assembly, famous in the congregation, men of renown:

> 16:3 And they gathered themselves together against Moses and against Aaron, and said unto them, [Ye take] too much upon you, seeing all the congregation [are] holy, every one of them, and the LORD [is] among them: wherefore then lift ye up yourselves above the congregation of the LORD?

225. Why would God allow for Jude to use the Old Testament reference to the rebellion of Korah, regarding people rebelling against the hierarchy established under Moses if there were not a hierarchy in place in New Testament times? A last reference to the apostolic hierarchy in New Testament times is found in Jude:

> *Jude* 11 Woe unto them! for they have gone in the way of Cain, and ran greedily after the error of Balaam for reward, and perished in the gainsaying of Core [Korah].

Tim Staples, a Catholic convert from the Assembly of God, has given a powerful testimony and witness of his conversion in "The Bible Made Me Do It," in Patrick Madrid, ed., *Surprised by Truth*, (San Diego, CA: Basilica Press, 1994). Further elaborating on the crucial impact of the Book of Jude in confirming for him the necessity for and functioning of the Catholic hierarchy during New Testament times, he weaves together Jude 11 with Numbers, Chapter 16. Mr. Staples vividly describes how the author of Jude warns the Church about the dire consequences of attacking and then usurping the position of the Church's hierarchy:

> "Scripture scholars point to two main heretical sects the Epistle of Jude deals with and condemns: the gnostics and the anti-nomians. These condemnations were not only for the first century Church; they are for the Church in the twentieth century as well. . . .
> "The allusion to the rebellion of Korah (Jude 11) is evidence of Jude's condemnation of the anti-nomians. In particular, the Nicolaitans. Perhaps founded by the deacon, Nicholas, mentioned in Acts 6:5, this sect was libertine in

nature. Claiming St. Paul as their authority, they claimed 'freedom' in Christ; therefore, the decrees of the Council of Jerusalem (Acts 15:28-29) were not necessary to follow. 'Who are these apostles anyway?' they would claim. 'They are mere men and sinners just like us.'

"Jude compares these heretics to Korah and his followers who rebelled against Moses and Aaron in Numbers 16. The argument of Korah went along the same lines. Korah and his followers were Levites; they were leaders in the congregation. They said to Moses and Aaron:

> "'You take too much upon you, *seeing all the congregation are holy*, every one of them, and the Lord is among them: why then do you lift yourselves up above the congregation of the Lord?' (Numbers 16:3)

"Their rebellion was against the hierarchy and the result was divine condemnation (Numbers 16:32). The Nicolaitans rebelled against the hierarchy claiming St. Paul as their authority and the result was the same. Jesus condemned them in Revelation 2:6, 14 and 20, not for rejecting the Bible, rather for rejecting the hierarchy. 'If they reject you, they reject me' (Luke 10:16).

"Here clearly, Scripture speaks of an authoritative hierarchy that the faithful are bound in conscience to follow. There is no evidence that this hierarchy does not exist anymore. If fact, Hebrews 13:7, 17 says:

> "'Remember them which have the rule over you, who have spoken unto you the word of God: *whose faith follow* . . . Obey them that have the rule over you, *and submit yourselves: for they watch for your souls...*'

"There is no Protestant hierarchy that even claims this kind of authority, yet the true Church founded by Christ must possess it.

"Why would St. Jude use this example of Korah when dealing with the anti-nomian Nicolaitans if there were no authoritative hierarchy to which to refer? More importantly, why would our Lord place this warning to the whole Church against following in the way of Korah in the New

Testament, if the New Testament does not have an authoritative hierarchy?

"As a Protestant, studying this text after I had been challenged by my Catholic friend concerning a New Testament hierarchy, I found myself in the precarious position of the Nicolaitans and the followers of Korah, 'despising Lordship, speaking evil of dignities' (Jude 8) and speaking evil of 'those things which [I] understand not' (Jude 10). I found myself following in the 'gainsaying of Korah' (Jude 11)." Tim Staples, letter to authors, 10 October 1994, 1-2.

After contemplating the various Biblical approaches to the Papacy, one may ask further questions. What do the Fathers and early writers of the Church historically believe to be the proper interpretations of certain key scriptural passages set forth in Part One of this handbook? How did the Fathers and early writers of the Church view the office of Peter and the role of the Roman Church? In Part Two of this volume are various sources from the early Church relative to Peter as the Rock and Key-holder, Peter as the Chief Apostle, Peter as the Chief Shepherd of the Church of Christ, and the Primacy of Peter and the Roman Church.

PART TWO

HISTORICAL SOURCES ON THE PRIMACY OF PETER AND THE ROMAN CHURCH

What follows are essentially the statements of early writers and Fathers of the Church on various passages of Scripture and on the primacy of the Roman See in the Church of Christ. Additional commentary is minimal. Some quotations apply to more than one category of reference.

JESUS, PETER AND THE KEYS

CHAPTER VI

ST. PETER AS THE ROCK AND KEY HOLDER OF MATTHEW 16:18-19

Matthew 16:18 And I say also unto thee, That thou art Peter, and upon this rock I will build my church; and the gates of hell shall not prevail against it.

16:19 And I will give unto thee the keys of the kingdom of heaven: and whatsoever thou shalt bind on earth shall be bound in heaven: and whatsoever thou shalt loose on earth shall be loosed in heaven.

Tertullian (ca. 200-220 A.D.):

"Tertullian, the son of a proconsular centurion, was born at Carthage about A.D. 150, and brought up for the profession of a Roman advocate. He embraced Christianity A.D. 185, was ordained priest in 192, became a Montanist in 199, and died about 220. His works, many of which are extant, are highly esteemed, since even those which were written after he had fallen into heresy bear important testimony regarding the faith, practice, and discipline of the Church in his time. Of his style, which is extremely terse and vigorous, St. Vincent of Lérins said: 'Who can express the praises which he deserves, . . . whose so many words almost are so many sentences, whose so many senses so many victories. This knew Marcion, Apelles, Praxeas, and Hermogenes, Jews, Gentiles, Gnostics, and many others, whose blasphemous opinions he hath overthrown with his many and great volumes, as it had been with thunderbolts' (*Commonit.* c. 18.) His treatise on *Prescription against Heretics* was written whilst he was a Catholic. His works were published by Erasmus (1520), Pamelius (1568), Rigalt (1648), Fell (Oxford, 1682), and others. The best edition is the Benedictine (Maran, Paris, 1726), and Migne (*Patr. Lat.* vols. iv. v.). English translations have been published in the Oxford *Library of the Fathers*, and in Clarke's *Ante-Nicene Christian Library*." Charles F. B. Allnatt, ed., *Cathedra Petri—The Titles and Prerogatives of St. Peter*, (London: Burns & Oates, 1879), 12.

"Was anything hidden from Peter, who was called the Rock whereon the Church was to be built; who obtained the keys of the kingdom of heaven, and the power of loosing and of binding in heaven and on earth?" (Tertullian, *De Praescript Haeret* n. 22, p. 209, in Colin Lindsay, *The Evidence for the Papacy*, (London: Longmans, 1870), 19.

"For if thou thinkest heaven is still closed, remember that the Lord left here the keys thereof to Peter, and through him to the Church; which keys every one that is here questioned and confesses, shall carry with him." (Tertullian, *Scorpiace*, n. x. p. 496), in Colin Lindsay, *The Evidence for the Papacy*, (London: Longmans, 1870), 19.

Tertullian eventually became a Montanist, a heretical group which was not as forgiving as the Church was in forgiving heretics. The following quote contains some heretical material that claims that only Peter personally, and his successors, hold the power of the keys. It was never a position of the Church, which believes that all of the successors of the Apostles have received the power of binding and loosing, retaining and forgiving, from Jesus Christ himself:

"I now inquire into your opinion, to see whence you usurp this right for the Church. Do you presume, because the Lord said to Peter, 'On this rock I will build my Church, I have given you the keys of the kingdom of heaven' [Matt. 16:18-19a] or "whatever you shall have bound or loosed on earth will be bound or loosed in heaven" [Matt. 16:19b] that the power of binding and loosing has thereby been handed on to you, that is, to every church akin to Peter? What kind of man are you, subverting and changing what was the manifest intent of the Lord when he conferred this personally upon Peter? On you, he says, I will build my Church; and I will give to you the keys, not to the Church; and whatever you shall have bound or you shall have loosed, not what they shall have bound or they shall have loosed" (Tertullian, *On Modesty* 21:9-10), in W. A. Jurgens, *The Faith of the Early Fathers*, vol. 1, (Collegeville, MN: The Liturgical Press, 1970), 160.

"It was His pleasure to communicate to the most highly esteemed of his disciples, in a peculiar manner, a name (Peter) drawn from the figures of Himself." (Tertullian, *Adv. Marcion.* lib. iv. c. 13), in Charles F. B. Allnatt, ed., *Cathedra Petri—The Titles and Prerogatives of St. Peter*, (London: Burns & Oates, 1879), 48.

St. Hippolytus (ca. 225 A.D.):

"Hippolytus (St.), a disciple of St. Irenaeus, came to Rome during the Pontificate of Zephyrinus, who, after a reign of eighteen years, was succeeded, A.D. 218, by Callistus. In combatting the heretics of his time (the Sabellians and Noetians, who maintained the Patripassian doctrine), Hippolytus himself fell into an opposite extreme of error (Subordinationism) and he also opposed the mitigated system of penance which had been approved by Pope Zephyrinus. When Callistus, to whom he showed a strong personal enmity, was elected Pope, Hippolytus, who had become Bishop of Pontus, set himself to oppose him, and 'declaring that a heretic could not be Pope, and that those who adhered to him were not the faithful, but formed "a school" and not the Church, he came to the conclusion that he himself was Pope, and that such as remained to him of his flock in the Tiburtine Way were the true Church. Thus he speaks of himself in a stately plural as "the successors of the Apostles, the partakers of the same grace, supreme priesthood, and doctorship, and the guardians of the Church."' (*Month*, Feb. 1878). The small schism thus caused continued for some years; but before his martyrdom, which probably occurred at the same time as that of Pope Pontian, A.D. 235, Hippolytus was reconciled to the Holy See." (Prudent., *Hymn in S. Hippol.*) See Dollinger's *Hippol. and Callist.*, Eng. trans. 1876), and *The Lives of SS. Callist. and Hippol.* in *Month* of February and March 1878. His collected works are published in Galland (tom. ii.) and Migne (*Patr. Graec.* vol. x.). He is now generally considered to have been the author of the *Philosophumena*, or *Confutation of all Heresies*, in ten books, which the first editor, Miller (Oxford, 1851), attributed to Origen. His *Chronicle*, which appeared in the year 235, contained a catalogue of the early Bishops of Rome, counting St. Peter as the first; but the portion containing it was supposed to be lost until restored by Mommsen, who proved 'that the earlier part of the celebrated *Liberian Catalogue* is derived from the list of Roman Bishops given by St. Hippolytus (*Dict. of Christ. biog. and Lit.* vol. i. p. 506, 7, 555, 7)." Charles F. B. Allnatt, ed., *Cathedra Petri—The Titles and Prerogatives of St. Peter*, (London: Burns & Oates, 1879), 7-8.

"Peter, . . . The Rock of the Church." Hippolytus, *In S. Theophan.* n. 9, *Galland*, ii. p. 494), in Charles F. B. Allnatt, ed., *Cathedra Petri—The Titles and Prerogatives of St. Peter*, (London: Burns & Oates, 1879), 16-17.

"Peter, the Rock of the faith, whom Christ our Lord called blessed, the teacher of the Church, the first disciple, he who has the keys of the kingdom." (Hippolytus, *Ex Fabricio, Op. Hippol. tom.* ii. *De Fine Mundi et de Antichristo*, n. 9), in Charles F. B. Allnatt, ed., *Cathedra Petri—The Titles and Prerogatives of St. Peter*, (London: Burns & Oates, 1879), 17.

Origen (ca. 230-250 A.D.):

"Origen was born at Alexandria about A.D. 185. His instructors in theology were Pantaenus and Clement of Alexandria; and in 203 he became head of the Catechetical School in that city. During the Pontificate of Zephyrinus, about A.D. 211, Origen went to Rome, . . . (Euseb. *Hist. Ecc.* vi. 14); but, returning to Alexandria, at the desire of his bishop, Demetrius, he there wrote many of his great works on the Scriptures. He was subsequently sent by Demetrius into Achaia, and during his stay at Caesarea in Palestine, he was ordained priest, A.D. 228. He returned to Alexandria in 230, and was treated with severity by his Bishop on account of the irregularity of his ordination, and some heretical doctrines attributed to him, for which also he was condemned in two Synods. He died at Tyre in 254. The best edition of his works is the *Benedictine* (De la Rue, Paris, 1743, 4 vols. fol.), republished by Oberthur (*Coll. PP. Graec.* vols. vii.-xxi.), and Migne (vols. xi.-xvii.)." Charles F. B. Allnatt, ed., *Cathedra Petri—The Titles and Prerogatives of St. Peter*, (London: Burns & Oates, 1879), 11.

"See what is said by the Lord to [Peter], that great foundation of the Church, and most solid rock, upon which Christ founded the Church [Matt. 16:18]. 'O thou of little faith! Why didst thou doubt?' [Matt. 14:31]." (Origen, *In Exod. Hom.* v. n. 4, tom. ii. p. 145, ed. Del la Rue, Migne), in Charles F. B. Allnatt, ed., *Cathedra Petri—The Titles and Prerogatives of St. Peter*, (London: Burns & Oates, 1879), 15-16.

"Upon him (Peter), as on the earth, the Church was founded." (Origen, *In Epist. ad Rom.* lib. v. c. 10, tom. iv. p. 568), in Charles F. B. Allnatt, ed., *Cathedra Petri—The Titles and Prerogatives of St. Peter*, (London: Burns & Oates, 1879), 16.

"Peter upon whom is built Christ's Church, against which the gates of hell shall not prevail." (Origen, *T. iv. In Joan. Tom. v.* p. 95 (Ex Euseb. *Hist. Eccles.* lib. vi. c. 25), in Colin Lindsay, *The Evidence for the Papacy*, (London: Longmans, 1870), 21. See also Allan Menzies, ed., *Ante-Nicene Fathers*, 4th ed., vol. 9, (Peabody, MA: Hendrickson, 1994), 346; G. A. Williamson, trans., *The History of the Church*, (New York: Barnes & Noble, 1965), 265; and Charles F. B. Allnatt, ed., *Cathedra Petri—The Titles and Prerogatives of St. Peter*, (London: Burns & Oates, 1879), 18.

"[Peter] a truly blessed rock, in which we too are placed."
(Origen, *In Matt.* x. 34, *Ex. Sirmond.* tom. vi. p. 1177, ed.
Migne), in Charles F. B. Allnatt, ed., *Cathedra Petri—The
Titles and Prerogatives of St. Peter*, (London: Burns & Oates,
1879), 17-18.

"What, in a previous passage (Matt. xvi. 19), was granted
to Peter alone, seems here (Matt. xviii. 18) to be shown to
be granted to all who have addressed three admonitions to
all sinners, in order that, if they be not listened to, they may
bind on earth the person condemned to be as a heathen and
a publican, since such a one is bound in heaven. But, as it
was fit,—even though something in common was spoken
of Peter, and of those who should thrice admonish the brethren,—that Peter should have something peculiar above those
who should thrice admonish; this was previously ordained
separately respecting Peter; thus, 'I will give to thee the keys
of the kingdom of heaven,' before (it was said) 'and whatsoever ye shall bind on earth,' and what follows; and truly,
if we sedulously attend to the evangelical writings, even in
them we may discover,—with regard even to those things
which seem to be common to Peter and to those who have
thrice admonished the brethren,—much difference and pre-
eminence in the words spoken to Peter, beyond those spoken to in the second place." (Origen, T. iii. *Comm. in Matt.*
Tom. xiii. n. 31, pp. 613-4), in Joseph Berington, John Kirk,
eds., and James Waterworth, rev., *The Faith of Catholics*,
vol. 2, (New York: Pustet & Co., 1884), 6-7.

"Peter likewise, on whom the Church was founded by the
good pleasure of the Lord, lays it down in his epistle, &c."
(Origen, *De Bono Patient.* p. 494), in Joseph Berington, John
Kirk, eds., and James Waterworth, rev., *The Faith of Catholics*, vol. 2, (New York: Pustet & Co., 1884), 10.

St. Cyprian (ca. 246 A.D.):

"Cyprian (St.), Bishop of Carthage from A.D. 248 to 257,
was born early in the third century, and became a convert to
Christianity A.D. 246. He suffered martyrdom A.D. 258.
The reader will find an interesting account of his life and

writings in *Dict. of Christ. Biog. and Literat.* vol. i. pp. 739-755; and in Mgr. Freppel's *S. Cyprien*, Paris, 1865. The best editions of his works are those of Erasmus (Basil, 1520); Paul Manutius (Rome, 1563); Pamelius (Antw. 1568); Rigaltius (Paris, 1648); Fell (Oxford, 1682); Baluzius and Dom. Prud. Maranus (the celebrated Benedictine edit., Paris 1726; republished by Migne, *Patr. Lat.* vols. iii. iv.); Goldhorn (*Cyp. Op. Genuina*, Lipsiae, 1838); and J. Hartel (1868-71). An English translation of Cyprian's works has been published in the Oxford *Library of the Fathers*, and another by Messrs. Clark of Edinburgh, in their *Ante-Nicene Christian Library*." Charles F. B. Allnatt, ed., *Cathedra Petri—The Titles and Prerogatives of St. Peter*, (London: Burns & Oates, 1879), 5.

"The Lord says to Peter: 'I say to you,' He says, 'that you are Peter, and upon this rock I will build my Church, and the gates of hell will not overcome it. And to you I will give the keys of the kingdom of heaven: and whatever things you bind on earth shall be bound also in heaven, and whatever you loose on earth, they shall be loosed also in heaven' [Matt. 16:18-19]). And again He says to him after His resurrection: 'Feed my sheep' [John 21:17]. On him He builds the Church, and to him He gives the command to feed the sheep; and although He assigns a like power to all the Apostles, yet He founded a single chair, and He established by His own authority a source and an intrinsic reason for that unity. Indeed, the others were that also which Peter was; but a primacy is given to Peter, whereby it is made clear that there is but one Church and one chair. So too, all are shepherds, and the flock is shown to be one, fed by all the Apostles in single-minded accord. If someone does not hold fast to this unity of Peter, can he imagine that he still holds the faith? If he desert the chair of Peter upon whom the Church was built, can he still be confident that he is in the Church?" Cyprian, *De ecclesiae catholicae unitate* 4 [first edition], in W. A. Jurgens, *The Faith of the Early Fathers*, vol. 1, (Collegeville, MN: The Liturgical Press, 1970), 220. See also Cyprian, *De Unitate*, p. 195, in Colin Lindsay, *The Evidence for the Papacy*, (London: Longmans, 1870), 23; Alexander Roberts and James Donaldson, eds., *Ante-Nicene*

Fathers, vol. 5, (Peabody, MA: Hendrickson, 1994), 422 [wherein the editors presume that Cyprian only wrote one version of his treatise, with references to Rome being later additions; scholarship has shown that there are in fact two versions of *De Unitate* written by Cyprian.]

"Peter, on whom the Church had been built by the Lord Himself, one speaking for all, and replying with the voice of the Church, says, 'Lord, to whom shall we go?'" Cyprian, *Ep. lv. Ad Cornel.* p. 83, in Colin Lindsay, *The Evidence for the Papacy*, (London: Longmans, 1870), 22.

"Our Lord, whose precepts we ought to fear and observe, in establishing the office of a bishop and the constitution of His Church in the Gospel, speaks and says to Peter: 'I say unto thee that thou art Peter . . . be loosed in heaven.' Hence, through the changes and successions of time, the establishment of bishops and the constitution of the Church are handed down, so that the Church is constituted upon bishops, and every act of the Church is directed by these same prelates." Cyprian, *Epistle 33*, I, in Dom John Chapman, *Bishop Gore and Catholic Claims* (London: Longmans, Green, and Co., 1905), 54-55.

"For first to Peter, upon whom He built the Church, and from whom He appointed and showed that unity should spring, the Lord gave this power that that should be in heaven which he should have loosed on earth. And, after the resurrection also, He speaks to the Apostles, saying, 'As My Father hath sent me, even so send I you,'" Cyprian, *Ep. lxxiii ad Fubaian.* p. 131, in Colin Lindsay, *The Evidence for the Papacy*, (London: Longmans, 1870), 23.

"Peter, also to whom the Lord commends His sheep to be fed and guarded, on whom He laid and founded the Church." Cyprian, *De Habitu Virg.* p. 176, in Colin Lindsay, *The Evidence for the Papacy*, (London: Longmans, 1870), 23.

"God is one, and Christ is one, and the Church is one, and the Chair one, founded, by the Lord's word, upon a rock, another altar and a new priesthood, besides the one altar and the one priesthood, cannot be set up." Cyprian, *Ep. xl. ad Pleb.* p. 53, in Colin Lindsay, *The Evidence for the Papacy*, (London: Longmans, 1870), 23.

Bishop Firmilian (ca. 254 A.D.):

> "Firmilian, Bishop of Caesarea, in Cappadocia, was a contemporary of St. Cyprian, and died A.D. 269. His Epistle to St. Cyprian is published with that Father's works. See Mgr. Freppel's *St. Cyprien*, p. 427 *seq.*" Charles F. B. Allnatt, ed., *Cathedra Petri—The Titles and Prerogatives of St. Peter*, (London: Burns & Oates, 1879), 6.

Firmilian "is remembered mostly for the moral support that he gave to Cyprian when the Bishop of Carthage was quarreling with Pope Stephen over the question of the Baptism of heretics" (W. A. Jurgens, *The Faith of the Early Fathers*, vol. 1, (Collegeville, MN: The Liturgical Press, 1970), 244). While disagreeing and denying the validity of baptism by heretics, Firmilian still upheld the authority of Pope Stephen:

> "But how great his ([Pope] Stephen's) error, how exceeding his blindness, who says remission of sins can be given in the synagogues of the heretics, not abiding on the foundation of the one Church, which was once first established by Christ on a Rock, may hence be understood that to Peter alone Christ said, 'Whatsoever thou shalt bind, &c.'; and again, in the Gospel, when Christ breathed on the Apostles alone, saying, 'Receive ye the Holy Ghost, &c.' The power, therefore, of forgiving sins, was given to the Apostles, and to the Churches which they, sent forth by Christ, founded, and to the bishops who, by vicarious ordination, have succeeded to them . . . And here, in this matter, I am justly indignant at this so open and manifest folly of Stephen, that he who so prides himself on the place of his episcopate, and contends that he holds the succession of Peter, upon whom the foundations of the Church were laid, introduces many other rocks . . . and sets up the new buildings of many Churches, while by his own authority he maintains that there is baptism amongst them . . . Stephen, who proclaims that

he occupies by succession the Chair of Peter, is moved with no kind of zeal against heretics." Firmilian, *Inter Ep. S. Cyp. Ep. lxxv.* p. 148, in Colin Lindsay, *The Evidence for the Papacy*, (London: Longmans, 1870), 25.

Bishop Eusebius (325 A.D.):

"Eusebius (Pamphilus), Bishop of Caesarea, and commonly called 'The Father of Ecclesiastical History,' was born between A.D. 260 and 270. He died about 340. In his *Ecclesiastical History* many valuable extracts from the works of earlier writers (since lost) are preserved. His complete works are published by Migne in six vols. (*Patr. Graec.* xix.-xxiv.). An English translation (not always perfectly accurate) of his *Ecclesiastical History* is published in Bohn's *Theological Library*." Charles F. B. Allnatt, ed., *Cathedra Petri— The Titles and Prerogatives of St. Peter*, (London: Burns & Oates, 1879), 6.

"That powerful and great one of the Apostles, who, on account of his excellence, was the leader of all the rest" (*Hist. Eccl.* lib. ii. c. 14). "The very head of the Apostles" (*Com. in Ps.* lxviii. 9, tom. v. p. 737). "Set above all the rest" *Demonstrat. Evang.* lib. iii. c. 7). "Peter, that *coryphaeus*, after having first founded the Church at Antioch, went away to Rome preaching the Gospel; and he also, after the Church in Antioch, presided over that of Rome until his death." (Eusebius, *Chron. ad Ann.* 44, tom. i. p. 539, Migne), in Charles F. B. Allnatt, ed., *Cathedra Petri—The Titles and Prerogatives of St. Peter*, (London: Burns & Oates, 1879), 49.

Juvencus (326 A.D.):

"Juvencus, a Christian poet of the fourth century, translated portions of the Scriptures into Latin verse; but only his *Book on Genesis* and *Gospel History* (4 books) are extant. Galland (tom. iv.), Migne (*Patr. Lat.* v. xix.)." Charles F. B. Allnatt, ed., *Cathedra Petri—The Titles and Prerogatives of St. Peter*, (London: Burns & Oates, 1879), 9.

"Then the Lord thus answers to Peter: 'Thou shalt be blessed.' Thou supportest the name of Peter with worthy fortitude; and upon this foundation and upon the strength of this rock I will place My edifice that shall stand for ever with everlasting walls." (Juvencus, *Hist. Evang. in Matt.* xvi. lib. iii. Galland, tom. iv. p. 618), in Charles F. B. Allnatt, ed., *Cathedra Petri—The Titles and Prerogatives of St. Peter*, (London: Burns & Oates, 1879), 18.

Aphraates the Persian Sage (ca. 336 A.D.):

"Of Aphraates, the oldest of the Fathers of the Syrian Church, there is virtually a total lack of biographical information. He was born about the year 280 A.D., and died after 345 A.D. He is invariably known as the 'Persian sage'; he was an ascetic; and probably he was a bishop, but his see is not known." W. A. Jurgens, *The Faith of the Early Fathers*, vol. 1, (Collegeville, MN: The Liturgical Press, 1970), 302.

"The earliest of the Syrian fathers of importance is Aphraates, who . . . urges his listeners to imitate Simon, '. . . the chief of the disciples . . . the Lord accepted him, set him up as the foundation, called him the rock and structure of the church." Aphraates, *Homily* 7:15, *De Paenitentibus*, ed. Parisot in *Patrologia Syriaca*, vol. 1, col. 335, in Michael M. Winter, *St. Peter and the Popes*, (Baltimore: Helicon, 1960), 58.

"And Jesus handed over the keys to Simon, and ascended and returned to Him who had sent Him." Aphraates, *Treatises* [21, 13] in W. A. Jurgens, *The Faith of the Early Fathers*, vol. 1, (Collegeville, MN: The Liturgical Press, 1970), 305.

"Aphraates gives the following references to S. Peter:

"1. 'And also Simon, who was called Cephas, because of his faith was called the firm rock,' I, 17, p. 351.
"2. 'David. . . . the chief of the kings of Israel, confessed his iniquity and was forgiven; Simon, too, the chief of the disciples. . . . when he repented. . . . our Lord received him and made him the foundation, and called him Cephas, the edifice of His Church,' VII, 15 (Dom. J. Parisot, *Patrologia Syriaca Aphraatis Demonstrationes*).

"3. 'He chose and instructed excellent leaders, and committed the sheep into their hands and gave them authority over all His flock. For He said to Simon Cephas, "Feed My sheep and My lambs and My ewes." So Simon fed His sheep, and he fulfilled his time and handed over the flock to you and departed' (x, 4).

"4. 'Jesus the son of Nun set up stones for a testimony in Israel; and Jesus our Saviour called Simon the firm Stone, and set him up as a faithful witness among the nations' (xi, 12). (Parisot.)

"5. 'Moses brought out water from the rock for his people, and Jesus sent Simon Cephas (the rock) to carry His doctrine among the peoples' (xxi, 10).

"6. 'David handed over the kingdom to Solomon, and was gathered to his people; and Jesus handed over the keys to Simon, and ascended and returned to Him who sent Him' (xxi, 13).

"7. 'Simon Cephas the foundation of the Church. . . . James and John firm pillars of the Church (xxiii).'" Aphraates, in S. Herbert Scott, *The Eastern Churches and the Papacy*, (London: Sheed & Ward, 1928), 60.

St. James of Nisibis (340 A.D.):

"James of Nisibis (St.), Bishop of Nisibis, in Mesopotamia, was illustrious in the annals of the Church of Syria, which venerated him as one of her greatest doctors. He was present at the Council of Nice, A.D. 325. His sermons, which were commended by St. Athanasius (*Epist. Encly. ad Episc. Egypt. et Lyb.*), and of which Gennadius gives the titles, were published entire at Rome in 1766, with a Latin translation from the Armenian, by Nicholas Antonelli." Charles F. B. Allnatt, ed., *Cathedra Petri—The Titles and Prerogatives of St. Peter*, (London: Burns & Oates, 1879), 9.

"Simon, who was called a rock, was deservedly called a rock because of his faith." (James of Nisibis, *Serm. i. de Fide*, n. i. 13, Galland, tom. v. p. 9), in Charles F. B. Allnatt, ed., *Cathedra Petri—The Titles and Prerogatives of St. Peter*, (London: Burns & Oates, 1879), 18.

"And Simon, the Head of the Apostles, he who denied Christ, saying 'I saw Him not,' and cursed and swore that he knew him not, as soon as he offered to God contrition and penitence, and washed his sins in the tears of his grief, our Lord received him , and made him the Foundation, and called him the Rock of the edifice of the Church." James of Nisibis, *Orat. vii. De Paenit. no. 6, p. lvii. Galland. t.v. p. lxxxiv.*, in Colin Lindsay, *The Evidence for the Papacy*, (London: Longmans, 1870), 27.

St. Ephraem the Syrian (ca. 350-370 A.D.):

"Ephraem Syrus (St.), deacon or priest of the Church of Edessa, was born about A.D. 306, at Nisibis, in Mesopotamia, and died after A.D. 379. His extant works, in Syriac and Greek (latter probably translated in his time), fill six vols. folio, and were edited by J. Assemani, at Rome, in 1732 and 1747. A Greek edition was published at Oxford in 1709 by Mr. Edward Thwaites; a Latin translation of all his works (Syriac and Greek) at Venice, in 1775." Charles F. B. Allnatt, ed., *Cathedra Petri—The Titles and Prerogatives of St. Peter*, (London: Burns & Oates, 1879), 6.

"Simon my follower, I have made you the foundation of the holy Church [Matt. 16:18]. I betimes called you Peter, because you will support all its buildings. You are the inspector of those who will build on earth a Church for Me. If they should wish to build what is false, you, the foundation, will condemn them. You are the head of the fountain from which My teaching flows, you are the chief of My disciples. Through you I will give drink to all peoples. Yours is the life-giving sweetness which I dispense. I have chosen you to be, as it were, the first-born in My institution, and so that, as the heir, you may be executor of My treasures. I have given you the keys of My kingdom. Behold, I have given you authority over all my treasures!" (Ephraem, *Homilies* 4:1), in W. A. Jurgens, *The Faith of the Early Fathers*, vol. 1, (Collegeville, MN: The Liturgical Press, 1970), 311.

"To whom, O Lord, didst Thou entrust that most precious pledge of the heavenly keys? To Bar Jonas, the Prince of the Apostles, with whom, I implore thee, may I share thy bridal chamber; and thee, most holy assembly of Apostles . . . to you also, ye Prophets, &c." (Ephraem, T. iii. *Syr. Paraen.* 33, p. 486), in Colin Lindsay, *The Evidence for the Papacy*, (London: Longmans, 1870), 31.

"Peter, who was called Cephas, he who was captured on the sea-shore, and who received a testimony from the great Pastor, that 'Upon this rock I will build by church,' by means of the priesthood received also the keys of heaven, as worthy (of them)." (Ephraem, T. iii. *Gr. De Sacerd.* p. 3), in Colin Lindsay, *The Evidence for the Papacy*, (London: Longmans, 1870), 31.

"Thee, O Simon Peter, will I proclaim the blessed, who holdest the keys, which the Spirit made. A great and ineffable word, that he binds and looses those in heaven, and those under the earth. . . . O thou blessed one, that obtainest the Place of the Head and of the tongue, in the body of the brethren, which (body) was enlarged out of the disciples and sons of thy Lord." (Ephraem, *Asseman. Bibl. Orient.* t. i. p. 95), in Colin Lindsay, *The Evidence for the Papacy*, (London: Longmans, 1870), 31.

"We hail thee, Peter, the Tongue of the disciples; the Voice of the heralds; the Eye of the Apostles; the Keeper of heaven; the First-born of those that bear the keys." (Ephraem, T. iii. *Gr. in SS. Apost.* p. 464), in Colin Lindsay, *The Evidence for the Papacy*, (London: Longmans, 1870), 31.

"On the words 'Thou art the Rock' Ephraem writes: 'That Rock (namely) which He set up that Satan might stumble thereon, Satan, on the other hand, wished to put this Rock in the way of the Lord, that He might stumble upon it, when Peter said "Far be it from Thee, Lord." We should not have said that Satan had devised this unless He Who knew all had made it manifest, saying, "Get thee behind Me, Satan, for thou art a stumbling-block to Me." But the Lord took this Rock and cast it behind Him that the sectaries of Satan should stumble thereon.'" S. Herbert Scott, *The Eastern Churches and the Papacy*, (London: Sheed & Ward, 1928), 62.

"In his homily 'On Our Lord' ([Ephraem,] *Post-Nicene Fathers*, xiii, p. 329) he says: 'And that our Lord might show that he received the keys from former stewards, he said to Simeon, "To thee will I give the keys of the doors." But how would He have given them to another had He not received them from another? So then the keys which He had received from Simeon the priest, He gave to another, Simeon the Apostle, that even though the people had not hearkened to the former Simeon, the people might hearken to the latter Simeon.'" S. Herbert Scott, *The Eastern Churches and the Papacy*, (London: Sheed & Ward, 1928), 62.

"And commenting on the Transfiguration he [Ephraem] speaks of Peter as 'the Second Moses.'

"'There were both the prince of the Old and the prince of the New Testament confronting one another. There the saintly Moses beheld the sanctified Simon the steward of the Father, the procurator of the Son. He who forced the sea asunder to let the people walk across the parted waves, beheld him who raised the new tabernacle and built the Church.'

"In the same sermon he speaks of him as the 'Key-bearer.'

"'If we remain here, how will those things I told thee come to pass? How will the Church be built up? How shalt thou receive the keys of the kingdom of heaven? Whom wilt thou bind? Whom wilt thou loose?' (Ephraem, *Sermo de Transfig. Dom.*, Sec. IV. *Edit. Rom. Syro-Graecolatina* Vol. II).

"And once again:

"'Hail! Peter, tongue of the disciples, voice of the preachers, eye of the apostles, guardian of heaven, first-born of those who bear the keys!' (Ephraem, *Encom. S.S. Petri et Pauli*)." S. Herbert Scott, *The Eastern Churches and the Papacy*, (London: Sheed & Ward, 1928), 62-63.

"He was the prince of the Apostles, and had received the keys, and was accounted the shepherd of the flock." (Ephraem, Tom. ii. *Syr. lvi. Adv. Haer.*), in Charles F. B. Allnatt, ed., *Cathedra Petri—The Titles and Prerogatives of St. Peter*, (London: Burns & Oates, 1879), 41.

"Our Lord chose Simon Peter and appointed him chief of the apostles, foundation of the holy Church and guardian of his establishment. He appointed him head of the apostles and commanded him to feed his flock and teach it laws for preserving the purity of its beliefs." (Ephraem, *S. Ephraemi Syri Hymni et Sermones*, ed. and trans. T. J. Lamy, I, 411-412, *Prolegomena*, LXXV), in James T. Shotwell and Louise Ropes Loomis, *The See of Peter*, (New York: Columbia University, 1991), 665-666.

"Peter the Rock shunned honour, he who was head of the Apostles." (Ephraem, *HArm.* 44, *PO* xxx, 208-9), in Robert Murray, *Symbols of Church and Kingdom: A Study in Early Syriac Tradition*,(London: Cambridge, 1975), 217.

"Blessed are you also, Simon Kepha, who hold the keys which the Spirit forged. Great is the word and ineffable, that could bind and loose above and below! Blessed the flocks he gave you! How they have multiplied since you set up the cross over the waters! Through love of it the sheep have borne all manner of virgins and saints!" (Ephraem, *HVirg.* 15, 6, CSCO 223, *Syr.* 94, p. 53) Robert Murray, *Symbols of Church and Kingdom: A Study in Early Syriac Tradition*, (London: Cambridge, 1975), 183.

"Let us consider what happened to Simon, thanks to his chastity; for [Jesus] made him the foundation of the Church and made him hold authority, made him the chief of the Apostles and gave him the keys of souls. He made him pasture his sheep. He gave him power to loose and to bind." (Ephraem, *Dialogues of (married) Continence and Virginity*), in Robert Murray, *Symbols of Church and Kingdom: A Study in Early Syriac Tradition*,(London: Cambridge, 1975.), 183-184.

St. Hilary of Poitiers (356 A.D.):

"Hilary of Poitiers (St.), was born about A.D. 320, became Bishop of Poitiers in 355, and was banished the next year by the Emperor Constantius for his zealous defence of Athanasius against Saturninus. He returned to his see in 359, and died in 366. In 1852 he was declared 'Doctor of the Universal Church' by Pope Pius IX. The best edition of his works is the *Benedictine* (Coustant, Paris, 1693), enlarged by Maffei in 1730 (2 vols. fol.), and Migne (*Patr. Lat.* vols. ix. x.)." Charles F. B. Allnatt, ed., *Cathedra Petri—The Titles and Prerogatives of St. Peter*, (London: Burns & Oates, 1879), 7.

"Blessed Simon, who after his confession of the mystery was set to be the foundation-stone of the Church, and received the keys of the kingdom." Hilary, *De Trinitate* 6:20 [360 A.D.] in Philip Schaff and Henry Wace, eds., *Nicene and Post-Nicene Fathers—Hilary of Poitiers, John of Damascus*, 2nd series, vol. 9, (Peabody, MA: Hendrickson, 1994), 105. See also Michael M. Winter, *Saint Peter and the Popes*, (Baltimore: Helicon, 1960), 56.

"Thus our one immovable foundation, our one blissful rock of faith, is the confession from Peter's mouth, 'Thou art the Son of the Living God" Hilary, *De Trinitate* 2:23 [360 A.D.] in Philip Schaff and Henry Wace, eds., *Nicene and Post-Nicene Fathers—Hilary of Poitiers, John of Damascus*, 2nd series, vol. 9, (Peabody, MA: Hendrickson, 1994), 58. See also Michael M. Winter, *Saint Peter and the Popes*, (Baltimore: Helicon, 1960), 56.

"On an occasion that the Only Begotten spoke to His disciples certain things concerning His Passion, and Peter expressed his abhorrence, as if it were unworthy of the Son of God, He took up Peter—to whom He had just before given the keys of the kingdom of heaven, upon whom He was about to build the Church, . . . against which the gates of hell should not in any way prevail, who, whatsoever he should bind or loose on earth, that should abide bound or loosed in heaven, this same Peter then, when expressing his abhorrence in such reproachful terms, He took up with, 'Get behind me, Satan, thou art an offence to Me.' For it was with Him so sacred a thing to suffer for the salvation of the human race, as thus to designate with the reproachful name Satan, Peter, the first Confessor of the Son of God, the Foundation of the Church, the Door-keeper of the heavenly kingdom, and in his judgment on earth a Judge of heaven." Hilary, *Tract in Ps. cxxxi.* n. 4, p. 447, in Colin Lindsay, *The Evidence for the Papacy*, (London: Longmans, 1870), 27.

"And in sooth [truth] Peter's confession obtained a worthy recompense. Blessed is he that is praised as having both remarked and seen beyond the ken of human eyes,not regarding what was of flesh and blood, but by the revelation of the heavenly Father, beholding the Son of God, and judged worthy to be the first to acknowledge what was in the Christ of God. Oh! in thy designation by a new name, happy Foundation of the Church, and a Rock worthy of the building up of that which was to scatter the infernal laws, and the gates of hell, and all the bars of death! O blessed Keeper of the gate of heaven, to whose disposal are delivered the keys of the entrance into eternity; whose judgment on earth is an authority prejudged in heaven, so that the things that are either loosed or bound on earth, acquire in heaven too a like state of settlement." Hilary, *Comm. in Matt.* c. xvi. n. 7, p. 690, 691 in Colin Lindsay, *The Evidence for the Papacy*, (London: Longmans, 1870), 27-28.

St. Zeno of Africa (362 A.D.):

"Zeno (St.), an African by birth, became eighth Bishop of Verona in A.D. 362. He died about 383. The best edition of his works is that of the brothers Ballerini (Verona, 1739), republished by Galland (tom. v.) and Migne (*Pat. Lat.* vol. xi.)." Charles F. B. Allnatt, ed., *Cathedra Petri—The Titles and Prerogatives of St. Peter*, (London: Burns & Oates, 1879), 13.

"Simon, on whom He built his Church." (Zeno, *Tract. xiii. de Circumcis.* 8, Galland, v. p. 127), in Charles F. B. Allnatt, ed., *Cathedra Petri—The Titles and Prerogatives of St. Peter*, (London: Burns & Oates, 1879), 19.

St. Cyril of Jerusalem (ca. 363 A.D.):

"Cyril of Jerusalem (St.), was born in Jerusalem about A.D. 315. He succeeded Maximus as Bishop of Jerusalem, A.D. 350. His eighteen *Catechetical Lectures*, addressed to Catechumens, and five *Mystagogical Lectures*, addressed to the newly baptized, were composed about A.D. 347, while he was still a priest. See *Dict. of Christ. Biog. and Literat.* vol. i. p. 762. The best editions of his works are those of Milles

(Oxford, 1703), and the *Benedictine* (Paris, 1720, and Venice, 1761), republished by Migne (*Patrol. Graec.* vol. xxxiii.).” Charles F. B. Allnatt, ed., *Cathedra Petri—The Titles and Prerogatives of St. Peter*, (London: Burns & Oates, 1879), 5.

“Our Lord Jesus Christ then became man, but by the many He was not known. But wishing to teach that which was not known, having assembled the disciples, He asked, ‘Whom do men say that I the Son of Man am?’ . . . . And all being silent (for it was beyond man to learn) Peter, the Foremost of the Apostles, and Chief Herald of the Church, not using language of his own finding, nor persuaded by human reasoning, but having his mind enlightened from the Father, says to Him, ‘Thou art the Christ,’ not simply that, but, ‘the Son of the living God.’ And a blessing follows the speech . . . . ‘Blessed art thou, &c.’” Cyril, *Catech.* xi. n. 3, p. 150, in Colin Lindsay, *The Evidence for the Papacy*, (London: Longmans, 1870), 29.

“For Peter was there, who carrieth the keys of heaven:” Cyril, *Catechetical Lectures* 6:15 [A.D. 350], in Philip Schaff and Henry Wace, eds., *Nicene and Post-Nicene Fathers—Cyril of Jerusalem, Gregory Nazianzen*, 2nd series, vol. 7, (Peabody, MA: Hendrickson, 1994), 38.

“He said to Peter, ‘And upon this Rock I will build my Church, and the gates of hell shall not prevail against it.” Cyril, *Catechetical Lectures* 18:25 [A.D. 350], in Philip Schaff and Henry Wace, eds., *Nicene and Post-Nicene Fathers—Cyril of Jerusalem, Gregory Nazianzen*, 2nd series, vol. 7, (Peabody, MA: Hendrickson, 1994), 140.

St. Optatus, of Milevis (ca. 370 A.D.):

“Optatus (St.), Bishop of Milevis in Africa, wrote his treatise *De Schism. Donat. cont. Parmenian.* about the year 370, and lived to see the accession of Pope Siricius (whose name he added to the list of Popes in lib. ii. c. 3) in 384. St. Jerome speaks of the treatise as containing six books (*De Vir. Illust.* c. 121); but the most ancient [manuscript] and editions contain a seventh, which was originally, it is supposed, regarded as an appendix, or added by the author when he revised his work (Dupin, *Praef. ad Op.* Sec. 2; Fessler, *Inst. Patr.* vol. ii. Sec. 255). St. Augustine (*De Doct. Christ.* ii. 40; *Cont. Epist. Parmenian*, lib. i. c. 3) reckons Optatus amongst the most renowned writers of the Church. The earlier editions of his treatise were very inaccurate, according to Dupin, who, after collating many [manuscripts], published his highly esteemed edition at Paris (in 1700), Amstelod (1701), and Antwerp (1702). This edition has been republished with select notes by Oberther (Wincel. 1790, 2 vols.), Galland (tom. v.), Migne (*P. Lat.* v. xi.), Hurter (*Patr. Opusc.* vol. x. 1870)." Charles F. B. Allnatt, ed., *Cathedra Petri—The Titles and Prerogatives of St. Peter*, (London: Burns & Oates, 1879), 10-11.

"Blessed Peter, to whom after his denial, it were enough if he obtained pardon, merited both to be preferred before all the Apostles, and he alone received of the kingdom of heaven the keys to be communicated to the others. . . . The Head of the Apostles could so have governed himself as not to incur a crime of which he would have to repent." Optatus, *De Schism. Don. l. vii. n. 3, Galland. t. v.* p. 501, in Colin Lindsay, *The Evidence for the Papacy*, (London: Longmans, 1870), 30.

St. Gregory of Nazianzen (370 A.D.):

"Gregory of Nazianzen (St.), a renowned champion of the Catholic faith against the Arians, was born about A.D. 329. He became Metropolitan of Caesarea about A.D. 370, and Bishop of Constantinople in 380, but soon resigned that see and retired to his native country, where he died A.D. 389. The best edition of his works is that of the Benedictines and A. B. Caillau (2 vols. fol. Paris, 1778-1849), republished by Migne (*Patr. Graec.* vols. xxxv.-xxxviii.)." Charles F. B. Allnatt, ed., *Cathedra Petri—The Titles and Prerogatives of St. Peter*, (London: Burns & Oates, 1879), 6.

"Seest thou that of the disciples of Christ, all of whom were great and deserving of the choice, one is called a Rock and is entrusted with the Foundations of the Church; whilst another is the best beloved, and reposes on the breast of Jesus; and the rest bear with the Prior Honour (thus bestowed)." Gregory Nazianzen, *T. i. or.* xxxii. n. 18, p. 591, in Colin Lindsay, *The Evidence for the Papacy*, (London: Longmans, 1870), 33.

"Peter, the Chief of the disciples, but he was a Rock, not as a fisherman, but because full of zeal." Gregory Nazianzen, *T. ii.* p. 790, in Colin Lindsay, *The Evidence for the Papacy*, (London: Longmans, 1870), 33.

"That unbroken rock, who had the key." (Gregory Nazianzen, *Sect. ii. Poem. Moral.* tom. ii. p. 325), in Charles F. B. Allnatt, ed., *Cathedra Petri—The Titles and Prerogatives of St. Peter*, (London: Burns & Oates, 1879), 19.

St. Gregory of Nyssa (371 A.D.):

"Gregory of Nyssa (St.), was the younger brother of Basil the Great, and became Bishop of Nyssa, in Cappadocia, A.D. 371; but was deposed and banished by the Arians in 375. He acted a prominent part at the General Council of Constantinople, A.D. 381, and died A.D. 395. The best edition of his works is that of Morell, republished by Migne (*Patr. Graec.* vols. xliv.-xlvi.)." Charles F. B. Allnatt, ed., *Cathedra Petri—The Titles and Prerogatives of St. Peter*, (London: Burns & Oates, 1879), 6-7.

"Peter, with his whole soul, associates himself with the Lamb; and, by means of the change of his name, he is changed by the Lord into something more divine; instead of Simon being both called and having become a Rock (Peter) . . . . The great Peter did not by advancing by little and little attain unto this grace, but at once he listened to his brother, believed in the Lamb, and was through faith perfected, and, having cleaved to the Rock, became Peter (a Rock)." Gregory Nyssa, *T. i. Hom. xv. in C. Cantic.* p. 691, in Colin Lindsay, *The Evidence for the Papacy*, (London: Longmans, 1870), 32.

"The memory of Peter, the Head of the Apostles, is celebrated; and magnified indeed with him are the other members of the Church; but (upon him) is the Church of God firmly established. For he is, agreeably to the gift conferred upon him by the Lord, that unbroken and most firm Rock upon which the Lord built His Church." Gregory Nyssa, *Alt. Or. De S. Steph.* Galland. t. vi. p. 600, in Colin Lindsay, *The Evidence for the Papacy*, (London: Longmans, 1870), 32.

St. Basil the Great, Bishop of Caesarea (371 A.D.):

"Basil the Great (St.), Bishop of Caesarea, in Cappadocia, was born A.D. 329, and died A.D. 379. See account of his life and writings in *Dict. of Christ. Biog.* vol. i. pp. 283-297. The best edition of his works is the *Benedictine*, by Julian Garnier (Paris, 1721-30, 3 vols. fol.); republished by Gaume (Paris, 1839, 3 vols.), and Migne (*Patr. Graec.* vols. xxix-xxxii.)." Charles F. B. Allnatt, ed., *Cathedra Petri— The Titles and Prerogatives of St. Peter*, (London: Burns & Oates, 1879), 3.

"The house of God, which is the Church of the living God, the foundations of which are on the holy mountains, for it is built upon the foundation of Apostles and Prophets. One also of these mountains was Peter, upon which Rock the Lord promised to build His Church." (Basil, T. i. *Comment. in Esai.* c. ii. n. 66, p. 427), in Colin Lindsay, *The Evidence for the Papacy*, (London: Longmans, 1870), 34-35.

"Who [referring to Peter], on account of the pre-eminence of his faith, received on himself the building of the Church. (Basil, *Adversus Eunomius* 2:4, Migne, *Patr. Graec.* vol. 29 col. 577), in Michael M. Winter, *Saint Peter and the Popes*, (Baltimore: Helicon, 1960), 55.

"And when he, the instrument of such and so great a judgment; he the minister of the so great wrath of God upon a sinner; that blessed Peter, who was preferred before all the disciples; who alone received a greater testimony and blessing than the rest; he to whom were entrusted the keys of the kingdom of heaven, &c." (Basil, T. ii. p. 1. *Procem. de Judic. Dei*, n. 7, p. 221), in Colin Lindsay, *The Evidence for the Papacy*, (London: Longmans, 1870), 35.

"Truly indeed and by highest right are sublime and elevated souls, souls which raise themselves above earthly things, called 'mountains.' The soul of the blessed Peter was called a lofty rock because he had a strong mooring in the faith and bore constantly and bravely the blows inflicted by temptations. All, therefore, who have acquired an understanding of the godhead—on account of the breadth of mind and of those actions which proceed from it—are the peaks of mountains, and upon them the house of God is built." (Basil, *Sermon 1 de Fide* I.13.), J. Waterworth, *A Commentary By Writers Of The First Five Centuries On The Place Of St. Peter In The New Testament And That Of St. Peter's Successors In The Church,* (London: Thomas Richardson, 1871), 39-40.

Pacian (372 A.D.):

"Pacian (St.), was Bishop of Barcelona from A.D. 370 to 391. His works are in Galland (tom. v.), and Migne (*Patr. Lat.* vol. xi.)." Charles F. B. Allnatt, ed., *Cathedra Petri— The Titles and Prerogatives of St. Peter*, (London: Burns & Oates, 1879), 11.

"The Lord spoke to one (Peter), that thus He might lay the foundation of unity from one." (Pacian, *Epist.* iii. n. II, p. 264, Galland, tom. vii.), in Charles F. B. Allnatt, ed., *Cathedra Petri—The Titles and Prerogatives of St. Peter*, (London: Burns & Oates, 1879), 20.

Ambrosiaster (ca. 380-384 A.D.):

"Ambrosiaster is the name given to a writer who was a contemporary of St. Ambrose and of Pope Damasus, and whose *Commentary on the Thirteen Epistles of St. Paul* was formerly attributed to St. Ambrose, and printed with his works." Charles F. B. Allnatt, ed., *Cathedra Petri—The Titles and Prerogatives of St. Peter*, (London: Burns & Oates, 1879), 2.

"The Lord said to Peter: 'On this rock I will build my church'; that is, in this confession of catholic faith I will consolidate the faithful for life." (Ambrosiaster, *Comm. on*

Ephesians, Migne *Patr. Lat.* vol. 17, col. 380), in Michael M. Winter, *Saint Peter and the Popes*, (Baltimore: Helicon, 1960), 62.

"The first Apostle, to whom the Lord gave the keys of the kingdom of heaven." (Ambrosiaster, *Com. in Ep. ad Galat.* ii. II, Ap. Op. St. Ambros.), in Charles F. B. Allnatt, ed., *Cathedra Petri—The Titles and Prerogatives of St. Peter*, (London: Burns & Oates, 1879), 33.

Pope Damasus (382 A.D.):

"Damasus (St. and Pope), succeeded Liberius A.D. 366, after violent opposition, leading to bloodshed, on the part of the Arian faction and the ante-Pope Ursicinus. 'Damasus,' says a Protestant writer, 'used his success well, and the chair of Peter . . . was never more respected nor more vigorous than during his bishopric. He appears as a principal defender of orthodoxy against Arian and other heretics' (*Dict. of Chris. Biog.* vol. i. p. 783). 'His correspondence with Jerome, his attached friend and secretary, begins A.D. 376, and closes only with his death, A.D. 384.'" Charles F. B. Allnatt, ed., *Cathedra Petri—The Titles and Prerogatives of St. Peter*, (London: Burns & Oates, 1879), 5-6.

"[3] Likewise it is decreed: . . . we have considered that it ought to be announced that although all the Catholic Churches spread abroad through the world comprise but one bridal chamber of Christ, nevertheless, the holy Roman Church has been placed at the forefront not by the conciliar decisions of other Churches, but has received the primacy by the evangelic voice of our Lord and Savior, who says: 'You are Peter, and upon this rock I will build My Church, and the gates of hell will not prevail against it; and I will give to you the keys of the kingdom of heaven, and whatever you shall have bound on earth will be bound in heaven, and whatever you shall have loosed on earth shall be loosed in heaven' [Matt. 16:18-19]. . . .

"The first see, therefore, is that of Peter the Apostle, that of the Roman Church, which has neither stain nor blemish nor anything like it." (Damasus, *The Decree of Damasus* 3 [382 A.D.]), in W. A. Jurgens, *The Faith of the*

Early Fathers, vol. 1, (Collegeville, MN: The Liturgical Press, 1970), 406.

Pope St. Siricius (ca. 384-386 A.D.):

"Siricius (St. and Pope), succeeded Damasus in A.D. 384, and died in 389. *Epistles* in Galland (tom. vii.), after Coustant." Charles F. B. Allnatt, ed., *Cathedra Petri—The Titles and Prerogatives of St. Peter*, (London: Burns & Oates, 1879), 12.

"[To Himerius, Bishop of Tarragona in Spain] Taking into account my office, it is not for me to choose,—on whom it is incumbent that there should be a zeal for the Christian religion greater than that of all other persons,—to dissemble, and remain silent. I bear the burdens of all who are heavily laden; yea, rather in me that burden is borne by the blessed Apostle Peter, who we trust, in all things, protects, and has regard to us who are the heirs of his Government.

"Let it suffice that faults have hitherto been committed in this matter; and now let the above-named rule be observed by all priests (Bishops) who do not wish to be rent from that solid Apostolic Rock upon which Christ constructed the Universal Church." (Siricius, *Ep. i. Ad Himer Tarrac.* n. i. 2. *Galland* t. vii. p. 533, 4), in Colin Lindsay, *The Evidence for the Papacy*, (London: Longmans, 1870), 227-228.

Didymus the Blind (385 A.D.):

"Didymus, born at Alexandria about the year 313 A.D., was blind from about the age of four. Yet he became one of the most learned men and one of the most prolific authors of his age. Under St. Athanasius, Didymus was made head of the catechetical school at Alexandria and was in fact its last head. At his death the school removed to Side, and shortly closed. Among Didymus' more famous students were Jerome and Rufinus." W. A. Jurgens, *The Faith of the Early Fathers*, vol. 2, (Collegeville, MN: The Liturgical Press, 1970), 60.

"In his [Didymus's] treatise on the Trinity he identifies Peter as the rock spoken of in Matthew 16, and extends the notion to his controlling thereby the entry into the church."

(Didymus, *De Trinitate*, 1:30, Migne, *Patr. Graec.*, vol. 39, col. 416), in Michael M. Winter, *Saint Peter and the Popes*, (Baltimore: Helicon, 1960), 57.

"How powerful is Peter's faith and his confession that Christ is the only-begotten God, the word, the true Son of God, and not merely a creature. Though he saw God on earth clothed in flesh and blood, Peter did not doubt, for he was willing to receive what 'flesh and blood have not revealed to you.' ... Upon this rock the Church was built, the Church which the gates of hell—that is, the arguments of heretics—will not overcome. The keys to the kingdom of heaven were given to Peter in order that, 'baptizing them in the name of the Father, and Son, and the Holy Spirit,' he might open the gates of God's kingdom to those whose faith agreed both with his own confession and with those things which he and the other apostles heard from Christ. To those, however, who do not, by like confession, offer a hymn of praise, Peter shuts the most blessed and hoped for entrance." (Didymus, *De Trinitate Liber Primus* I.30), in Migne, *Patr. Graec.*, vol. 39, col. 416, trans. John Collorafi.

St. Epiphanius (ca. 385 A.D.):

"Epiphanius (St.), Archbishop of Salamis, in the island of Cyprus, was born about A.D. 310, in Palestine, and died A.D. 403. His great work, entitled *Panarion*, or, *Box of Antidotes against all Heresies*, appeared in 374. The best editions of his complete works are those of Petavius (2 vols. fol. Colon. 1622); Dindorf (5 vols. 8vo, Lipsiae, 1859-63); Migne (*Patrol. Graec.* vols. xli. xlii.)." Charles F. B. Allnatt, ed., *Cathedra Petri—The Titles and Prerogatives of St. Peter*, (London: Burns & Oates, 1879), 6.

". . . And the blessed Peter, who for awhile denied the Lord, Peter who was the Chiefest of the Apostles, he who became unto us truly a firm Rock upon which is based the Lord's faith, upon which (Rock) the Church is in every way built; first, in that he confessed that Christ was the Son of the living God, and heard that upon this Rock of firm faith I will build my Church . . . . Further, he then also became a firm rock of the building, and Foundation of the house of

God, in that having denied Christ, and being again converted, being both found of the Lord and found worthy to hear, 'Feed my sheep and feed my lambs.'" Epiphanius, *Adv. Haeres.* p. 500, in Colin Lindsay, *The Evidence for the Papacy*, (London: Longmans, 1870), 35-36.

"Holy men are therefore called the temple of God, because the Holy Spirit dwells in them; as that Chief of the Apostles testifies, he that was found worthy to be blessed by the Lord, because the 'Father had revealed unto him.' To him then did the Father reveal His true Son, and he is blessed; and the same (Peter) furthermore reveals the Holy Ghost. This was befitting in that First of the Apostles, that firm Rock upon which the Church of God is built, and 'the gates of hell shall not prevail against it.' 'The gates of hell' are heretics and heresiarchs. For in every way was the faith confirmed in him who received the keys of heaven; who looses on earth and binds in heaven. For in him are found all subtle questions of faith . . . . He was aided by the Father, so as to be (or, lay) the Foundation of the security (firmness) of the faith . . . . He heard from that same God, Peter, 'feed My lambs;' to him was entrusted the flock; he leads the way admirably in the power of his own Master." Epiphanius, *T. ii. in Anchor.* n. 9, p. 14, 15 in Colin Lindsay, *The Evidence for the Papacy*, (London: Longmans, 1870), 36.

St. Ambrose (ca. 385-389 A.D.):

"Ambrose (St.), Archbishop of Milan from A.D. 374 to 397, was born about the year 335, and died in 397. See account of his life and writings in *Dict. of Christ. Biog. and Literat.* vol. i. pp. 91-99. The best edition of his works is the *Benedictine* (Paris, 1686 and 1690), republished by Migne, Paris, in 4 vols. (*Patrolog. Lat.* vols. xiv.-xvii.).)" Charles F. B. Allnatt, ed., *Cathedra Petri—The Titles and Prerogatives of St. Peter*, (London: Burns & Oates, 1879), 2.

"It is that same Peter to whom He said, 'Thou art Peter, and upon this rock I will build my Church.' Therefore where Peter is, there is the Church; where the Church is, there death is not, but life eternal; and therefore it was added, and 'the gates of hell shall not prevail against it,' and, 'I will give to thee the keys of the kingdom of heaven.' Blessed Peter, against whom the gates of hell prevailed not, nor were the gates of heaven closed against him; but who, on the contrary, destroyed the porches of hell and opened the heavenly places." Ambrose, *T. i. In Ps. xl.* n. 30, p. 879, 880 in Colin Lindsay, *The Evidence for the Papacy*, (London: Longmans, 1870), 37.

"Further, that thou mayest know that, as man, He prays; as God, He commands; thou hast in the Gospel that He said to Peter, 'I have prayed for thee that thy faith fail not.' But to that same Peter when He said on an earlier occasion, "Thou art the Christ, the Son of the living God, He answered, 'Thou art Peter, and upon this Rock I will build my Church, and I will give unto thee the keys of the kingdom of heaven.' How could he not confirm his faith, unto whom of His own authority He gave the kingdom, and whom when He styles a Rock, He pointed out the Foundation of the Church?" Ambrose, *T. ii. l. iv. De Fide*, c. v. n. 56, p. 531, in Colin Lindsay, *The Evidence for the Papacy*, (London: Longmans, 1870), 38.

"Peter is called the 'rock' because, like an immovable rock, he sustains the joints and mass of the entire Christian edifice." Ambrose, *Sermon 4*, in *The Great Commentary of Cornelius Lapide*, II, Catholic Standard Library, trans. Thomas Mossman, (John Hodges & Co., 1887), 220, in Michael Malone, ed., *The Apostolic Digest*, (Irving, TX: Sacred Heart, 1987), 248.

"Christ is the Rock, 'For they drank of that spiritual Rock that followed them, and that Rock was Christ,' and He did not refuse to bestow the favour of this title even upon His disciple, so that he, too, might be Peter [or Rock], in that he has from the Rock a solid constancy, a firm faith." (Ambrose, *Expos. in Luc.* Ib. l. vi. n. 97, pp. 1406-7), in Colin Lindsay, *The Evidence for the Papacy*, (London: Longmans, 1870), 37.

St. Asterius, Bishop of Amasea in Pontus (387 A.D.):

"Asterius (St.), Bishop of Amasea, in Pontus, was a contemporary of St. Chrysostom, and wrote about A.D. 387. His works were published by F. Combefis, in his *Auctuarium* to the *Bibl. Patrum* (Paris, 1648), and a more complete edition by Migne (*Patr. Graec.* vol. xl.)." Charles F. B. Allnatt, ed., *Cathedra Petri—The Titles and Prerogatives of St. Peter*, (London: Burns & Oates, 1879), 2.

"The Only-begotten denominates Peter the foundation of the Church. . . . 'Other foundation no man can lay but that which is laid, which is Jesus Christ.' But with a like appellation (to His own) did He adorn also that first disciple of His, denominating him a rock of the faith. Through Peter, therefore, . . . the stability of the Church is preserved incapable of fall and unswerving. . . . Peter is called the rock of faith, and the foundation and substructure of the Church of God." (Asterius, *Homily* 8 in *SS. Pet. et Paul.* tom. ii. p. 127, *seq.* Combefis. Paris, 1648; Migne, *Patr. Graec.* tom. xl. pp. 268, 280), in Charles F. B. Allnatt, ed., *Cathedra Petri—The Titles and Prerogatives of St. Peter*, (London: Burns & Oates, 1879), 21-22.

"Peter went not away unrequited and unrewarded; but, declared 'Blessed' by the truly blessed, he is called the rock of faith, and the foundation and substructure of the Church of God. He receives, too, by promise, 'the keys of the kingdom,' and becomes the Lord of the gates thereof, so as to open them to whom he may choose, and to close them against those against whom they justly ought to be shut,—plainly against the defiled and profane, and the deniers of this confession, through which, as a careful guardian of the wealth of the Churches, he was appointed to preside over the entrances into the Kingdom." (Asterius, *Hom. in Apost. Pet. et Paul.* tom. ii. p. 127 *seq.*), in Charles F. B. Allnatt, ed., *Cathedra Petri—The Titles and Prerogatives of St. Peter*, (London: Burns & Oates, 1879), 32-33.

St. John Chrysostom (ca. 387 A.D.):

"Chrysostom (St. John), born A.D. 347, was priest and preacher at Antioch from A.D. 381 to 398, and Bishop of Constantinople from A.D. 398 to 404. The surname of 'golden-mouthed' was given to him on account of the extraordinary brilliancy of his eloquence. See account of his life and writings in *Dict. of Christ. Biog. and Lit.* pp. 518-535. The best edition of his works is the *Benedictine*, by Montfaucon (13 vols. fol. Paris, 1718), reprinted by Gaume (Paris, 1834-39), and by Migne (16 vols. 8vo, Paris, 1863, in *Patr. Graec.* vols. xlvii.-lxiv.)." Charles F. B. Allnatt, ed., *Cathedra Petri—The Titles and Prerogatives of St. Peter*, (London: Burns & Oates, 1879), 4.

"There is nothing equal to the Church. Do not talk to me about ramparts and armaments, for they grow old with time, but the Church never grows old. . . O man, nothing is more powerful than the Church! . . . The Church is stronger than heaven, for 'Heaven and Earth shall pass away, but My words shall not pass away' [Mark 13:31]. What words? 'Thou art Peter, and upon this rock I will build My Church, and the gates of hell shall not prevail against it' [Matthew 16:18]. If you will not believe the word, believe the fact." Chrysostom, "De Capto Eutropio," no. 6, in Joseph Berington and John Kirk, rev. James Waterworth, *The Faith of Catholics*, vol. 1, (San Marino, CA: Victory Publications, 1985), 232-234, in Michael Malone, ed., *The Apostolic Digest*, (Irving, TX: Sacred Heart, 1987), 245.

"Peter himself the Head or Crown of the Apostles, the First in the Church, the Friend of Christ, who received a revelation, not from man, but from the Father, as the Lord bears witness to him, saying, 'Blessed art thou, & c.' This very Peter—and when I name Peter I name that unbroken Rock, that firm Foundation, the Great Apostle, the First of the disciples, the First called, and the First who obeyed—he was guilty of a deed not slight, but exceeding great, even denying of the Lord." (Chrysostom, *T. ii. Hom. iii. de Paenit.* n. 4, p. 300), in Colin Lindsay, *The Evidence for the Papacy*, (London: Longmans, 1870), 41.

"Peter, the Leader of the choir of the Apostles, the Mouth of the disciples, the Pillar of the Church, the Buttress (foundation) of the faith, the Foundation of the confession, the Fisherman of the universe." (Chrysostom, *T. iii. Hom. de Dec. Mill. Talent.* n. 3, p. 4, 5), in Colin Lindsay, *The Evidence for the Papacy*, (London: Longmans, 1870), 41.

"Peter, that Leader of the choir, that Mouth of the rest of the Apostles, that Head of the brotherhood, that One set over the entire universe, that Foundation of the Church." (Chrysostom, *In illud, hoc Scitote*, n. 4, p. 282), in Colin Lindsay, *The Evidence for the Papacy*, (London: Longmans, 1870), 41.

"Chrysostom, for instance, is fond of passages like these: 'Peter, that head of the Apostles, the first in the Church, the friend of Christ, who received the revelation not from man but from the Father . . . this Peter, and when I say Peter, I mean the unbroken Rock, the unshaken foundation, the great Apostle, the first of the disciples, the first called, the first to obey'; 'Peter, the coryphaeus of the choir of the Apostles, the mouth of the disciples, the foundation of the Faith, the base of the confession, the fisherman of the world'; 'the first of the Apostles, the foundation of the Church, the coryphaeus of the choir of the Apostles'; 'the foundation of the Church, the vehement lover of Christ . . . he who ran throughout the world, who fished the whole world'; 'this holy coryphaeus of the blessed choir, the lover of Christ, the ardent disciple, who was entrusted with the keys of heaven, who received the spiritual revelation'; 'Peter, the coryphaeus of the choir, the mouth of all the Apostles, the head of that company, the ruler of the whole world, the foundation of the Church, the fervent lover of Christ.' These passages are from Chrysostom, *De Eleemos*, iii. 4; *Hom. de decem mille tal.* 3; *ad eos qui scandal. sunt* 17; *in illud. Vidi Dmn.* iv. 3; *In Act. App.* vi. I; *in illud. Scitote quod in noviss. dieb.* 4." Dom John Chapman, *Bishop Gore and Catholic Claims* (London: Longmans, Green, and Co., 1905), 48.

St. Jerome (ca. 393-398 A.D.):

"Jerome (St.), a profound Biblical scholar, and the author of the translation of the whole Bible known as the *Latin*

Vulgate, was born at Stridon, in Dalmatia, about A.D. 340. His youth was passed at Rome, where he studied almost every branch of learning, especially rhetoric, Hebrew, and theology. After leading for four years a solitary life in the deserts of Syria, he went to Antioch, and was ordained priest, A.D. 377. In 381 he went to Constantinople, and from thence passed to Rome, where he became the friend and secretary of Pope Damasus. After the death of Damasus, Jerome quitted Rome (385) and retired to the Holy Land, where he superintended several monasteries, until his death at Bethlehem in 420. Besides his translation of the Scriptures (of which, according to Hain, in his *Repertorium Biliographicum*, ninety-eight distinct editions were printed between the year 1460 and the close of the fifteenth century), his entire works were published by Erasmus (Basil, ap. Froben, 1516 *et seq.*, in 9 vols. fol.), and at Rome (9 vols. fol.) in 1565. The Benedictine edition (Pouget and Martianay) appeared in 1693-1706, in 5 vols. fol. The best edition was that of Vallarsius (Verona, 1734, 12 vols. fol.). Migne's edition is reprinted from the two last named, in 9 vols. roy. 8vo (*Patr. Lat.* vols. xxii.-xxx.)." Charles F. B. Allnatt, ed., *Cathedra Petri—The Titles and Prerogatives of St. Peter*, (London: Burns & Oates, 1879), 9.

"But you say, the Church was founded upon Peter: although elsewhere the same is attributed to all the Apostles, and they all receive the keys of the kingdom of heaven, and the strength of the Church depends upon them all alike, yet one among the twelve is chosen so that when a head has been appointed, there may be no occasion for schism." (Jerome, *Against Jovinianus* 1:26 [ca. 393 A.D.], in Philip Schaff and Henry Wace, eds., *Nicene and Post-Nicene Fathers— Jerome: Letters and Select Works*, 2nd series, vol. 6, (Peabody, MA: Hendrickson, 1994), 366.

"[1] Since the East, shattered as it is by the long-standing feuds, subsisting between its peoples, is bit by bit tearing into shreds the seamless vest of the Lord, 'woven from the top throughout,' since the foxes are destroying the vineyard of Christ, and since among the broken cisterns that hold no water it is hard to discover 'the sealed fountain' and 'the garden inclosed,' I think it my duty to consult the chair of Peter, and to turn to a church whose faith has been praised by Paul. I appeal for spiritual food to the church whence I have received the garb of Christ. The wide space of sea and land that lies between us cannot deter me from searching for 'the pearl of great price.' 'Wheresoever the body is, there will the eagles be gathered together.'

"[2] . . . My words are spoken to the successor of the fisherman, to the disciple of the cross. As I follow no leader save Christ, so I communicate with none but your blessedness, that is with the chair of Peter. For this, I know, is the rock on which the church is built! This is the house where alone the paschal lamb can be rightly eaten. This is the ark of Noah, and he who is not found in it shall perish when the flood prevails." (Jerome, *Letters* 15 [ca. 375 A.D.]), in Philip Schaff and Henry Wace, eds., *Nicene and Post-Nicene Fathers—Jerome: Letters and Select Works*, 2nd series, vol. 6, (Peabody, MA: Hendrickson, 1994), 18.

"'Thou art Peter, and upon this rock I will build my Church.' As He bestowed light on His Apostles, so that they were to be called 'the light of the world,' and as they obtained other titles from the Lord, so also to Simon, who believed on the Rock Christ, was given the name Peter (Rock). And in accordance with the metaphor of a rock, it is justly said to him, 'I will build my Church upon thee.'" [385-398 A.D.] (Jerome, Ib. l. iii. *Comm. in Matt.*, *Patr. Lat.* i. col. 74), in Colin Lindsay, *The Evidence for the Papacy*, (London: Longmans, 1870), 40.

"As Christ himself gave light to the apostles, that they might be called the light of the world, and as they obtained other names also from the Lord, so to Simon also, who believed in the rock Christ, He bestowed the name Peter; and according to the metaphor of a rock, it is rightly said of him 'I will build my church upon thee.'" Jerome, *Comm. on Matthew III*, 16, 18, Migne, *Patr. Lat.*, vol. 26, col. 117), in Michael M. Winter, *Saint Peter and the Popes*, (Baltimore: Helicon, 1960), 63.

"[2] If, then, the apostle Peter, upon whom the Lord has founded the Church, has expressly said that the prophecy and promise of the Lord were then and there fulfilled [in Acts 2:14-18], how can we claim another fulfillment for ourselves?" (Jerome, *Letters* 16 [385 A.D.]), in Philip Schaff and Henry Wace, eds., *Nicene and Post-Nicene Fathers— Jerome: Letters and Select Works*, 2nd series, vol. 6, (Peabody, MA: Hendrickson, 1994), 55.

"Christ is not alone in being the rock [see Christ as Rock in I Cor. 10:4], for He granted to the apostle Peter that he should be called 'Rock.'" Jerome, *Comm. on Jeremias* 3:65, *Corpus Scriptorum Ecclesiasticorum Latinorum* (Vienna), vol. 59, 202 [415 A.D.], in Michael M. Winter, *Saint Peter and the Popes*, (Baltimore: Helicon, 1960), 63.

"[C] What has Paul to do with Aristotle? Or Peter with Plato? For as the latter [Plato] was the prince of philosophers, so was the former [Peter] chief of the Apostles: on him the Lord's Church was firmly founded, and neither rushing flood nor storm can shake it." Jerome, *Against the Pelagians* 1:14a [417 A.D.], in Philip Schaff and Henry Wace, eds., *Nicene and Post-Nicene Fathers—Jerome: Letters and Select Works*, 2nd series, vol. 6, (Peabody, MA: Hendrickson, 1994), 455.

St. Augustine (ca. 400 A.D.):

"Augustine (St.), the great Bishop of Hippo, in Africa, was born A.D. 354, and died A.D. 430. The best edition of his voluminous writings is the *Benedictine* (11 vols. fol. Paris, 1679-1700), republished by Leclerc (Antwerp, 1700-3, 12 vols. fol.), by Guame (Paris, 1836-39, 22 vols. roy. 8vo), Antonelli (Venice, 1858-60, 14 vols. fol.), and Migne (Paris, 16 vols. in *Patr. Lat.* xxxii.-xlvii.). An English translation of his principal works has been published by Messrs. Clark of Edinburgh, in 16 vols. 8vo." Charles F. B. Allnatt, ed., *Cathedra Petri—The Titles and Prerogatives of St. Peter*, (London: Burns & Oates, 1879), 2.

"Amongst the Apostles almost everywhere Peter alone merited to bear the person of the Church. On account of this very person, which he alone of the whole Church bore, he merited to hear, 'To thee I will give the keys of the kingdom of heaven.' For these keys not one man, but the unity of the Church received. Hence the excellence of Peter is set forth, because he bore the figure of that very universality and unity of the Church when to him was said, ' To thee' I deliver what was delivered to all" (Augustine, Tom. v. *Serm.* ccxcv. in *Nat. App. Pet. et Paul.* n. 2) in Charles F. B. Allnatt, ed., *Cathedra Petri—The Titles and Prerogatives of St. Peter*, (London: Burns & Oates, 1879), 33.

"Peter bore the person of the Church." (Augustine, *Sermon* 149:7 Migne, *Patr. Lat.* v. 38, col. 802), in Michael M. Winter, *Saint Peter and the Popes*, (Baltimore: Helicon, 1960), 69.

"If the order of bishops succeeding to each other is to be considered, how much more securely, and really beneficially, do we reckon from Peter himself, to whom, bearing a Figure of the Church, the Lord says, 'Upon this rock I will build my Church.'" (Augustine, *T. ii. E. liii. Generos* col. 91), in Colin Lindsay, *The Evidence for the Papacy*, (London: Longmans, 1870), 45.

"Of this Church, Peter, the Apostle, on account of the Primacy of his Apostleship, bore a character which represented the whole Church. For as to what personally regards him, he was by nature but one man, by grace one Christian, by a more abundant grace, one, and that the First Apostle; but when there was said to him, 'I will give unto him the keys, &c.,' He signified the whole Church, which, in this world, is, by divers trials, as it were, by rains, rivers, and tempests, agitated, but fall not, because it was built upon a Rock, whence Peter derived his name. For a rock (*petra*) is not derived from Peter (*Petro*), but Peter from a Rock, as Christ is not derived from Christian, but Christian from Christ. For therefore does the Lord say, 'Upon this rock I will build my Church,' because Peter had said, 'Thou art the Christ, the Son of the living God.' Upon this Rock, therefore, which thou hast confessed, I will build My Church. For Christ was the Rock; upon which Foundation, even Peter himself was built. 'For other foundation can no man lay but that which is laid, which is Christ Jesus.' The Church therefore which is founded on Christ, received in Peter the keys of the kingdom of heaven from Him, that is, the power of binding and of loosing sins." (Augustine, *T. iii. Tract. cxxiv. in Joan. n. 5*, co. 599), in Colin Lindsay, *The Evidence for the Papacy*, (London: Longmans, 1870), 45-46.

"In St. Augustine the same idea occurs frequently; the keys, he says, were given to Peter as bearing the figure of the Church, and more than once he explains that it is because of his primacy that he thus represented the Church. I repeat the following references from an elaborate footnote on the subject in the *Revue Bened*, Jan., 1903, pp. 37, 38, directed against the misunderstandings of Father Puller: 'To Peter bearing the figure of the Church' (*de agone* 30; *Serm.* 149, 6; 4 18; *Retract.* i. 21; *Tract* 118 *in Joann.*). 'Almost everywhere Peter merited to bear the person of the whole Church' (*Serm.* 295 2; 75 9) etc., 'on account of the primacy which he had among the disciples' (*Enarr. in Ps.* 108 1), 'the first and chief in the order of the Apostles, in whom the Church was figured' (*Serm.* 76 3). 'To Peter first, because among the Apostles Peter is first' (*Serm.* 295 4), etc." Dom John Chapman, *Bishop Gore and Catholic Claims* (London: Longmans, Green, and Co., 1905), 50-51.

"Number the bishops from the see
   of Peter itself.
And in that order of Fathers see
   who succeeded whom.
That is the rock against which the
   gates of hell do not prevail."

(Augustine, *Psalmus contr. Partem Donati*, str. 18 [written in 393 A.D. as an acrostic hymn meant to be memorized and sung by the people as an antidote to the Donatists]), in Dom John Chapman, *Bishop Gore and Catholic Claims* (London: Longmans, Green, and Co., 1905), 51.

"Peter, who had confessed Him the Son of God, and in that confession had been called the rock upon which the Church should be built." (Augustine, *In Ps.* lxix. n. 4, tom. iv. p. 1020, ed. Bened. 1836), in Charles F. B. Allnatt, ed., *Cathedra Petri—The Titles and Prerogatives of St. Peter*, (London: Burns & Oates, 1879), 23.

"For what the Church is essentially in Christ, such representatively is Peter in the rock (*petra*); and in this representation Christ is to be understood as the Rock, Peter as the Church." (Tract. 124, ch. 19-25, Par. 5, Augustine, *Homilies on the Gospel of St. John*), in Philip Schaff, ed., *Nicene and Post-Nicene Fathers—Augustin: Homilies on the Gospel of John, Homilies on the First Epistle of John, Soliloquies*, 1st series, vol. 7, (n.p.: Christian Literature Pub. Co., 1888; repr. Peabody, MA: Hendrickson, 1994), 450.

"[In my first book against Donatus] I mentioned somewhere with reference to the apostle Peter that 'the Church is founded upon him as upon a rock.' This meaning is also sung by many lips in the lines of blessed Ambrose, where, speaking of the domestic cock, he says: 'When it crows, he, the rock of the Church, absolves from sin.' But I realize that I have since frequently explained the words of our Lord: 'Thou art Peter and upon this rock I will build my church,' to the effect that they should be understood as referring to him whom Peter confessed when he said: 'Thou art the Christ, the Son of the living God,' and as meaning that Peter, having been named after this rock, figured the person of the Church, which is built upon this rock and has received the keys of the kingdom of heaven. For what was said to him was not 'Thou art the rock,' but 'Thou art Peter.' But the rock was Christ, having confessed whom (even as the whole Church confesses) Simon was named Peter. Which of these two interpretations is the more likely to be correct, let the reader choose." (Augustine, *Retractations*, Book 1, Chapter 21, J. P. Migne, *Patr. Lat.* 32.618), in E. Giles, ed., *Documents Illustrating Papal Authority—A.D. 96-454*, (London: S.P.C.K., 1952), 177.

"St. Augustine invented a new exegesis [of Matthew 16:18-19]—that the rock is Christ. The last opinion may be at once pronounced impossible. It rests on a distinction between *Petra* and *Petrus* which could not have been made in the language which our Lord was using (St. Augustine invested this interpretation as a part of his argument against the Donatists that the validity of the sacraments does not depend on the sanctity of the minister, because Christ acts in the minister. Peter has his name from Christ, *Petrus a Petra.*); it would be hardly comprehensible unless our Lord said, '*but* upon this rock,' instead of '*and* upon this rock'; and if St. Matthew had meant us to understand him thus, he would have told us that Christ pointed to himself as He spoke. . . .

"He says in the *Retractations* that he is now inclined to think another explanation of the text more correct; but the doctrine founded on it (which is of course an infinitely more important matter) he leaves untouched. He had not ceased to believe that the Roman See, to the enumeration of whose bishops he so frequently appeals, was truly the rock upon which the Church is founded, and against which the gates of hell do not prevail. He had originally meant to emphasise in a telling way the position of that Church with which the Donatists were not in communion; and the remembrance of St. Peter the rock naturally suggested a transference (occasionally but rarely met with elsewhere among ancients and moderns) of the metaphor to Peter's see. Never does he suggest that though the metaphor might be mistaken, the fact expressed by it was doubtful." Dom John Chapman, *Bishop Gore and Catholic Claims* (London: Longmans, Green, and Co., 1905), 51-52.

"These miserable wretches, refusing to acknowledge the Rock as Peter, and to believe that the Church has received the keys to the Kingdom of Heaven, have lost these very keys from their own hands." (Augustine, *Christian Combat*, in J. P. Migne, ed., *Patrologiae Cursus Completus: Series Latina*, 40:289), in Michael Malone, ed., *The Apostolic Digest*, (Irving, TX: Sacred Heart, 1987), 246.

Victor of Antioch (405 A.D.):

> "To Simon he gave the name Peter [Rock], that the name may anticipate the event itself; because as Christ the Lord was about to build His Church on Peter—that is, on the unbroken and sound doctrine of Peter and his unshaken faith—therefore, in prophetic spirit does He call him Peter." (Victor, *In Evang. Marc.* c. 3, p. 277, *Bibl. Max. Pat.* t. v.), in Charles F. B. Allnatt, ed., *Cathedra Petri—The Titles and Prerogatives of St. Peter*, (London: Burns & Oates, 1879), 24.

Pope St. Zosimus (417 A.D.):

> "That he was a Greek, the son of Abram, is all that is known of the early life of St. Zosimus [Pope, 417-418]. His pontificate, however, though short, is important for a climax in the fight against Pelagianism. . . . Pelagianism denied original sin and the necessity of divine grace to perform meritorious acts, indeed even to win heaven itself. . . . Once Pope Zosimus was convinced . . . [of] the heretical doctrine, he spoke out strongly in a famous *Epistola tractoria* or encyclical letter which clearly and forcefully condemned Pelagius and Pelagianism. Of this epistle, worthy to be ranked with the great modern encyclicals, Prosper of Acquitaine said that it put the sword of Peter into the hands of every bishop." Joseph S. Brusher, *Popes Through the Ages*, 3rd ed., (San Rafael, CA: Neff-Kane, 1980), 82.

> "Although the tradition of the Fathers has assigned so great an Authority to the Apostolic See, that no one should dare to dispute about a Judgment given by it, and that See, by laws and regulations, has kept to this; and the discipline of the Church, in the laws which it yet follows, still pays to the name of Peter, from whom that See (or discipline) descends, the reverence due,—for canonical antiquity, by universal consent, willed that so great a Power should belong to that Apostle, a Power also derived from the actual promise of Christ our God, that it should be his to loose what was bound, and to bind what was loosed, an equal state of Power being bestowed upon those who, by His will, should be found worthy to inherit his See, for he has charge both of all the

Churches, and especially of this One wherein he sat; nor does he allow any storm to shake one particle of the Privilege, or any part of the Sentence of that See to which he has given his name as a foundation firm and not to be weakened by any violence whatever, and which no one can rashly attack but at his peril;—seeing then, that Peter is a Head of such great authority, and that he has confirmed the subsequent decrees (or statutes) of the Fathers; that, by all laws and regulations, both human and divine, the Roman Church is strengthened; and you are not ignorant, you know, dearest brethren, and as priests you are not ignorant, that we rule over his Place, and are in possession also of the Authority of his name, nevertheless, though so great be our Authority that none may refuse (or reconsider) our Sentence, we have not done anything, which we have not, of our will referred by letter to your knowledge, conceding this to the Brotherhood." (Zosimus *Ep. xi. Ad Africanos*, *Galland* T. ix. pp. 15, 16), in Colin Lindsay, *The Evidence for the Papacy*, (London: Longmans, 1870), 232-233.

Paulus Orosius, Disciple of Augustine (ca. 414-419 A.D.):

"Paulus Orosius was a priest of Bracara in Spain, and a disciple of S.S. Jerome and Augustine. Writings in Galland (tom. ix.), and Migne (vol. xxxi.)." Charles F. B. Allnatt, ed., *Cathedra Petri—The Titles and Prerogatives of St. Peter*, (London: Burns & Oates, 1879), 11.

"Paul Orosius, the Spanish priest who was a contemporary and disciple of Augustine, holds fast to the identification of Peter and the rock foundation of the church." [414 A.D.] (Orosius, *Liber Apologeticus contra Pelagianum de arbitrii libertate* 23:5, 27:3, *Corpus Scriptorum Ecclesiasticorum Latinorum* (Vienna) vol. 5 pp. 641, 747), in Michael M. Winter, *Saint Peter and the Popes*, (Baltimore: Helicon, 1960), 70.

"Peter, . . . constituted the rock of the foundation of the Church." (Orosius, *De Lib. Arbit.* n. 23, p. 165 Galland, ix.), in Charles F. B. Allnatt, ed., *Cathedra Petri—The Titles and Prerogatives of St. Peter*, (London: Burns & Oates, 1879), 24.

"Peter, upon which rock Christ built His Church." (Orosius, *De Lib. Arbit.* n. 27, p. 166, Galland, ix.), in Charles F. B. Allnatt, ed., *Cathedra Petri—The Titles and Prerogatives of St. Peter*, (London: Burns & Oates, 1879), 24.

Paulinus of Nola, Deacon of Milan (418 A.D.):

"Paulinus, deacon of Milan, wrote about the year 418. Galland. (tom. ix.)." Charles F. B. Allnatt, ed., *Cathedra Petri—The Titles and Prerogatives of St. Peter*, (London: Burns & Oates, 1879), 11.

"The same opinion [as that of Paulus Orosius] is voiced by another of Augustine's circle, Paulinus of Nola, who adopts a more comprehensive view, since he calls Peter the rock, though he is aware that the title is primarily Christ's in accordance with I Corinthians." (Paulinus, *Epis.* 23:43, *Corpus Scriptorum Ecclesiasticorum Latinorum* (Vienna), vol. 29 p. 198), in Michael M. Winter, *Saint Peter and the Popes*, (Baltimore: Helicon, 1960), 70.

Pope St. Celestine (ca. 423 A.D.):

"Celestine (St.), the forty-second Bishop of Rome, succeeded Boniface I., A.D. 422, and died in 432. This Pope sent Germanus, Bishop of Auxerre, and Lupus, Bishop of Troyes, to repress the Pelagian heresy in Britain, and SS. Palladius and Patrick to convert the Irish. Hence St. Prosper of Acquitaine said of him, that 'whilst he took pains to keep the Roman island (Britain) Catholic, he made the barbarian island (Ireland) to become Christian." (*Prosp. Adv. Collator.* 41), in Charles F. B. Allnatt, ed., *Cathedra Petri—The Titles and Prerogatives of St. Peter*, (London: Burns & Oates, 1879), 4.

"[To the Bishop of Illyricum] We in a special manner are constrained by our charge, which regards all men, we on whom Christ has, in the Person of the holy Peter the Apostle, when He gave him the keys to open and to shut, imposed as a necessity to be engaged about all men." (Celestine *Ep. iii. Ad Episc. Illyr. Galland* t. ix. p. 292), in Colin Lindsay, *The Evidence for the Papacy*, (London: Longmans, 1870), 234.

St. Maximus of Turin (424 A.D.):

"Maximus of Turin (St.), was celebrated in the fifth century as a Christian orator, and was called by Gennadius, 'Vir divinis Scripturis satis intentus, et ad docendum ex tempore plebem sufficiens' (*De Script. Eccl.* c. 40). He acted a prominent part in the Council of Milan, A.D. 451, and at the Council of Rome, A.D. 465. The best edition of his works is that of P. Brunnus (Rome, 1784), republished by Migne (*Patr. Lat.* vol. lvii.)." Charles F. B. Allnatt, ed., *Cathedra Petri— The Titles and Prerogatives of St. Peter*, (London: Burns & Oates, 1879), 10.

"On account of this confession, the blessed Apostle merited to hear from the mouth of the Lord, 'Thou art Peter, and upon this rock, &c.' That is, thou art the First to confess Me on earth, and I will make thee to have a perpetual Primacy in heaven, and in My Kingdom. And what more just than that the Church should be built on him, who gives so mighty a Foundation to the Church. What could be more religiously done, than that he should receive the 'keys of heaven,' he who revealed the Lord of the heavenly kingdom; inasmuch as he who opened to believers the gates of faith, the same would also open for them the gates of heaven." (Maximus, *Serm. lxxii. De Dict. Ev. "Vos estis sal terrae."* Galland. t. ix. p. 393), in Colin Lindsay, *The Evidence for the Papacy*, (London: Longmans, 1870), 49.

"This is Peter on whom Christ freely bestowed a sharing in his name. For just as Christ is the rock, as the Apostle Paul taught, so through Christ Peter is made a rock, when the Lord says to him: 'Thou art Peter and upon this rock I will build my church.'" (Maximus, *Homily 63, In nativitate Petri et Pauli*, Migne, *Patr. Lat.*, vol. 57, col. 394), in Michael M. Winter, *Saint Peter and the Popes*, (Baltimore: Helicon, 1960), 62. [408 A.D.].

St. Cyril of Alexandria (424 A.D.):

"Cyril of Alexandria (St.), was Archbishop of Alexandria, and the great opponent of the Nestorian heresy. He succeeded

Theophilus A.D. 412, and died A.D. 444. He presided, as Pope Celestine's Legate, over the General Council of Ephesus. The best edition of his works is that of Aubert (6 vols. Paris, 1658), republished by Migne (*Patrol. Graec.* vols. lxviii.-lxxvii.)." Charles F. B. Allnatt, ed., *Cathedra Petri—The Titles and Prerogatives of St. Peter*, (London: Burns & Oates, 1879), 5.

"He suffers him no longer to be called Simon, exercising authority and rule over him already as having become His own. But by a title suitable to the thing, He changed his name into Peter, from the word *petra* (rock); for on him He was afterwards to found His Church [commenting on John 1:42, alluding to Matthew 16:18]." (Cyril, *T. iv. Comm. in Joan.*, p. 131), in Colin Lindsay, *The Evidence for the Papacy*, (London: Longmans, 1870), 50.

"'Blessed art thou . . .,' calling, I imagine, nothing else the rock, in allusion to his name, but the immovable and stable faith of the disciple on which the Church of Christ is founded and fixed without danger of falling." (Cyril, *On the Holy Trinity* [426 A.D.]), in E. Giles, *Documents Illustrating Papal Authority A.D. 96-454*, (London: SPCK, 1952), 258.

"He [Christ] promises to found the church, assigning immovableness to it, as He is the Lord of strength, and over this he sets Peter as shepherd." (Cyril, *Comm. on Matt.*, *ad. loc.*, Migne, *Patr. Graec.*, vol. 72, col. 424), in Michael M. Winter, *Saint Peter and the Popes*, (Baltimore: Helicon, 1960), 74. [429 A.D.]

John Cassian, Monk (430 A.D.):

"Cassian, a monk of Scythia, brought up in the monastery of Bethlehem, and who afterwards became celebrated as a founder of Western monachism, was born about the year 350, and died about 440. His writings were published in *Bibl. Max. Pat.* (tom. vii.), Migne (vols. xlix., l.)." Charles F. B. Allnatt, ed., *Cathedra Petri—The Titles and Prerogatives of St. Peter*, (London: Burns & Oates, 1879), 4.

"O Peter, Prince of the Apostles, it is just that you should teach us, since you were yourself taught by the Lord; and also that you should open to us the gate of which you have received the key. Keep out all those who are undermining the heavenly House; turn away those who are trying to enter through false caverns and unlawful gates since it is certain that no one can enter in at the gate of the kingdom except the one unto whom the key, placed by you in the churches, shall open it." John Cassian, *The Seven Books of John Cassian on the Incarnation of the Lord, Against Nestorius*, 3:12, in Michael Malone, *The Apostolic Digest*, (Irving, TX: Sacred Heart, 1987), 243-244.

Council of Ephesus (431 A.D.):

"Ephesus, the (Third Ecumenical) Council of, was held A.D. 431, and presided over by St. Cyril of Alexandria (having plenary power from Pope Celestine), and the Papal Legates. About 200 Bishops were present [among whom was Philip, who spoke to the Council]." Charles F. B. Allnatt, ed., *Cathedra Petri—The Titles and Prerogatives of St. Peter*, (London: Burns & Oates, 1879), 13.

"Philip the presbyter and legate of the Apostolic See said: 'There is no doubt, and in fact it has been known in all ages, that the holy and most blessed Peter, prince and head of the Apostles, pillar of the faith, and foundation of the Catholic Church, received the keys of the kingdom from our Lord Jesus Christ, the Saviour and Redeemer of the human race, and that to him was given the power of loosing and binding sins: who down even to to-day and forever both lives and judges in his successors. The holy and most blessed Pope Coelestine, according to due order, is his successor and holds his place." (*Extracts from the Acts [of the Council of Ephesus]*, session 3, in Labbe and Cossart, *Concilia*, Tom. III, col. 621), in Philip Schaff and Henry Wace, eds., *Nicene and Post-Nicene Fathers—The Seven Ecumenical Councils*, 2nd series, vol. 14, (Peabody, MA: Hendrickson, 1994), 223.

St. Peter Chrysologus, Bishop of Ravenna (432 A.D.):

"Chrysologus (St. Peter), Archbishop of Ravenna, A.D. 433 to 454, was born at Imola about 405, and died there A.D.

454. Like Chrysostom, he obtained the name by which he was usually known by the golden brilliancy of his oratory. His extant works are published in *Bibl. Max. Pat.* (tom. vii.), and by Migne (*Patr. Lat.* vol. lii.). Numerous works of his perished by fire, partly in the siege of Imola by Theodoric in 524; partly in the conflagration of the Archbishop's library at Ravenna, A.D. 700." Charles F. B. Allnatt, ed., *Cathedra Petri—The Titles and Prerogatives of St. Peter*, (London: Burns & Oates, 1879), 4.

"Just as Peter received his name from the rock, because he was the first to deserve to establish the Church, by reason of his steadfastness of faith, so also [Pope] Stephen was named from a crown. . . . Let Peter hold his ancient primacy of the Apostolic choir. Let him open to those who enter the kingdom of heaven. Let him bind the guilty with his power and absolve the penitent in kindness." (Peter Chrysologus, *Sermon 154*, Migne, *Patr. Lat.* V52 C608), in E. Giles, *Documents Illustrating Papal Authority A.D. 96-454*, (London: SPCK, 1952), 283.

"For though to be called Peter is elsewhere merely to receive a name, in this place it is a sign of strength. Truly, blessed Peter, that immovable foundation of salvation, showed himself to be such in the priestly office as they who desire the priesthood would wish to see . . . Peter is the guardian of the faith, the rock of the Church, and the gatekeeper of heaven. He was chosen to be an apostolic fisher and with the hook of sanctity he brought to himself crowds submerged in waves of error, while by the nets of his teaching he brought from the multitude an abundance of men. Moreover, he was a most blessed and apostolic bird catcher, who reached the souls of youths flying through the air with the rod of the divine word." (Peter Chrysologus, *Sermon 107*, Migne, *Patr. Lat.*, vol. 57, col. 498), trans. John Collorafi.

St. Proclus, Patriarch of Constantinople (434 A.D.):

"Proclus (St.), a disciple of St. Chrysostom, became Patriarch of Constantinople in A.D. 434, and was a zealous opponent of Nestorianism. He died in 447. His letters and homilies were published by Riccardi (Rome, 1630), Combefis (*Auctuar.* tom. i.), Galland (tom. xix.), Migne

(*Patr. Graec.* vol. lxv.)." Charles F. B. Allnatt, ed., *Cathedra Petri—The Titles and Prerogatives of St. Peter*, (London: Burns & Oates, 1879), 11.

"Proclus shows implicitly, in his sermon on the Transfiguration, that Peter is the foundation of the Church, and his witness is all the more valuable since he was from 434 to 446 bishop of Constantinople." *Eastern Liturgy*, Migne, *Patr. Graec.*, vol. 65, col. 768; Michael M. Winter, *Saint Peter and the Popes*, (Baltimore: Helicon, 1960), 75.

St. Sechnall, or Secundinus (ca. 440 A.D.):

"[A disciple of St. Patrick, whom he assisted in the administration of the See of Armagh until his death in 448, St. Sechnall says:] he is constant in the service of God, and immoveable in the faith as Peter, upon whom the Church is built, and whose apostolate he received from God, against whose bulwark the assaults of hell cannot prevail." (*Lib. Hymn.* p. 12, Publ. of I. A. S. 1855), in Charles F. B. Allnatt, ed., *Cathedra Petri—The Titles and Prerogatives of St. Peter*, (London: Burns & Oates, 1879), 27.

Pope St. Leo (ca. 440-461 A.D.):

"Leo the Great (St. and Pope), succeeded Sixtus III, A.D. 440, and died in 461. It was this great Pontiff who, by his confidence in God and noble and courageous conduct, saved Rome from being pillaged by the Huns under 'the Scourge of God,' Attila, A.D. 452; and again, in 455, he saved the city from destruction by the awe which he inspired in the fierce Gesneric [Gaiseric], King of the Vandals. 'The Pontificate of Leo the Great,' says the Protestant Milman, 'is one of the epochs of Latin, or rather of universal Christianity. Christendom, wherever mindful of its Divine origin, and of its proper humanising and hallowing influence, might turn away in shame from the melancholy and disgraceful (religious) contests in the East. On the throne of Rome alone, of all the greater sees, did religion maintain its majesty, its sanctity, its piety; and if it demanded undue deference, the world would not be rigidly inclined to question pretensions supported as well by such conscious power as by such singular and unimpeachable virtue; and by such inestimable benefits conferred on Rome, on the empire, on civilisation' (*Hist. of Latin Christ.* book ii. ch. 4). It was this Pope who summoned, and by his Legates, presided over the General Council of Chalcedon, A.D. 451; and it was his famous Epistle to Flavian, Patriarch of Constantinople, that elicited from the assembled prelates the exclamation, 'Peter hath spoken by the mouth of Leo.' The best edition of his works is that of the brothers Ballerini (1753, in 3 vols. fol.). They are also published by Migne (*Patr. Lat.* vols liv.-lvi.); and his *Epistolae Selectae* and *Sermones Selecti* by Hurter (*Patr. Opusc. Select.* Eniponti, 1868-74, vols. xiv., xxv., xxvi.)." Charles F. B. Allnatt, ed., *Cathedra Petri—The Titles and Prerogatives of St. Peter*, (London: Burns & Oates, 1879), 10.

"Though Peter alone received many things, nothing passed unto any one else without his participation in it. . . . Out of the whole world the one Peter is chosen, to be set over the vocation of all the nations, and over all the Apostles, and all the Fathers of the Church; that so, though there be in the people of God, many priests and many pastors, Peter especially (or, of his own right) may rule all, whom Christ also rules primarily (or, as the Head). . . He is the First in the apostolic dignity. When he said, 'Thou art the Christ, the Son of the living God,' Jesus answers him, 'Blessed art thou, Simon; My Father which is in heaven. . . and I say to thee,' that is, as My Father has manifested to thee My Divinity, so do I make known to thee thy excellence. For 'thou art Peter'; that is, whereas I am the inviolable Rock; I that Chief Corner-stone; I who make both one (Eph. ii. 6), I the Foundation besides which no one can lay other, nevertheless thou also art a Rock, because thou art consolidated by My power, that what things are mine by My power, may be common to thee by being made partaker of them with Me. Upon this strength, he says, I will raise an everlasting temple, and the lofty building of My Church, reaching unto heaven, shall arise on the firmness of this faith. The "gates of hell" shall not hold, the bonds of death shall not bind, this confession; for this word (voice), is the word (voice) of life." (Leo, *T. i. Serm. iv. in Anniver. Assumpt. c. i.-iv.*, col. 16-19), in Colin Lindsay, *The Evidence for the Papacy*, (London: Longmans, 1870), 52-53.

"But the Lord willed the sacrament of this office (of the apostolic trumpet) to pertain to all the Apostles in such manner, as that He placed it principally in the blessed Peter, the Chief of all the Apostles, and wishes His gifts to flow unto the whole body, from him (Peter) as from a Head; that whoso should dare withdraw from the solidity of Peter, might know himself to be an alien from the divine mystery. For it was His will that this man whom He had taken into the fellowship of an indivisible unity (or, taken for the connexion of an indivisible unity) should be named that which Himself was (i.e., the Rock), by saying, 'Thou art Peter, and upon this rock I will build My Church,' that the building of an everlasting temple might, by the marvelous gift of the grace of God, be compacted together in the Solidity of Peter, by this Firmness strengthening His Church, so as that neither human temerity should be able to injure (assault) it, nor the 'gates of hell prevail against it.'" (Leo, *T. i. Ep. x. ad Episcopos per Provinc. Viennens. contitutos, in caussa Hilarii Arelat. Epis. c. 1, 2*, col. 633-35), in Colin Lindsay, *The Evidence for the Papacy*, (London: Longmans, 1870), 53-54.

"[2] [T]he Lord says, 'Blessed art thou, Simon Bar-Jonah, because flesh and blood hath not revealed it to thee, but My Father, which is in heaven. And I say to thee, that thou art Peter, and upon this rock I will build My Church, and the gates of Hades shall not prevail against it. And I will give unto thee the keys of the kingdom of heaven. And whatsoever thou shalt bind on earth, shall be bound in heaven; and whatsoever thou shalt loose on earth, shall be loosed also in heaven.'

"[3] The dispensation of Truth therefore abides, and the blessed Peter persevering in the strength of the Rock, which he has received, has not abandoned the helm of the Church, which he undertook. For he was ordained before the rest in such a way that from his being called the Rock, from his being pronounced the Foundation, from his being constituted the Doorkeeper of the kingdom of heaven, from his being set as the Umpire to bind and loose, whose judgments shall retain their validity in heaven, from all these mystical titles we might know the nature of his association with Christ." (Leo, *Sermons* 3:2-3 [442 A.D.]), in Philip

Schaff and Henry Wace, eds., *Nicene and Post-Nicene Fathers—Leo the Great, Gregory the Great*, 2nd series, vol. 12, (Peabody, MA: Hendrickson, 1994), 117.

"Our Lord Jesus Christ, Saviour of Mankind, instituted the observance of the Divine religion which He wished by the grace of God to shed its brightness upon all nations and all peoples. . . . But this mysterious function the Lord wished to be indeed the concern of all the apostles, but in such a way that He has placed the principal charge on the blessed Peter, chief of all the Apostles: and from him as from the Head wishes His gifts to flow to all the body: so that any one who dares to secede from Peter's solid rock may understand that he has no part or lot in the divine mystery. For He wished him who had been received into partnership in His undivided unity to be named what He Himself was, when He said: 'Thou art Peter, and upon this rock I will build My Church:' that the building of the eternal temple by the wondrous gift of God's grace might rest on Peter's solid rock: strengthening His Church so surely that neither could human rashness assail it nor the gates of hell prevail against it." (Leo, *Letters* 10:1 [450 A.D.]) in Philip Schaff and Henry Wace, eds., *Nicene and Post-Nicene Fathers—Leo the Great, Gregory the Great*, 2nd series, vol. 12, (Peabody, MA: Hendrickson, 1994), 8.

"[F]or not only was the power of binding and loosing given to Peter before the others, but also to Peter more especially was entrusted the care of feeding the sheep. Yet anyone who holds that the headship must be denied to Peter, cannot really diminish his dignity: but is puffed up with the breath of his pride, and plunges himself to the lowest depth." (Leo, *Letters* 10:2 [450 A.D.]) in Philip Schaff and Henry Wace, eds., *Nicene and Post-Nicene Fathers—Leo the Great, Gregory the Great*, 2nd series, vol. 12, (Peabody, MA: Hendrickson, 1994), 9.

"Since, therefore, the Universal Church has become a rock (*petra*) through the building up of that original Rock, and the first of the Apostles, the most blessed Peter, heard the voice of the Lord saying, 'Thou art Peter, and upon this rock (*petra*) I will build My Church,' who is there who dare assail such impregnable strength, unless he be either antichrist or the devil, who, abiding unconverted in his wickedness, is anxious to sow lies by the vessels of wrath which are suited to his treachery, whilst under the false name of diligence he pretends to be in search of the Truth." (Leo, *Letter* 156:2 [458 A.D.]), in Philip Schaff and Henry Wace, eds., *Nicene and Post-Nicene Fathers—Leo the Great, Gregory the Great*, 2nd series, vol. 12, (Peabody, MA: Hendrickson, 1994), 100.

"The rock of the Catholic faith, which name the blessed Apostle Peter received from the Lord, admits no trace of either (the Nestorian or Eutychian impiety)." (Leo, T. i. *Ep. cxix. ad Max. Antioch. Ep.* c. n. 2, p. 1213.), in Joseph Berington, John Kirk, eds., and James Waterworth, rev., *The Faith of Catholics*, vol. 2, (New York: Pustet & Co., 1884), 57.

Theodoret, Bishop of Cyrus (ca. 450 A.D.):

"Theodoret, Bishop of Cyrus in Palestine [Syria], was born at Antioch about A.D. 393, and died about 458. He was accused of sympathising with the heretical Patriarch Nestorius, but justified himself before the Council of Chalcedon by anathematising Nestorius and his doctrines. His works were published by Sirmond (Paris, 1642); Garnier (1684); Schulze (Halle, 1769) in 8vo, 5 vols.); Migne (*Patr. Graec.* vols. lxxx.-lxxxiv.)." Charles F. B. Allnatt, ed., *Cathedra Petri— The Titles and Prerogatives of St. Peter*, (London: Burns & Oates, 1879), 12.

"The great foundation of the Church was shaken, and confirmed by the Divine grace. . . . And the Lord commanded him to apply the same care to the brethren: 'And thou,' He says, 'converted, confirm thy brethren.'" (Theodoret, Tom. iv. *Haeret. Fab.* lib. v. c. 28, p. 478), in Charles F. B. Allnatt, ed., *Cathedra Petri—The Titles and Prerogatives of St. Peter*, (London: Burns & Oates, 1879), 38.

St. Prosper of Acquitaine (450 A.D.):

> "Prosper of Acquitaine (St.), a zealous disciple of St. Augustine, and opponent of the Pelagian heresy, flourished about A.D. 428. He died in 455. The best edition of his works is that of Paris (fol. 1671 and 1711), republished by Mangeant (Venice, 1744 and 1782), and Migne (*Patr. Lat.* vol. li.)." Charles F. B. Allnatt, ed., *Cathedra Petri—The Titles and Prerogatives of St. Peter*, (London: Burns & Oates, 1879), 11.

> "Peter derived his quality of being the 'rock' solely by dependence on Christ. This view he [St. Prosper of Aquitaine] expresses in the book, *The Calling of all Nations*, where he describes Peter as 'the most firm rock, who from the principal Rock received a share of his virtue and his name.'" (Prosper, *De Vocatione Omnium Gentium*, 2:28 Migne, *Patr. Lat.*, vol. 51, col. 714), in Michael M. Winter, *Saint Peter and the Popes*, (Baltimore: Helicon, 1960), 70-71.

Council of Chalcedon (451 A.D.):

> "Chalcedon, the (Fourth Ecumenical) Council of, was held A.D. 451, under the four Legates of Pope Leo I. About 600 Bishops were present, almost all of the Eastern Church." Charles F. B. Allnatt, ed., *Cathedra Petri—The Titles and Prerogatives of St. Peter*, (London: Burns & Oates, 1879), 13.

> "Wherefore the most holy and blessed Leo, archbishop of the great and elder Rome, through us, and through this present most holy synod together with the thrice blessed and all-glorious Peter the Apostle, who is the rock and foundation of the Catholic Church, and the foundation of the orthodox faith, hath stripped him [Dioscorus] of the episcopate, and hath alienated from him all hieratic worthiness. Therefore let this most holy and great synod sentence the before mentioned Dioscorus to the canonical penalties." (*Extracts from the Acts of the Council of Chalcedon*, Session 3), in Philip

Schaff and Henry Wace, eds., *Nicene and Post-Nicene Fathers—The Seven Ecumenical Councils*, 2nd series, vol. 14, (Peabody, MA: Hendrickson, 1994), 259-260.

Pope St. Felix (490 A.D.):

"Felix III, St. Pope from 483-492. The successor to St. Simplicius, he was elected on March 13. He is most remembered for excommunicating Acacius, patriarch of Constantinople, in 484, for supporting the cause of Monophysitism. The excommunication helped cause the so-called Acacian Schism that divided the Eastern and Western Churches for nearly thirty-five years. Felix was a member of a Roman senatorial family and an ancestor of Pope St. Gregory the Great." *Our Sunday Visitor's Encyclopedia of Catholic History*, 1995 ed., s.v. "Felix III, St.".

"I am also cheered by the purport of your letter, wherein you have not omitted to state that blessed Peter is the Chief of the Apostles and the Rock of faith, and have judiciously proved that to him were intrusted the keys of the heavenly mysteries." (Felix, *Ep. iv. Imper. Zenoni*, Galland, t. x. p. 671-72), in Colin Lindsay, *The Evidence for the Papacy*, (London: Longmans, 1870), 55.

"[To Flavian, Bishop of Constantinople:] There are many circumstances which cause me to rejoice at the ordination of your friendliness. . . . Because also the letters of your friendliness confesses [*sic*] that blessed Peter was the Chief of the Apostles, and the Rock of faith, as having the keys committed to him, the dispenser of heavenly mystery." (Felix, *Ep. v. ad Flavian. Episc. Constantinop.* Ib. pp. 672, 3.), in Colin Lindsay, *The Evidence for the Papacy*, (London: Longmans, 1870), 239-240.

Pope St. Gelasius (ca. 492 A.D.):

"Gelasius I. (St. and Pope), occupied the chair of Peter from A.D. 492 to 496. Eighteen of his *Decretal Epistles* are published in Labbe (*Concil.* t. iv.); Migne (*Patr. Lat.* vol. lix.); and Thiel (*Epist. Rom. Pont.* tom. i. 1867)." Charles F. B.

Allnatt, ed., *Cathedra Petri—The Titles and Prerogatives of St. Peter*, (London: Burns & Oates, 1879), 6.

"Referring to the adjudication of the Primacy to Rome, he says, 'as being men who bore in mind the Lord's sentence, "Thou art Peter, and upon this rock I will build My Church, &c." And again to the same Peter, "Lo! I have prayed for thee that thy faith fail not, and converted, confirm the brethren," and that sentence, "If thou lovest Me, feed my sheep." Wherefore, then, is the Lord's discourse so frequently directed to Peter? Was it that the rest of the holy and blessed Apostles were not clothed with his virtue? Who dare assert this? No, but that, by a Head being constituted, the occasion of schism might be removed; and that the compact bond of the body of Christ, thus uniformly tending, by the fellowship of the most glorious love, to one Head, might be shown to be one; and that there might be one Church faithfully believed in, and one house of the one God and of the one Redeemer, wherein we might be nourished with one bread and one chalice. . . . There were assuredly twelve Apostles, endowed with equal merits and equal dignity; and whereas they all shone equally with spiritual light, yet was it Christ's will that One amongst them should be the Ruler (prince) (*principem*), &c." (Gelasius, in Galland, t. x. p. 677), in Colin Lindsay, *The Evidence for the Papacy*, (London: Longmans, 1870), 55-56.

"Granting to the See, which he himself (Peter) blessed, that, in accordance with the Lord's promise, it should never be conquered by 'the gates of hell,' and be the safest harbour of those tossed by the waves." (*Epist.* xiv. p. 1216, Galland, x.; *Tract.* ii. n. 10, ed. Thiel. p. 259), in Charles F. B. Allnatt, ed., *Cathedra Petri—The Titles and Prerogatives of St. Peter*, (London: Burns & Oates, 1879), 66.

Pope Hormisdas (519 A.D.):

"Hormisdas (Pope), was elected in the year 514. At the request of the Emperor Justin, and John, Patriarch of Constantinople, this Pope sent a deputation to bring about the re-union of the Monophysites with the Church. This was to be effected by the proposal of a profession of faith—com-

monly called the 'Formula of Pope Hormisdas'—to be signed
by the Eastern Bishops. It was accepted and signed by all of
them (including those who had joined the Acacian schism),
as also by the Emperor Justinian, and by the Patriarchs of
Constantinople—Epiphanius, John, and Mennas [signed by
2500 Oriental Bishops, per Dollinger, vol. ii. p. 221, Eng.
trans.]. It was also signed by every Bishop before taking his
seat in the eighth General Council, held A.D. 869." Charles
F. B. Allnatt, ed., *Cathedra Petri—The Titles and Prerogatives of St. Peter*, (London: Burns & Oates, 1879), 7.

"In the Formula of Pope Hormisdas, . . . it is said:—'Because the statement of our Lord Jesus Christ, when He said,
"Thou art Peter, and upon this rock I will build My Church,"
&c., cannot be set aside; this, which is said, is proved by the
results; for in the Apostolic See religion has always been
preserved without spot. . . . In which (See) is set the perfect
and true solidity of the Christian religion.'" (Hormisdas,
Form. Hormisd. Ep. Orient. Praescript. Denzinger's
Enchirid. p. 42), in Charles F. B. Allnatt, ed., *Cathedra
Petri—The Titles and Prerogatives of St. Peter*, (London:
Burns & Oates, 1879), 68.

Eulogius of Alexandria (581 A.D.):

"[Eulogius] Bishop. Born in Syria, he became a monk and
then abbot of Mother of God monastery at Antioch. In 579
he was made patriarch of Alexandria, Egypt. On a journey
to Constantinople he met St. Gregory the Great; some of
their correspondence is extant, notably one letter referring
to Augustine's work in England. Eulogius was most active
in combating Monophysitism and other heresies." John J.
Delaney and James Edward Tobin, *Dictionary of Catholic
Biography*, (Garden City, NY: Doubleday, 1961), 389.

"Neither to John, nor to any other of the disciples, did our
Savior say, 'I will give to thee the keys of the kingdom of
heaven,' but to Peter." (Eulogius, *Lib. ii. Cont. Novatian.
ap. Photium*, Biblioth, cod. 280), in Charles F. B. Allnatt,
ed., *Cathedra Petri—The Titles and Prerogatives of St. Peter*, (London: Burns & Oates, 1879), 35.

Pope Pelagius II (ca. 579-590 A.D.):

> "Pelagius II. Pope from 579-590. Born in Rome, Pelagius was a Goth by descent. Elected to succeed Benedict I in August 579, he came to the papacy during the Lombard siege of Rome." *Our Sunday Visitor's Encyclopedia of Catholic History*, 1995 ed., s.v. "Pelagius II".

> "You know that the Lord proclaims in the Gospel: 'Simon, Simon, behold: Satan has desired to possess you, so that he might sift you like wheat. But I have prayed for you, that your faith may not fail. And you, once you have converted, confirm your brethren!' [Luke 22:31-32]. Consider that the Truth could not have lied, nor will the faith of Peter be able to be shaken or changed for ever. For, although the devil desired to sift all the disciples, the Lord testifies that He Himself asked for Peter alone, and wished that the others be confirmed by him; and to Peter also was committed the care of 'feeding the sheep' [John 21:15]; and to him also did the Lord hand over the 'keys to the kingdom of Heaven' [Matthew 16:19], and upon him did He promise to 'build His Church' [Matthew 16:18]; and He testified that 'the gates of hell would not prevail against it' [Matthew 16:19]. . . If, however, anyone either suggests or believes contrary to this faith, let him know that he is condemned and anathematized. Consider, therefore, the fact that whoever has not been in the peace and unity of the Church cannot have the Lord. . . . On the Day of Judgment, no one can excuse himself. For the Church of God is established among those known to preside over the Apostolic Sees through succession, and whoever separates himself from the authority of these Sees is manifestly in schism. Those not willing to be at agreement in the Church of God cannot abide with God." Pelagius II, "Quod Ad Dilectionem"; "Dilectionis Vestrae," in Henry Denzinger, *Enchiridion Symbolorum*, 30th Ed., (London: B. Herder Book Co., 1957), Para. 246, 247, in Michael Malone, ed., *The Apostolic Digest*, (Irving, TX: Sacred Heart, 1987), 206.

Pope St. Gregory the Great (ca. 600 A.D.):

"Gregory the Great (St. and Pope), was born about A.D.
520, and died in 604. To the mission of Augustine and his
monks by this Pope England owes its conversion to Christianity. The best edition of his works is the *Benedictine* (Paris,
1705, 4 vols. fol. and Venice, 1768-76, 4 vols.), republished
by Migne (*Patr. Lat.* vols. lxxv.-lxxix.)." Charles F. B.
Allnatt, ed., *Cathedra Petri—The Titles and Prerogatives
of St. Peter*, (London: Burns & Oates, 1879), 7.

"Who could be ignorant of the fact that the holy church is
consolidated in the solidity of the prince of the Apostles,
whose firmness of character extended to his name so that
he should be called Peter after the 'rock,' when the voice of
the Truth says, 'I will give to thee the keys of the kingdom
of heaven.' To him again is said 'When after a little while
thou hast come back to me, it is for thee to be the support of
thy brethren.'" (Gregory, *Letter 40* in Book 6, Migne, *Patr.
Lat.*, vol. 77, col. 898), in Michael M. Winter, *Saint Peter
and the Popes*, (Baltimore: Helicon, 1960), 65-66.

"It is evident to all who know the Gospel, that by the voice
of the Lord the care of the whole Church was committed to
holy Peter, the prince of all the Apostles. For to him it is
said, . . . 'Thou art Peter, and upon this rock I will build My
Church. And to thee will I give the keys of the kingdom of
heaven.' Behold, he receives the keys of the heavenly kingdom; the power of binding and of loosing is given to him;
to him the care and government of the whole Church is committed." (Gregory, *Epist. ad Maurit. August.* lib. iv. epist.
32), in Charles F. B. Allnatt, ed., *Cathedra Petri—The Titles
and Prerogatives of St. Peter*, (London: Burns & Oates,
1879), 35-36.

"For the more you fear the Creator of all, the more fully
may you love the Church of him to whom it was said, 'Thou
art Peter, and upon this rock I will build by Church, and the
gates of hell shall not prevail against it'; and to whom it is
said, 'To thee I will give the keys of the kingdom of heaven;
and whatsoever thou shalt bind on earth shall be bound in

heaven; and whatsoever thou shalt loose on earth shall be loosed in heaven.' (Matth. xv.[*sic*] 18). Whence it is not doubtful to us with what strong love you will bind yourself to him through whom you earnestly desire to be loosed from all sins." (Gregory, *Letter to Leontia, Empress*, Book 13, Letter 39), in Philip Schaff and Henry Wace, eds., *Nicene and Post-Nicene Fathers—Gregory the Great (II), Ephraim Syrus, Aphrahat*, 2nd series, vol. 13, (Peabody, MA: Hendrickson, 1994), 101.

"Yet I exhort thee that, as long as some time of life remains for thee, thy soul may not be found to be divided from the church of the same blessed Peter, to whom the keys of the heavenly kingdom were entrusted and the power of binding and loosing was granted, lest if his benefit be despised down here, he may close up the entrance to life up there." (Gregory, *The Great Epistles*, B IV, Ep. 41), in J. P. Migne, *Patr. Lat.*, trans. John Collorafi.

Stephen, Bishop of Dora in Palestine (ca. 645 A.D.):

"And for this cause, sometimes we asked for water to our head and to our eyes a fountain of tears, sometimes the wings of a dove, according to holy David, that we might fly away and announce these things to the Chair which rules and presides over all, I mean to yours, the head and highest, for the healing of the whole wound. For this it has been accustomed to do from of old and from the beginning with power by its canonical or apostolical authority, because the truly great Peter, head of the Apostles, was clearly thought worthy not only to be entrusted with the keys of heaven, alone apart from the rest, to open it worthily to believers, or to close it justly to those who disbelieve the Gospel of grace, but because he was also first commissioned to feed the sheep of the whole Catholic Church; for 'Peter,' saith He, 'lovest thou Me? Feed My sheep.' And again, because he had in a manner peculiar and special, a faith in the Lord stronger than all and unchangeable, to be converted and to confirm his fellows and spiritual brethren when tossed about, as having been adorned by God Himself incarnate for us with power and sacerdotal authority. (*Mansi*, x, 893) . . . And Sophronius

of blessed memory, who was Patriarch of the holy city of
Christ our God, and under whom I was Bishop, conferring
not with flesh and blood, but caring only for the things of
Christ with respect to your Holiness, hastened to send my
nothingness without delay about this matter alone to this
Apostolic and great See. . . . Swiftly pass, therefore, from
one end of the world to the other, until thou come to the
Apostolic See, where are the foundations of the holy doc-
trines." (Stephen, *Mansi*, x, 893), in Dom John Chapman,
"The Condemnation of Pope Honorius," *Dublin Review*,
(July-October, 1906), 136-137.

St. Maximus the Confessor (650 A.D.):

"Maximus the Confessor, St. (c. 580-662). Byzantine theologian who was also known as Maximus the Theologian
and Maximus of Constantinople. A native of Constantinople
and a member of a noble Byzantine family, he served as a
respected secretary of Emperor Heraclius before becoming
a monk around 614 at the monastery of Chrysopolis. In 626
and the Persian invasion of the region, Maximus fled to
Africa. There he became an outspoken opponent of
Monothelitism at African synods and at the Lateran Council of 649. In 653, however, Maximus and Pope St. Martin I
were arrested by Emperor Constans II and, as they refused
to accept his decrees, the *Typos*, were exiled. Martin was
sent to Crimea and Maximus was sent to Thrace. Brought
back to Constantinople in 661, he once again refused to yield
and so his tongue and right hand were chopped off and numerous humiliations were heaped upon him. . . . One of the
great theologians of the Church, Maximus is honored with
the title of 'The Theologian' and is ranked as a Doctor [of
the Church] for his contributions to the theology of the Incarnation." *Our Sunday Visitor's Encyclopedia of Catholic
History*, 1995 ed., s.v. "Maximus the Confessor".

"The same opinion [like Proclus, that Peter is the foundation of the Church] is found again in the first half of the
seventh century in the works of the monk John Moschus
(*Pratum Spirituale*, Migne, *Patr. Graec.*, vol. 87, (iii), col.
3012) and his friend Sophronius, the celebrated patriarch of

Jerusalem (*Sermon on SS. Cyrus and John*, Migne, *Patr. Graec.*, vol. 87, (iii), col. 369) who was the first opponent of the monothelite heresy. Another famous champion of orthodoxy against the Monothelites was Maximus the Confessor, who died in 662. His attitude to St. Peter must be inferred from his opinion of the Bishop of Rome. He attributed to Rome a superior authority in matters of faith which he related to the power of the keys. It is reasonable therefore to conclude that he must have recognized some kind of superiority for St. Peter (Maximus, *Opuscula Ad Petr. Ill.*, Migne, *Patr. Graec.*, vol. 91, col. 144; *Letters to Rome*, Migne, *Patr. Graec.*, vol. 91, cols. 137, 139)." Michael M. Winter, *Saint Peter and the Popes*, (Baltimore: Helicon, 1960), 75.

"The extremities of the earth, and everyone in every part of it who purely and rightly confess the Lord, look directly towards the Most Holy Roman Church and her confession and faith, as to a sun of unfailing light, awaiting from her the brilliant radiance of the sacred dogmas of our Fathers, according to that which the inspired and holy Councils have stainlessly and piously decreed. For, from the descent of the Incarnate Word amongst us, all the churches in every part of the world have held that greatest Church alone to be their base and foundation, seeing that, according to the promise of Christ Our Savior, the gates of hell never prevail against her, that she has the keys of orthodox confession and right faith in Him, that she opens the true and exclusive religion to such men as approach with piety, and she shuts up and locks every heretical mouth which speaks against the Most High." (cf. Maximus, *Opuscula theologica et polemica*, Migne, *Patr. Graec.* vol. 90), in Michael Malone, ed., *The Apostolic Digest*, (Irving, TX: Sacred Heart, 1987), 251.

St. John Damascene (ca. 680-740 A.D.):

"Born of a wealthy Christian family at Damascus, he [John Damascene] spent all his life under Mohammedan rule. He was educated by a brilliant monk named Cosmas, who had been captured in a Mohammedan raid on Sicily and was bought by John's father, Mansur. John succeeded his father as chief revenue officer and counselor of Caliph Abdul

Malek. In 726, when Emperor Leo the Isaurian issued his first edict prohibiting the veneration of images, John defended the practice and soon became a leading champion of the Catholic position, arousing the bitter enmity of the Byzantine Emperors, who could not molest him physically, since he was under the caliph's rule and protection. He resigned his position about 726, and with his adopted brother, another Cosmas, became a monk at St. Sabas' laura outside Jerusalem. He was denounced at a pseudosynod in Constantinople by iconoclast Emperor Constantine Copronymus, successor of Emperor Leo the Isaurian, but was ordained in Constantinople by Patriarch John V, who also appointed Cosmas bishop of Majuma. John soon after returned to the monastery and led the defenders of orthodoxy and expounders of the Catholic position in the iconoclasm controversy. Among his outstanding writings are the *Fount of Wisdom*, on philosophy, heresies, and the orthodox faith; *De Fide Orthodoxa*, a comprehensive presentation of the teachings of the Greek Fathers on the main Christian doctrines; and *Sacra Parallela*, a compilation of scriptural and patristic texts on Christian moral and ascetical works. His writings, especially his *De Fide Orthodoxa*, one of the most notable theological works of antiquity, has had great influence on theologians of both East and West. He also wrote poetry, and some of his poems are used in the Greek liturgy. The elegance of his Greek caused him to be called Chrysorrhoas (gold-pouring). He died at Sabas, probably on December 5, the last of the Greek Fathers, and was made a Doctor of the Church by Pope Leo XIII in 1890." John J. Delaney and James Edward Tobin, *Dictionary OF Catholic Biography*, (Garden City, NY: Doubleday, 1961), 320-21.

French scholar Martin Jugie characterizes the thoughts of St. John Damascene (from his various writings on the papacy), as follows:

"The church was monarchial from the beginning, for the Apostle Peter whom our Doctor considers the first-called and the first to follow the Savior." (*Homily on the Transfiguration* 6; pg. 96, col. 553D)

"[Peter] was predestined by Jesus Christ to be the worthy head of the Church." (*Homily on Holy Saturday* 33, col. 636C. *Ibid.*, col. 560C)

"It is to him, as to the most faithful servant, that Jesus entrusted the rudder of all the Church, this Church which he acquired with his blood." (*Ibid.*, col. 556B.)

"John gives an excellent commentary on the words 'Thou art Peter,' and the expressions he uses are enough to shut up the chicanery of all anti-Catholic polemics. Peter is compared to Moses. He is placed at the head of the New Covenant as Moses presided over the old." (*Ibid.*, 2, col. 548B)

"Peter's faith is undoubtedly the unshakable rock upon which the Church rests, but this faith is not separable from Peter's person: it is indeed Peter who is the rock." (*Ibid.*, 6, col. 556B.)

"He is at the same time the key-bearer of the kingdom of heaven." (*Ibid.*, col. 556C)

"Orderer of the Universal Church." (*Ibid.*, 16, col. 569D)

"The regulator responsible for the power of the keys." (*Ibid.*, 6, col. 556C)

"It was not of tents that the Master constituted thee the orderer, but of the Universal Church. Thy disciples, thy sheep, which the Good Shepherd entrusted to thee as head, have fulfilled thy desire. They have raised one tent to Christ, one to Moses and Elias, his servants, and we now celebrate our feasts there." (*Homily on the Transfiguration, Ibid.* 16, col. 569D). Martin Jugie, "Doctrine of Saint John Damascene on the Church [in French]," *Echos d' Orient*, (October, 1924), trans. John Collorafi.

Third Council of Constantinople (680 A.D.):

"ConstantinoConstantinopleple, the Third Council of (Sixth Ecumenical), composed of 170 Eastern Bishops, was held A.D. 680, and its decisions were confirmed by the Legates of Pope Agatho. In the letter written by the Synod to the Pope, he is called 'The Head of the Church,' and his chair, 'The First See of the Ecumenical Church.' (Hardouin, tom. iii. p. 1632)." Charles F. B. Allnatt, ed., *Cathedra Petri— The Titles and Prerogatives of St. Peter*, (London: Burns & Oates, 1879), 13.

Pope St. Agatho (680 A.D.):

> "Agatho, St. Pope from 678-681. He was active in combating the heresy of Monothelitism with a council in Rome in 680 that would produce a formula to be used later that year against the Monothelite supporters at the Sixth General Council (Third Council of Constantinople)." *Our Sunday Visitor's Encyclopedia of Catholic History*, 1995 ed., s.v. "Agatho, St.".

> "This Apostolic Church never turned away from the way of truth nor held any kind of error. This is the rule of faith. All who wish to please God must study to conform to the Apostolic rule of the primitive faith founded on the rock Peter, and kept by him from error." Cf. Agatho, "Epistle to Emperor Constantine Pogonatus," confirmed by III Constantinople; Archbp. John Mansi, *Sacrorum Conciliorium*, Vol. XI, (Thomas Florentiae, 1759), 635, in Michael Malone, ed., *The Apostolic Digest*, (Irving, TX: Sacred Heart, 1987), 252.

Venerable Bede (700 A.D.):

> "Bede (the Venerable), the historian of the Anglo-Saxon Church, and called by the Protestant Neander 'emphatically the teacher of England (Bohn's *Neander*, v. 210), was born at Jarrow, in Northumbria, A.D. 673, and died A.D. 735. His collected works have been published by Dr. Giles, in 12 vols. (London and Oxford, 1843), and by Migne (*Patr. Lat.* vols. xc.-xcv.). An English translation of his *Ecclesiastical History* is published in Bohn's *Antiquarian Library*, and one of his *Explanation of the Apocalypse*, by E. Marshall, Oxford, Parker & Co., 1878." Charles F. B. Allnatt, ed., *Cathedra Petri—The Titles and Prerogatives of St. Peter*, (London: Burns & Oates, 1879), 3.

> "Blessed Peter in a special manner received the keys of the kingdom of heaven and the headship of judiciary power, that all believers throughout the world might understand that all those who in any way separate themselves from the unity of this faith and communion,—such can neither be absolved from

the bonds of their sins, nor enter the gate of the heavenly kingdom." (Bede, *Bede. Ven Hom. in die S.S. Pet. et Paul.*), in Charles F. B. Allnatt, ed., *Cathedra Petri—The Titles and Prerogatives of St. Peter*, (London: Burns & Oates, 1879), 36.

"Peter received the keys to heaven as a sign to all the children of the Church, so that if they separate from the one faith which he teaches, they give up all hope of being acquitted of their guilt and of entering the eternal portals . . . And I say unto you that Peter is the doorkeeper whom I will not contradict, but I will obey his decrees in everything, lest when I come to the gates of the kingdom of Heaven there should be no one to open them, since he will be my adversary who is proven to have possession of the keys." (Bede, in Colman Barry, *Readings in Church History* (Westminster, MD: Newman Press, 1957), vol. 1, 273), in Michael Malone, *The Apostolic Digest*, (Irving, TX: Sacred Heart, 1987), 243.

The works of Bede should be understood in the context of his time and interpreted in light of Vatican II's clarification of "outside the Church there is no salvation."

St. Theodore the Studite (759-826 A.D.):

"A native of Constantinople who became a monk at the monastery of the Studium (more correctly Studios) in that city. His uncle was St. Plato, abbot of Saccudium. He entered his uncle's abbey and after ordination in 787, became abbot in 794, his uncle resigning in his favour. His community became involved in the internal quarrels of the imperial house, and as a result this abbey was closed and he was banished to Thessalonica. A reversal of fortunes led to the renewal of the community at the abbey of Studios in Constantinople in 799 and under his rule the monastery developed into a centre from which a monastic revival spread throughout the East, its influence reaching to Mt. Athos and later to Russia, Rumania and Bulgaria. Studium stood for all that is lasting in monastic observance: liturgical prayer, community life, enclosure, poverty, studies and manual work (the monks excelled in calligraphy). The community, with St. Theodore at their head, uncompromisingly defended the veneration of images (against a series of iconoclastic emperors), and opposed Caesaropapism in every form. Theodore suffered banishment several times on this account. He is one of the great figures of monastic history, and his austerity and patience under suffering and persecution are a witness to his sincerity and holiness. His uncompromising orthodoxy is a hallmark of a truly monastic spirit, valid in any age." Benedictine monks of St. Augustine's Abbey, Ramsgate., *The Book Of Saints*, 6th ed., (Wilton: CN, Morehouse Publishing, 1989), 535-536.

Theodore the Studite wrote to Leo III:

"Since to great Peter Christ our God gave the office of Chief Shepherd after entrusting him with the keys of the kingdom of heaven, to Peter or his successor must of the necessity every novelty in the Catholic Church . . . be referred. . . . Save us, most divine Head of all Heads, Chief Shepherd of the Church under Heaven." (Theodore the Studite, Bk. I. Ep. 23, *Patr. Graec.* 99, 1017; cp. Ep. 34, pp. 1021 and 1025), in Dom John Chapman, *The First Eight General Councils and Papal Infallibility*, 3rd ed., (London: Catholic Truth Society, 1928), 74.

"Hear [Pope Paschal], O apostolic head, divinely appointed Shepherd of Christ's sheep, keybearer of the kingdom of heaven, rock of the faith, upon whom is built the Catholic Church. For Peter art thou, who adornest and governest the chair of Peter. . . . Hither, then, from the West, imitator of Christ, arise and repel not for ever (*Ps.* xliii. 23). To thee spake Christ our Lord: 'And thou being one day converted, shalt strengthen thy brethren.' Behold the hour and the place. Help us, thou that art set by God for this. Stretch forth thy hand so far as thou canst. Thou hast strength with God, through being the first of all." (*Letter of St. Theodore and four other Abbots to Pope Paschal*, Bk. ii Ep. 12, *Patr. Graec.* 99, 1152-3), in Dom John Chapman, *The First Eight General Councils and Papal Infallibility*, 3rd ed., (London: Catholic Truth Society, 1928), 74.

"[To Emperor Michael] order that the declaration from old Rome be received, as was the custom by the tradition of our Fathers from of old and from the beginning. For this, O Emperor, is the highest of the Churches of God, in which first Peter held the chair, to whom the Lord said: 'Thou art Peter . . . prevail against it.'" (Theodore the Studite, Bk. II. Ep. 86, *Patr. Graec.* 99, 1331.), in Dom John Chapman, *The First Eight General Councils and Papal Infallibility*, 3rd ed., (London: Catholic Truth Society, 1928), 75.

"I witness now before God and men, they have torn themselves away from the Body of Christ, from the supreme see, in which Christ placed the keys of the faith, against which the gates of hell (I mean the mouths of heretics) have not prevailed, and never will until the consummation, according to the promise of Him who cannot lie. Let the most blessed and apostolic Paschal rejoice therefore, for he has fulfilled the work of Peter" (Theodore the Studite, Bk. II Ep. 63, *Patr. Graec.* 99, 1281), in Dom John Chapman, *The First Eight General Councils and Papal Infallibility*, 3rd ed., (London: Catholic Truth Society, 1928), 75-76.

JESUS, PETER AND THE KEYS

CHAPTER VII

PETER FORESHADOWED AS THE CHIEF APOSTLE IN LUKE 22:32

Luke 22:32 {But I have prayed for thee, that thy faith fail not: and when thou art converted, strengthen thy brethren.}

Ambrosiaster (ca. 380-384 A.D.):

"After the Saviour all were included in Peter; for He constituted him to be their head, that he might be the shepherd of the Lord's flock. . . . And He says to Peter, 'Behold, Satan hath desired to have you, that he may sift you as wheat. But I have prayed for thee, that thy faith fail not; and thou, being once converted, confirm thy brethren.' What doubt is there? He prayed for Peter, but prayed not for James and John, not to mention the others. It is manifest that all are included; for, praying for Peter, He is seen to have prayed for all; for a people is ever blamed or praised in him that is set over it." (Ambrosiaster, *Quaest.* 75, *ex N. Test. in App. St. August.* tom. iii. 2894), in Charles F. B. Allnatt, ed., *Cathedra Petri—The Titles and Prerogatives of St. Peter*, (London: Burns & Oates, 1879), 43.

St. Ambrose (ca. 385-389):

> "Peter, after having been tempted by the devil, is set over the Church. The Lord, therefore, signified beforehand what that is, that He afterwards chose him the pastor of the Lord's flock. For to him He said, 'But thou, when thou art converted, confirm thy brethren'" (*In Ps.* xliii. n. 40, p. 1109). "To whom He gave the kingdom, his faith could He not confirm?" (Ambrose, *De Fide*, lib. iv. c. 5, n. 56), in Charles F. B. Allnatt, ed., *Cathedra Petri—The Titles and Prerogatives of St. Peter*, (London: Burns & Oates, 1879), 36-37.

> "Further, that thou mayest know that, as man, He prays; as God, He commands; thou hast in the Gospel that He said to Peter, 'I have prayed for thee that thy faith fail not.' But to that same Peter when He said on an earlier occasion, 'Thou art the Christ, the Son of the living God,' He answered, 'Thou art Peter, and upon this Rock I will build my Church, and I will give unto thee the keys of the kingdom of heaven.' How could he not confirm his faith, unto whom of His own authority He gave the kingdom, and whom when He styles a Rock, He pointed out the Foundation of the Church?" Ambrose, *T. ii. l. iv. De Fide*, c. v. n. 56, p. 531, in Colin Lindsay, *The Evidence for the Papacy*, (London: Longmans, 1870), 38.

St. Chrysostom (ca. 387 A.D.):

> "In those days Peter rose up in the midst of the disciples" (Acts i. 15): "Both as being ardent, and as intrusted by Christ with the flock, . . . he first acts with authority in the matter, as having all put into his hands; for to him Christ had said, 'And thou, being converted, confirm thy brethren.'" (Chrysostom, *Hom.* iii. in *Act. Apost.* tom. ix. p. 26), Charles F. B. Allnatt, ed., *Cathedra Petri—The Titles and Prerogatives of St. Peter*, (London: Burns & Oates, 1879), 37.

> "He passed over his fall, and appointed him first of the Apostles; wherefore He said: 'Simon, Simon,' etc." (in Ps.cxxix. 2). "God allowed him to fall, because He meant

to make him ruler over the whole world, that, remembering his own fall, he might forgive those who should slip in the future. And that what I have said is no guess, listen to Christ Himself saying: 'Simon, Simon, etc." (John Chrysostom, *Hom. quod frequenter conveniendum sit 5*, cf. *Hom. 73 in Joan. 5*), in Dom John Chapman, *Bishop Gore and Catholic Claims*,(London: Longmans, Green, and Co., 1905), 59.

"Again, that coryphaeus Peter, after a thousand wonders and signs and so much warning and counsel, did He not rebuke him when he had fallen this grave fall? Nay, He passed it over, and appointed him first of the apostles. Wherefore he said: 'Simon, Simon, behold Satan hath desired to sift thee as wheat, and I have prayed for thee that thy faith fail not'." (John Chrysostom, *In Psalm CXXIX*, 2 vol. v. p. 375(369)), in Dom John Chapman, *Studies on the Early Papacy*, (London: Sheed & Ward, 1928), 84.

St. Cyril of Alexandria (ca. 424 A.D.):

"Therefore, when the Lord had hinted at the disciple's denial in the words that he used, 'I have prayed for thee that thy faith fail not,' he at once introduced a word of consolation, and said: 'And do thou, when once thou art converted, strengthen thy brethren.' That is, 'Be thou a support and a teacher of those who through faith come to me.' Again, marvel also at the insight of that saying and at the completeness of the divine gentleness of spirit. For so that he should not reduce the disciple to despair at the thought that after his denial he would have to be debarred from the glorious distinction of being an apostle, he fills him with good hope, that he will attain the good things promised. In fact he says 'And when thou art converted, strengthen thy brethren.' O loving kindness! The sin was not yet committed, and he already extends his pardon and sets him again in his apostolic office." Alexandria, *Commentary on Luke's Gospel* in J. P. Migne, ed., *Patrologiae Cursus Completus: Series Graeca*, (Paris, 1866), 72:916 in E. Giles, *Documents Illustrating Papal Authority A.D. 96-454*, (London: SPCK, 1952), 259.

Pope St. Leo the Great (ca. 440-461 A.D.):

"Again as his passion pressed on, which was to shake the firmness of the disciples, the Lord says, 'Simon, behold Satan has desired to have you that he may sift you as wheat, but I have prayed for thee that thy faith fail not, and when thou art converted, confirm thy brethren, that ye enter not into temptation.' The danger from the temptation of fear was common to all apostles, and they equally needed the help of divine protection, since the devil desired to harass and shatter all; and yet special care is taken of Peter by the Lord, and he asks specially for the faith of Peter, as if the state of the others would be more certain if the mind of the chief were not overcome. So then in Peter the strength of all is fortified, and the help of divine grace is so ordered that the stability which through Christ is given to Peter, through Peter is conveyed to the apostles." Leo, *Sermo 4—Gaudeo, dilectissimi* in J. P. Migne, ed., *Patrologiae Cursus Completus: Series Latina*, (Paris, 1866), 54:149 in E. Giles, *Documents Illustrating Papal Authority A.D. 96-454*, (London: SPCK, 1952), 280.

"Since then, beloved, we see such a protection divinely granted to us, reasonably and justly do we rejoice in the merits and dignity of our leader, rendering thanks to the eternal King, our Redeemer, the Lord Jesus Christ, for having given so great a power to him whom he made chief of the whole Church, that if anything, even in our time, by us be rightly done and rightly ordered, it is to be ascribed to his working, to his guidance, unto whom it was said, 'And thou, when thou art converted, confirm thy brethren'; and to whom the Lord after his resurrection, in answer to the triple profession of eternal love, thrice said, with mystical intent, 'Feed my sheep.' And this, beyond a doubt, the pious shepherd does even now, and fulfils the charge of his Lord, confirming us with his exhortations, and not ceasing to pray for us, that we may be overcome by no temptation. But if, as we must believe, he extends this care of his piety to all God's people everywhere, how much more will he condescend to grant his help unto us his children, among whom, on the sacred couch of his blessed repose, he rests in the same flesh in which he ruled! To him, therefore, let us ascribe this anniversary day of us his servant, and this festival, by whose patronage we have been thought worthy to share his seat itself, the grace of our Lord Jesus Christ helping us in all things, who liveth and reigneth with God the Father and the Holy Ghost for ever and ever. Amen." (Leo, *Sermo 4—Gaudeo, dilectissimi* in J. P. Migne, ed., *Patrologiae Cursus Completus: Series Graeca*, (Paris, 1866), 54:149), in E. Giles, *Documents Illustrating Papal Authority A.D. 96-454*, (London: SPCK, 1952), 280-281.

Theodoret, Bishop of Cyrus (ca. 450 A.D.):

"The great foundation of the Church was shaken, and confirmed by the Divine grace. . . . And the Lord commanded him to apply the same care to the brethren: 'And thou,' He says, 'converted, confirm thy brethren.'" (Theodoret, Tom. iv. *Haeret. Fab.* lib. v. c. 28, p. 478), in Charles F. B. Allnatt, ed., *Cathedra Petri—The Titles and Prerogatives of St. Peter*, (London: Burns & Oates, 1879), 38.

"'For as I,' he says, 'did not despise thee when tossed, so be thou a support to thy brethren in trouble, and the help by which thou wast saved do thou thyself impart to others, and exhort them not while they are tottering, but raise them up in their peril. For this reason I suffer thee also to slip, but do not permit thee to fall, [thus] through thee gaining steadfastness for those who are tossed.' So this great pillar supported the tossing and sinking world, and permitted it not to fall entirely and gave it back stability, having been ordered to feed God's sheep." Theodoret, *Oratio de Caritate* in J. P. Migne, ed., *Patrologiae Cursus Completus: Series Graeca*, (Paris, 1866), 82:1509 in E. Giles, *Documents Illustrating Papal Authority A.D. 96-454*, (London: SPCK, 1952), 292. See also Charles F. B. Allnatt, ed., *Cathedra Petri—The Titles and Prerogatives of St. Peter*, (London: Burns & Oates, 1879), 38.

Pope St. Gelasius (ca. 492 A.D.):

"For the government of the Apostolic See, engaged without ceasing in the care of the whole flock of the Lord, which care was delegated to the blessed Peter by the voice of our Saviour Himself, 'And thou, converted, confirm thy brethren,' we neither can, nor ought to, dissemble such things as constrain our solicitude." (Gelasius, *Epist. v. ad. Honorium Dalmat. Episc.* Labbe, iv. p. 1170), in Charles F. B. Allnatt, ed., *Cathedra Petri—The Titles and Prerogatives of St. Peter*, (London: Burns & Oates, 1879), 39.

"Referring to the adjudication of the Primacy to Rome, he says, 'as being men who bore in mind the Lord's sentence, "Thou art Peter, and upon this rock I will build My Church, etc." And again to the same Peter, "Lo! I have prayed for thee that thy faith fail not, and converted, confirm the brethren," and that sentence, "If thou lovest Me, feed my sheep." Wherefore, then, is the Lord's discourse so frequently directed to Peter? Was it that the rest of the holy and blessed Apostles were not clothed with his virtue? Who dare assert this? No, but that, by a Head being constituted, the occasion of schism might be removed; and that the compact bond of the body of Christ, thus uniformly tending, by the fellowship of a most glorious love, to one Head, might be shown to be one; and that there might be one Church faithfully believed in, and one house of the one God and of the one Redeemer, wherein we might be nourished with one bread and one chalice. . . . There were assuredly twelve Apostles, endowed with equal merits and equal dignity; and whereas they all shone equally with spiritual light, yet was it Christ's will that One amongst them should be the Ruler (prince—*principem*), etc." (Gelasius, in Galland, t. x. p. 677), in Colin Lindsay, *The Evidence for the Papacy*, (London: Longmans, 1870), 55-56.

Pope Pelagius II (ca. 579-590 A.D.):

"You know that the Lord proclaims in the Gospel: 'Simon, Simon, behold: Satan has desired to possess you, so that he might sift you like wheat. But I have prayed for you, that your faith may not fail. And you, once you have converted, confirm your brethren!' [Luke 22:31-32]. Consider that the Truth could not have lied, nor will the faith of Peter be able to be shaken or changed for ever. For, although the devil desired to sift all the disciples, the Lord testifies that He

Himself asked for Peter alone, and wished that the others be confirmed by him; and to Peter also was committed the care of 'feeding the sheep' [John 21:15]; and to him also did the Lord hand over the 'keys to the kingdom of Heaven' [Matthew 16:19], and upon him did He promise to 'build His Church' [Matthew 16:18]; and He testified that 'the gates of hell would not prevail against it' [Matthew 16:19]. . . If, however, anyone either suggests or believes contrary to this faith, let him know that he is condemned and anathematized." Pelagius II, "Quod Ad Dilectionem"; "Dilectionis Vestrae," in Henry Denzinger, *Enchiridion Symbolorum*, 30th Ed., (London: B. Herder Book Co., 1957), Para. 246, 247, in Michael Malone, ed., *The Apostolic Digest*, (Irving, TX: Sacred Heart, 1987), 206.

Patriarch John VI of Constantinople (715 A.D.):

"[The Pope] the head of the Christian priesthood, whom, in Peter, the Lord commanded to confirm his brethren." (John VI, *Epist. ad Constantin. Pap. ap.* Combefis, *Auctuar. Bibl. P.P. Graec.* tom. ii. p. 211, *seq.*), in Charles F. B. Allnatt, ed., *Cathedra Petri—The Titles and Prerogatives of St. Peter*, (London: Burns & Oates, 1879), 105.

JESUS, PETER AND THE KEYS

CHAPTER VIII

ST. PETER AS THE CHIEF SHEPHERD OF JOHN 21:15

John 21:15 So when they had dined, Jesus saith to Simon Peter, Simon, [son] of Jonas, lovest thou me more than these? He saith unto him, Yea, Lord; thou knowest that I love thee. He saith unto him, Feed my lambs.

Origen (ca. 216 A.D.):

> "When the Chief Authority as regards the feeding of the sheep was delivered to Peter; and on him, as on earth, the Church was founded; of no other virtue was the confession required, than that of love." Origen, *T. iv. l. 5, in Ep. ad Rom. n. 1*, p. 568, in Colin Lindsay, *The Evidence for the Papacy*, (London: Longmans, 1870), 21.

St. Cyprian (ca. 246 A.D.):

> "The Lord says to Peter, 'I say unto thee,' says he, 'that thou art Peter. . . shall be loosed in heaven.' And to the same after his resurrection, he says to him 'Feed my sheep.' Upon him he builds the Church, and he commits to him the sheep to feed, and though to all the apostles he gives an equal power, yet he founded one chair, and by his authority ap-

pointed the source and system of unity. Certainly the rest were as Peter was, but primacy is given to Peter and one Church and one chair is shown; and they are all shepherds, but one flock is exhibited, which is fed by all the apostles with unanimous consent. And he who does not hold this unity of his Church, does he think he holds the faith? He who deserts the chair of Peter, upon whom the Church was founded, does he trust himself to be in the Church? The episcopate is one, part of which is held by each one in solidity." (Cyprian, *De Catholicae Ecclesiae Unitate*), in E. Giles, *Documents Illustrating Papal Authority A.D. 96-454*, (London: SPCK, 1952), 52-53.

"Peter also to whom the Lord commends His sheep to be fed and guarded, on whom He laid and founded the Church." Cyprian, *De Habitu Virg.* p. 176, in Colin Lindsay, *The Evidence for the Papacy*, (London: Longmans, 1870), 23.

Aphraates the Persian Sage (ca. 336 A.D.):

"He chose and instructed excellent leaders, and committed the sheep into their hands and gave them authority over all His flock. For He said to Simon Cephas, 'Feed My sheep and My lambs and My ewes.' So Simon fed His sheep, and he fulfilled his time and handed over the flock to you and departed' (Aphraates, x, 4)." S. Herbert Scott, *The Eastern Churches and the Papacy*, (London: Sheed & Ward, 1928), 60.

Lucifer, Bishop of Cagliari (ca. 340-350 A.D.):

"Bishop, must have been born in the early years of the fourth century; d. in 371. His birthplace and the circumstances of his youth are unknown. He first appears in ecclesiastical history, in full maturity of strength and abilities, in 354 when he was deputed by Pope Liberius, with the priest Pancratius and the deacon Hilary, to request the Emperor Constantius to convene a council, to deal with the accusations directed against St. Athanasius and his previous condemnation. This council was convened at Milan." Charles G. Herbermann, *The Catholic Encyclopedia*, vol. 9, (New York: The Encyclopedia Press, Inc., 1907-13), 410.

"The Lord says to blessed Peter, 'Feed my lambs,' and again, 'Feed my sheep': and thou, coming as a wolf, willest those to play the part of hirelings who are found to have been the successors of blessed Peter, and whom by Jeremias He has long ago promised to his people: 'And I will give you pastors according to my own heart, and they shall feed you.' (iii. 15)." (Bishop Lucifer, *De non parcendo in Deum delinq.* n. 15.—*Ib.* p.228.), in Joseph Berington, John Kirk, eds., and James Waterworth, rev., *The Faith of Catholics*, vol. 1, (New York: Pustet & Co., 1884), 270.

St. Ephraem the Syrian (ca. 350-370 A.D.):

"He was the prince of the Apostles, and had received the keys, and was accounted the shepherd of the flock." (Ephraem, Tom. ii. *Syr. lvi. Adv. Haer.*), in Charles F. B. Allnatt, ed., *Cathedra Petri—The Titles and Prerogatives of St. Peter*, (London: Burns & Oates, 1879), 41.

"Ephraem wrote a commentary on the Diatessaron of Tatian. Speaking of John the Baptist, he says: 'When he saw that the course of his life was finished, he handed over his flock to the Chief of the Pastors, even as the Lord at the time of His death handed over His flock to Peter, the presbyter of pastors, in order to show the pastoral solicitude which He had for it' (Ephraem, in Mosinger's Latin translation, p. 101)." S. Herbert Scott, *The Eastern Churches and the Papacy*, (London: Sheed & Ward, 1928), 61.

"The Lord of the flock, as he ate with his shepherds, took and delivered his flock to Simon who obeyed him. He spoke once, twice and again, to stress his concern. Three pledges he took from him as shepherd, that with love he should shepherd his lambs, and should visit his sheep with mercy, and should guard his ewes with fear." (Ephraem, *HVirg.* 36, 6 (CSCO 223, Syr. 94, p. 131)), in Robert Murray, *Symbols of Church and Kingdom: A Study in Early Syriac Tradition*, (London: Cambridge, 1975), 190.

Ambrosiaster (ca. 380-384 A.D.):

> "After the Saviour all were included in Peter; for He constituted him to be their head, that he might be the shepherd of the Lord's flock. . . . And He says to Peter, 'Behold, Satan hath desired to have you, that he may sift you as wheat. But I have prayed for thee, that thy faith fail not; and thou, being once converted, confirm thy brethren.' What doubt is there? He prayed for Peter, but prayed not for James and John, not to mention the others. It is manifest that all are included; for, praying for Peter, He is seen to have prayed for all; for a people is ever blamed or praised in him that is set over it." (Ambrosiaster, *Quaest.* 75, *ex N. Test. in App. St. August.* tom. iii. 2894), in Charles F. B. Allnatt, ed., *Cathedra Petri—The Titles and Prerogatives of St. Peter*, (London: Burns & Oates, 1879), 43.

St. Ambrose (385 A.D.):

> "[Peter] set over the Church . . . the pastor of the Lord's flock." (Ambrose, *In Ps.* xliii. n. 40), in Charles F. B. Allnatt, ed., *Cathedra Petri—The Titles and Prerogatives of St. Peter*, (London: Burns & Oates, 1879), 41.

> "Him whom, as He is about to be raised to heaven, He was leaving to us, as it were, the Vicar of His love. For thus you have it: 'Simon, son of John, lovest thou Me? . . . Feed My sheep. . . . Because he alone out of all makes this profession (of love), he is preferred before all. . . . And now he is not ordered, as at first, to 'feed His lambs,'. . . but 'His sheep,' that the more perfect might govern the more perfect." (Ambrose, *In Lucam*, lib. x. p. 1848, tom. ii.), in Charles F. B. Allnatt, ed., *Cathedra Petri—The Titles and Prerogatives of St. Peter*, (London: Burns & Oates, 1879), 41-42.

> "To Pope Siricius, who had ordered that Jovinian and others should be excommunicated in the Church of Milan: 'We have recognised in the letter of your Holiness the watchfulness of the good shepherd, who dost faithfully keep the gate intrusted to thee, and with pious solicitude dost guard the fold of Christ, worthy, indeed, that the Lord's sheep should

hear and follow thee." (Ambrose, *Epist. xliii. Siricio.* tom. ii. p. 966), in Charles F. B. Allnatt, ed., *Cathedra Petri—The Titles and Prerogatives of St. Peter*, (London: Burns & Oates, 1879), 108.

"Therefore did Christ also commit to Peter to feed His flock, and to do the will of the Lord, because He knew his love." (Ambrose, *Ib.in. Ps. cxviii.* (Mem) n. 3, p. 1131.), in Joseph Berington, John Kirk, eds., and James Waterworth, rev., *The Faith of Catholics*, vol. 2, (New York: Pustet & Co., 1884), 26.

St. Epiphanius (ca. 385 A.D.):

". . . And the blessed Peter, who for awhile denied the Lord, Peter who was the Chiefest of the Apostles, he who became unto us truly a firm upon which is based the Lord's faith, upon which (Rock) the Church is in every way built; first, in that he confessed that Christ was the Son of the living God, and heard that upon this Rock of firm faith I will build my Church . . . . Further, he then also became a firm rock of the building, and Foundation of the house of God, in that having denied Christ, and being again converted, being both found of the Lord and found worthy to hear, 'Feed my sheep and feed my lambs.'" Epiphanius, *Adv. Haeres.* p. 500, in Colin Lindsay, *The Evidence for the Papacy*, (London: Longmans, 1870), 35-36.

"He heard from that same God, 'Peter, feed My lambs;' to him was intrusted the flock; he leads the way admirably in the power of his own Master." (Epiphanius, Tom. ii. *In Anchorat.* n. 9), in Charles F. B. Allnatt, ed., *Cathedra Petri—The Titles and Prerogatives of St. Peter*, (London: Burns & Oates, 1879), 42.

St. Orsiesius (ca. 380 A.D.):

"Orsiesius, born in Egypt, he embraced the monastic or ascetic life, under St. Pachomius, whom he succeeded in the year 349. He died in 380. His treatise on the monastic state is given by Galland, t. v." Joseph Berington, John Kirk, eds., and James Waterworth, rev., *The Faith of Catholics*, vol. 2, (New York: Pustet & Co., 1884), 14.

"He said to Peter, the prince of the Apostles, 'Simon, son of John, lovest thou me more than these? &c.' (John xxi. 15, 16) Three times did He bid him 'feed His sheep,' and thereby has He imposed this duty upon us all, to feed diligently the Lord's sheep." (Orsiesius, *Doctrina de Instit. Monach.* n. 17, p. 42, t.v. Galland.), in Joseph Berington, John Kirk, eds., and James Waterworth, rev., *The Faith of Catholics*, vol. 2, (New York: Pustet & Co., 1884), 14.

St. John Chrysostom (ca. 387 A.D.):

"The apostles do not see their own affairs, but those of others, all together and each separately. Peter, the leader of the choir, the mouth of all the apostles, the head of that tribe, the ruler of the whole world, the foundation of the Church, the ardent lover of Christ; for he says 'Peter, lovest thou me more than these?' I speak his praises that you may learn that he loves Christ, for the care of the slaves is the greatest proof of love to the Lord. It is not I who say these things, but the beloved Lord. 'If thou lovest me,' he says, 'feed my sheep.' Let us see whether he has the primacy of a shepherd." Chrysostom, *Homily on 2 Timothy 3.1*, in J. P. Migne, ed., *Patrologiae Cursus Completus: Series Graeca*, (Paris, 1866), 56:275 in E. Giles, *Documents Illustrating Papal Authority A.D. 96-454*, (London: SPCK, 1952), 162-163.

"And why, then, passing by the others, does He converse with Peter on these things? (John 21:15). He was the chosen one of the Apostles, and the mouth of the disciples, and the leader of the choir. On this account, Paul also went up on a time to see him rather than the others [Galatians 1:18]. And withal, to show him that he must thenceforward have confidence, as the denial was done away with, He puts into his hands the presidency over the brethren. And He brings not forward the denial, nor reproaches him with what had past, but says, 'If thou lovest Me, preside over the brethren, . . . and the third time He gives him the same injunction, showing at what a price He sets the presidency over his own sheep. And if any one should say, How then did James receive the throne of Jerusalem? This I would answer, that He appointed this man (Peter) teacher, not of that throne, but of the world." (Chrysostom, *In Joan. Hom.* lxxxviii. n. 1, tom. viii. pp. 526, 7), in Charles F. B. Allnatt, ed., *Cathedra Petri—The Titles and Prerogatives of St. Peter*, (London: Burns & Oates, 1879), 42-43.

"Why did He shed His blood? That He might gain possession of those sheep which He intrusted to Peter and to his successors." (Chrysostom, *De Sacerdot.* lib. ii. c. 1, p. 371), in Charles F. B. Allnatt, ed., *Cathedra Petri—The Titles and Prerogatives of St. Peter*, (London: Burns & Oates, 1879), 43.

St. Asterius (395 A.D.):

"Asterius (St.), Bishop of Amasea, in Pontus, was a contemporary of St. Chrysostom, and wrote about A.D. 387. His works were published by F. Combefis, in his *Auctuarium* to the *Bibl. Patrum* (Paris, 1648), and a more complete edition by Migne (*Patr. Graec.* vol. xl.)." Charles F. B. Allnatt, ed., *Cathedra Petri—The Titles and Prerogatives of St. Peter*, (London: Burns & Oates, 1879), 2.

"In order that he may show his power, God has endowed none of his disciples with gifts like Peter. But, having raised him with heavenly gifts, he has set him above all. And, as first disciple and greater among the brethren, he has shown, by the test of deeds, the power of the Spirit. The first to be called, he followed at once. . . . The Saviour confided to this man, as some special trust, the whole Universal Church, after having asked him three times 'Lovest thou me?'. And he received the world in charge, as one flock one shepherd, having heard, 'Feed my lambs'; and the Lord gave, well nigh in his own stead, that most faithful disciple to the proselytes as a father, and shepherd and instructor." (Asterius, *Homily On the Chief Holy Apostles, Peter and Paul*, in J. P. Migne, ed., *Patrologiae Cursus Completus: Series Graeca*, (Paris, 1866), 40:273), in E. Giles, *Documents Illustrating Papal Authority A.D. 96-454*, (London: SPCK, 1952), 145-146.

St. Augustine (ca. 400 A.D.):

> "Deservedly also, after his resurrection, the Lord commended his sheep to Peter himself to feed; for he was not the only one among the disciples who was thought worthy to feed the Lord's sheep, but when Christ speaks to one, unity is commended—and to Peter for the first time, because Peter is first among the apostles." Augustine, *Sermo. 295*, in J. P. Migne, ed., *Patrologiae Cursus Completus: Series Latina*, (Paris, 1866), 38:802 in E. Giles, *Documents Illustrating Papal Authority A.D. 96-454*, (London: SPCK, 1952), 176.

> "I am held in the communion of the Catholic Church by . . . the succession of priests from the very Chair of the Apostle Peter, to whom the Lord, after his resurrection, committed His sheep to be fed, even to the present Episcopate." (Augustine, Tom. viii. *Cont. Epist. Manich. Fund.* n. 5 p. 269), in Charles F. B. Allnatt, ed., *Cathedra Petri—The Titles and Prerogatives of St. Peter*, (London: Burns & Oates, 1879), 43-44.

> "Peter was made the pastor of the Church, as Moses was made the ruler of the Jewish people." (Augustine, *Cont. Faustum*, lib. xxii. c. 70), in Charles F. B. Allnatt, ed., *Cathedra Petri—The Titles and Prerogatives of St. Peter*, (London: Burns & Oates, 1879), 44.

> "Peter, to whom He commended His sheep as another self, He wished to make one with Himself, that so He might commend the sheep to him; that he might be the head, he bear the figure of the Body—that is, of the Church—and as husband and wife be two in one flesh." (Augustine, Tom. v. *Serm.* xlvi. n. 30, p. 345), in Charles F. B. Allnatt, ed., *Cathedra Petri—The Titles and Prerogatives of St. Peter*, (London: Burns & Oates, 1879), 44.

St. Boniface (419 A.D.):

> "As you have loyally said in your letters, the most blessed apostle Peter watches with his eyes in what manner you

exercise the office of rector. He who was appointed shepherd of the Lord's sheep in perpetuity cannot but be very close to you, cannot but watch over any church, no matter where it is situated, in which we have laid a foundation-stone of the Universal Church." Boniface, *Ep. 5, to Rufus, Bishop of Thessalonica, 19 September 419*, in J. P. Migne, ed., *Patrologiae Cursus Completus: Series Latina*, (Paris, 1866), 20:762 in E. Giles, *Documents Illustrating Papal Authority A.D. 96-454*, (London: SPCK, 1952), 229.

Theodoret, Bishop of Cyrus (ca. 420 A.D.):

"'For as I,' he says, 'did not despise thee when tossed, so be thou a support to thy brethren in trouble, and the help by which thou wast saved do thou thyself impart to others, and exhort them not while they are tottering, but raise them up in their peril. For this reason I suffer thee also to slip, but do not permit thee to fall, [thus] through thee gaining steadfastness for those who are tossed.' So this great pillar supported the tossing and sinking world, and permitted it not to fall entirely and gave it back stability, having been ordered to feed God's sheep." Theodoret, *Oratio de Caritate* in J. P. Migne, ed., *Patrologiae Cursus Completus: Series Graeca*, (Paris, 1866), 82:1509 in E. Giles, *Documents Illustrating Papal Authority A.D. 96-454*, (London: SPCK, 1952), 292. See also Charles F. B. Allnatt, ed., *Cathedra Petri—The Titles and Prerogatives of St. Peter*, (London: Burns & Oates, 1879), 38.

St. Maximus of Turin (424 A.D.):

"Peter found a grace greater than that which he had lost. As a good shepherd, he received the flock to guard, that he, who before had been weak in his own case, might become a support to all . . . and a foundation to the rest by stability of faith." (Maximus, *Hom.* iv. *De Pet. Apost. Bibl. Max. Pat.* vi. 24), in Charles F. B. Allnatt, ed., *Cathedra Petri—The Titles and Prerogatives of St. Peter*, (London: Burns & Oates, 1879), 44.

"This is Peter to whom Christ entrusted the feeding of his sheep and lambs just before he ascended to the Father. As Christ had redeemed these by the compassion of his obedient service, so Peter served them by virtue of his faith. And rightly did that witness of mysteries, the Son of God, commit the feeding and tending of sheep to Peter whom he knew would not desist in his enthusiasm and faithfulness in nourishing the Lord's flock." (Maximus, *Homily LXVIII, In Nativitate Petri et Pauli*), in J. P. Migne, *Patr. Lat.*, vol. 57, col. 394, trans. John Collorafi.

Cyril of Alexandria (ca. 424 A.D.):

"For the wondrous Peter, overcome by uncontrollable fear, denied the Lord three times. Christ heals the error done, and demands in various ways the threefold confession. . . . For although all the holy disciples alike fled . . . still Peter's fault in the threefold denial was in addition, special and peculiar to himself. Therefore by the threefold confession of blessed Peter, the fault of triple denial was done away. Further by the Lord's saying 'Feed my lambs,' we must understand a renewal as it were of the apostleship already given to him, washing away the intervening disgrace of his fall, and the littleness of human infirmity." Cyril, *Commentary on John's Gospel, Book 12*, in J. P. Migne, ed., *Patrologiae Cursus Completus: Series Graeca*, (Paris, 1866), 74:749 in E. Giles, *Documents Illustrating Papal Authority A.D. 96-454*, (London: SPCK, 1952), 258.

"Over the Church He sets Peter as shepherd." (Cyril, *In Matt.* xvi. tom. v. p. 25), in Charles F. B. Allnatt, ed., *Cathedra Petri—The Titles and Prerogatives of St. Peter*, (London: Burns & Oates, 1879), 44.

St. Peter Chrysologus, Bishop of Ravenna (432 A.D.):

"Hence it is that the Master Himself seeks for helpers, for associates to take charge of the whole world, saying, 'Sing joyfully to God, all the earth' (Ps. xcix). Hence it is that, when about to return to heaven, He commends His sheep to be fed by Peter, in his Stead. Peter, says He, 'lovest thou Me? Feed My sheep.'" Peter Chrysologus, *Serm. vi. In Ps. xcix.*, p. 10, in Colin Lindsay, *The Evidence for the Papacy*, (London: Longmans, 1870), 51-52.

"As Peter obtained his name from a Rock, because he was the First, that merited to found the Church by the firmness of his faith, so Stephen was so called from a crown, because he was the first who merited to engage in conflict for the name of Christ. . . . Let Peter hold his long-established Princedom (*principatum*) over the Apostolic Choir; let him open the kingdom of heaven for those who enter in; let him with power bind the guilty; with clemency absolve the penitent." (Peter Chrysologus, *Serm. cliv.* p. 217), in Colin Lindsay, *The Evidence for the Papacy*, (London: Longmans, 1870), 52.

Arnobius Junior (440 A.D.):

"Arnobius Junior was a priest or bishop of Gaul, who flourished about A.D. 440. His *Commentary on the Psalms* is dedicated to Leontius, Bishop of Arles, and to Rusticus, Bishop of Narbonne. Published in *Bibl. Max. Pat.* (tom. viii.)." Charles F. B. Allnatt, ed., *Cathedra Petri—The Titles and Prerogatives of St.* Peter, (London: Burns & Oates, 1879), 2.

"Behold, that succour is given to a penitent Apostle, who is the Bishop of bishops, and a greater rank is restored to him now weeping than was taken from him when he 'denied.' That I may prove this, I show that no other Apostle received the name of Shepherd. For the Lord Jesus alone said, 'I am the Good Shepherd;' and again, 'My sheep,' He says, 'Follow Me.' This holy name, therefore, and the power of the same name, He, after the resurrection, conceded to the penitent Peter; and the Denied bestowed on him who denied Him this power which he alone had; that he might be proved not only to have recovered what he had lost, but also to have acquired even much more by being penitent than he had lost by denying." (Arnobius Junior, *Com. in Ps.* cxxxviii. tom. viii. *Bib. Max. Pat.* p. 320), in Charles F. B. Allnatt, ed., *Cathedra Petri—The Titles and Prerogatives of St. Peter*, (London: Burns & Oates, 1879), 46.

St. Eucherius, Bishop of Lyons (ca. 440):

"Eucherius, Saint, Bishop of Lyons, theologian, born in the latter half of the fourth century; died about 449. . . . Though imitating the virtues of the Egyptian solitaries, he kept in touch with men renowned for learning and piety, e.g. Cassian, St. Hilary of Arles, St. Honoratus, later Bishop of Marseilles, and Valerian, to whom he wrote. . . . The fame of Eucherius was soon so widespread in southeastern Gaul, that he was chosen Bishop of Lyons . . . probably in 434. [The text of his works] is most accessible in Migne, *Patr. Lat.*, L, 685-894." *The Catholic Encyclopedia*, 1913 ed., s.v. "Eucherius," by Leon Clugnet.

"First He committed to him the lambs, then the sheep; because He constituted him not only shepherd, but the shepherd of shepherds. Therefore, Peter feeds the lambs, he feeds also the sheep; he feeds the offspring, he feeds also the mothers; he rules both subjects and prelates. He is the shepherd, therefore, of all, because, besides lambs and sheep, there is nothing in the Church." (Eucherius, *Serm. de Natal. SS. Apost. Petri et Pauli*), in Charles F. B. Allnatt, ed., *Cathedra Petri—The Titles and Prerogatives of St. Peter*, (London: Burns & Oates, 1879), 45-46.

Pope St. Leo the Great (ca. 440-461 A.D.):

"[F]or not only was the power of binding and loosing given to Peter before the others, but also to Peter more especially was entrusted the care of feeding the sheep. Yet anyone who holds that the headship must be denied to Peter, cannot really diminish his dignity: but is puffed up with the breath of his pride, and plunges himself to the lowest depth." (Leo, *Letters* 10:2 [450 A.D.]) in Philip Schaff and Henry Wace, eds., *Nicene and Post-Nicene Fathers—Leo the Great, Gregory the Great*, 2nd series, vol. 12, (Peabody, MA: Hendrickson, 1994), 9.

"Since then, beloved, we see such a protection divinely granted to us, reasonably and justly do we rejoice in the merits and dignity of our leader, rendering thanks to the eternal King, our Redeemer, the Lord Jesus Christ, for having given so great a power to him whom he made chief of the whole Church, that if anything, even in our time, by us be rightly done and rightly ordered, it is to be ascribed to his working, to his guidance, unto whom it was said, 'And thou, when thou art converted, confirm thy brethren'; and to whom the Lord after his resurrection, in answer to the triple profession of eternal love, thrice said, with mystical intent, 'Feed my sheep.' And this, beyond a doubt, the pious shepherd does even now, and fulfils the charge of his Lord, confirming us with his exhortations, and not ceasing to pray for us, that we may be overcome by no temptation. But if, as we must believe, he extends this care of his piety to all God's people everywhere, how much more will he condescend to grant his help unto us his children, among whom, on the sacred couch of his blessed repose, he rests in the same flesh in which he ruled! To him, therefore, let us ascribe this anniversary day of us his servant, and this festival, by whose patronage we have been thought worthy to share his seat itself, the grace of our Lord Jesus Christ helping us in all things, who liveth and reigneth with God the Father and the Holy Ghost for ever and ever. Amen." (Leo, *Sermo 4—Gaudeo, dilectissimi* in J. P. Migne, ed., *Patrologiae Cursus Completus: Series Latina*, (Paris, 1866), 54:149), in E. Giles, *Documents Illustrating Papal Authority A.D. 96-454*, (London: SPCK, 1952), 280-281.

Pope St. Simplicius (468 A.D.):

"Simplicius (St. and Pope), sat from A.D. 468 to 483. His epistles are in Labbe (*Concil.* tom. iv.), &c." Charles F. B. Allnatt, ed., *Cathedra Petri—The Titles and Prerogatives of St. Peter*, (London: Burns & Oates, 1879), 12.

"Him on whom the Lord enjoined the care of all the sheepfold." (Simplicius, *Epist.* iv. *ad Basil August.* Labbe, iv. p. 1071), in Charles F. B. Allnatt, ed., *Cathedra Petri— The Titles and Prerogatives of St. Peter*, (London: Burns & Oates, 1879), 46.

"This same norm of apostolic doctrine persists in the successors of him to whom the Lord enjoined the care of the entire sheepfold." (Simplicius, *Simplic. Pap. ep. 4 ad Zenon. Imp.*), in Dr. Hergenrother, trans. J. B. Robertson, *Anti-Janus: An Historico-Theological Criticism Of The Work, Entitled 'The Pope And The Council', By Janus.* (Dublin: W. B. Kelly, 1870), 63 [textual Latin trans. by John Collorafi].

Pope St. Gelasius (ca. 492 A.D.):

"For the government of the Apostolic See, engaged without ceasing in the care of the whole flock of the Lord, which care was delegated to the blessed Peter by the voice of our Saviour Himself, 'And thou, converted, confirm thy brethren,' we neither can, nor ought to, dissemble such things as constrain our solicitude." (Gelasius, *Epist. v. ad. Honorium Dalmat. Episc.* Labbe, iv. p. 1170), in Charles F. B. Allnatt, ed., *Cathedra Petri—The Titles and Prerogatives of St. Peter*, (London: Burns & Oates, 1879), 39.

"Referring to the adjudication of the Primacy to Rome, he says, 'as being men who bore in mind the Lord's sentence, "Thou art Peter, and upon this rock I will build My Church, etc." And again to the same Peter, "Lo! I have prayed for thee that thy faith fail not, and converted, confirm the brethren," and that sentence, "If thou lovest Me, feed my sheep." Wherefore, then, is the Lord's discourse so frequently directed to Peter? Was it that the rest of the holy and blessed Apostles were not clothed with his virtue? Who dare assert this? No, but that, by a Head being constituted, the occasion of schism might be removed; and that the compact bond of the body of Christ, thus uniformly tending, by the fellowship of a most glorious love, to one Head, might be shown to be one; and that there might be one Church faithfully believed in, and one house of the one God and of the one Redeemer, wherein we might be nourished with one bread and one chalice. . . . There were assuredly twelve Apostles, endowed with equal merits and equal dignity; and whereas they all shone equally with spiritual light, yet was it Christ's will that One amongst them should be the Ruler (prince—*principem*), etc." (Gelasius, in Galland, t. x. p. 677), in Colin Lindsay, *The Evidence for the Papacy*, (London: Longmans, 1870), 55-56.

Pope Pelagius II (ca. 579-590 A.D.):

" Consider that the Truth could not have lied, nor will the faith of Peter be able to be shaken or changed for ever. For, although the devil desired to sift all the disciples, the Lord testifies that He Himself asked for Peter alone, and wished that the others be confirmed by him; and to Peter also was committed the care of 'feeding the sheep' [John 21:15]; and to him also did the Lord hand over the 'keys to the kingdom of Heaven' [Matthew 16:19], and upon him did He promise to 'build His Church' [Matthew 16:18]; and He testified that 'the gates of hell would not prevail against it' [Matthew 16:19]. . . If, however, anyone either suggests or believes contrary to this faith, let him know that he is condemned and anathematized." Pelagius II, "Quod Ad Dilectionem"; "Dilectionis Vestrae," in Henry Denzinger, *Enchiridion Symbolorum*, 30th Ed., (London: B. Herder Book Co., 1957), Para. 246, 247, in Michael Malone, ed., *The Apostolic Digest*, (Irving, TX: Sacred Heart, 1987), 206.

Pope St. Gregory the Great (ca. 600 A.D.):

"By the voice of the Lord, the care of the whole Church was committed to Peter, the head of all the Apostles; for to him it was said, 'Peter, lovest thou Me? Feed My sheep.'" (Gregory, Lib. iv. *Epist.* 32), in Charles F. B. Allnatt, ed., *Cathedra Petri—The Titles and Prerogatives of St. Peter*, (London: Burns & Oates, 1879), 46-47.

JESUS, PETER AND THE KEYS

CHAPTER IX

PRIMACY OF THE POPE AND THE ROMAN CHURCH

Origen (ca. 230-250 A. D.):

"Peter, the Prince of the Apostles." (Origen, *In Lucam, Hom.* xvii. tom. iii. p. 953), and "More honour than the rest." (Origen, Tom. xxxii in *Joann.* n. 5 tom. iii. p. 413), both in Charles F. B. Allnatt, ed., *Cathedra Petri—The Titles and Prerogatives of St. Peter*, (London: Burns & Oates, 1879), 48.

"[Origen] on the words in Matt. xvii. 26 [27] he remarks, that the disciples 'considered that this was a very great favour to Peter on the part of Jesus, as having adjudged him greater than the other disciples.'" (Origen, Tom. xiii. *in Matt.* n. 14, tom. iii. p. 588), in Charles F. B. Allnatt, ed., *Cathedra Petri—The Titles and Prerogatives of St. Peter*, (London: Burns & Oates, 1879), 48.

"There is one baptism, and one Holy Ghost, and one Church, founded by Christ our Lord upon Peter, for (or from) an original and principle of unity." (Origen, *Ep. lxx. ad Januar. et Ep. Numid.* p. 270.), in Joseph Berington, John Kirk, eds., and James Waterworth, rev., *The Faith of Catholics*, vol. 2, (New York: Pustet & Co., 1884), 8.

"To the seven children there is evidently conjoined their mother, the origin and root, which afterwards bare seven churches, herself having been founded first and alone, by the voice of the Lord, upon Peter." (Origen, *De Exhort. Martyr.* pp. 522-3), in Joseph Berington, John Kirk, eds., and James Waterworth, rev., *The Faith of Catholics*, vol. 2, (New York: Pustet & Co., 1884), 10.

St. Cyprian (ca. 246 A.D.):

"The Lord says to Peter, 'I say unto thee,' says he, 'that thou art Peter. . . shall be loosed in heaven.' And to the same after his resurrection, he says to him 'Feed my sheep.' Upon him he builds the Church, and he commits to him the sheep to feed, and though to all the apostles he gives an equal power, yet he founded one chair, and by his authority appointed the source and system of unity. Certainly the rest were as Peter was, but primacy is given to Peter and one Church and one chair is shown; and they are all shepherds, but one flock is exhibited, which is fed by all the apostles with unanimous consent. And he who does not hold this unity of his Church, does he think he holds the faith? He who deserts the chair of Peter, upon whom the Church was founded, does he trust himself to be in the Church? The episcopate is one, part of which is held by each one in solidity." Cyprian, *De Catholicae Ecclesiae Unitate* in E. Giles, *Documents Illustrating Papal Authority A.D. 96-454*, (London: SPCK, 1952), 52-53.

"Moreover, after all this, having had a pseudo-bishop set up for themselves by heretics, they dare to sail, and to carry letters, from schismatic and profane men, to the chair of Peter, and to the principal Church whence the unity of the priesthood took its rise; nor do they consider that the Romans are those (whose faith was praised in the preaching of the Apostle) to whom faithlessness cannot have access." (Cyprian, *Ep. lv. ad Cornel.* pp. 182-3.), in Joseph Berington, John Kirk, eds., and James Waterworth, rev., *The Faith of Catholics*, vol. 1, (New York: Pustet & Co., 1884), 309-10.

Auctor de Rebaptismate (254 A.D.):

> "Auctor de Rebaptismate. This anonymous author is proved by Tillemont, Gallandi, and Dom Ceillier to have written against St. Cyprian about the year 254. His treatise is published in Galland (tom. iii.), and by Migne (*Patr. Lat.* vol. iii. p. 1187 sq.), in Charles F. B. Allnatt, ed., *Cathedra Petri— The Titles and Prerogatives of St. Peter*, (London: Burns & Oates, 1879), 2.

> "Peter, the leader and prince of the Apostles." (Auctor, *Auct. de Rebapt.* n. 10, Galland, ii. p. 366), in Charles F. B. Allnatt, ed., *Cathedra Petri—The Titles and Prerogatives of St. Peter*, (London: Burns & Oates, 1879), 49.

St. Peter, Bishop of Alexandria (ca. 306-311 A.D.):

> "It is generally assumed that Peter, although he was an anti-Origenist, was head of the catechetical school in Alexandria prior to his being made bishop of that see about the year 300 A.D. After being bishop of Alexandria for about eleven years he died a martyr's death.
>
> "Except for a very short letter to the clergy of Alexandria in reference to Meletius of Lycopolis, who had usurped the see of Alexandria when Peter withdrew from the city during the persecution, and who had thereby instigated the so-called Meletian schism, which persisted for several centuries, his writings are extant only in fragments." W. A. Jurgens, *The Faith of the Early Fathers*, vol. 1, (Collegeville, MN: The Liturgical Press, 1970), 259.

> "Peter, set above the Apostles." (Peter of Alexadria, *Canon.* ix. Galland, iv. p. 98), in Charles F. B. Allnatt, ed., *Cathedra Petri—The Titles and Prerogatives of St. Peter*, (London: Burns & Oates, 1879), 49.

Council of Nicaea (325 A.D.):

(From the *Arabic Canons of the Council of Nicaea*):

"[CANON XXXIX] Of the care and power which a Patriarch has over the bishops and archbishops of his patriarchate; and of the primacy of the Bishop of Rome over all.

"Let the patriarch consider what things are done by the archbishops and bishops in their provinces; and if he shall find anything done by them otherwise than it should be, let him change it, and order it, as seemeth him fit; for he is the father of all, and they are his sons. And although the archbishop be among the bishop as an elder brother, who hath the care of his brethren, and to whom they owe obedience because he is over them; yet the patriarch is to all those who are under this power, just as he who holds the seat of Rome, is the head and prince of all patriarchs; inasmuch as he is first, as was Peter, to whom power is given over all Christian princes, and over all their peoples, as he who is the Vicar of Christ our Lord over all peoples and over the whole Christian Church, and whoever shall contradict this, is excommunicated by the Synod. [While not a part of the generally accepted canons of the Council of Nicaea, these canons promulgated from the Eastern Church give a mind's eye view of the thinking of Eastern Christianity.]" Philip Schaff and Henry Wace, eds., *Nicene and Post-Nicene Fathers—The Seven Ecumenical Councils*, vol. 14, (Peabody, MA: Hendrickson, 1994), 48.

Eusebius (ca. 325 A.D.):

"The providence of the universal Ruler led as it were by the hand to Rome, that most powerful and great one of the Apostles, and, on account of his virtue, the mouthpiece (or, leader) of the rest, Peter, against that sad destroyer of the human race (Simon Magus). He, as a noble general (appointed) of God, armed with heavenly weapons, brought the precious merchandise of intellectual light from the east to the dwellers in the west." (Eusebius, *H. E.l. ii.* c. 14, pp. 63-4.), in Joseph Berington, John Kirk, eds., and James

Waterworth, rev., *The Faith of Catholics*, vol. 2, (New York: Pustet & Co., 1884), 12-13.

"He became a stranger to these his brethren (ps. lxviii. 9), at the time of His Passion, when all his disciples leaving Him fled, and he the very head (Coryphaeus) of the Apostles, Peter, denied Him thrice." (Eusebius, *Comm. in Ps. lxix.* t. i. p. 373, Nov. Collect.), in Joseph Berington, John Kirk, eds., and James Waterworth, rev., *The Faith of Catholics*, vol. 2, (New York: Pustet & Co., 1884), 13.

St. Anthony of Egypt (330 A.D.):

"Anthony (St.), the great founder of monasticism, was born A.D. 250, at Coma, on the borders of Upper Egypt, and died A.D. 355, at the age of 105. His extant writings are in Galland (tom. iv.)." Charles F. B. Allnatt, ed., *Cathedra Petri—The Titles and Prerogatives of St. Peter*, (London: Burns & Oates, 1879), 2.

"[Peter] the Prince of the Apostles." (Anthony, *Epist.* xvii. Galland, iv. p. 687), in Charles F. B. Allnatt, ed., *Cathedra Petri—The Titles and Prerogatives of St. Peter*, (London: Burns & Oates, 1879), 49.

Pope St. Julius I (342 A.D.):

"Julian I, St. Pope from 337-352. A strong opponent of Arianism, Julius spent much of his reign upholding Christian orthodoxy against the Arians. . . . He gave refuge in Rome to St. Athanasius of Alexandria in 339 after the bishop had been deposed and expelled from his see by the Arians. Julius reaffirmed Athanasius' right to the see at the Council of Rome in 340, and then convoked the Council of Sardica (342-343) to combat Arianism and to bolster the West against its spread. The council gave Julius acknowledgment of his supreme ecclesiastical authority, particularly the right to judge cases involving episcopal sees. Emperor Constantius II, an Arian, confirmed Julius's restoration of Athanasius, a statement of Julius's abilities as pontiff. Letters from Julius

were preserved in Athanasius' *Apology Against the Arians.*"
Our Sunday Visitor's Encyclopedia of Catholic History, 1995
ed., s.v. "Julius I, St.".

"It behoved [behooved] you, beloved, to come hither
(Rome), and not to refuse, in order that this business may
be terminated; for reason requires this. . . . Oh, beloved!
The judgments of the Church are no longer in accordance
with the Gospel, but are (by you, Arians) to the inflicting of
exile and of death. For even though any transgression had
been committed, as you pretend, by these men (i.e. S.
Athanasius, Paul of Constantinople, &c.), the judgment
ought to have been in accordance with the ecclesiastical rule,
and not thus. It behoved you to write to all of us, that thus
what was just might be decreed by all. For they who suffered were Bishops, and the Churches that suffered no common ones, over which the Apostles ruled in person. And
why were we not written to concerning the Church, especially of Alexandria? Or, are you ignorant that this has been
the custom first to write to us, and thus what is just be decreed from this Place (Rome)? If, therefore, any such suspicion fell upon the Bishop there (Alexandria), it was befitting to write to this Church (Rome). But now they who acquainted us not, but did what they themselves chose, proceed to wish us, though unacquainted with the facts, to become supporters of their views. Not thus were Paul's ordinances, not thus have the Fathers handed down to us, this is
another form, and a new institution. Bear with me cheer-
fully, I beseech you, for what I write is for the common
good. For what we have received from the blessed Apostle
Peter, the same do I make known to you; and these things I
would not have written to you, deeming them manifest to
you all, had not what has been done confounded us." (Julius,
Ep. ad Eusebian. n. 6, 21. *Galland.* T. v. p. 6, 13), in Charles
F. B. Allnatt, ed., *Cathedra Petri—The Titles and Prerogatives of St. Peter*, (London: Burns & Oates, 1879), 222.

St. Ephraem the Syrian (ca. 350-370 A.D.):

"He was the prince of the Apostles, and had received the
keys, and was accounted the shepherd of the flock."

(Ephraem, Tom. ii. *Syr. lvi. Adv. Haer.*), in Charles F. B. Allnatt, ed., *Cathedra Petri—The Titles and Prerogatives of St. Peter*, (London: Burns & Oates, 1879), 41.

"Then Peter deservedly received the Vicariate (of Christ) over His people." (Ephraem, *in Sermone de Martyrio. SS. App. Petri et Pauli*), in S. Herbert Scott, *The Eastern Churches and the Papacy*, (London: Sheed & Ward, 1928), 62.

St. Athanasius (362 A.D.):

"Athanasius (St.), Archbishop of Alexandria, and the great champion of orthodoxy against the Arians, was born A.D. 296, and died A.D. 373. See account of his life and writings in *Dict. of Christ. Biog. and Literat.* vol. i. pp. 179-203. The best edition of his works is the *Benedictine*, by Montfaucon (2 vols. fol. Paris, 1698), republished, with additions, by Migne, in 4 vols. (*Patr. Graec.* vols. xxv.-xxviii.)." Charles F. B. Allnatt, ed., *Cathedra Petri—The Titles and Prerogatives of St. Peter*, (London: Burns & Oates, 1879), 2.

Rome is called, "The Apostolic throne." (Athanasius, *Hist. Arian. ad Monach.* n. 35), in Charles F. B. Allnatt, ed., *Cathedra Petri—The Titles and Prerogatives of St. Peter*, (London: Burns & Oates, 1879), 61.

"The Chief, Peter." (Athanasius, *In Ps.* xv. 8, tom. iii. p. 106, Migne), in Charles F. B. Allnatt, ed., *Cathedra Petri— The Titles and Prerogatives of St. Peter*, (London: Burns & Oates, 1879), 50.

St. Cyril of Jerusalem (ca. 363 A.D.):

"Peter, the chiefest and foremost (leader) of the Apostles, before a little maid thrice denied the Lord, but, moved to penitence, he wept bitterly." (Cyril, *Catech. ii.* n. 15, p. 31), in Joseph Berington, John Kirk, eds., and James Waterworth, rev., *The Faith of Catholics*, vol. 2, (New York: Pustet & Co., 1884), 16.

"In the power of the same Holy Spirit, Peter, also the foremost of the Apostles and the key-bearer of the kingdom of heaven, healed Aeneas the paralytic in the name of Christ. (Cyril, *Catech. xvii.* n. 27, p. 227.), in Joseph Berington, John Kirk, eds., and James Waterworth, rev., *The Faith of Catholics*, vol. 2, (New York: Pustet & Co., 1884), 17.

St. Optatus, of Milevis (ca. 370 A.D.):

"You cannot deny that you know that in the city of Rome the Chair was first conferred on Peter, in which the prince of all the Apostles, Peter, sat, . . . in which Chair unity should be preserved by all, so that he should now be a schismatic and a sinner who should set up another Chair against that unique one. Therefore in the Single Chair, which is the first of the endowments [enumerated by Parmenian, the writer's Donatist adversary] sat first Peter, to whom succeeded Linus [a list of the Popes follows] . . . to Damasus succeeded Siricius, who is our colleague, with whom the whole world together with us is united in one fellowship of communion by the interchange of letters." Optatus, *De schismate Donatistorum—Contra Parmen.* 2:2, in Dom John Chapman, *Bishop Gore and Catholic Claims* (London: Longmans, Green, and Co., 1905), 55.

"Whence then is it that you strive to usurp unto yourselves the keys of the kingdom of heaven, you who sacrilegiously fight against the chair of Peter, by your presumption and audacity?" (Optatus, *De Schism. Donat.* l. ii. n. 4, 6), in Joseph Berington, John Kirk, eds., and James Waterworth, rev., *The Faith of Catholics*, vol. 1, (New York: Pustet & Co., 1884), 311-12.

"Having established the primacy of the see of Rome, he says: 'But you say that you have a certain share in the city of Rome. This is a branch of your error, shooting forth from false-hood, not from the root of truth. In fact, if Macrobius be asked what chair he fills in that city, can he answer, 'Peter's chair?' which I do not know that he even knows by sight, and unto whose memorial, like a schismatic, he has not ap-proached, acting in opposition to the Apostle, who says, Communicating with the memories of the saints (Rom. xii. 13). Lo! there are the memorials of the two Apostles."

(Optatus, *De Schism. Donat.* l. ii. n. 4, 6), in Joseph Berington, John Kirk, eds., and James Waterworth, rev., *The Faith of Catholics*, vol. 1, (New York: Pustet & Co., 1884), 310, 312.

St. Gregory Nazianzen (370 A.D.):

"The faith (of Rome) was of old, and still is now, right, binding the whole West by the saving word, as is just in her who presides over all, reverencing the whole harmonious teaching of God." (Gregory Nazianzen, *Carm. de Vita Sua*, vv. 568-573, tom. ii. p. 704), in Charles F. B. Allnatt, ed., *Cathedra Petri—The Titles and Prerogatives of St. Peter*, (London: Burns & Oates, 1879), 70.

St. Gregory of Nyssa (371 A.D.):

"The leader and *coryphaeus* of the Apostolic choir, . . . The head of the Apostles." (Gregory Nyssa, *Alt. Orat. de S. Steph.* tom. iii p. 730, 4), in Charles F. B. Allnatt, ed., *Cathedra Petri—The Titles and Prerogatives of St. Peter*, (London: Burns & Oates, 1879), 50.

St. Macarius of Egypt (371 A.D.):

"Macarius of Egypt (St.), was born A.D. 300, and in 330 entered on a life of rigid monasticism, dying in 399. Works published by Galland (tom. viii.), and Migne (*Patr. Gr.* vol. xxxiv.)." Charles F. B. Allnatt, ed., *Cathedra Petri—The Titles and Prerogatives of St. Peter*, (London: Burns & Oates, 1879), 10.

"The Chief, Peter." (Macarius, *De Patientia*, n. 3, p. 180, Galland, vii. p. 180), in Charles F. B. Allnatt, ed., *Cathedra Petri—The Titles and Prerogatives of St. Peter*, (London: Burns & Oates, 1879), 50-51.

"Moses was succeeded by Peter, who had committed to his hands the new Church of Christ, and the true priesthood." (Macarius, *Hom.* xxvi. n. 23, p. 101), in Charles F. B. Allnatt, ed., *Cathedra Petri—The Titles and Prerogatives of St. Peter*, (London: Burns & Oates, 1879), 51.

Edict of Emperor Theodosius (380 A.D.):

> "We will that all people who are governed by our clemency should practise the same religion as the divine Apostle Peter delivered to the Romans, as the religion proclaimed by him up to this time declares it; and which it is clear the Pontiff Damasus follows, and Peter, the Bishop of Alexandria, a man of apostolic sanctity-that is, &c. Those who follow this law we order to take the name of Catholic Christians." (*Theodosian Code* 16.1.22 (*cunctos populos*), 27 February 380 [J. P. Migne, *Patr. Lat.* 13.530]), in Luke Rivington, *The Primitive Church and the See of St. Peter*, (London: Longmans, Green and Co., 1894), 244.

Ambrosiaster (ca. 380-384 A.D.):

> "It was right indeed that he [Paul] should be anxious to see Peter; for he was the first among the apostles, and was entrusted by the Savior with the care of the churches." (Ambrosiaster, *Comm. on Galatians*, Migne *Patr. Lat.*, vol. 17, col. 344), in Michael M. Winter, *Saint Peter and the Popes*, (Baltimore: Helicon, 1960), 62.

> "Whereas the whole world is God's, yet is the Church said to be His house, of which Damasus [pope for whom St. Jerome translated the Vulgate Bible] is at this day the ruler." (Ambrosiaster, *Comment. in Epist. i. ad Tim.* Inter. Op. S. Ambros.), in Charles F. B. Allnatt, ed., *Cathedra Petri— The Titles and Prerogatives of St. Peter*, (London: Burns & Oates, 1879), 107.

Pope Damasus (382 A.D.):

> "[3] Likewise it is decreed: . . . we have considered that it ought to be announced that although all the Catholic Churches spread abroad through the world comprise but one bridal chamber of Christ, nevertheless, the holy Roman Church has been placed at the forefront not by the conciliar decisions of other Churches, but has received the primacy by the evangelic voice of our Lord and Savior, who says:

'You are Peter, and upon this rock I will build My Church, and the gates of hell will not prevail against it; and I will give to you the keys of the kingdom of heaven, and whatever you shall have bound on earth will be bound in heaven, and whatever you shall have loosed on earth shall be loosed in heaven' [Matt. 16:18-19]. . . .

"The first see, therefore, is that of Peter the Apostle, that of the Roman Church, which has neither stain nor blemish nor anything like it." (Damasus, *The Decree of Damasus* 3 [382 A.D.]), in W. A. Jurgens, *The Faith of the Early Fathers*, vol. 1, (Collegeville, MN: The Liturgical Press, 1970), 406.

St. Faustinus (383 A.D.):

"Faustinus is the sole author of *De Trinitate* or *De fide contra Arianos*; and he shows himself a much better theologian than Lucifer. . . . Faustinus' work on the Trinity is in seven short books, the seventh being devoted to the theology of the Holy Spirit in refutation of the homoiousian and pneumatomachian Macedonians. The work never uses the term Macedonian, however, a fact which led A. Wilmart to date the work as early as ca. 380 A.D. His reasoning seems quite valid; for it is soon after 380 that the term Macedonian becomes common enough in literature." W. A. Jurgens, *The Faith of the Early Fathers*, vol. 2, (Collegeville, MN: The Liturgical Press, 1970), 145.

"[Peter] Prince of the Apostles." (Faustinus, *De Trinitate*, c. 5, n. 3, Galland, vii. p. 455), in Charles F. B. Allnatt, ed., *Cathedra Petri—The Titles and Prerogatives of St. Peter*, (London: Burns & Oates, 1879), 51.

St. Ambrose (385 A.D.):

"St. Ambrose . . . declares union with the Roman See to be union with the Catholic Church. Speaking of his brother Satyrus, who had arrived, after shipwreck, in a place of doubtful orthodoxy, he says: 'He called the Bishop to him, and not accounting any grace true which was not of the true faith, he inquired of him whether he agreed with the Catholic Bishops, that is, with the Roman Church. (Ambrose, *De Excessa Frat.* n. 46, tom. ii. p. 1126), in Charles F. B. Allnatt, ed., *Cathedra Petri—The Titles and Prerogatives of St. Peter*, (London: Burns & Oates, 1879), 94.

"From this Church [of Rome] the rights of venerable communion flow unto all." (Ambrose, *Epist.* xi. n. 4), in Charles F. B. Allnatt, ed., *Cathedra Petri—The Titles and Prerogatives of St. Peter*, (London: Burns & Oates, 1879), 94.

St. John Chrysostom (ca. 387 A.D.):

"The apostles do not see their own affairs, but those of others, all together and each separately. Peter, the leader of the choir, the mouth of all the apostles, the head of that tribe, the ruler of the whole world, the foundation of the Church, the ardent lover of Christ; for he says 'Peter, lovest thou me more than these?' I speak his praises that you may learn that he loves Christ, for the care of the slaves is the greatest proof of love to the Lord. It is not I who say these things, but the beloved Lord. 'If thou lovest me,' he says, 'feed my sheep.' Let us see whether he has the primacy of a shepherd." John Chrysostom, *Homily on 2 Timothy 3.1*, in J. P. Migne, ed., *Patrologiae Cursus Completus: Series Graeca*, (Paris, 1866), 56:275 in E. Giles, *Documents Illustrating Papal Authority A.D. 96-454*, (London: SPCK, 1952), 162-163.

"Peter so washed away that denial as to be even made the first Apostle, and to have the whole world committed to him." (John Chrysostom, Tom. i. *Orat.* viii. n. 3), in Charles F. B. Allnatt, ed., *Cathedra Petri—The Titles and Prerogatives of St. Peter*, (London: Burns & Oates, 1879), 46.

"And should any one say, 'Why then did James receive the throne of Jerusalem?:' this is my answer: that He appointed this man (Peter) not teacher of that throne, but of the habitable globe." (John Chrysostom, *Ib. Hom. lxxxviii.* n. 6, p. 600.), in Joseph Berington, John Kirk, eds., and James Waterworth, rev., *The Faith of Catholics*, vol. 2, (New York: Pustet & Co., 1884), 34.

Pope Anastasius I (399 A.D.):

> "Anastasius I, St. Pope from 399-401. The successor to Pope
> Siricius and a Roman by birth, Anastasius was best known
> for his condemnation of various writings by the influential
> early Christian theologian Origen. He was praised by St.
> Augustine, St. Jerome and St. Paulinus of Nola." *Our Sun-
> day Visitor's Encyclopedia of Catholic History*, 1995 ed.,
> s.v. "Anastasius I, St.".

> "Far be this from the Catholic discipline of the Roman
> Church . . . Assuredly care shall not be wanting on my part
> to guard the faith of the Gospel for my people; and to visit
> by Letter, as far as I be able, the members of my body,
> throughout the divers regions of the earth, to prevent any
> beginning of a profane interpretation from creeping in, which
> may have for its object to confound devout minds, by spread-
> ing its darkness." (Anastasius, *Ep. i. Ad Joan. Jerosol* n. 5,
> *Galland.* t. viii. p. 247, 8), in Colin Lindsay, *The Evidence
> for the Papacy*, (London: Longmans, 1870), 228.

St. Augustine (ca. 400 A.D.):

> "Of this Church, Peter, the Apostle, on account of the Pri-
> macy of his Apostleship, bore a character which represented
> the whole Church. For as to what personally regards him,
> he was by nature but one man, by grace one Christian, by a
> more abundant grace, one, and that the First Apostle; but
> when there was said to him, 'I will give unto him the keys,
> &c.,' He signified the whole Church, which, in this world,
> is, by divers trials, as it were, by rains, rivers, and tempests,
> agitated, but falls not, because it was built upon a Rock,
> whence Peter derived his name. For a rock (*petra*) is not
> derived from Peter (*Petro*), but Peter from a Rock, as Christ
> is not derived from Christian, but Christian from Christ. For
> therefore does the Lord say, 'Upon this rock I will build my
> Church,' because Peter had said, 'Thou art the Christ, the
> Son of the living God.' Upon this Rock, therefore, which
> thou hast confessed, I will build My Church. For Christ was
> the Rock; upon which Foundation, even Peter himself was
> built. 'For other foundation can no man lay but that which
> is laid, which is Christ Jesus.' The Church therefore which

is founded on Christ, received in Peter the keys of the kingdom of heaven from Him, that is, the power of binding and
of loosing sins." (Augustine, *T. iii. Tract. cxxiv. in Joan. n.
5*, co. 599), in Colin Lindsay, *The Evidence for the Papacy*,
(London: Longmans, 1870), 45-46.

"In St. Augustine the same idea occurs frequently; the keys,
he says, were given to Peter as bearing the figure of the
Church, and more than once he explains that it is because of
his primacy that he thus represented the Church. I repeat
the following references from an elaborate footnote on the
subject in the *Revue Bened*, Jan., 1903, pp. 37, 38, directed
against the misunderstandings of Father Puller: 'To Peter
bearing the figure of the Church' (*de agone* 30; *Serm.* 149,
6; 4 18; *Retract.* i. 21; *Tract* 118 *in Joann.*). 'Almost everywhere Peter merited to bear the person of the whole Church'
(*Serm.* 295 2; 75 9) etc., 'on account of the primacy which
he had among the disciples' (*Enarr. in Ps.* 108 i), 'the first
and chief in the order of the Apostles, in whom the Church
was figured' (*Serm.* 76 3). 'To Peter first, because among
the Apostles Peter is first' (*Serm.* 295 4), etc." Dom John
Chapman, *Bishop Gore and Catholic Claims* (London:
Longmans, Green, and Co., 1905), 50-51.

"This is also one privilege of our city, that it received in the
beginning for its teacher the chief of the Apostles. For it was
befitting that city which, before the rest of the world, was
crowned with the name of Christian, should receive as shepherd the first of the Apostles. But, after having had him as
our teacher, we did not retain him, but surrendered him to
Imperial Rome." (Augustine, Tom. iii. *Hom.* ii. in *Inscript.
Act.* n. 6, p. 70), in Charles F. B. Allnatt, ed., *Cathedra Petri—
The Titles and Prerogatives of St. Peter*, (London: Burns &
Oates, 1879), 33.

"The Roman Church, in which the Primacy of the Apostolic
See has always been in force." (Augustine, *Epist.* xlii.), in

Charles F. B. Allnatt, ed., *Cathedra Petri—The Titles and Prerogatives of St. Peter*, (London: Burns & Oates, 1879), 73.

"Peter . . . head of the Apostles, doorkeeper of heaven and foundation of the church." (Augustine, *Ep.* 36, J. P. Migne, *Patrologiae Cursus Completus Series Latina* (Paris, 1844-1855), trans. John Collorafi.

"Pastoral vigilance is common to all of us who exercise the episcopal office, although you have the preeminence on a loftier summit" (Augustine, *L. i. ad Bonif.* c. I (Coust. p. 1024)), in Dr. Hergenrother, *Anti-Janus: An Historico-Theological Criticism Of The Work, Entitled 'The Pope And The Council', By Janus.* (Dublin: W. B. Kelly, 1870), p. 96 [Lat. trans. John Collorafi].

"To be unwilling to give the primacy [*primas*] to the Roman Church either stems from the utmost impiety or from rash arrogance." (Augustine, *De Util. Cred.* c. 17), in Dr. Hergenrother, *Anti-Janus: An Historico-Theological Criticism Of The Work, Entitled 'The Pope And The Council', By Janus.* (Dublin: W. B. Kelly, 1870), p. 96 [Lat. trans. John Collorafi].

Prudentius (405 A.D.):

"Prudentius, a Christian poet, was born at Saragossa, in Spain, A.D. 348, and died about A.D. 413. The latest editions of his poems are those of Dressel (Lipsiae, 1860), and Migne (*Patr. Lat.* vols. lix. lx.)." Charles F. B. Allnatt, ed., *Cathedra Petri—The Titles and Prerogatives of St. Peter*, (London: Burns & Oates, 1879), 11.

"Possessing the first chair, he [Peter] throws open the gates of eternity, that have been intrusted to him." (Prudentius, *Hymn. ii. in St. Laurent.* Galland, viii. p. 440), in Charles F. B. Allnatt, ed., *Cathedra Petri—The Titles and Prerogatives of St. Peter*, (London: Burns & Oates, 1879), 34.

"The highest disciple of God [Peter]." (Prudentius, *Cont. Symmachum*, lib. ii. Galland, viii. p. 509), in Charles F. B.

Allnatt, ed., *Cathedra Petri—The Titles and Prerogatives of St. Peter*, (London: Burns & Oates, 1879), 53.

Pope St. Innocent I (410 A.D.):

"Innocent I (St. and Pope), succeeded Anastasius I in the year 402, and died in 417. His epistles are published in Galland (tom. viii.), after Coustant." Charles F. B. Allnatt, ed., *Cathedra Petri—The Titles and Prerogatives of St. Peter*, (London: Burns & Oates, 1879), 8.

"Peter, through whom both the apostolate and episcopate took its beginning in Christ." (Innocent, *Epist. ii. ad Victric.* n. 2, p. 546, Galland, viii.), in Charles F. B. Allnatt, ed., *Cathedra Petri—The Titles and Prerogatives of St. Peter*, (London: Burns & Oates, 1879), 53.

"[Peter] from whom the episcopate itself, and the whole authority of this name, has sprung." (Innocent, *Epist. xxix. ad Concil. Carth.* n. 1, p. 599), in Charles F. B. Allnatt, ed., *Cathedra Petri—The Titles and Prerogatives of St. Peter*, (London: Burns & Oates, 1879), 53.

"As often as a principle of faith is ventilated, I am of opinion that all our brethren and fellow-bishops ought not to refer save to Peter, that is, to the author of their name and dignity." (Innocent, *Epist. xxx. ad Concil. Milev.* n. 1, p. 602), in Charles F. B. Allnatt, ed., *Cathedra Petri—The Titles and Prerogatives of St. Peter*, (London: Burns & Oates, 1879), 53.

"These, then, are the things which it behoves every Catholic Bishop, having before his eyes the judgment of God, hence-forward to observe. . . . That if any causes, or contentions, arise between clergy of the higher, or even of an inferior order, the dispute be settled agreeably to the Synod of Nicaea, by an assembly of the Bishops of that same province; and that it be not lawful for any one . . . to leave these priests (Bishops), who by the will of God govern the Church of God, and to have recourse to other provinces. If any greater causes shall have been brought forward (or discussed), let them, after episcopal judgment, be referred to the Apostolic See, as the synod (of Nicaea) resolved, and a blessed custom requires." (Innocent, *Ep. ii. ad Victric.* n. 1,

2, 3, 5, 6, *Galland*. t. viii. p. 547), in Colin Lindsay, *The Evidence for the Papacy*, (London: Longmans, 1870), 228.

"[To Decentius, Bishop of Gubbio] For who knows not, or notices not, that what was delivered to the Roman Church by Peter, the Prince of the Apostles, and is to this day guarded, ought to be observed by all men, and that nothing ought to be superinduced (or, introduced), which has not (that) authority, or which may seem to derive its precedent elsewhere,—clear especially as it is that no one has founded churches throughout the whole of Italy, Gaul, Spain, Africa, and Sicily, and the inter-adjacent islands, except those whom the venerable Apostle Peter, or his Successors, appointed Priests (i.e. Bishops). . . . But if they read of no other, for they never can find any other, they ought to follow what is observed by the Roman Church, from which there is no doubt that they derived their origin, lest whilst they court strange assertions, they be seen to set aside the Head (*caput*) of their institutions." (Innocent, *Ep. xxv. ad Decent.* n. 1, 3. Ib. p. 586), in Colin Lindsay, *The Evidence for the Papacy*, (London: Longmans, 1870), 230.

"[To the Council of Milevis] Yea, why have you confirmed this by your own act, but that you know that, throughout all the provinces, answers to questions always emanate from the Apostolic Spring. Especially, as often as questions of faith are agitated, I am of opinion that all our brethren and fellow-Bishops ought not to refer but to Peter—that is, to the Author of their name and honour—even as your friendliness has now referred (to ascertain) what may be for the common weal of all the churches throughout the whole world. For the authors of these evils must needs be more cautious, in seeing themselves, upon the report of two synods, separated from the communion of the Church, by the Decree of our sentence." (Innocent, *Ep. xxx. ad Concil. Milev.* n. 1, 2, 6. Ib. p. 602-3), in Colin Lindsay, *The Evidence for the Papacy*, (London: Longmans, 1870), 231.

Paulinus Orosius (418 A.D.):

"I appeal to the justice of your Holiness, my Lord Zosimus, venerable Pope. The true faith is never troubled, and this especially in the Apostolic Church, wherein the teachers of a corrupt faith are as easily detected as they are truly punished . . . that they may have in them that true faith which the Apostles taught, and which is held by the Roman Church, and by all the teachers of the Catholic faith." (Paulinus Orosius, *Libell. adv. Celest. Zozimo oblatus*, n. 1, *Galland.* t. ix. p. 32), in Colin Lindsay, *The Evidence for the Papacy*, (London: Longmans, 1870), 161.

Bachiarius, Monk (420 A.D.):

"Bachiarius was a monk of the early part of the fifth century. His *Libellus de fide Apologeticus* was written 'to satisfy the Bishop of Rome of his orthodoxy,' and 'its date is fixed approximately at about the middle of the fifth century' (*Dict. of Christ. Biog.* p. 236). This and another treatise are published by Galland (tom. ix.)and by Migne (*Patr. Lat.* vol. xx)." Charles F. B. Allnatt, ed., *Cathedra Petri—The Titles and Prerogatives of St. Peter*, (London: Burns & Oates, 1879), 3.

"If, for one man's fault, the population of a whole province is to be anathematised, then will be condemned also that most blessed disciple (of Peter), Rome to wit, out of which there have sprung up not one, but two or three, or even more heresies, and yet not one of them has been able either to have possession, or to move the Chair of Peter, that is, the Seat of Faith. . . . Seeing that the institutes of the Apostolic doctrine exhort us, to produce to all that ask us the reason of the faith and hope that is in us, we will not delay to place the rule of our faith before your Holiness, who are the builder of that edifice." (Bachiarius, *De Fide*, n. 2, p. 183, 184 *Galland*, ix.), in Colin Lindsay, *The Evidence for the Papacy*, (London: Longmans, 1870), 162. See also, Charles F. B. Allnatt, ed., *Cathedra Petri—The Titles and Prerogatives of St. Peter*, (London: Burns & Oates, 1879), 67-68.

Pope St. Boniface (ca. 420 A.D.):

"Boniface (St. and Pope), succeeded Zosimus, A.D. 418. He was 'an unswerving supporter of orthodoxy and Augustine in the contest against Pelagius" (*Dict. of Christ. Biog.* vol. i. p. 328). His epistles are in Galland (tom. ix.), after

Coustant; and a selection of them is contained in Hurter's *Patrum Opusc. Select.* (vol. xviii. 1872)." Charles F. B. Allnatt, ed., *Cathedra Petri—The Titles and Prerogatives of St. Peter*, (London: Burns & Oates, 1879), 3.

"Peter, to whom the highest place of the priesthood was granted by the voice of the Lord." (Boniface, *Epist. iv. Rufo*, n. 1, Galland, ix. p. 47), in Charles F. B. Allnatt, ed., *Cathedra Petri—The Titles and Prerogatives of St. Peter*, (London: Burns & Oates, 1879), 24.

"The institution of the universal nascent Church took its beginning from the honour of blessed Peter, in whom its government and headship reside." (Boniface, *Epist. xiv. Rufo*, n. 1, p. 57), in Charles F. B. Allnatt, ed., *Cathedra Petri— The Titles and Prerogatives of St. Peter*, (London: Burns & Oates, 1879), 233.

"[To the Bishops in Thessaly:] The institution of the Universal Church took its beginning from the honour bestowed on blessed Peter, in whom its Government and Headship reside. For from him, as its Source, did ecclesiastical discipline flow over all the churches, when the culture of religion had begun to make progress. The precepts of the Synod of Nicaea bear no other testimony; insomuch that that Synod did not attempt to make any regulations in his regard, as it saw that nothing could be conferred that was superior to his won dignity (merit); it knew, in fine, that everything had been bestowed on him by the Word of the Lord. It is, therefore, certain that this Church is to the churches spread over the whole world, as the Head is to its own members; from which Church whoso has cut himself off becomes an alien from the Christian religion, whereas he has begun not to be in the same bonds of fellowship. Now I hear that certain Bishops, the Apostolic right despised, are attempting a novelty which is in direct opposition to the special Injunctions of Christ, seeing that they are trying to separate themselves from communion, or, to speak more correctly, from the communion of the Apostolic See; seeking aid from men to whom the regulations of the Church have never given their sanction that they should be of superior authority. . . . Receive, therefore, from us an admonition, and a rebuke, of which we offer one to the Prelates (who side with us), the other to the separatists (quoting I Cor. iv. 21). . . . For you know that both are in blessed Peter's Power,—to rebuke, that is, with meekness the meek, and the proud with a rod. Wherefore, show to the Head the honour due to it; for we would not have the members at variance with each other, as the strife between them reaches unto us, when our brother and fellow-Bishop, Rufus, is accounted by you a person to be contemned. . . . It is not becoming in the brethren to feel galled at another's power. Assuredly, as the Apostolic See holds the Princedom for this, that it may receive the lawful complaints of all, if in anything his correction seemed to be excessive, it became you, by sending an embassy to appeal to us, upon whom you may see the charge of everything devolves. . . . Let this novel presumption cease. Let every one who accounts himself a Bishop, obey our ordinance. Let no one presume to ordain Bishops throughout Illyricum, without our fellow-Bishop Rufus privy to it." (Boniface, *Ep. xiv. Epis. Thess.* Ib. p. 57), in Colin Lindsay, *The Evidence for the Papacy*, (London: Longmans, 1870), 233-234.

Zacchaeus (421 A.D.):

"Peter, into whose person the power of all priests is gathered together." (Zacchaeus, Lib. ii. *Consult. Zacch.* c. 18, Galland, ix. p. 238), in Charles F. B. Allnatt, ed., *Cathedra Petri—The Titles and Prerogatives of St. Peter*, (London: Burns & Oates, 1879), 32.

Pope St. Celestine (ca. 423 A.D.):

"Therefore let all those whom he has separated from his communion understand that they continue in ours, and that from this time he himself (Nestorius) cannot continue in communion with us, if he persists in opposing the Apostolic doctrine. Wherefore you shall execute this Judgment with the Authority of our See, acting in our Stead, and having our Power delegated to you; and that if, in the space of ten days after he has received this admonition, he does not expressly anathematise his impious doctrines, and promise to confess, for the future, that faith which the Roman Church and your Church and all Christendom teach concerning the generation of Jesus Christ our God, your Holiness may forthwith set about to provide for this Church (of Constantinople) under the full assurance that in such a case it is necessary that he should be utterly separated from our body." (Celestine, *Labbe, Concil.* T. iii. col. 898-9), in Colin Lindsay, *The Evidence for the Papacy*, (London: Longmans, 1870), 234.

"Placed as we are by God on a watchtower, . . . our spiritual care fails not as regards places however distant, but extends through all places where the name of God is preached." (Celestine, *Epist.* iv. *Univ. Episc. per Vienn et Narbonens Prov.* n. 1, Galland, ix.), in Charles F. B. Allnatt, ed., *Cathedra Petri—The Titles and Prerogatives of St. Peter*, (London: Burns & Oates, 1879), 110.

St. Cyril of Alexandria (ca. 424 A.D.):

"They (the Apostles) strove to learn through one, that preeminent one, Peter." (Cyril, *Ib.* l. ix. p. 736. He is spoken of again in the same words, *Ibid.* p. 772, C.), in Joseph Berington, John Kirk, eds., and James Waterworth, rev., *The Faith of Catholics*, vol. 2, (New York: Pustet & Co., 1884), 46.

"And even the blessed Peter, though set over the holy disciples, says, 'Lord, be it far from Thee, this shall be unto Thee.'" (Cyril, *Ibid.* l. xi.p. 924.), in Joseph Berington, John Kirk, eds., and James Waterworth, rev., *The Faith of Catholics*, vol. 2, (New York: Pustet & Co., 1884), 46.

"If Peter himself, that prince of the holy disciples, was, upon an occasion, scandalized, so as suddenly to exclaim, 'Lord, be it far from Thee;' what wonder that the tender mind of woman should be carried away?" (Cyril, *Ib.* l. xii. p. 1064.), in Joseph Berington, John Kirk, eds., and James Waterworth, rev., *The Faith of Catholics*, vol. 2, (New York: Pustet & Co., 1884), 46.

"That the Spirit is God we shall also learn hence. That prince of the Apostles, to whom 'flesh and blood,' as the Saviour says, 'did not reveal' the divine mystery, says to Ananias, 'Why hath Satan tempted thy heart, &c.'" (Cyril, *T. v. Par. 1, Thesaur.* p. 340.), in Joseph Berington, John Kirk, eds., and James Waterworth, rev., *The Faith of Catholics*, vol. 2, (New York: Pustet & Co., 1884), 46.

"Besides all these, let there come forward that leader of the holy disciples, Peter, who, when the Lord, on a certain occasion, asked him, Whom do men say that the Son of man is? instantly cried out, Thou art the Christ the Son of the living God." (Cyril, *T. v. P.2, Hom. viii. De Fest. Pasch.* p. 105.), in Joseph Berington, John Kirk, eds., and James Waterworth, rev., *The Faith of Catholics*, vol. 2, (New York: Pustet & Co., 1884), 46.

"If I wash thee not, thou shalt have no part with me. When the coryphaeus had heard these words he began to change." (Cyril, *Ib. Hom. in Myst. Coen.* p. 376.), in Joseph Berington, John Kirk, eds., and James Waterworth, rev., *The Faith of Catholics*, vol. 2, (New York: Pustet & Co., 1884), 47.

"This bold man (Julian), besides all this, cavils at Peter, the chosen one of the holy Apostles." (Cyril, *T. vi.l. ix. Contr. Julian.* p. 325.), in Joseph Berington, John Kirk, eds., and James Waterworth, rev., *The Faith of Catholics*, vol. 2, (New York: Pustet & Co., 1884), 47.

St. Maximus of Turin (424 A.D.):

"On account of this confession, the blessed Apostle merited to hear from the mouth of the Lord, 'Thou art Peter, and upon this rock, &c.' That is, thou art the First to confess Me on earth, and I will make thee to have a perpetual Primacy in heaven, and in My Kingdom. And what more just than that the Church should be built on him, who gives so mighty a Foundation to the Church. What could be more religiously done, than that he should receive the 'keys of heaven,' he who revealed the Lord of the heavenly kingdom; inasmuch as he who opened to believers the gates of faith, the same should also open for them the gates of heaven." (Maximus, *Serm. lxxii. De Dict. Ev. "Vos estis sal terrae."* Galland. t.

ix. p. 393), in Colin Lindsay, *The Evidence for the Papacy*, (London: Longmans, 1870), 49.

"Of how great merit before his God was Peter, that, after rowing his little boat, there should be consigned to him the helms of the whole Church." (Maximus, *Hom. iii. De Eod. Fest.* ib. p. 35.), in Joseph Berington, John Kirk, eds., and James Waterworth, rev., *The Faith of Catholics*, vol. 2, (New York: Pustet & Co., 1884), 43.

"In the additional sermons published by Gallandius, he is called 'the principal of the Apostles.'" (Maximus, *Serm. iv. de Pasch.* t. ix. p. 363.), in Joseph Berington, John Kirk, eds., and James Waterworth, rev., *The Faith of Catholics*, vol. 2, (New York: Pustet & Co., 1884), 44.

John Cassian, Monk (430 A.D.):

"[T]hat great man, the disciple of disciples, that master among masters, who wielding the government of the Roman Church possessed the authority [*principatum*] in faith and priesthood. Tell us therefore, tell us we beg of you, Peter, prince of the Apostles, tell us how the churches must believe in God." (John Cassian, *Contra Nestorium*, III, 12, CSEL, vol. 17, p. 276), in Michael M. Winter, *Saint Peter and the Popes*, (Baltimore: Helicon, 1960), 61.

St. Isidore of Pelusium (ca. 430 A.D.):

"A Greek priest who served as superior of the monastery at Pelusium, he was so devoted in his religious duties that he served as a model of conduct for St. Cyril. Some 2000 letters of pious exhortation and theological instruction are extant." John J. Delaney and James Edward Tobin, *Dictionary of Catholic Biography*, (Garden City, NY: Doubleday, 1961), 595.

"[St. Isidore] Calls St. Peter by the usual title, 'the coryphaeus of the choir of the disciples.'(Isidore, *L. 1, Ep. cxlii.* p. 44; also L. ii. Ep. lviii. p. 148, et alib.), in Joseph Berington, John Kirk, eds., and James Waterworth, rev., *The Faith of Catholics*, vol. 2, (New York: Pustet & Co., 1884), 42.

St. Peter Chrysologus, Bishop of Ravenna (ca. 432 A.D.):

> "Just as Peter received his name from the rock, because he was the first to deserve to establish the Church, by reason of his steadfastness of faith, so also Stephen was named from a crown. . . . Let Peter hold his ancient primacy of the Apostolic choir. Let him open to those who enter the kingdom of heaven. Let him bind the guilty with his power and absolve the penitent in kindness." (Peter Chrysologus, *Sermon 154*, Migne, *Patr. Lat.* vol. 52, col. 608), in E. Giles, *Documents Illustrating Papal Authority A.D. 96-454*, (London: SPCK, 1952), 283.

> "We exhort you, honourable brother, that you obediently listen to what has been written by the blessed Pope of the city of Rome, since Blessed Peter, who lives and presides in his own see, offers the truth of faith to those who seek. For we, in our zeal for peace and faith, cannot decide questions of faith apart from the consent of the Bishop of Rome. May the Lord vouchsafe to preserve your love for us a very long time, our most dear and honoured son." (Peter Chrysologus, *Ad Eutychem.* (Feb. 449), *Sermon 25:2*), in E. Giles, *Documents Illustrating Papal Authority A.D. 96-454*, (London: SPCK, 1952), 282-283.

> "Peter denies Him; John flies; Thomas doubts; all abandon Him: to whom had not Christ given His 'peace,' both Peter, who was the first of all of them, might have been thought inferior, and the follower might perhaps have been unduly lifted up against the chief." (Peter Chrysologus, *Serm. lxxxiv.* p. 129.), in Joseph Berington, John Kirk, eds., and James Waterworth, rev., *The Faith of Catholics*, vol. 2, (New York: Pustet & Co., 1884), 49-50.

Pope St. Sixtus III (434 A.D.):

> "Sixtus III, St. Pope from 432-440. Also known as Xystus III, he was a Roman by birth. Prior to his election, Sixtus had served under Popes Zosimus, Boniface I, and Celestine I. . . . Elected to succeed St. Celestine, he approved the acts

of the Council of Ephesus (431) and worked with much vigor to restore unity in the Eastern Church that had been threatened with dispute between St. Cyril of Alexandria and John of Antioch begun during the Council of Ephesus over the Nestorian Controversy. . . . He also defended the rights of the papacy in Illyricum in the face of the local ambition of the bishops and the interference of Proclius, patriarch of Constantinople." *Our Sunday Visitor's Encyclopedia of Catholic History*, 1995 ed., s.v. "Sixtus III, St.".

"[To John, Bishop of Antioch] You have learned by the result of this present business what it is to agree in sentiment with us. The blessed Apostle Peter, in his Successors, has transmitted what he received. Who would separate himself from his doctrine, whom the Master Himself declared to be the First amongst the Apostles?" (Sixtus, *Ep. vi. Ad. Joan.* n. 5, Galland T. ix. p. 529), in Colin Lindsay, *The Evidence for the Papacy*, (London: Longmans, 1870), 235.

St. Proclus (ca. 434 A.D.):

"Peter, the coryphaeus of the disciples, and the one set over (or the chief of) the Apostles. . . . Art not thou he that didst say, 'Thou art the Christ the Son of the living God?' Thou Bar-Jonas (son of the dove) hast thou seen so many miracles, and art thou still but Simon (a hearer)? He appointed thee the key-bearer of heaven, and hast thou not as yet laid aside thy fisherman's clothing?" (Proclus, *Or. viii. In Dom. Transfig.* t. ix. Galland. pp. 650-1.), in Joseph Berington, John Kirk, eds., and James Waterworth, rev., *The Faith of Catholics*, vol. 2, (New York: Pustet & Co., 1884), 48.

Spanish Bishop (ca. 440 A.D.):

"The most blessed Peter, the supremacy of whose vicar, as it is eminent, so is it to be feared and loved by all." (*Epist. Episc. Tarracan. Hilario*, col 1033, Labbe, tom. iv.), in Charles F. B. Allnatt, ed., *Cathedra Petri—The Titles and Prerogatives of St. Peter*, (London: Burns & Oates, 1879), 101.

Paul of Emesa (ca. 440):

> "Paul was consecrated bishop of Emesa just after 410 A.D. He took part in the Council of Ephesus and was ambassador for John of Antioch in his talks of reconciliation with Cyril of Alexandria." William Webster, *Peter and the Rock*, (Battle Ground, WA: Christian Resources, 1996), 114.

> "Upon this faith the Church of God has been founded. With this expectation, upon this rock the Lord God placed the foundations of the Church. When then the Lord Christ was going to Jerusalem, He asked the disciples, saying, 'Whom do men say that the Son of Man is?' The apostles say, 'Some Elias, others Jeremias, or one of the prophets.' And He says, but you, that is, My elect, you who have followed Me for three years, and have seen My power, and miracles, and beheld Me walking on the sea, who have shared My table, 'Whom do you say that I am?' Instantly, the Coryphaeus of the apostles, the mouth of the disciples, Peter, 'Thou art the Christ, the Son of the living God.' (Paul of Emesa, *Hom. de Nativ.* p. 1437, *Inter. Opp. S. Cyril. Alex.* T. x.), in J. Waterworth, *A Commentary by Writers of the First Five Centuries on the Place of St. Peter in the New Testament and that of St. Peter's Successors in the Church* (London: Thomas Richardson, 1871), 148.

Arnobius Junior (ca. 440 A.D.):

> "[Peter] the bishop of bishops." (Arnobius Junior, *Episcopus episcoporum. Comment. in Ps.* cxxxviii. p. 320), in Charles F. B. Allnatt, ed., *Cathedra Petri—The Titles and Prerogatives of St. Peter*, (London: Burns & Oates, 1879), 55.

Salvian the Presbyter (ca. 440 A.D.):

> "Born probably in Treves, Gaul, which was overrun four times by barbarians during a life which spanned most of the century, he married, but his wife entered a convent when he went to Lérins, where he seems to have been ordained. He taught rhetoric there to SS. Caesarius, Hilary and Honoratus among others. He wrote on the Church, the sacraments, scrip-

tural commentaries, homilies, letters, and the particularly important *The Present Judgement* and *The Governance of God*, which laid bare the greed and injustice of his day, particularly among officials and the landed aristocracy." John J. Delaney and James Edward Tobin, *Dictionary of Catholic Biography*, (Garden City, NY: Doubleday, 1961), 680.

"[Salvian] calls St. Peter 'the prince of the Apostles'" (Salvian, *L. vi. De Dei Gubern. n. 1*, t. x. *Galland.* p. 33), in Joseph Berington, John Kirk, eds., and James Waterworth, rev., *The Faith of Catholics*, vol. 2, (New York: Pustet & Co., 1884), 48.

St. Vincent of Lérins (445 A.D.):

"Vincent of Lérins (St.), was, according to Gennadius, 'by birth a Gaul, a presbyter in a monastery in the island of Lérins, a man learned in the Holy Scriptures, and well instructed in the knowledge of the doctrines of the Church.' His celebrated *Commonitorium* against heretics appeared in the year 434." Charles F. B. Allnatt, ed., *Cathedra Petri— The Titles and Prerogatives of St. Peter*, (London: Burns & Oates, 1879), 13.

"Pope Stephen of blessed memory, Prelate of the Apostolic See, in conjunction indeed with his colleagues but yet himself the foremost, withstood it [rebaptism], thinking it right, I doubt not, that as he exceeded all others in the authority of his place, so he should also in the devotion of his faith." (Vincent Lérins, *Commonit. Adv. Haer.* 6:16), in Philip Schaff and Henry Wace, eds., *Nicene and Post-Nicene Fathers—Sulpitius Severus, Vincent of Lérins, John Cassian*, 2nd series, vol. 11, (Peabody, MA: Hendrickson, 1994), 135.

St. Basil of Seleucia (448 A.D.):

"Basil of Seleucia (St.), Bishop of Seleucia, in Isauria, took a leading part in the Council of Constantinople, A.D. 448, at which Eutyches was condemned. His homilies were first published, in Greek, by Commelin (Lugd. Bat. 1596), and also at the end of the works of St. Gregory Thaumaturgus

(Paris, 1672)." Charles F. B. Allnatt, ed., *Cathedra Petri— The Titles and Prerogatives of St. Peter*, (London: Burns & Oates, 1879), 3.

"Likewise, for Basil, St. Peter is the leader (*coryphaeus*) of the apostles, and the chief (*prostates*) of the disciples of Christ." (Basil, *Oratio XVII, MPG*, vol. 85, col. 217), in Michael M. Winter, *Saint Peter and the Popes*, (Baltimore: Helicon, 1960), 74.

"Peter is again called 'the coryphaeus of the Apostles.'" (Basil, *Orat. xxv.* p. 138), in Joseph Berington, John Kirk, eds., and James Waterworth, rev., *The Faith of Catholics*, vol. 2, (New York: Pustet & Co., 1884), 49.

St. Nilus (448 A.D.):

"Nilus (St.), flourished under the Emperors Arcadius and Theodosius, and died about A.D. 450. He had for his master the great St. Chrysostom. His letters were published by Allatius (Rome, 1668), and his treatises by Suarez (Rome, 1673)." Charles F. B. Allnatt, ed., *Cathedra Petri—The Titles and Prerogatives of St. Peter*, (London: Burns & Oates, 1879), 10.

"[Peter] the Head of the choir of the Apostles." (Nilus, Lib. ii. *Epist.* cclxi. p. 252, *Bib. M.* xxvi.), in Charles F. B. Allnatt, ed., *Cathedra Petri—The Titles and Prerogatives of St. Peter*, (London: Burns & Oates, 1879), 55.

"Peter, who was foremost in the choir of the Apostles, and always ruled amongst them." (Nilus, *Tract. ad Magnam.* c. 8, p. 244), in Charles F. B. Allnatt, ed., *Cathedra Petri— The Titles and Prerogatives of St. Peter*, (London: Burns & Oates, 1879), 55.

Theodoret, Bishop of Cyrus (ca. 450 A.D.):

"I, therefore, beseech your holiness to persuade the most holy and blessed Archbishop (Leo) to use his apostolic power, and to order me to hasten to your Council.. For that most holy throne has the sovereignty over the churches throughout the universe on many grounds." (Theodoret, Tom. iv. *Epist. cxvi. Renato*, p. 1197), in Charles F. B. Allnatt, ed., *Cathedra Petri—The Titles and Prerogatives of St. Peter*, (London: Burns & Oates, 1879), 107-108.

"It pertains to you (Pope Leo) to hold the primacy in all things, for your throne is adorned with many prerogatives." (Theodoret, *Ib. Epist. cxiii. Leoni*, p. 1187), in Charles F. B. Allnatt, ed., *Cathedra Petri—The Titles and Prerogatives of St. Peter*, (London: Burns & Oates, 1879), 108.

"If Paul, the herald of the truth, the trumpet of the Holy Ghost, hastened to the great Peter, to convey from him the solution to those at Antioch, who were at issue about living under the law, how much more do we, poor and humble, run to the Apostolic Throne, to receive from you (Pope Leo) healing for the wounds of the Churches. For it pertains to you to have the primacy in all things; for your throne is adorned with many prerogatives." (Theodoret, *Epist. cxiii. Leoni*, tom. iv. p. 1187), in Charles F. B. Allnatt, ed., *Cathedra Petri—The Titles and Prerogatives of St. Peter*, (London: Burns & Oates, 1879), 66-67.

"For that all holy throne has the office of heading the Churches of the whole world, for many reasons; and, above all others, because it has remained free of the communion of heretical taint, and no one holding heterodox sentiments ever sat in it, but it has preserved the Apostolic grace unsullied." (Theodoret, *Epist. cxvi. Renato*, p. 1197), in Charles F. B. Allnatt, ed., *Cathedra Petri—The Titles and Prerogatives of St. Peter*, (London: Burns & Oates, 1879), 67.

"But this man will not abide by the decrees (of Nicaea), but brings forward at every turn that his is the throne of Mark; and yet he knows well that the great city of Antioch has the throne of Peter, who was both the teacher of Mark, and the first and the leader (coryphaeus) of the choir of the Apostles." (Theodoret, *T. iv. Ep. lxxxvi. Flavian.* Ep. C.P. p. 1157), in Joseph Berington, John Kirk, eds., and James Waterworth, rev., *The Faith of Catholics*, vol. 2, (New York: Pustet & Co., 1884), 48.

"He calls Peter 'that divine Peter, the coryphaeus of the Apostles.'" (Theodoret, *T. i. In Ps. ii.* p. 616, and so again *Ib.* p. 622.), in Joseph Berington, John Kirk, eds., and James Waterworth, rev., *The Faith of Catholics*, vol. 2, (New York: Pustet & Co., 1884), 47.

St. Leo the Great (ca. 450 A.D.):

"It behooves your friendliness to see clearly, with all your soul, over the government of what Church the Lord has willed you to preside, and to be mindful of that doctrine which the most blessed Peter, the chief of all the Apostles, established throughout the whole world indeed by a uniform teaching, but by a special instruction in the cities of Antioch and of Rome." (Leo, T. i. *Ep. cxix. ad Max. Antioch.* c. 3, p. 121.), in Joseph Berington, John Kirk, eds., and James Waterworth, rev., *The Faith of Catholics*, vol. 1, (New York: Pustet & Co., 1884), 319.

"The following is to Dioscorus, bishop of Alexandria: 'As the most blessed Peter received the apostolic primacy from the Lord, and the Roman Church continues in his institutions, it is criminal to believe that his holy disciple, Mark, who was the first that governed the church of Alexandria, formed decrees by other rules of his own traditions; since without doubt from the same source of grace was the spirit both of the disciple and of his master." (Leo, T. i. *Ep. ix. ad Diosc. Ep. Alex.* pp. 628-9.), in Joseph Berington, John Kirk, eds., and James Waterworth, rev., *The Faith of Catholics*, vol. 2, (New York: Pustet & Co., 1884), 54.

The Bishops of Moesia wrote to Pope Leo:

"That it had been by the command of Pope Leo, who was truly the head of bishops, convened." (*Hard., Conc. II.*, 710.), Dr. Hergenrother, *Anti-Janus: An Historico-Theological Criticism Of The Work, Entitled 'The Pope And The Council', By Janus.* (Dublin: W. B. Kelly, 1870), 121.

Canon of St. Patrick (450 A.D.):

"If any case of extreme difficulty shall arise, . . . let it be referred to the See of the chief Bishop of the Irish (that is, of Patrick). . . . But if it cannot easily be decided in that See, . . . we have decreed that it be sent to the Apostolic See, that is, to the Chair of the Apostle Peter, which holds authority of the city of Rome. (*Can. S. Patric.* vide Moran's *Essays on the Early Irish Church*, 1864, c. ii. p. 120, *et seq.*; and Appendix, no. vi., p. 304), in Charles F. B. Allnatt, ed., *Cathedra Petri—The Titles and Prerogatives of St. Peter*, (London: Burns & Oates, 1879), 64.

St. Prosper of Acquitaine (450 A.D.):

"Rome, the See of Peter, . . . made to the world the head of pastoral honour, possesses by religion what it did not possess by arms." (Prosper, *Carm. de Ingratis*, p. 106, *Bibl. Max. Pat.* tom. viii.), in Charles F. B. Allnatt, ed., *Cathedra Petri—The Titles and Prerogatives of St. Peter*, (London: Burns & Oates, 1879), 76-77.

"Rome the See of Peter, which has been made to the whole world the head of the pastoral office." (Prosper, *Carm. de Ingratis*, p. 106, *Bibl. Max. Pat.* tom. viii.), in Luke Rivington, *The Primitive Church and the See of St. Peter*, (London: Longmans, Green and Co., 1894.) p. 245 [Lat. trans. John Collorafi].

Emperor Valentinian III (ca. 450 A.D.):

"[Peter] the prince of the episcopal crown [455 A.D.]." (Valentinian, *In Constit. de Epp. Ord. Vide* Hallam's *Middle Ages*, chap. vii. note), in Charles F. B. Allnatt, ed., *Cathedra Petri—The Titles and Prerogatives of St. Peter*, (London: Burns & Oates, 1879), 55.

"The primacy of the Apostolic See having been established by the merit of the Apostle Peter, by the dignity of the city of

Rome, and by the authority of the holy Synod, no pretended power shall arrogate to itself anything against the authority of that See. For peace can be universally preserved only when the whole Church acknowledges its ruler [445 A.D.]." (Valentinian, in Ap. Neander, *Hist. of Ch.* iii. p. 246), in Charles F. B. Allnatt, ed., *Cathedra Petri—The Titles and Prerogatives of St. Peter*, (London: Burns & Oates, 1879), 107.

Council of Chalcedon (451 A.D.):

"Chalcedon, the (Fourth Ecumenical) Council of, was held A.D. 451, under the four Legates of Pope Leo I. About 600 Bishops were present, almost all of the Eastern Church." Charles F. B. Allnatt, ed., *Cathedra Petri—The Titles and Prerogatives of St. Peter*, (London: Burns & Oates, 1879), 13.

"Wherefore the most holy and blessed Leo, archbishop of the great and elder Rome, through us, and through this present most holy synod together with the thrice blessed and all-glorious Peter the Apostle, who is the rock and foundation of the Catholic Church, and the foundation of the orthodox faith, hath stripped him [Dioscorus] of the episcopate, and hath alienated from him all hieratic worthiness. Therefore let this most holy and great synod sentence the before mentioned Dioscorus to the canonical penalties." (*Extracts from the Acts of the Council of Chalcedon*, Session 3), in Philip Schaff and Henry Wace, eds., *Nicene and Post-Nicene Fathers—The Seven Ecumenical Councils*, 2nd series, vol. 14, (Peabody, MA: Hendrickson, 1994), 259-260.

"Leo can never be charged with weakness. His rejection of the [28th] canon [wherein a pressured council attempted to make a political see at Constantinople ('which is honoured with the Sovereignty and the Senate, and enjoys equal privileges with the old imperial Rome') the equivalent of the Roman See] was absolute and unequivocal. In writing to the Emperor he says that Anatolius only got the See of Constantinople by his consent, that he should behave himself modestly, and that there is no way he can make of Constantinople 'an Apostolic See,' and adds that 'only from love of peace and for the restoration of the unity of the faith' he has 'abstained from annulling this ordination.' (*Ep. civ.*) . . .

"Leo never gave over his opposition, although the breach was made up between him and Anatolius by an apparently insincere letter on the part of the latter (*Ep.* cxxxii.). Leo's successors followed his example in rejecting the canons, both of the IIId of Constantinople and the XXVIIIth of Chalcedon." Philip Schaff and Henry Wace, eds., *Nicene and Post-Nicene Fathers—The Seven Ecumenical Councils*, 2nd series, vol. 14, (Peabody, MA: Hendrickson, 1994), 287, 289.

Macedonius, Patriarch of Constantinople (466-516 A.D.):

"A patriarch of Constantinople who suffered deportation for his zeal in defence of the council of Chalcedon. He died in exile." The Benedictine Monks of St. Augustine's Abbey, Ramsgate, *The Book of Saints*, (Wilton, CN: Morehouse, 1989), 358.

"Declared, when desired by the Emperor Anastasius to condemn the Council of Chalcedon, that such a step, without an Ecumenical Synod presided over by the Pope, was impossible." (Macedonius, *Patr. Graec.* 108: 360a (*Theophan. Chronogr.* pp. 234, 242, 346, seq.)), in Dr. Hergenrother, *Anti-Janus: An Historico-Theological Criticism Of The Work, Entitled 'The Pope And The Council', By Janus.* (Dublin: W. B. Kelly, 1870) 122.

Sedulius (ca. 480 A.D.):

"A priest and poet who flourished about the middle of the fifth century. The edition used is that given in the (*Bibl. Maxim.* SS. PP. t. vi.; also, *Galland.* t. ix.)", in Joseph Berington, John Kirk, eds., and James Waterworth, rev., *The Faith of Catholics*, vol. 2, (New York: Pustet & Co., 1884), 58.

"The weakness of the Galatians forces him to state, that not only had not the other Apostles aided him in anything, and that he had not been less than they, but that he had corrected something in Peter, who was the prince of the Apostles." (Sedulius, *Collect. in Ep. ad Galat.* c. 2, p 557, t. vi. Bibl. Max. SS. PP.), in Joseph Berington, John Kirk, eds., and James Waterworth, rev., *The Faith of Catholics*, vol. 2, (New York: Pustet & Co., 1884), 58.

Victor of Vita (ca. 485 A.D.):

"Very little is known of Victor, Bishop of Vita in the African province of Byzacena. He is the author of a *Historia persecutionis Africanae provinciae*, which recounts the terrible sufferings of Catholics in Africa in the time of the Vandal kings Geiserich (428-477 A.D.) and Hunerich (477-484 A.D.)." W. A. Jurgens, *The Faith of the Early Fathers*, vol. 3, (Collegeville, MN: The Liturgical Press, 1970), 281.

"The Roman Church, which is the head of all the churches." (Victor, *De Persecut. Afric.* [480 A.D.] lib. iii. p. 682, *Bibl. Max.* viii.), in Charles F. B. Allnatt, ed., *Cathedra Petri— The Titles and Prerogatives of St. Peter*, (London: Burns & Oates, 1879), 78.

Pope St. Gelasius (ca. 492 A.D.):

"Referring to the adjudication of the Primacy to Rome, he says, 'as being men who bore in mind the Lord's sentence, "Thou art Peter, and upon this rock I will build My Church, etc." And again to the same Peter, "Lo! I have prayed for thee that thy faith fail not, and converted, confirm the brethren," and that sentence, "If thou lovest Me, feed my sheep." Wherefore, then, is the Lord's discourse so frequently directed to Peter? Was it that the rest of the holy and blessed Apostles were not clothed with his virtue? Who dare assert this? No, but that, by a Head being constituted, the occasion of schism might be removed; and that the compact bond of the body of Christ, thus uniformly tending, by the fellowship of a most glorious love, to one Head, might be shown to be one; and that there might be one Church faithfully believed in, and one house of the one God and of the one Redeemer, wherein we might be nourished with one bread and one chalice. . . . There were assuredly twelve Apostles, endowed with equal merits and equal dignity; and whereas they all shone equally with spiritual light, yet was it Christ's will that One amongst them should be the Ruler (prince— *principem*), etc." (Gelasius, in Galland, t. x. p. 677), in Colin Lindsay, *The Evidence for the Papacy*, (London: Longmans, 1870), 55-56.

"The canons themselves willed the appeals of the whole Church to be referred to the examination of this See. From it they decreed also that no appeal whatever ought to be made; and thereby that it judged of the whole Church, and that itself passed under the judgment of none. . . . Timothy of Alexandria, Peter of Antioch, Peter, Paul, John, not one, but many, bearing the name of the priesthood, were deposed by the sole authority of the Apostolic See. . . . The canons cannot summon the Apostolic See to judgment. . . . Therefore we are in no fear lest the Apostolic judgment be reversed, which both the voice of Christ and the tradition of the fathers, as also the authority of the canons support, in such wise that rather it always may judge the whole Church." (Gelasius, *Epist.* iv. *Commonitor ad Faustum*, pp. 1169-1171, Labbe, iv.; and *Epist. Rom. Pont.* ed. Thiel, 1867, tom. i. p. 343, *Epist.* x. n. 5).

"The first See both confirms every synod by its authority, and guards by its continuous rule, by reason, to wit, of its supremacy, which, received by the Apostle Peter from the mouth of the Lord, the Church nevertheless seconding, it both always has held and retains. . . . We will not pass over in silence what every Church throughout the world knows, that the See of the Blessed Apostle Peter has the right to absolve from what has been bound by the sentence of any prelates whatsoever, in that it has the right of judging of the whole Church; neither is it lawful for any one to pass judgment on its judgment, seeing that the canons have willed that it may be appealed to from any part of the world, but that from it no one be permitted to appeal." (Gelasius, *Epist. xiii. ad Episc. Dardan*, p. 1200, Labbe; and Thiel, *Epist. xxvi.* n. 5, tom. i. p. 399), in Charles F. B. Allnatt, ed., *Cathedra Petri—The Titles and Prerogatives of St. Peter*, (London: Burns & Oates, 1879), 79-80.

"Although the universal Catholic Church all over the world is one bridal chamber of Christ, nevertheless the Holy Roman Church did not obtain the primacy by any synodical constitutions, but by the evangelical voice of our Lord and Savior: 'Thou art Peter and upon this rock.'" (Gelasius, *Ep. 33*, no. 5), in Dr. Hergenrother, *Anti-Janus: An Historico-Theological Criticism Of The Work, Entitled 'The Pope And The Council', By Janus.* (Dublin: W. B. Kelly, 1870), p. 62 [Lat. trans. John Collorafi].

Acclamation of the clergy to Pope Gelasius:

"We see thee, the Vicar of Christ, we see thee, the Apostle Peter." (*Ep. 27*, n. 15), in Dr. Hergenrother, *Anti-Janus: An Historico-Theological Criticism Of The Work, Entitled 'The Pope And The Council', By Janus.* (Dublin: W. B. Kelly, 1870), p. 103 [Lat. trans. John Collorafi].

The Bishops of Dardania (writing to Pope Gelasius ca. 494 A.D.):

"We who desire to serve the Apostolic see without blame, according to the divine precepts and statutes of the Fathers." (*Mansi*, viii, 13), in Dom John Chapman, *Bishop Gore and the Catholic Claims*, (London: Longmans, Green, and Co., 1905), 92.

"It is a protestation of the fidelity of Eastern bishops to the Apostolic See, that they observe in everything the precepts of their fathers and follow inviolably the rules of the holy canons, and so endeavour to obey all, with a common faith and an equal devotion to the Apostolic See of the Roman pontiff exalted and angelic." (Bishops of Dardania, *Mansi*, viii, 13), in S. Herbert Scott, *The Eastern Churches and the Papacy*, (London: Sheed & Ward, 1928), 214-215 [expanding foregoing quotation].

St. Avitus (ca. 495 A.D.):

"Avitus (St.), Archbishop of Vienne, in Gaul, was born about A.D. 450, and died in 523. His works are published in

Galland (tom. x.), and by Migne (*Patr. Lat.* vol. lix.), with the exception of some discoveries of M. Delisle, published in 1866." Charles F. B. Allnatt, ed., *Cathedra Petri—The Titles and Prerogatives of St. Peter*, (London: Burns & Oates, 1879), 3.

"We were anxious in mind and fearful in the cause of the Roman Church, as feeling our own position tottering in the head assailed . . . [t]he chief of the Universal Church. . . . If the Pope of that city is called into doubt, not a Bishop, but the Episcopate will at once seem to be in danger." (Avitus, *Epist.* xxxi. p. 724, Galland, tom. x.), in Charles F. B. Allnatt, ed., *Cathedra Petri—The Titles and Prerogatives of St. Peter*, (London: Burns & Oates, 1879), 105.

"You know that the Synodal laws have it that if any doubt arise in matters pertaining to the state of the Church, we have recourse to the Bishop of the Roman Church as to our head." (Avitus, *Ep. 36.*), in Dr. Hergenrother, *Anti-Janus: An Historico-Theological Criticism Of The Work, Entitled 'The Pope And The Council', By Janus.* (Dublin: W. B. Kelly, 1870), p. 118 [Lat. trans. John Collorafi].

"Peter, the head of the Apostles, that is, the prince of the princes." (Avitus, *Fragm. i.*, p. 746, t. x. *Galland.*), in Joseph Berington, John Kirk, eds., and James Waterworth, rev., *The Faith of Catholics*, vol. 2, (New York: Pustet & Co., 1884), 59.

Pope Anastasius II (496 A.D.):

"Anastasius II. Pope from 496-498. His main contribution was attempting a reconciliation between the Eastern and Western Churches, as both had been in a state of schism since the reign of Pope Felix III, who in 484 had excommunicated Acacius, patriarch of Constantinople, starting the Acacian Schism." *Our Sunday Visitor's Encyclopedia of Catholic History*, 1995 ed., s.v. "Anastasius II".

"Through the ministry of my lowliness . . . may the See of blessed Peter hold the Princedom assigned to it by the Lord our God in the Universal Church." (Anastasius, *Epist. ad Anast. Aug.* Labbe, tom. iv. p. 1278), in Colin Lindsay, *The Evidence for the Papacy*, (London: Longmans, 1870), 275.

Pope Symmachus (498-514 A.D.):

"[Symmachus] Pope. A native of Sardinia, the son of Fortunatus, he became archdeacon under Pope Anastasius II, whom he succeeded on Nov. 22, 498. He was immediately faced with an antipope, Laurence, who had been elected by a minority of the clergy of Byzantine leanings and who was supported by Emperor Anastasius of Constantinople. Both claimants appealed to Theodoric, the Gothic king at Ravenna, who ruled that Symmachus had been lawfully elected. However, his pontificate was repeatedly disturbed by this conflict. He aided the victims of barbarian raids and Arian persecutions, helped the poor, and built several new basilicas." John J. Delaney and James Edward Tobin, *Dictionary of Catholic Biography*, (Garden City, NY: Doubleday, 1961), 1094.

A letter from the Eastern Bishops to Pope Symmachus:

"But for the precious salvation, not only of the East, but of three parts almost of the inhabited world, redeemed, not with corruptible gold or silver, but with the precious Blood of the Lamb of God, according to the doctrine of the blessed Prince of the glorious Apostles, whose See Christ, the Good Shepherd, has entrusted to Your Blessedness. . . . You are not ignorant of his malice, you whom Peter, your blessed Doctor, teaches always to shepherd, not by violence but by an authority fully accepted, the sheep of Christ which are entrusted to You in all the habitable world." (*Letter to Pope Symmachus, Mansi.*, viii, 221 seq.), in S. Herbert Scott, *The Eastern Churches and the Papacy*, (London: Sheed & Ward, 1928), 216-217.

Andrew of Caesarea (ca. 515 A.D.):

"[Andrew,] Bishop of that see in Cappadocia, assigned by Krumbacher to the first half of the sixth century, though he is yet variously placed by others from the fifth to the ninth century. His principal work is a commentary on the Apocalypse (*Patr. Graec.*, CVI, 215-458, 1387-94)." Charles G. Herbermann and others, *The Catholic Encyclopedia*, vol. 1, (New York: Robert Appleton, 1907; Encyclopedia Press, 1913), 473.

"[Andrew of Caesarea] calls St. Peter 'the coryphaeus of the choir of disciples.' " (Andrew of Caesarea, *Comm. in cap. xiii. Apoc. cap. xxxvii.* t. v. p. 613, *Bib. Maxim.* SS. PP.), in Joseph Berington, John Kirk, eds., and James Waterworth, rev., *The Faith of Catholics*, vol. 2, (New York: Pustet & Co., 1884), 44.

Pope Hormisdas (ca. 519 A.D.):

"In the Formula of Pope Hormisdas, . . . it is said:—'Because the statement of our Lord Jesus Christ, when He said, "Thou art Peter, and upon this rock I will build My Church," &c., cannot be set aside; this, which is said, is proved by the results; for in the Apostolic See religion has always been preserved without spot. . . . In which (See) is set the perfect and true solidity of the Christian religion.'" (Hormisdas, *Form. Hormisd. Ep. Orient. Praescript.* Denzinger's *Enchirid.* p. 42), in Charles F. B. Allnatt, ed., *Cathedra Petri—The Titles and Prerogatives of St. Peter*, (London: Burns & Oates, 1879), 68.

The formula of Pope Hormisdas, A.D. 519, by the Eastern Emperor, Patriarch, and Bishops (and confirmed in 869 by the Fathers of the Eighth General Council) is as follows:

"In the Apostolic See the Catholic religion has always been kept undefiled and her holy doctrine proclaimed. Desiring, therefore, not to be in the least degree separated from the faith and doctrine of that See, we hope that we may deserve to be in the one communion with you which the Apostolic See preaches, in which is the entire and true solidity of the

Christian religion: promising also that the names of those who are cut off from the communion of the Catholic Church, that is, not consentient with the Apostolic See, shall not be recited during the sacred mysteries. This is my profession, I have subscribed with my own hand, and delivered to you Hormisdas, the holy and venerable pope of the city of Rome." (*Form. Hormisd. Episc. Orient. Praescript.* Denzinger's *Enchirid.* p. 42, ed. 1874), in Charles F. B. Allnatt, ed., *Cathedra Petri—The Titles and Prerogatives of St. Peter*, (London: Burns & Oates, 1879), 92.

Emperor Justinian I (520-533 A.D.):

"Justinian I (483-565). Byzantine Emperor from 527-565 who has been called the 'Last Roman' and the First Byzantine Emperor" and was responsible for the return of the empire to greatness. . . . His main achievements were in acting as a patron of the Church. In Constantinople, he built the Santa (or Hagia) Sophia, one of the greatest churches in Christendom, and other basilicas were erected elsewhere, particularly at Ravenna. . . . In 552, he summoned the Second Council of Constantinople in an effort to reconcile the Monophysites." *Our Sunday Visitor's Encyclopedia of Catholic History*, 1995 ed., s.v. "Justinian I".

"Nor do we allow that any of these things, concerning ecclesiastical institution, should fail to be brought before his Holiness, as being the head of all the holy Priests of God, and because as often as heretics have arisen in these parts, Justinianhave been repressed by the sentence and judgment of that holy See." (Justinian, *Epist. ad Epiphan. Cod. Justinian*, lib. i. tom. i. n. 7), in Charles F. B. Allnatt, ed., *Cathedra Petri—The Titles and Prerogatives of St. Peter*, (London: Burns & Oates, 1879), 102.

"Yielding honour to the Apostolic See, and to your Holiness, and honouring your Holiness, as one ought to honour a father, . . . we have hastened to subject all the priests of the whole Eastern district, and to unite them to the See of your Holiness. . . . For we do not allow of any point, however manifest and indisputable it be, which relates to the state of the Churches, not being brought to the cognizance of your Holiness, since you are the Head of all holy churches." (Justinian, *Epist. ad Pap. Joan.* ii. *Cod. Justin.* lib. i. tit. 1), in Charles F. B. Allnatt, ed., *Cathedra Petri— The Titles and Prerogatives of St. Peter*, (London: Burns & Oates, 1879), 102-103.

"Let your apostleship show, . . . that you have worthily suc-ceeded to the Apostle Peter, since the Lord will work through you, as Supreme Pastor, the salvation of all." (*Coll. Avell. Ep. 196*, July 9th, 520, Justinian to the Pope), in Dom John Chapman, *Studies on the Early Papacy*, (London: Sheed & Ward, 1928), 215.

Bishop of Patara writing to Justinian:

"Reminding Justinian of God's judgement for the exile of Pope Silverius, 'In this world there are many kings, not one, like that Pope who is over the church of the whole world.'" (Liberatus [in his *Brevarium*, c. 22]), in Dr. Hergenrother, *Anti-Janus: An Historico-Theological Criticism Of The Work, Entitled 'The Pope And The Council', By Janus.* (Dublin: W. B. Kelly, 1870), 103.

St. Fulgence [Fulgentius] of Ruspe (523 A.D.):

"St. Fulgence, born in 467 A.D., was the son of a wealthy and influential family, and was well-educated in both Latin and Greek. At one time a tax-collector in his native town of Telepte in the African Province of Byzacena, he afterwards became a monk. About the year 502 A.D. he was made Bishop of Ruspe. A year later, in the Arian-Vandal persecu-tion, he was exiled with more than sixty other Catholic Bish-ops to Sardinia. With the exception of a two-year period when he was at Carthage, sometime between 510 and 517 A.D., he remained in Sardinia until the death of Trasamund, the Vandal King, in 523. Fulgence was then able to return to Ruspe, where he remained until his death on January 1, 527 A.D." W. A. Jurgens, *The Faith of the Early Fathers*, vol. 3, (Collegeville, MN: The Liturgical Press, 1970), 285.

"To Peter, that is, to his Church, he gave the power of re-taining and forgiving sins on earth." (Fulgence, *De Remissione Peccatorum* 2:20 Migne *Patr. Lat.* vol. 65, col. 571), in Michael M. Winter, *Saint Peter and the Popes*, (Baltimore: Helicon, 1960), 71.

"That which the Roman Church—which is the summit of the world enlightened with resplendent rays by the words of two great luminaries, namely Peter and Paul, and deco-rated with their bodies—holds and teaches, the entire Christian world unhesitatingly believes and professes with her, unto righteousness and salvation." (Fulgence, *Ep. 18*, J. P. Migne, *Patrologiae Cursus Completus Series Latina* (Paris, 1844-1855), trans. John Collorafi.

"Only in the Catholic Church, therefore, is the remission of sins given and received, which the spouse himself calls his dove, his only chosen one, which he founded upon a rock to which he gave the keys of the kingdom of heaven, to which he also granted the power of binding and loosing, as truth itself promised with veracity to blessed Peter, saying: 'Thou art Peter and upon this rock I will build my church, and the gates of hell shall not prevail against it; I shall give to thee the keys of the kingdom of heaven, and whatsoever thou shall bind on earth shall be bound in heaven, and whatso-ever thou shall loose on earth shall be loosed in heaven.'" (Fulgentius, *On the Remission of Sins, to Euthymius*, Book I, ch. 19., in J. P. Migne, *Patrologiae Cursus Completus Series Latina* (Paris, 1844-1855), trans. John Collorafi.

Roman Synod in 531 writing to Pope Boniface II:

"Nor is it lawful for us to dissent in any way from the height of Your Apostleship, whom Christ our Lord willed, in his place, to be the head of us all on earth." (*Ep. ad Bonif.*) in Dr. Hergenrother, *Anti-Janus: An Historico-Theological Criticism Of The Work, Entitled 'The Pope And The Coun-cil', By Janus.* (Dublin: W. B. Kelly, 1870), 103.

Pelagius I (561 A.D.):

> [Writing to the Western Bishops who resisted the fifth General Council:] "That they ought to have referred their doubts to the Apostolic See; that they would be separated from the communion of the whole world, if they omitted in the Mass the commemoration of the Pope, in whom now rests the solidity of the Holy See." (Pelagius I, *Ep. 2 ad Narset. Patric. Op. 6 ad Episc. Tusc.*), in Dr. Hergenrother, *Anti-Janus: An Historico-Theological Criticism Of The Work, Entitled 'The Pope And The Council', By Janus*. (Dublin: W. B. Kelly, 1870), 68-69 [Lat. trans. John Collorafi].

St. Venantius Honorius Clementianus Fortunatus (570 A.D.):

> "[Venantius] Poet. Born near Treviso, Italy, he was educated in Ravenna, and in 565 went to Germany." John J. Delaney and James Edward Tobin, *Dictionary of Catholic Biography*, (Garden City, NY: Doubleday, 1961), 1157.

> "He (Paul) was more learned in his admonitions; (Peter) was higher in rank." (Venantius, *Lib. iii. Carm. 7*) "Peter was prince by virtue of the key; Paul was also first by his teaching." (Venantius, *Lib. ix. Carm. 2*), in Charles F. B. Allnatt, ed., *Cathedra Petri—The Titles and Prerogatives of St. Peter*, (London: Burns & Oates, 1879), 34.

Pope Pelagius II (ca. 579-590 A.D.):

> "Pope, born in Rome, son of the vicar of one of the two districts into which Rome was then divided, he accompanied Pope Agapetus I to Constantinople and was appointed nuncio by Agapetus [or, Agapitus] just before his death there in 536. He returned to Rome when Pope Silverius was driven from the city by Belisarus, agent of Empress Theodora, and on Vigilius' accession to the papal throne in 537 became a trusted adviser of Emperor Justinian." John J. Delaney and James Edward Tobin, *Dictionary of Catholic Biography*, (Garden City, NY: Doubleday, 1961), 909.

"Since the authority of convoking General Synods by a singular privilege has been delivered to the Apostolic See of Blessed Peter, and we do not read that any synod was ever considered ratified which was not supported by Apostolic authority." (Pope Pelagius II, *Ep. 6 ad Orient*), in Dr. Hergenrother, *Anti-Janus: An Historico-Theological Criticism Of The Work, Entitled 'The Pope And The Council', By Janus.* (Dublin: W. B. Kelly, 1870), p. 121 [Lat. trans. John Collorafi].

"You know that the Lord proclaims in the Gospel: 'Simon, Simon, behold: Satan has desired to possess you, so that he might sift you like wheat. But I have prayed for you, that your faith may not fail. And you, once you have converted, confirm your brethren!' [Luke 22:31-32]. Consider that the Truth could not have lied, nor will the faith of Peter be able to be shaken or changed for ever. For, although the devil desired to sift all the disciples, the Lord testifies that He Himself asked for Peter alone, and wished that the others be confirmed by him; and to Peter also was committed the care of 'feeding the sheep' [John 21:15]; and to him also did the Lord hand over the 'keys to the kingdom of Heaven' [Matthew 16:19], and upon him did He promise to 'build His Church' [Matthew 16:18]; and He testified that 'the gates of hell would not prevail against it' [Matthew 16:19]. . . If, however, anyone either suggests or believes contrary to this faith, let him know that he is condemned and anathematized. Consider, therefore, the fact that whoever has not been in the peace and unity of the Church cannot have the Lord. . . . On the Day of Judgment, no one can excuse himself. For the Church of God is established among those known to preside over the Apostolic Sees through succession, and whoever separates himself from the authority of these Sees is manifestly in schism. Those not willing to be at agreement in the Church of God cannot abide with God." Pelagius II, "Quod Ad Dilectionem"; "Dilectionis Vestrae," in Henry Denzinger, *Enchiridion Symbolorum*, 30th Ed., (London: B. Herder Book Co., 1957), Para. 246, 247, in Michael Malone, ed., *The Apostolic Digest*, (Irving, TX: Sacred Heart, 1987), 206.

St. Gregory the Great (ca. 590 A.D.):

Gregory receives this oath from a bishop returning from schism: "And therefore after I discovered the snare of division by which I was held, I humbly and spontaneously was led by divine grace to return to the unity of the apostolic see (Rome) and lest I be thought to return not through a pure intention but deceitfully, I swear, under pain of the loss of my order, and under the bond of anathema, and promise to thee, and through thee to Saint Peter, prince of the apostles, and to his vicar, the most blessed Gregory or his successors, that I will never, through anyone's persuasion or in any other way return to schism, from which I have been delivered through the mercy of our redeemer, but shall always remain, throughout all things, in the unity of the holy Catholic Church and the communion of the Roman pontiff." (St. Gregory the Great, *Register of Epistles*, Book XII, Ep. 7), in J. P. Migne, *Patrologiae Cursus Completus Series Latina* (Paris, 1844-1855), trans. John Collorafi.

St. Gregory writes in his *Letter to John, Bishop of Syracuse*: "St. Gregory the Great in reference to a later Bishop of Constantinople: 'As to what he says, that he is subject to the Apostolic See, I know not what bishop is not subject to it, if any fault be found in bishops.'" in Luke Rivington, *The Primitive Church and the See of St. Peter*, (London: Longmans, Green and Co., 1894), 174.

St. Gregory the Great regularly refers to Peter as 'Prince of the Apostles.' (See, e.g. *Register of his Epistles*, Book IX Ep. 131, 155, and *passim*. Book VI, Ep. 22, etc., in J. P. Migne, *Patrologiae Cursus Completus Series Latina* (Paris, 1844-1855), trans. John Collorafi.

St. Columbanus (ca. 600 A.D.):

"Columbanus (St.), a celebrated Irish monk, was born in Leinster, A.D. 543, and was brought up in the monastery of Bangor on the coast of Down, under St. Comgall, by whom he was sent, A.D. 590, with twelve other monks, to preach the Gospel to the tribes dwelling on the borders of the Frankish kingdom. He subsequently founded the great monasteries of Anegrey, Luxeuil, Fontaines, and Bobbio. See the account of his life and labours in Montalembert's *Monks of the West*, vol. ii. b. vii. His writings are published in Fleming's *Collectanea Sacra* (Lovan. 1667), and Galland (tom. xii.). Charles F. B. Allnatt, ed., *Cathedra Petri—The Titles and Prerogatives of St. Peter*, (London: Burns & Oates, 1879), 4-5.

"The celebrated Irish Liturgy known as the Missal of St. Columbanus contains the following Collect in the Mass assigned for the *Cathedra Sancti Petri*: 'O God! who on this day didst give to St. Peter, after Thyself, the headship of the whole Church, we humbly pray Thee that, as Thou didst constitute him pastor for the safety of the flock, and that Thy sheep might be preserved from error, so now Thou mayest save us through his intercession." (*Museum Italicum*, vol. i. p. 297, a D. J. Mabillon, Paris, 1724), in Charles F. B. Allnatt, ed., *Cathedra Petri—The Titles and Prerogatives of St. Peter*, (London: Burns & Oates, 1879), 47.

"[Rome] the principal See of the orthodox faith." (Columbanus, *Epist. ad. Bonif. Pap.* p. 353, Galland, tom. xii.), in Charles F. B. Allnatt, ed., *Cathedra Petri—The Titles and Prerogatives of St. Peter*, (London: Burns & Oates, 1879), 69.

"We are Irish, inhabitants of the furthermost part of the world, receiving nothing beyond the evangelic and apostolic doctrine. None of us has been a heretic, none a Jew, none a schismatic; but the faith, just as it was at first delivered by you, the successors, to wit, of the holy Apostles, is held unshaken. . . . Purity is to be reputed not to the stream, but to the fountain-head. . . . We are, as I said before, bound to the Chair of Peter. For although Rome is great and illustrious, it is only through this Chair that she is great and bright among us, . . . and if it can be said, on account of Christ's two Apostles (Peter and Paul), . . . You are almost heavenly, and Rome is the head of the churches of all the world, saving the singular prerogative of the place of the Lord's resurrection." (Columbanus, *Epist. ad Bonif. Pap.* pp. 352, 354, Galland, tom. xii.), in Charles F. B. Allnatt, ed., *Cathedra Petri—The Titles and Prerogatives of St. Peter*, (London: Burns & Oates, 1879), 80-81.

St. Isidore of Seville (620 A.D.):

"Bishop and Doctor of the Church. Born in Cartegena, Spain, brother of SS. Leander, Fulgentius, and Florentina, he was educated by his elder brother and succeeded him as bishop of Seville about 600. He continued the conversion of the Arian Visigoths, reorganized the discipline of the Church at several councils, saw to it that seminaries were built in each diocese, and completed the Mozarabic liturgy. An exceptionally well-read scholar, he organized schools which taught the arts (including Hebrew and Greek) as well as medicine and law. His encyclopedic *Etymologies* was a textbook until the sixteenth century; he also wrote histories, including a significant account of the Goths, biographies, treatises on astronomy and geography, rules for monastic life, and theological studies. He was declared a Doctor of the Church in 1722 by Pope Benedict XIV." John J. Delaney and James Edward Tobin, *Dictionary of Catholic Biography*, (Garden City, NY: Doubleday, 1961), 595.

"We know who is in charge in the Church of Christ to the extent that we reverently, humbly and devoutly profess more especially to give due obedience in all things to the Roman Pontiff as God's Vicar. Whoever proudly resists this principle, we decree, is altogether outside the fellowship of the faithful, as a heretic." (Isidore, *Ep. ad Claud. ducem*), in Dr. Hergenrother, *Anti-Janus: An Historico-Theological Criticism Of The Work, Entitled 'The Pope And The Council', By Janus.* (Dublin: W. B. Kelly, 1870), p. 105 [Lat. trans. John Collorafi].

St. Sophronius, Patriarch of Jerusalem (ca. 638 A.D.)

"[Sophronius] Patriarch. Born in Damascus, Syria, he probably traveled through Syria and Egypt before he became a recluse in 580 with John Moschus in sanctuaries directed by SS. Sabas and Theodius. He became patriarch of Jerusalem after 620, fought the Monothelite heresy, and sent his associate Stephen to Rome to have the papacy take a strong stand against it. Honorius took no action, but Pope Martin I eventually condemned the heresy at the Lateran Council of 649. Sophronius wrote a number of doctrinal treatises, biographies, homilies, and poems before the Saracens overran his see." John J. Delaney and James Edward Tobin, *Dictionary of Catholic Biography*, (Garden City, NY: Doubleday, 1961), 1071.

"Teaching us all orthodoxy and destroying all heresy and driving it away from the God-protected halls of our holy Catholic Church. And together with these inspired syllables and characters, I accept all his [the pope's] letters and teachings as proceeding from the mouth of Peter the Coryphaeus, and I kiss them and salute them and embrace them with all my soul. . . . I recognize the latter as definitions of Peter and the former as those of Mark, and besides, all the heaven-taught teachings of all the chosen mystagogues of our Catholic Church, etc." (Sophronius, *Mansi*, xi, 461-509), in Dom John Chapman, "The Condemnation of Pope Honorius," *Dublin Review*, (July-October, 1906), 135.

"Traverse quickly all the world from one end to the other until you come to the Apostolic See, where are the foundations of the orthodox doctrine, make clearly known to the most holy personages of that throne the questions agitated among us. Cease not to pray and to beg then until their apostolic and Divine wisdom shall have pronounced the victorious judgment and destroyed from the foundation . . . the new heresy." (Sophronius [quoted by Bishop Stephen of Dora to Martin I at Lateran Council], *Mansi*, x, 893), in S. Herbert Scott, *The Eastern Churches and the Papacy*, (London: Sheed & Ward, 1928), 269.

Sergius, Metropolitan of Cyprus, to Pope Theodore (649 A.D.):

"O holy Head, Christ our God hath destined thy Apostolic See to be an immovable foundation, and a pillar of the faith [cf. I Tim. 3:15]. For thou art, as the divine Word truly saith, Peter, and on thee as a foundation-stone have the pillars of the Church been fixed." (Sergius, *Ep. ad Theod. lecta* in Sess. ii., Concil. Lat., anno 649), in Dr. Hergenrother, *Anti-Janus: An Historico-Theological Criticism Of The Work, Entitled 'The Pope And The Council', By Janus.* (Dublin: W. B. Kelly, 1870), 63.

Theodore I (649 A.D.):

"[Theodore I] Pope. A Greek of Jerusalem and son of a bishop, he became pope on Nov. 24, 642. He vigorously opposed Monothelitism, which was to plague his pontificate; refused to recognize Paul as patriarch of Constantinople, since his predecessor, Pyrrhus, had been illegally deposed; and attempted unsuccessfully to win back Pyrrhus and Paul, both of whom he was forced to excommunicate in 648 and 649 respectively. His actions against Monothelitism were approved by the bishops of Cyprus, Palestine, and Africa, but Emperor Constans II refused to withdraw the *Ecthesis*, merely issuing the *Type*, at Paul's instigation, forbidding discussion of the doctrine of one or two wills in Christ, a step which was denounced by the West." John J. Delaney and James Edward Tobin, *Dictionary of Catholic Biography*, (Garden City, NY: Doubleday, 1961), 1108.

"Three Councils of Africa, in their Synodical letter sent to Pope Theodore, and read in the Council of Rome under Martin I, A.D. 646:—'No one can doubt that there is in the Apostolic See a great unfailing fountain, pouring forth waters for all Christians; whence rich streams proceed, bountifully irrigating the whole Christian World; to which See also, in honour of blessed Peter, the decrees of the Fathers gave special veneration in searching out the things of God, which ought by all means to be carefully examined; and above all, and justly, by the Apostolic Head of Bishops, whose care from of old it is, as well to condemn evils as to commend the things that are to be praised. For by the ancient discipline it is ordained that whatsoever be done, even in provinces remote and afar off, shall neither be treated or nor accepted, unless it be first brought to the knowledge of your August See, so that a just sentence may be confirmed by its authority, and that the other Churches may thence receive the original preaching as from its native source, and that the mysteries of saving faith may remain in uncorrupt purity throughout the various regions of the world.'" (*Epist. Synod. ad Pap. Theod. lect. in Concil. Rom. ann. 649*, sub. P. Mart.), in Charles F. B. Allnatt, ed., *Cathedra Petri—The Titles and Prerogatives of St. Peter*, (London: Burns & Oates, 1879), 108.

St. Maximus the Confessor (650 A.D.):

"How much more in the case of the clergy and Church of the Romans, which from of old until now, as the of all the Churches which are under the sun, presides over all? Having surely received this canonically, as well from councils and the apostles, as from the princes of the latter, and being numbered in their company, she is subject to no writings or issues of synodical documents, on account of the eminence of her pontificate, even as in all these things all are equally subject to her according to sacerdotal law. And so when, without fear but with all holy and becoming confidence, those ministers of the truly firm and immovable rock, that is of the most great and Apostolic Church at Rome." (Maximus, in J. B. Mansi, ed. *Amplissima Collectio Conciliorum*, vol. 10, (Florence, 1764-65), 677-78), in Dom John Chapman, "The Condemnation of Pope Honorius," *Dublin Review*, (July-October, 1906), 139.

"If the Roman See recognizes Pyrrhus to be not only a reprobate but a heretic, it is certainly plain that every one who anathematizes those who have rejected Pyrrhus, anathematizes the See of Rome, that is, he anathematizes the Catholic Church. I need hardly add that he excommunicates himself also, if indeed he is in communion with the Roman See and the Catholic Church of God. . . . Let him hasten before all things to satisfy the Roman See, for if it is satisfied, all will agree in calling him pious and orthodox. For he only speaks in vain who thinks he ought to persuade or entrap persons like myself, and does not satisfy and implore the blessed Pope of the most holy Church of the Romans, that is, the Apostolic See, which from the incarnate Son of God Himself, and also by all holy synods, according to the holy canons and definitions has received universal and supreme dominion, authority and power of binding and loosing over all the holy Churches of God which are in the whole world." (Maximus, *Letter to Peter*, in Mansi x, 692), in Dom John Chapman, "The Condemnation of Pope Honorius," *Dublin Review*, July-October, 1906), 146-147.

Venerable Bede (ca. 700 A.D.):

"Because they had seen Peter, James, and John led aside up to the mountain . . . and that earlier on the keys of the kingdom of heaven had been promised to Peter, and that the Church was to be built upon him, they thought that either those three were set over the rest or that Peter was set over all the apostles." (Venerable Bede, *On Luke* Bk.III, ch. 9), in J. P. Migne, *Patrologiae Cursus Completus Series Latina* (Paris, 1844-1855), trans. John Collorafi.

Theodore the Studite (759-826 A.D.) wrote to Leo III:

"In truth we have seen that a manifest successor of the prince of the Apostles presides over the Roman Church. We truly believe that Christ has not deserted the Church here (at Constantinople), for assistance from you has been our one and only aid from of old and from the beginning by the providence of God in the critical times. You are, indeed, the untroubled and pure fount of orthodoxy from the beginning, you the calm harbour of the whole Church, far removed from the waves of heresy, you the God-chosen city of refuge." (*Letter of St. Theodore and four other Abbots to Pope Paschal*, Bk. ii Ep. 12, *Patr. Graec.* 99, 1153), in Dom John Chapman, *The First Eight General Councils and Papal Infallibility*, 3rd ed., (London: Catholic Truth Society, 1928), 75.

"Let him (the Patriarch Nicephorus) assemble a synod of those with whom he has been at variance, if it is impossible that representatives of the other Patriarchs should be present, a thing which might certainly be, if the Emperor should wish the Western (Patriarch) to be present, to whom is given the authority over an ecumenical synod; but let him make peace and union, by sending his synodical letters to the prelate of the first see.' (Theodore the Studite, *Patr. Graec.* 99, 1420), in Dom John Chapman, *The First Eight General Councils and Papal Infallibility*, 3rd ed., (London: Catholic Truth Society, 1928), 75.

St. Nicephorus, Patriarch of Constantinople (758-828 A.D.):

"Patriarch. Philosopher, musician, and statesman in the service of Constantine VI, he was secretary to the second Nicaean Council. Though a layman, he was elected patriarch of Constantinople to succeed St. Tarasius and swore to uphold the freedom to venerate icons, for which stand his father had been scourged and exiled. He was briefly out of favor with St. Theodore Studites, who condemned him for reinstating a priest who had permitted Constantine to contract a bigamous marriage. He spent his last fifteen years in exile after Emperor Leo I revived the Iconoclast heresy, dying on June 2 in a monastery on the Bosphorus. His writings include a defense of icons and two historical chronicles." John J. Delaney and James Edward Tobin, *Dictionary of Catholic Biography*, (Garden City, NY: Doubleday, 1961), 848-849.

"Without whom (the Romans presiding in the seventh Council) a doctrine brought forward in the Church could not, even though confirmed by canonical decrees and by ecclesiastical usage, ever obtain full approval or currency. For it is they (the Roman Pontiffs) who have had assigned to them the rule in sacred things, and who have received into their hands the dignity of headship among the Apostles." (Nicephorus, *Niceph. Cpl. pro. s. imag.* c 25 (Mai N. Bibl. pp. ii. 30)), in Dr. Hergenrother, *Anti-Janus: An Historico-Theological Criticism Of The Work, Entitled 'The Pope And The Council', By Janus.* (Dublin: W. B. Kelly, 1870), 125-126.

Alcuin (780 A.D.):

"Alcuin (Flaccus Albinus), an English monk, who became renowned throughout Christendom for his great learning, was born of noble Northumbrian parentage about A.D. 735, and brought up from infancy in the celebrated school of York (founded by Archbishop Egbert, the disciple and friend of Ven. Bede), of which he became the head A.D. 780. He was sent to Rome A.D. 781, and shortly afterwards, at the request of the Emperor Charlemagne, went to France, where he spent the remainder of his life in various literary and scholastic labours, dying at Tours in 804. 'His services to religion and literature in Europe,' says a Protestant writer, 'based indeed on the foundation of Bede, were more widely extended, and in themselves inestimable' (*Dict. of Christ. Biog. and Literat.* vol. i. p. 74). The best editions of his writings are those of Froben (Ratisbon, 1777, 2 vols. fol.), and Migne (*Patrol. Lat.* vols. c., ci.)." Charles F. B. Allnatt, ed., *Cathedra Petri—The Titles and Prerogatives of St. Peter*, (London: Burns & Oates, 1879), 1.

"To Leo [III] the Pope, the most blessed Lord, . . . As much as ever I could, have I always loved the most blessed princes, and shepherds of the holy Roman See; wishful to be numbered, through their most holy intercessions, among Christ's sheep, which Christ our God intrusted unto the blessed Peter, Prince of the Apostles, to be fed. This, I acknowledge, was truly becoming, that the multitude of this flock, though abiding in sundry pastures of the earth, should, by the one faith of love, be placed under its Shepherd, whom, as a godly Pastor, it becometh to have a great care for the flock intrusted to his keeping, . . . Behold, thou art, most holy Father, the Pontiff chosen by God, the Vicar of the Apostles, the heir of the Fathers, the Prince of the Church, the Nourisher of the one Spotless Dove. In the kindness of fatherly feeling, by thy most holy prayers, and sweetest exhortations of sacred writings, gather us unto God's holy Church, within the very strong bonds of the Church's soundness; lest any of us, wandering about, should be met on the outside to be devoured by the ravenousness of the wolf." (Alcuin, *Alcuin. Epist.* Op. tom i. p. 30, ed. Froben.), in Charles F. B. Allnatt, ed., *Cathedra Petri—The Titles and Prerogatives of St. Peter*, (London: Burns & Oates, 1879), 111.

"Lest he be found a schismatic or a non-Catholic, let him follow the most approved authority of the Roman Church, so that we may ever have the examples of our salvation from the same place we received the beginnings of the Catholic faith. Let not the members be separated from the Head; let not the key-bearer of the heavenly kingdom cast out those whom he knows have deviated from his teachings." (Alcuin, *Ep. 70*), in Dr. Hergenrother, *Anti-Janus: An Historico-Theological Criticism Of The Work, Entitled 'The Pope And The Council', By Janus.* (Dublin: W. B. Kelly, 1870), p. 105 [Lat. trans. John Collorafi].

EPILOGUE

The issue of leadership and the mechanism of providing divine guidance is as old as the Church. However, questions regarding it would have seemed superfluous immediately after the Ascension of Jesus since the great expectation was of an imminent return of Jesus, an early second coming. There would be no recognition of a need to address leadership if there were to be no change from what had existed earlier. Peter had a recognized role as spokesman for the Twelve that continued in what seemed to be a mere interlude, as he humbly assumed the cloak of authority.

Paul's writings were the first to appear within the first two decades of the new church, a community forming within Judaism. When Paul initiates the New Testament writings, the picture of a belief in an early second coming appears to exist (I Thessalonians 4:15). Paul recognizes Peter as a leader among the disciples (Galatians 1:18-29), and claims their approval of his own mission as justification that it had broad approval (Galatians 2:1-10), even as he criticized publicly a personal lapse by Peter (Galatians 2:11-14). The only comprehensive view of those early years is Luke's record in Acts, written perhaps more than a half-century after the Resurrection. From the vantage point of seeing how the Church developed after the death of Peter and Paul, how she was organized after she separated from Judaism, Luke presents a picture in which Peter is the prominent leader, even though one may describe the purpose of Acts as showing the expansion of the kingdom to

Gentiles, and the contribution of Paul. The picture presented should reflect what was commonly accepted by Christians up to that time, not some later view to influence Church organization.

There were great issues addressed by the early Church, which may not have been clear in how the message of Jesus had been presented to the early disciples. The questions of persecution, the separation from Judaism, the meaning of kingdom after the separation, and the divinity of Jesus Christ were certainly major for Christians who were simply waiting for his second coming. Responding to each issue, the Church reviewed the events, sayings and teachings of Jesus, and then assembled those related to such questions into the four Gospel accounts included in the New Testament. Jesus may not have appeared clearly to address the various individual questions, but from the remembered accounts of his public life a very clear response could be obtained. Anyone who reviewed the Gospel accounts would recognize that the stories they had all known individually would reflect the Lord's direction when seen as an assembled document.

Questions about certain aspects of the nature of Church leadership either did not arise or were never of such importance that they were addressed directly in writing. Historical questions occurred at much later times when the Papacy played a role in a western empire in conflict with the remnant of the old Roman Empire ruled from Constantinople. Some of those questions regarding Papal Authority were addressed after Eastern Orthodox Churches became separated from Rome. However, the most direct questions raised in regard to the Papacy are seen as coming from the disputes rising out of the Protestant Reformation. Yet, the primary issue is not how to settle a question of leadership that came from a troubled time of difficulty within the Christian family. Rather, it should be addressed in terms of the statements from the Revelation which comes in the very words and teachings of Jesus Christ.

The subject of leadership was not analyzed in great detail during the lifetime of the disciples who heard Jesus speak or who collected the stories from eyewitnesses, as much as were the major issues that framed the Gospel accounts. Yet, the issue of Church leadership and the application of a revealed message on situations facing the Church nearly 2,000 years after the Resurrection are of sufficient magnitude that they would have been touched in the collections of stories used to produce the four Gospels. The issue of leadership and preservation of teaching deserves a searching answer from that same source.

This preparation of responses to a series of questions which can be raised about the Papacy is the result of such a search. It is a search for answers which predate the actual questions. It represents a collection of views from Jesus as understood by the Church on a single issue separated from his views on other subjects in order to provide clarity. Other sections of Scripture are used where applicable since that represents the earliest Church view. Quotations are used from early Church writings to reflect the continuity of genuine teachings after the New Testament period, in both Parts I and II. Scholarly works of the present time are included to provide a better understanding of language and early information. Certain of the great theological opinions of later times are not used because they do not represent common ground for all sides of this issue. The answers that are found in the early records are the most convincing and when they can be traced back to the words of Jesus, the subject should be settled among Christians.

Anyone could propose a means to lead a kingdom of one and a half billion disciples. One might advance arguments for a new type of Church leadership, or a changed organization might be presented in a very convincing manner. Yet, the record of proposals that have been put forth and tried, apart from the Catholic hierarchical model, is one of constant fracturing. The very weakness of the alternatives is what causes the question to remain. If some human experiment had shown an objective improvement over what history records as the original approach, there would be no reason for discussion. Moreover, if the divine plan which came to earth with Jesus originated a means of preserving his kingdom as that kingdom expands, substituting the greatest of human proposals becomes self-defeating.

Like Jesus himself, there is always a human side to revelation and the Church in addition to the divine purpose and presence. If the earliest Church only recognized a human side to the community after the Ascension, it is reasonable that there would be a period of waiting for a second coming to reestablish a divine connection. However, with the recognition that the Holy Spirit was personally active in the Church, a delayed second coming was accepted. The end times continue. That the Church would function with divine guidance in a human framework was not found by happenstance, but was clearly expected, even foreseen. It was expected because the history of Revelation included in the Scriptures available to the earliest Church, our Old Testament, described God as working through his agents, and most of all through his anointed one.

Jesus was originally seen by many Jews as the greatest of those anointed ones, and by others as the divine one who would inaugurate the long-awaited Day of the Lord. Jesus was both the reestablishment of the dynasty of David and its divine perfection. That Jesus went far beyond the expectations of Judaism has been how God's actions were interpreted from the earliest days of Christianity.

The genre of this writing should not be of arguments put forth to force a conclusion. Rather, it is a reflection on the plan of the Lord—that Christianity in unity may speak for him both individually and officially. What the words of Jesus say on the subject of leadership and the protection of the message of Revelation in every age is what disciples everywhere should be able to accept.

APPENDIX

THE LANGUAGE OF MATTHEW

The Language of Jesus in the Gospel of Matthew

Matthew 16:13 When Jesus came into the coasts of Caesarea Philippi, he asked his disciples, saying, Whom do men say that I the Son of man am?

16:14 And they said, Some [say that thou art] John the Baptist: some, Elias; and others, Jeremias, or one of the prophets.

16:15 He saith unto them, But whom say ye that I am?

16:16 And Simon Peter answered and said, Thou art the Christ, the Son of the living God.

16:17 And Jesus answered and said unto him, Blessed art thou, Simon Bar-jona: for flesh and blood hath not revealed [it] unto thee, but my Father which is in heaven.

16:18 And I say also unto thee, That thou art Peter [*sur*, *kepha*, *petros*], and upon this rock [*sur*, *kepha*, *petra*] I will build my church; and the gates of hell shall not prevail against it.

16:19 And I will give unto thee the keys of the kingdom of heaven: and whatsoever thou shalt bind on earth shall be bound in heaven: and whatsoever thou shalt loose on earth shall be loosed in heaven.

226. In what language was Jesus speaking as he spoke to Peter in Matthew 16? Aramaic. In Matthew 16:13-19, the words "flesh and blood," "bind and loose," and "blessed art thou" are Aramaic phrases used in Scripture.

The renowned Swiss Protestant theologian Oscar Cullmann, declares that Jesus spoke Aramaic, lending support to the conclusion that Matthew was originally written in Aramaic:

> ". . . the great antiquity and the Palestinian origin of the section [Matthew 16:17 ff.] may today be considered beyond question. This is shown by the quite Semitic linguistic character of this section. . . . The parallelism of the two statements: 'you are rock, and upon this rock I will build . . .' shows that the second rock refers to nothing different from the first one. This is more clearly expressed in the Aramaic, where the same word *kepha* occurs both times, than it is in the Greek. . . . Thus here the name and the thing are exactly identical. Therefore, we must assume that the saying was originally coined in Aramaic." Oscar Cullmann, *Peter: Disciple, Apostle, Martyr*, trans. Floyd V. Filson, (Philadelphia: Westminster, 1953), 185, 206, 185.

From the Lutheran-Catholic Dialogue, there is the following quotation regarding the use of the Aramaic language in Matthew 16:

> "In Aramaic there is identity: 'You are *Kepha* and upon this *kepha* I will build.' Another Semitism, 'gates of Hades' for 'powers of death' (note 208 above), plus the Semitisms 'flesh and blood' in the preceding verse and 'bind and loose' in the following verse (also the presence of Semitic parallelism—see vs. 19 below), constitute impressive evidence for proposing that these verses originated in a setting where Aramaic was a native tongue, and this supports the thesis of a pre-Matthean origin of the basic material." Brown, Raymond E., Karl P. Donfried, and John Reumann, eds., *Peter in the New Testament*, (Minneapolis, MN: Augsburg; New York: Paulist: 1973), 90-91.

And, consider the following passages from Scripture:

> *Matthew* 27:46 And about the ninth hour Jesus cried with a loud voice, saying, Eli, Eli, lama sabachthani? that is to say, My God, my God, why hast thou forsaken me?

> *Mark* 15:34 And at the ninth hour Jesus cried with a loud voice, saying Eloi, Eloi, lama sabachthani? that is to say, My God, my God, why hast thou forsaken me?

This rendering of "Eloi, Eloi, lama sabachthani" is consistent with the Aramaic language spoken by Jesus and his original disciples in Jerusalem, albeit that *Eli* in the first verse is Hebrew. The rest of the phrasing is Aramaic and is reconciled thus:

> "In Mark [15:34] the verse is cited entirely in Aramaic, which Matthew partially retains but changes the invocation of God to the Hebrew *Eli*, possibly because it is more easily related to the statement of the following verse about Jesus calling for Elijah." Confraternity of Christian Doctrine, *The New American Bible* (Giant Print Edition), fn. [Matthew] 27:46, (Huntington, IN: Our Sunday Visitor, 1988), 1766.

The Original Language of Matthew According to the Early Church

227. In what language was the Gospel of Matthew originally written? Aramaic ("Hebrew"), according to Papias (130-150 A.D., Irenaeus (180 A.D.), Origen (244 A.D.), Eusebius (325 A.D.), Chrysostom (370 A.D.), Epiphanius (376 A.D.), Augustine (400 A.D.), and possibly Jerome (390 A.D.).

Eusebius, in his *History of the Church*, Book III, Chapter 39, cites from Papias, *Explanation of the Sayings of the Lord* (ca. 130 A.D.):

> "Matthew, indeed, composed the sayings in the Hebrew language; and each one interpreted them to the best of his ability [Gr. *dialekto Hebraico*, also translated from *Patrologiae cursus completus, Series graeca*, Volume 5, Migne, J. P. (Paris, 1857), p. 1257-1258, as "Hebraic dialect", not "He-

brew language", according to Bernadeane Carr, S.T.L., (personal conference of July 15, 1993), and Fr. Mitchell Pacwa, S.J. (telephonic conference of July 22, 1993)]." W. A. Jurgens, ed., *The Faith of the Early Fathers*, vol. 1, (Collegeville, MN: Liturgical, 1970), 39. Papias [born 69 A.D.] "'was a hearer of John and a companion of Polycarp [of Smyrna].'" W. A. Jurgens, ed., *The Faith of the Early Fathers*, vol. 1, (Collegeville, MN: Liturgical, 1970), 38.

From the Greek, the late G. A. Williamson (Senior Classics Master at Norwich School, England, from 1922 to 1960) translates a passage of Eusebius as follows:

"Such is Papias's account of Mark. Of Matthew he has this to say: 'Matthew compiled the *Sayings* in the Aramaic language, and everyone translated them as well as he could.'" Eusebius, *The History of the Church from Christ to Constantine*, trans. G. A. Williamson, (New York: Barnes & Noble, 1965), 152.

"Bartholomew, one of the apostles, had preached to them and had left behind Matthew's account in the actual Aramaic characters." Eusebius, *The History of the Church from Christ to Constantine*, trans. G. A. Williamson, (New York: Barnes & Noble, 1965), 213-214.

"Though the two languages, Hebrew and Aramaic, had co-existed for several centuries in the Near East before this [the Babylonian exile], Aramaic became the more important of the two, serving as the *lingua franca* during the latter part of the Neo-Assyrian empire and during the Persian period. Hebrew is usually regarded today as the more important of the two languages, because it is the tongue of the bulk of the OT. And yet, historically it was restricted to a small area on the south-eastern coast of the Mediterranean, whereas Official or Imperial Aramaic was used across a major portion of the Near Eastern world, from Egypt to Asia Minor to Pakistan. Indeed, it gradually supplanted Hebrew in most of Palestine itself as the common tongue." Joseph

A. Fitzmyer, *A Wandering Aramean: Collected Aramaic Essays*, (Ann Arbor, MI: Edwards Brothers, 1979), 29.

Irenaeus (180 A.D.), who was a pupil of St. Polycarp, writes in *Against Heresies* 3.1.1, quoted by Eusebius in *Hist. Eccl.* 5.8.2-4): "Matthew also issues among the Hebrews a written gospel in their own language, while Peter and Paul were evangelizing in Rome and laying the foundation of the Church." W. A. Jurgens, ed., *The Faith of the Early Fathers*, vol. 1, (Collegeville, MN: Liturgical, 1970), 89.

Origen (244 A.D.) wrote twenty-five books of commentaries on Matthew. He is quoted by Eusebius, in *History of the Church*, Book 6, Chapter 25: "As to the four Gospels, which alone are indisputable in the Church of God under heaven, I learned from tradition that the first to have been written was that of Matthew, who was formerly a tax collector, but later an Apostle of Jesus Christ. It was prepared for those who were converted from Judaism to the faith, and was written in Hebrew letters." W. A. Jurgens, ed., *The Faith of the Early Fathers*, vol. 1, (Collegeville, MN: Liturgical, 1970), 210.

Eusebius (325 A.D.) himself declared that "Matthew had begun by preaching to the Hebrews, and when he made up his mind to go to others too, he committed his own gospel to writing in his native tongue (Aramaic), so that for those with whom he was no longer present the gap left by his departure was filled by what he wrote." *History of the Church, Book 3, Chapter 24* in *The Ecclesiastical History of Eusebius Pamphilus: Bishop of Caesarea in Palestine*, trans. Christian F. Cruse, (Grand Rapids, MI: Baker, 1991), 108.

St. Athanasius (ca. 350 A.D.), "in his *Synopsis of Holy Scripture*, says, 'Matthew's Gospel was written by Matthew in the Hebrew dialect, published at Jerusalem, and a translation made by James, the Lord's brother.'" Cornelius A. Lapide, *The Great Commentary upon the Holy Scriptures*, trans. Thomas W. Mossman, (London: John Hodges, 1893), p. xxxvii.

St. John Chrysostom (ca. 370 A.D.) related, in his *Homilies on the Gospel of St. Matthew* writes:

> "Of Matthew again it is said, that when those who from amongst the Jews had believed came to him, and besought

him to leave to them in writing those same things, which he had spoken to them by word, he also composed his Gospel in the language of the Hebrews." *Homilies of St. John Chrysostom on the Gospel According to St. Matthew*, in Philip Schaff, ed., *Nicene and Post-Nicene Fathers—Chrysostom*, vol. 10, (n.p.: Christian Literature Pub. Co., 1888; repr. Peabody, MA: Hendrickson, 1994), 3.

Epiphanius (376 A.D.) in his work, entitled *Panarion*, wrote against eighty heresies. In the chapter entitled "The Nazoreans," Book 29, Chapter 9, verse 4, he stated: "They [the Nazoreans] have the complete gospel of Matthew in Hebrew. For there is no doubt that it is still preserved by them in Hebrew writing, just as it was originally written." Epiphanius, trans. Philip R. Amidon, *The Panarion of St. Epiphanius, Bishop of Salamis: Selected Passages*, (New York: Oxford, 1990), 93.

"The Ebionites [c. 1st - 3rd centuries A.D.; views lingered in the East until absorbed into Islam in 7th century], heretics who believed that Jesus was born from the seed of Joseph, observed Jewish ceremonial law, the Sabbath, and circumcision. As a Judaized heretical sect that insisted on calling itself 'Christian': 'They too accept the Gospel of Matthew, and like the followers of Cerinthus and Merinthus, they also use it alone. They call it the Gospel according to the Hebrews, to tell the truth, because Matthew alone in the New Testament expounded and declared the gospel in Hebrew and Hebrew letters.'" *The Panarion*, 95; *Encyclopaedia Britannica*, 11th ed., s.v. "Ebionites."

Jerome (390 A.D.) referred to Matthew as the "Hebrew" gospel. *The Homilies of Saint Jerome, Volume 1*, trans. Marie L. Ewald, in *The Fathers of the Church*, vol. 48, (Washington, DC: Catholic University, 1964), 355.

"S. Jerome declares that he had seen S. Matthew's Gospel, written in Hebrew, in the Library of Pamphilus the Martyr, at Caesarea, and from it had transcribed his own copy. This Hebrew text is now, however, lost." Cornelius A. Lapide, *The Great Commentary upon the Holy Scrip-*

tures, trans. Thomas W. Mossman, (London: John Hodges, 1893), p. xxxvii.

Augustine (ca. 400 A.D.), in *The Harmony of the Gospels*, wrote:

"4. Of these four [gospels], it is true, only Matthew is reckoned to have written in the Hebrew language; the others in Greek." *The Harmony of the Gospels*, 1:1:4, in Philip Schaff, ed., *Nicene and Post-Nicene Fathers—Augustin*, vol. 6, (n.p.: Christian Literature Pub. Co., 1888; repr. Peabody, MA: Hendrickson, 1994), 78.

228. What does patristic tradition have to say about Matthew? It was described as the Gospel that was: (i) complete (Irenaeus, Origen [from *Commentary on Matthew*, in Eusebius (Hist. Eccl. 6.25.4)], Eusebius, Augustine, Epiphanius); (ii) written in "Hebrew" or Aramaic (Papias, Irenaeus, Eusebius, Origen, Epiphanius, and Jerome); (iii) written by and for Jewish Christians (Irenaeus, Eusebius, Origen); (iv) written while Peter and Paul were evangelizing the Gentiles (Irenaeus); and (v) widely interpreted and variously translated (Papias).

"SS. Jerome and Augustine, Eusebius, and the rest of the ancients, unanimously affirm that Matthew wrote in Hebrew, and that he did so because he was asked by the Jews, when he was going away amongst the Gentiles, to leave them in writing what he had orally preached to them. This is asserted by S. Chrysostom, in his first Homily. The *Auctor Imperfecti* adds, 'The cause of S. Matthew's writing was this: at a time of severe persecution in Palestine, when all were in danger of being dispersed, in order that if the disciples were deprived of teachers of the faith, they might not be deprived of teaching, they asked Matthew to write them a history of all the words and deeds of Christ, that wheresoever they might be, they might have with them a statement of all that they believed." Cornelius A. Lapide, *The Great Commentary upon the Holy Scriptures*, trans. Thomas W. Mossman, (London: John Hodges, 1893), p. xxxvi.

The Language Jesus Spoke

Until recent times, Hebrew was not the vernacular spoken language of the Jews. At various times in Jewish history, other languages supplanted Hebrew (always a written language of Scripture, except for those Old Testament books and passages written in Aramaic and Greek). By the time of Christ, Aramaic had largely become the spoken, then the written, Jewish language.

"Before the Christian era Aramaic had in good part replaced Hebrew in Palestine as the vernacular of the Jews. It continued as their vernacular for centuries later." Kevin Cathcart, Martin McNamara, and Michael Maher, eds., *The Aramaic Bible: the Targums*, vol. 1A, trans. Martin McNamara, (Collegeville, MN: Liturgical, 1992), vii. In fact, the Targums are reflective of this Aramaic common language.

229. What were the Targums? The Targums were at first an oral, then a written, translation and interpretation of Scripture into Aramaic for the benefit of the people, who could not understand Hebrew. The Targums contain commentaries and homilies as well.

> "The use of the term 'Targum' by itself was restricted to the Aramaic version of the Bible (see Bacher, 'Wie Terminologie der Tannaiten, pp. 205 *et seq.*). In like manner, the Aramaic passages in Genesis, Jeremiah, Daniel, and Ezra were briefly called 'Targum,' while the Hebrew text was called 'Mikra' (see Yad. iv. 5; Shab. 115b).
>
> "As an interpretation of the Hebrew text of the Bible the Targum had its place both in the synagogal liturgy and in Biblical instruction, which the reading of the Bible text combined with the Targum in the presence of the congregation assembled for public worship was an ancient institution which dated from the time of the Second Temple, and was traced back to Ezra by Rab when he interpreted the word 'meforash' (Neh. viii. 8) as referring to the Targum (Meg. 3a; Ned. 37b; comp. Yer. Meg. 74d, line 48; Gen. R. xxxvi., end)." Isidore Singer, ed., *The Jewish Encyclopedia*, vol. 12, (Hoboken, NJ: Ktav, 1964), 57.

230. Why were Hebrew scriptures translated into (and commented upon) in Aramaic? Because most Jewish people did not speak Hebrew during that period.

231. What was the language that most Jews spoke? Aramaic, which had gradually replaced Hebrew as the vernacular in most of Palestine, and throughout the Near East.

232. When were the Targums first transmitted? Perhaps as early as the time of the second temple (537-520 B.C.), or perhaps later during the time when the Essenes occupied Qumran (200 B.C.-68 A.D.). See Allen C. Myers, ed., *The Eerdmans Bible Dictionary*, (Grand Rapids, MI: Eerdmans, 1987), 984-85, 991.

Modern scholarship has placed the *written* Targums earlier in time than those certain later medieval transcriptions:

> "The extant written Targums had their beginnings with the oral rendering into the Aramaic vernacular of portions of the Hebrew Bible that took place as part of the regular worship in synagogues during the centuries when the Jews of Palestine and Babylonia spoke dialects of Aramaic (cf. Ezra 8:7-8). Among the factors contributing to the recent upsurge of interest in the Targums are . . . the identification in 1956 of a nearly complete text of the Palestinian Targum to the Pentateuch (Codex Neofiti I of the Vatican Library), and the publication of Aramaic fragments from Qumran, including extensive fragments of a Targum of Job (11QtgJob). Allen C. Myers, ed., *The Eerdmans Bible Dictionary*, (Grand Rapids, MI: Eerdmans, 1987), 984-85.

Various written Targums existed at the time of Christ, but their extent or exact dating is not known. Other written works are susceptible to specific textual dating within the Christian period. Etan Levine provides the following analysis:

> "Some elements can be historically pinpointed with reasonable certainty. For example, in its homily on the Four Kingdoms (Hab. 3:17), the targum denounces the oppressive re-

gime by predicting that 'The Romans will be destroyed and they will not exact tribute from Jerusalem.' Had the destruction of the Temple (70 C.E.) ensued already, the targum would surely have related to that far greater tragedy. Instead it is indignant over the census tax: a levy imposed by the second Procurator Quirinius in 6 C.E. which aroused widespread resentment and antagonism from then until the general revolt of 66 C.E., since it was regarded as national bondage. The targum's homily, therefore, must have originated during that sixty-year period." Etan Levine, *The Aramaic Version of the Bible*, (New York: Walter de Gruyter, 1988), 21-22.

One logical conclusion as to the influence and usefulness of the Targums is as follows:

"Comparative studies of the early Bible versions reveal variant readings similar to those found in the targum, and New Testament quotations which depart from both the Hebrew and Greek texts are sometimes identical to targum readings, suggesting that the earliest Jewish-Christians too were dependent upon Aramaic for their understanding of Scripture, so that the Christian Church may have itself passed through a phase of targumism in emerging from the synagogue." Etan Levine, *The Aramaic Version of the Bible*, (New York: Walter de Gruyter, 1988), 20-21.

The Targums thus are an indicator that there were Aramaic writings in existence at the time of Christ and that it is likely that they had a significant effect upon the writing of the New Testament, whether the original version was written in Aramaic or Greek.

233. Did the Targums, as expansive translations and commentary, of Hebrew scriptures, continue to be written after the death of Christ? Yes, Targums were being written down many years after the time of Christ.

"Where does the Aramaic of the Palestinian Targum fit into the overall pattern? Paul Kahle strongly maintained that this Aramaic represented the spoken language of Palestine in the time of Jesus. It was the language of Jesus." Kevin Cathcart, Martin McNamara, and Michael Maher, eds., *The Aramaic Bible: the Targums*, vol. 1A, trans. Martin McNamara, (Collegeville, MN: Liturgical, 1992), 14.

234. What can we conclude from the Aramaic Targums? That the original of Matthew was probably written in Aramaic, "a Semitic language closely related to Hebrew." Allen C. Myers, ed., *The Eerdmans Bible Dictionary*, (Grand Rapids, MI: Eerdmans, 1987), 71). Logically, this writing was made in order that Palestinian Jews could read the Gospel of Matthew in their native tongue—Aramaic. An Aramaic rendering of Matthew also helps to solidify an understanding of how the followers of Jesus would have easily interpreted Simon's change in name to "Rock."

Aramaic was the spoken language of Galilee and Judea during the time of Jesus and may have been colloquially referred to as "Hebrew" by later writers. Aramaic could very well have been the original language in which Matthew was written. The Lord Jesus could foresee that his sayings would be spoken and written in Aramaic first and later translated into Greek, Hebrew and other languages, even into English.

JESUS, PETER AND THE KEYS

THE POPES OF THE CATHOLIC CHURCH

Peter (32-67)
Linus (67-76)
Anacletus (76-88)
Clement I (88-97)
Evaristus (97-105)
Alexander I (105-115)
Sixtus I (115-125)
Telesphorus (125-136)
Hyginus (136-140)
Pius I (140-155)
Anicetus (155-166)
Soter (166-175)
Eleutherius (175-189)
Victor I (189-199)
Zephyrinus (199-217)
Callistus I (217-222)
Urban I (222-230)
Pontain (230-235)
Anterus (235-236)
Fabian (236-250)
Cornelius (251-253)
Lucius I (253-254)
Stephen I (254-257)
Sixtus II (257-258)
Dionysius (259-268)

Felix I (269-274)
Eutychian (275-283)
Caius (283-296)
Marcellinus (296-304)
Marcellus I (308-309)
Eusebius (Apr.-Aug. 309/310)
Miltiades (311-314)
Sylvester I (314-335)
Marcus (Jan.-Oct. 336)
Liberius (352-366)
Damasus I (366-384)
Siricius (384-399)
Anastasius I (399-401)
Zosimus (417-418)
Boniface I (418-422)
Celestine I (422-432)
Sixtus III (432-440)
Leo I (440-461)
Hilarius (461-468)
Simplicius (468-483)
Felix III (II) (483-492)
Gelasius I (492-496)
Anastasius II (496-498)
Symmachus (498-514)
Hormisdas (514-523)

John I (523-526)
Felix IV (III) (526-530)
Boniface II (530-532)
John II (533-535)
Agapetus I ((535-536)
Silverius (536-537)
Vigilius (537-555)
Pelagius I (556-561)
John III (561-574)
Benedict I (575-579)
Pelagius II (579-590)
Gregory I (590-604)
Sabinian (604-606)
Boniface III (Feb.-Nov. 607)
Boniface IV (608-615)
Adeodatus I (615-618)
Boniface V (619-625)
Honorius I (625-638)
Severinus (May-Aug. 640)
John IV (640-642)
Theodore I (642-649)
Martin I (649-655)
Eugene I (655-657)
Vitalian (657-672)
Adeodatus II (672-676)
Donus (676-678)
Agatho (678-681)
Leo II (682-683)
Benedict II (684-685)
John V (685-686)
Conon (686-687)
Sergius I (687-701)
John VI (701-705)
John VII ((705-707)
Sisinnius (Jan.-Feb. 708)
Constantine (708-715)
Gregory II (715-731)
Gregory III (731-741)

Zachary (741-752)
Stephen II (III) (752-757)
Paul I (757-767)
Stephen III (IV) (768-772)
Adrian I (772-795)
Leo III (795-816)
Stephen IV (V) (816-817)
Paschal I (817-824)
Eugene II (824-827)
Valentine (Aug.-Sep. 827)
Gregory IV (827-844)
Sergius II (844-847)
Leo IV (847-855)
Benedict III (855-858)
Nicholas I (858-867)
Adrian II (867-872)
John VIII (872-882)
Marinus I (882-884)
Adrian III (884-885)
Stephen V (VI) (885-891)
Formosus (891-896)
Boniface VI (Apr. 896)
Stephen VI (VII) (896-897)
Romanus (Aug.-Nov. 897)
Theodore II (Nov.-Dec. 897)
John IX (898-900)
Benedict IV (900-903)
Leo V (Jul.-Dec. 903)
Sergius III (904-911)
Anastasius III (911-913)
Lando (913-914)
John X (914-928)
Leo VI (May-Dec. 928)
Stephen VII (VIII) (929-931)
John XI (931-935)
Leo VII (936-939)
Stephen VIII (IX) (939-942)
Marinus II (942-946)

Agapetus II (946-955)
John XII (955-963)
Leo VIII (963-965)
Benedict V (964-966)
John XIII (965-972)
Benedict VI (973-974)
Benedict VII (974-983)
John XIV (983-984)
John XV (985-996)
Gregory V (996-999)
Sylvester II (999-1003)
John XVII (Jun.-Dec. 1003)
John XVIII (1003-1009)
Sergius IV (1009-1012)
Benedict VIII (1012-1024)
John XIX (1024-1032)
Benedict IX (1032-1044)
Sylvester III (Jan.-Mar. 1045)
Benedict IX (Apr.-May 1045)
Gregory VI (1045-1046)
Clement II (1046-1047)
Benedict IX (1047-1048)
Damasus II (Jul.-Aug. 1048)
Leo IX (1049-1054)
Victor II (1055-1057)
Stephen IX (X) (1057-1058)
Nicholas II (1059-1061)
Alexander II (1061-1073)
Gregory VII (1073-1085)
Victor III (1086-1087)
Urban II (1088-1099)
Paschal II (1099-1118)
Gelasius II (1118-1119)
Callistus II (1119-1124)
Honorius II (1124-1130)
Innocent II (1130-1143)
Celestine II (1143-1144)
Lucius II (1144-1145)

Eugene III (1145-1153)
Anastasius IV (1153-1154)
Adrian IV (1154-1159)
Alexander III (1159-1181)
Lucius III (1181-1185)
Urban III (1185-1187)
Gregory VIII (1187)
Clement III (1187-1191)
Celestine III (1191-1198)
Innocent III (1198-1216)
Honorius III (1216-1227)
Gregory IX (1227-1241)
Celestine IV (Oct.-Nov. 1241)
Innocent IV (1243-1254)
Alexander IV (1254-1261)
Urban IV (1261-1264)
Clement IV (1265-1268)
Gregory X (1271-1276)
Innocent V (Jan.-Jun. 1276)
Adrian V (Jul.-Aug. 1276)
John XXI (1276-1277)
Nicholas III (1277-1280)
Martin IV (1281-1285)
Honorius IV (1285-1287)
Nicholas IV (1288-1292)
Celestine V (Jul.-Dec. 1294)
Boniface VIII (1294-1303)
Benedict XI (1303-1304)
Clement V (1305-1314)
John XXII (1316-1334)
Benedict XII (1334-1342)
Clement VI (1342-1352)
Innocent VI (1352-1362)
Urban V (1362-1370)
Gregory XI (1370-1378)
Urban VI (1378-1404)
Boniface IX (1389-1404)
Innocent VII (1404-1406)

Gregory XII (1406-1415)
Martin V (1417-1431)
Eugene IV (1431-1447)
Nicholas V (1447-1455)
Callistus III (1455-1458)
Pius II (1458-1464)
Paul II (1464-1471)
Sixtus IV (1471-1484)
Innocent VIII (1484-1492)
Alexander VI (1492-1503)
Pius III (Sep.-Oct. 1503)
Julius II (1503-1513)
Leo X (1513-1521)
Adrian VI (1522-1523)
Clement VII (1523-1534)
Paul III (1534-1549)
Julius III (1550-1555)
Marcellus II (Apr.-May. 1555)
Paul IV (1555-1559)
Pius IV (1559-1565)
Pius V (1566-1572)
Gregory XIII (1572-1585)
Sixtus V (1585-1590)
Urban VII (Sep. 1590)
Gregory XIV (1590-1591)
Innocent IX (Oct.-Nov. 1591)
Clement VIII (1592-1605)
Leo XI (Apr. 1605)
Paul V (1605-1621)
Gregory XV (1621-1623)
Urban VIII (1623-1644)
Innocent X (1644-1655)
Alexander VII (1655-1667)
Clement IX (1667-1669)
Clement X (1670-1676)
Innocent XI (1676-1689)
Alexander VIII (1689-1691)
Innocent XII (1691-1700)

Clement XI (1700-1721)
Innocent XIII (1721-1724)
Benedict XIII (1724-1730)
Clement XII (1730-1740)
Benedict XIV (1740-1758)
Clement XIII (1758-1769)
Clement XIV (1769-1774)
Pius VI (1775-1799)
Pius VII (1800-1823)
Leo XII (1823-1829)
Pius VIII (1829-1830)
Gregory XVI (1831-1846)
Pius IX (1846-1878)
Leo XIII (1878-1903)
Pius X (1903-1914)
Benedict XV (1914-1922)
Pius XI (1922-1939)
Pius XII (1939-1958)
John XXIII (1958-1963)
Paul VI (1963-1978)
John Paul I (Aug.-Sep. 1978)
John Paul II (1978-)

Source: "Annuario Pontificio," in Felician A. Foy, ed., *1991 Catholic Almanac*, (Huntington, IN: Our Sunday Visitor, 1990), 126-128.

A leading commentator on the history of the Popes is J. N. D. Kelly in *The Oxford Dictionary of the Popes* (Oxford: Oxford University Press, 1986).

BIBLIOGRAPHY

Akin, James. "The Office of the New Testament Priest." Unpublished paper, 1995.

Albright, W. F. and Mann, C. S. *The Anchor Bible: Matthew*. Garden City, NY: Doubleday, 1971.

Alford, Henry, *The New Testament for English Readers*. Grand Rapids, MI: Baker, 1983.

Allnatt, Charles F. B., ed. *Cathedra Petri—The Titles and Prerogatives of St. Peter*. London: Burns & Oates, 1879.

Augustine. *Saint Augustine Letters*, vol. 1, trans. Wilfrid Parsons, in Roy J. Deferrari, ed., *The Fathers of the Church*, vol. 12. New York: Fathers of the Church, Inc., 1951.

Baima, Thomas A. "Papal Claims: Beyond the Misconceptions." *Touchstone* 5.2 (1992).

Carson, Donald A. III. *Matthew*, in Kenneth L. Barker and John Kohlenberger, eds. *Zondervan NIV Bible Commentary—New Testament*, vol. 2. Grand Rapids, MI: Zondervan, 1994.

Barnes, Albert. *Notes on the New Testament*, ed. Robert Frew. Grand Rapids, MI: Baker, 1973.

Barnstone, Willis. *The Other Bible*. San Francisco, CA: Harper & Row, 1984. [Contains the *Letter to Flora* by Ptolemaeus, in Epiphanius, *Pan. haer.* xxxiii 3-7, 190, from Robert M. Grant, *Gnosticism*, New York: Harper & Brothers, 1961.]

Bermant, Chaim. *The Walled Garden: The Saga of Jewish Family Life and Tradition*. New York: Macmillan, 1975.

Benedictine Monks of St. Augustine's Abbey, Ramsgate. *The Book of Saints*, 6th ed. Wilton, CN: Morehouse, 1989.

Berington, Joseph and John Kirk, eds., rev. James Waterworth, *The Faith of Catholics: The Rule of Faith Confirmed by Scripture*, 2 volumes, 2nd ed. New York: Pustet & Co., 1884.

Bivin, B. "Queries and Comments." *Biblical Archaeology Review* 19:3 (May/June 1993).

Black, Matthew and H. H. Rowley, eds. *Peake's Commentary on the Bible*. London: Thomas Nelson, 1972.

Blomberg, Craig L. *The New American Commentary: Matthew*, vol. 22. Nashville: Broadman, 1992.

Boring, M. Eugene. "Matthew," in Pheme Perkins and others, eds., *The New Interpreter's Bible*, vol. 8. Nashville, TN: Abingdon Press, 1995.

Broadus, John A. *Commentary on the Gospel of Matthew*. Valley Forge, PA: Judson Press, 1886.

Brown, Colin. "The Gates of Hell and the Church," in James E. Bradley and Richard A. Muller, eds. *Church, Word, and Spirit*. Grand Rapids, MI: Eerdmans, 1987.

Brown, Raymond E., Karl P. Donfried, and John Reumann. *Peter in the New Testament*. Minneapolis, MN: Augsburg; New York: Paulist: 1973.

Bruce, F. F. *The Book of Acts*. Grand Rapids, MI: Eerdmans, 1988.

_____. *The Hard Sayings of Jesus*. Downers Grove, IL: Intervarsity, 1983.

Brusher, Joseph S. *Popes Through the Ages*, 3rd ed. San Rafael, CA: Neff-Kane, 1980.

Bunson, Matthew, ed. *Our Sunday Visitor's Encyclopedia of Catholic History*. Huntington, IN: 1995.

Butler, B. C. *The Church and Infallibility*. New York: Sheed & Ward, 1954.

Buttrick, George Arthur and others, eds. *The Interpreter's Bible*. New York: Abingdon, 1951.

Calvin, John. *Calvin's New Testament Commentaries—The Harmony of the Gospels Matthew, Mark, and Luke*, vol. 2, trans. T. H. L. Parker, ed. David W. Torrance and Thomas F. Torrance. Grand Rapids, MI: Eerdmans, 1972.

_____. *Commentary on the Book of the Prophet Isaiah*, vol. 2, trans. William Pringle. Grand Rapids, MI: Eerdmans, 1948.

Caragounis, Chrys C. *Peter and the Rock*. New York: Walter de Gruyter, 1990.

Carson, D. A. "Matthew," in Gaebelein, Frank E., ed. *The Expositor's Bible Commentary: Volume 8 (Matthew, Mark, Luke)*. Grand Rapids, MI: Zondervan, 1984.

Casciaro, Jose Maria and others, eds. *The Navarre Bible: The Gospel of Saint John*. Dublin: Four Courts Press, 1992.

_____. *The Navarre Bible: The Acts of the Apostles*. Dublin: Four Courts Press, 1992.

Catechism of the Catholic Church. London: Geoffrey Chapman—Libreria Editrice Vaticana, 1994.

Cathcart, Kevin, Martin McNamara, and Michael Maher, eds. *The Aramaic Bible: the Targums*, trans. Martin McNamara. Collegeville, MN: Liturgical, 1992.

Chamblin, J. Knox. "Matthew," in Walter A. Elwell, ed. *Evangelical Commentary on the Bible*. Grand Rapids, MI: Baker, 1989.

Chapman, Dom John. *Bishop Gore and the Catholic Claims*. New York: Longmans, 1905.

_____. *Studies on the Early Church*. Port Washington, NY: Kennikat Press, 1928.

_____. *Studies on the Early Papacy*. London: Sheed & Ward, 1928.

_____. "The Condemnation of Pope Honorius." *Dublin Review* (July-October, 1906).

_____. *The First Eight General Councils and Papal Infallibility*, 3rd ed. London: Catholic Truth Society, 1928.

Coats, George W. *Moses: Heroic Man, Man of God*. Sheffield, UK: Sheffield Academic Press, 1988.

Confraternity of Christian Doctrine. *The New American Bible*, (Giant Print Edition). Huntington, IN: Our Sunday Visitor, 1988.

Cullmann, Oscar. *Peter: Disciple, Apostle, Martyr*, trans. Floyd V. Filson. Philadelphia: Westminster, 1953.

Davies, W. D. and Dale C. Allison. *A Critical and Exegetical Commentary on the Gospel according to Saint Matthew*, vol. 11, in J. A. Emerton, C. E. B. Cranfield, and G. N. Stanton, eds. *The International Critical Commentary*. Edinburgh: Clark, 1991.

Deferrari, Roy J., ed. *The Fathers of the Church*, vol. 12, *Saint Augustine Letters*, vol. I (1-82), trans. Wilfrid Parsons. New York: Fathers of the Church, Inc., 1951.

Delaney, John J. and James Edward Tobin. *Dictionary of Catholic Biography*. Garden City, NY: Doubleday, 1961.

De Vaux, Roland. *Ancient Israel*, trans. John McHugh. New York: McGraw-Hill, 1961.

Di Berardino, Angelo, ed. *Encylclopedia of the Early Church*, trans. Adrian Walford. Cambridge: James Clarke & Co., 1992.

Dietrich, Suzanne de. *The Layman's Bible Commentary: Matthew*, vol. 16, trans. Donald G. Miller. Atlanta: John Knox Press, 1961.

Doyle, Stephen. *The Pilgrim's New Guide to the Holy Land*. Collegeville, MN: Liturgical Press, 1985.

Du Pont, J. "Le logion des douze trones," [trans. Bernadeane Carr, STL, 7/15/93]. *Biblica* 45 (1962).

Earle, Ralph. "Matthew," in A. F. Harper, W. M. Greathouse, Ralph Earle, and W. T. Purkiser, eds., *Beacon Bible Commentary*, vol.6. Kansas City, MO: Beacon Hill, 1964.

Early Christian Writings—The Apostolic Fathers, trans. Maxwell Staniforth. New York: Dorset Press, 1968.

Empie, Paul C. and T. Austin Murphy. *Papal Primacy and the Universal Church—Lutherans and Catholics in Dialogue V*. Minneapolis: Augsburg, 1974.

Encyclopaedia Britannica, The, 11th ed. Cambridge: Cambridge University, 1910-1911.

Encyclopaedia Judaica, 1971 ed. Jerusalem: Keter Publishing House, 1971.

Epiphanius. *The Panarion of St. Epiphanius, Bishop of Salamis: Selected Passages*, ed. and trans. Philip R. Amidon. New York: Oxford, 1990.

Eusebius. *The History of the Church from Christ to Constantine*, trans. G. A. Williamson. New York: Barnes & Noble, 1965.

_____. *History of the Church, Book 3, Chapter 24* in *The Ecclesiastical History of Eusebius Pamphilus: Bishop of Caesarea in Palestine*, trans. Christian F. Cruse. Grand Rapids, MI: Baker, 1991.

Farmer, William R. and Roch Kereszty. *Peter and Paul in the Church of Rome*. New York: Paulist, 1990.

Fitzmyer, Joseph A. *To Advance the Gospel*. New York: Crossroad, 1981.

_____. *A Wandering Aramean: Collected Aramaic Essays*. Ann Arbor, MI: Edwards Brothers, 1979.

Forberg, Tord. "Peter—the High Priest of the new Covenant?" *The East Asia Journal of Theology* 4:1 (1986).

Foy, Felician, ed. *1991 Catholic Almanac*. Huntington, IN: Our Sunday Visitor, 1990.

France, R. T. *The Gospel According to Matthew: An Introduction and Commentary*. Grand Rapids, MI: Eerdmans, 1989.

_____. *Matthew: Evangelist and Teacher*. Grand Rapids, MI: Zondervan, 1989.

Freedman, David Noel and others, eds. *The Anchor Bible Dictionary*. New York: Doubleday, 1992.

Freudmann, Lillian. "Paul Undermined Torah." *Bible Review* 9:4 (August 1993).

Friedrich, Gerhard, ed. and Geoffrey W. Bromley, trans. and ed. *Theological Dictionary of the New Testament*. Grand Rapids, MI: Eerdmans, 1968.

Fuller, Reginald C., Leonard Johnston, and Conleth Kearns, eds. *A New Catholic Commentary on Holy Scripture*. Nashville: Thomas Nelson, 1969.

Gasser, Vinzenz. "The Official Relatio on Infallibility of Bishop Vincent Gasser at Vatican Council I," in James T. O'Connor, trans. and ed., *The Gift of Infallibility*. Boston: Daughters of St. Paul, 1986.

Giles, E. ed. *Documents Illustrating Papal Authority—A.D. 96-454*. London: S.P.C.K., 1952.

Goldstein, David. *What Say You?* St. Paul, MN: Radio Replies, 1945.

Green, Jay P. Sr., ed. and trans. *The Interlinear Hebrew-Greek-English Bible One Volume Carrying Edition*. London: Trinitarian, 1981.

Guthrie, D., J. A. Motyer, A. M. Stibbs, and D. J. Wiseman. *The New Bible Commentary*. Grand Rapids, MI: Eerdmans, 1953 [reprinted by Inter-Varsity Press].

Hagner, Donald A. *Matthew 14-28*, in David A. Hubbard, Glenn W. Barker, John D. W. Watts, Ralph P. Martin, eds. *Word Biblical Commentary*, vol. 33b. Dallas: Word Books, 1995.

Hendriksen, William. *New Testament Commentary: Exposition of the Gospel According to Matthew*. Grand Rapids, MI: Baker, 1973.

Henry, Matthew. *Matthew Henry's Commentary: Matthew to John*, vol. 5. McLean, VA: MacDonald, n.d. [originally published 1721].

Herbermann, Charles G. and others. *The Catholic Encyclopedia*. New York: Robert Appleton Co., 1907; The Encyclopedia Press, 1913.

Hergenrother, Dr. *Anti-Janus: An Historico-Theological Criticism f The Work, Entitled 'The Pope And The Council', By Janus.* Dublin: W. B. Kelly, 1870.

Hill, David. "The Gospel of Matthew," in Ronald E. Clements and Matthew Black, eds., *The New Century Bible Commentary.* London: Marshall, Morgan & Scott, 1972.

Hyland, St. George Kieran. "The Papal Supremacy During the First Three Centuries." *The Irish Ecclesiastical Record* (July 1908).

Ide, Arthur. "An Apology for the Petrine Doctrine." M.A. thesis. University of Northern Iowa, 1968.

Jaki, S. L. *And On This Rock*, 2nd ed. Manassas, VA: Trinity, 1987.

Jaki, Stanley L. *The Keys of the Kingdom.* Chicago: The Franciscan Herald, 1986.

Jamieson, Robert, Andrew Robert Fausset, and David Brown. *One Volume Commentary.* Grand Rapids, MI: Associated Publishers, n.d. [197?].

Jerome. *The Homilies of Saint Jerome, Volume 1*, trans. Marie L. Ewald, in *The Fathers of the Church*, vol. 48. Washington, DC: Catholic University, 1964.

_____. "The Apology Against the Books of Rufinus," *Saint Jerome—Dogmatic and Polemical Works*, trans. Joseph N. Hritzu, in Roy Joseph Deferrari, ed., *The Fathers of the Church*, vol. 53:47. Washington, DC: Catholic University, 1965.

Jugie, Martin. "Doctrine of Saint John Damascene on the Church [in French]." *Echos d' Orient* (October, 1924) [trans. John Collorafi].

Jurgens, W. A., ed. *The Faith of the Early Fathers*, vols. 1-3. Collegeville, MN: Liturgical, 1970.

Keener, Craig S. *The IVP Bible Background Commentary New Testament*. Downer's Grove, IL: Intervarsity Press, 1993.

Kelly, J. N. D. *The Oxford Dictionary of the Popes*. Oxford: Oxford University Press, 1986.

Lachs, S. T. *A Rabbinic Commentary on the New Testament: The Gospels of Matthew, Mark, and Luke*. Hoboken, NJ: Ktav, 1987.

Lange, John Peter. *Lange's Commentary on the Holy Scriptures: The Gospel According to Matthew*, trans. Philip Schaff. Grand Rapids, MI: Zondervan, 1976.

Lapide, Cornelius A. *The Great Commentary upon the Holy Scriptures*, trans. Thomas W. Mossman. London: John Hodges, 1893.

Levine, Etan. *The Aramaic Version of the Bible*. New York: Walter de Gruyter, 1988.

Likoudis, James. *Ending the Byzantine Greek Schism*. New Rochelle, NY: Catholics United for the Faith, 1992.

Lindsay, Colin. *The Evidence for the Papacy*. London: Longmans, Green, 1870.

Lumen Gentium (Constitution on the Church, November 21, 1964). Washington, DC: United States Catholic Conference, n.d.

Luther, Martin. "The Keys," in Conrad Bergendoff, ed., *Luther's Works*, trans. Earl Beyer and Conrad Bergendoff, vol. 40. Philadelphia: Fortress, 1958.

Madrid, Patrick, ed. *Surprised by Truth*. San Diego, CA: Basilica Press, 1994.

Maier, Gerhard. "The Church in the Gospel of Matthew: Hermeneutical Analysis of the Current Debate," trans. Harold H. P. Dressler, in D.A. Carson, ed., *Biblical Interpretation and Church Text and Context*. Flemington Markets, NSW: Paternoster Press, 1984.

Malone, Michael. *The Apostolic Digest*. Irving, TX: Sacred Heart, 1987.

May, Herbert G. and Bruce M. Metzger, eds. *The New Oxford Annotated Bible, with Apocrypha*, Revised Standard Version. New York: Oxford, 1977.

McCumber, William E. "Matthew," in William M. Greathouse and Willard H. Taylor, eds., *Beacon Bible Expositions*, vol. 1. Kansas City, MO: Beacon Hill, 1975.

McDonnell, Kilian. "Papal Primacy: Development, Centralization, and Changing Styles," in Paul C. Empie and T. Austin Murphy, *Papal Primacy and the Universal Church—Lutherans and Catholics in Dialogue V*. Minneapolis: Augsburg, 1974.

McCue, James F. "The Roman Primacy in the Apostolic Era—The Beginnings Through Nicaea," in Paul C. Empie, and T. Austin Murphy, *Papal Primacy and the Universal Church—Lutherans and Catholics in Dialogue V*. Minneapolis: Augsburg, 1974.

Menzies, Allan, ed. *Ante-Nicene Fathers—Origen, et al.*, 4th ed., vol. 9. Peabody, MA: Hendrickson, 1994.

Meyendorff, J., A. Schmemann, N. Afanassieff, and N. Koulomzine. *The Primacy of Peter*. Aylesbury, Bucks, UK: The Faith Press, 1973.

Meyendorff, John, ed. *The Primacy of Peter*. Crestwood, NY: St. Vladimir's Seminary Press, 1992 [revised and expanded from 1992 edition].

Millgram, Abraham E. *Jewish Worship*. Philadelphia: Jewish Publication Society, 1971.

Morgan, G. Campbell. *The Acts of the Apostles*. Tarrytown, NY: Revell, 1924.

Murray, Robert. *Symbols of Church and Kingdom: A Study in Early Syriac Tradition*. London: Cambridge, 1975.

Myers, Allen C., ed. *The Eerdmans Bible Dictionary*. Grand Rapids, MI: Eerdmans, 1987.

New Catholic Encyclopedia, vol. 14. New York: McGraw-Hill, 1967. Neusner, Jacob. *First-Century Judaism in Crisis*. Nashville: Abingdon Press, 1975.

Oesterley, W. O. E., trans. *The Sayings of the Jewish Fathers (Pirke Aboth)*. New York: Macmillan, 1919.

Ott, Ludwig. *Fundamentals of Catholic Dogma*, 4th ed. (1960). Rockford, IL: TAN, 1974.

Migne, J. P. *Patrologiae cursus completus, Series graeca* [*PG*]. 161 volumes, Paris, 1857-1866 [part. trans. Bernadeane Carr, S.T.L., Fr. Mitchell Pacwa, S.J., and John Collorafi].

Migne, J. P. *Patrologiae cursus completus, Series latina* [*PL*]. 221 volumes, Paris, 1844-1855 [part. trans. John Collorafi].

Ridderbos, Herman N. *Bible Student's Commentary: Matthew*. Grand Rapids, MI: Zondervan, 1987.

Ripley, Francis J. *The Pope: Vicar of Jesus Christ*. Dublin: Catholic Truth Society, 1965.

Rivington, Luke. *The Primitive Church and the See of St. Peter*. (London: Longmans, Green and Co., 1894).

Roberts, Alexander and James Donaldson, eds., *Ante-Nicene Fathers*, vol. 1—*Apostolic Fathers, Justin Martyr, Irenaeus*. N.p.: Christian Literature Pub. Co., 1885; repr., Peabody, MA: Hendrickson, 1994.

Robinson, J. A. T. *Redating the New Testament*. Philadelphia: Westminster, 1976 [wherein Robinson believes that all twenty-seven books of the New Testament were written prior to the destruction of the Temple in 70 A.D.].

Sabourin, Leopold. *The Gospel According to St. Matthew*, vol. 1. Bandra, India: Bombay St. Paul Society, 1982.

Schaff, Philip. *Lange's Commentary on the Holy Scriptures: The Gospel According to Matthew*, vol. 8. Grand Rapids, MI: Zondervan, 1976.

Schaff, Philip, ed. *Nicene and Post-Nicene Fathers—Augustin: Homilies on the Gospel of John, Homilies on the First Epistle of John, Soliloquies*, 1st series, vol. 7. N.p.: Christian Literature Pub. Co., 1888; repr. Peabody, MA: Hendrickson, 1994.

Schaff, Philip, ed. *The Nicene and Post-Nicene Fathers of the Christian Church*, vol. 13, *Saint Chrysostom: Homilies on Galatians*, trans. Gross Alexander. Repr., Grand Rapids: Eerdmans; Edinburgh: T. & T. Clark, 1991.

Schaff, Philip and Henry Wace, eds. *Nicene and Post-Nicene Fathers*, 2nd series, 14 vols. New York: Charles Scribner's Sons, 1900; repr., Peabody, MA: Hendrickson, 1994.

Scott, S. Herbert. *The Eastern Churches and the Papacy*. London: Sheed & Ward, 1928.

Shelton, James B. Letter to authors, 21 October 1994.

Shotwell, James T. and Louise Ropes Loomis. *The See of Peter*. New York: Columbia University, 1991.

Simpson, J. A. and E. S. C. Weiner, eds. *The Oxford English Dictionary*, 2nd ed. Oxford: Oxford University, 1989.

Singer, Isidore, ed. *The Jewish Encyclopedia*, vol. 12. Hoboken, NJ: Ktav, 1964.

Solovyev, Vladimir. *Russia and the Universal Church*. London: Geoffrey Bles, 1948.

Stanford, Derek and Muriel Spark, eds. *The Letters of John Henry Newman*. Baltimore: Newman Press, 1957.

Staples, Tim. Letter to authors, 10 October 1994, 1-2.

Stern, David H. *Jewish New Testament Commentary*. Clarksville, MD: Jewish New Testament Publications, 1992.

Stravinskas, Peter M. J., ed. *Our Sunday Visitor's Catholic Encyclopedia*. Huntington, IN: Our Sunday Visitor, 1991.

Sukenik, E. L. *Ancient Synagogues in Palestine and Greece*. London: OUP, 1934.

Sungenis, Robert A. "The Precedent for Infallibility." Letter to authors, November 1993.

_____. "The Succession Motif in the Landowner/Servant Parables." Letter to authors, February 1994.

_____. "John 21:15-17." Letter to authors, June 1994.

_____. "The Palace Administrator." Letter to authors, June 1994.

_____. "Will the Real Rock Please Stand Up?" Letter to authors, June 1994.

_____. Letter to Greg Krehbiel, 22 September 1994.

_____. Letter to authors, 15 December 1994.

_____. Letter to authors, 13 January 1995.

_____. Letter to authors, 21 January 1995.

_____. Letter to authors, 16 March 1995.

_____. "Will the Real Rock Please Stand Up!" *The Catholic Answer* 9:2 (May/June 1995).

_____. "The Biblical Basis for Papal Succession." Letter to authors, 22 May 1995.

_____. "The Use of the Greek *Poimanao* in John 21:16." Letter to authors, 2 June 1995.

_____. "James's Use of the Imperative Mood in Acts 15:14." Letter to authors, 28 July 1995.

_____. Letter to authors, 7 November 1995.

Vaughn, Herbert Cardinal. *Ten Lectures delivered in Free Trade Hall, Manchester.* Manchester, UK: John Heywood, Excelsior Printing and Bookbinding Works, 1896.

Von Balthasar, Hans Urs. *The Office of Peter and the Structure of the Church*, trans. Andrée Emery. San Francisco, CA: Ignatius, 1986.

Waterworth, J. *A Commentary by Writers of the First Five Centuries on the Place of St. Peter in the New Testament and that of St. Peter's Successors in the Church.* London: Thomas Richardson, 1871.

Webster, William. *Peter and the Rock.* Battle Ground, WA: Christian Resources, 1996.

Wicks, Jared, ed. and trans. *Cajetan Responds.* Washington, DC: Catholic University, 1978.

Wigoder, Geoffrey and others, eds. *The Encyclopedia of Judaism.* Jerusalem: Jerusalem Publishing, 1989.

Willoughby, C. Allen. *The International Critical Commentary: St. Matthew.* Edinburgh: T. & T. Clark, 1977.

Winter, Michael M. *Saint Peter and the Popes.* Baltimore: Helicon, 1960.

INDEX OF QUESTIONS

JESUS, PETER AND THE KEYS

INDEX OF CITATIONS

Sacred Scripture

OLD TESTAMENT

NEW TESTAMENT

INDEX OF AUTHORS

INDEX OF PERSONS

JESUS, PETER AND THE KEYS

INDEX OF SUBJECTS

M

*Magisterial teaching
(Magisterium); xii, 72, 202*
Majordomo; 41, 46
Midrash (fragments); 8, 105, 157
*Ministry; xiv, 13, 65, 68, 80, 82,
85, 113, 125, 167, 174, 205, 341*
Mishna; 154, 155
Mitzvot; 207
Monophysitism; 266, 268
Monothelitism; 272, 276, 353
*Moses' Seat; 153, 154-160, 165,
182*
Mt. Hermon; 14

N

Nestorianism; 259
*New Testament; xi, xiv, 3, 6, 11,
14-16, 23, 26, 29, 49, 69, 72,
79, 82, 92, 96, 97, 100, 101,
114, 120, 125-127, 140, 142,
149, 155, 171, 186-189, 192,
193, 195, 210, 211, 212, 229,
359, 360, 361, 368, 372*
*Nicaea, Council of (also Nice);
175, 308*
*Noachide covenant(also Noachide
Laws); 103, 107, 109*
*Noachide Laws (also Noachide
Covenant); 102-107*

O

*Old Testament; xx, 6, 22, 44, 49,
54, 78, 82, 99, 152, 155, 157,
172, 186, 188, 189, 191, 210,
362*
Ordain; 74, 183, 190, 324
Overseer; 46, 81, 87

P

*Petra; 9, 10, 13, 15, 17-23, 28,
30-32, 35, 36, 251, 252, 257,
263, 264, 317, 363*
*Petros; 13, 15, 17-24, 26-32, 35,
36, 363*
*Papacy; ix, xii, xv, xvii, xxi, 3, 37,
46, 56, 156, 212, 269, 274, 329,
352, 360, 361*
Pelagianism; 253
*Persecution; 278, 307, 345, 360,
369*
*Pharisees; 63, 153, 154, 157,
158, 159, 160*
*plenary authority; 46, 47, 71,
258*
*Pontiff (Roman) (see also Pope,
Bishop of Rome, Patriarch of
the West); 64, 66, 72, 76, 91,
136, 137, 179, 201, 203, 260,
314, 351, 357*
*Pope; 17, 66, 72, 74, 76-78, 82,
84-86, 91, 97, 98, 110, 135,
137-139, 148, 151, 159, 160,
163, 165, 173, 179, 181-183,
196, 199-202, 217, 218, 223,
230, 233, 237-239, 246, 253,
255, 257, 258, 260, 261, 265-
267, 269, 270, 272, 275, 276,
278, 284-287, 290, 292, 300-
303, 305, 309, 314, 317, 320,
322, 324, 328, 331, 333, 334,
336-338, 340-347, 352-354,
357, 446, 450*
Pre-eminence; 4, 91, 220, 236
Presbuteros; 83, 88, 186, 187
*Priest (also presbuteros, presby-
ter, elder); 4, 13, 79, 82, 84,
87, 88, 112, 130, 152, 153, 154,
156, 159-161, 163, 187, 188,*

ENDORSEMENTS

This book is an invaluable tool for anyone willing to study – with an open mind – the meaning of Jesus' words in Mt. 16:17-19 in the light of their Old Testament background. The amount of useful and pertinent data in this veritable compendium is simply staggering. Whoever ignores it consigns his own work to irrelevance. In short, this book gives to the ongoing debate over Petrine primacy and succession a much sharper focus, and a new point of departure.

Scott Hahn, Ph.D.
Theology Department, Franciscan University of Steubenville

No longer may Protestants exclaim *"Sola Scriptura"* to rebuke Roman Catholic Papal dogma. Butler, Dahlgren, and Hess, have assembled an impressive work. The authority of Scripture is presented as a convincing apologetic for the Primacy of Peter. The Patristic evidence included in Part Two is clearly intended to support the Biblical evidence with historical precedence. This work demands serious attention by all students of Scripture and theology.

Rev. S.D. deHart
Adjunct Professor of Theology, St. Leo College
Rector, St. Andrew's (traditional) Episcopal Church, Gainsville, FL

Jesus, Peter and the Keys raises issues that no serious student of the Bible can blithely ignore. The time has come for Protestants to set aside their aversions to Roman Catholicism which color their interpretation of the New Testament and let the text speak for itself. When one does so, the prominent and pre-eminent role of Peter among the apostles stands out clearly. This should be the first step in honest dialogue among divided brethren wishing to mend the tear in the seamless robe of Christ.

James B. Shelton, Ph.D., Associate Professor
Oral Roberts University, School of Theology and Mission

If you wish to find the simplest hypothesis that explains the most data from Scripture and the early Church, and if, for the sake of the search, you are willing to entertain the hypothesis that our Lord intended something like the Roman Papacy from the beginning of His earthly ministry, the results are startling. Bible verses suddenly leap to life with hitherto unimagined significance, and the once confusing jigsaw puzzle of early Church history comes together into a picture of disarming clarity. *Jesus, Peter and the Keys* serves up an avalanche of incontrovertible evidence, more overwhelming than any single argument – much of it, remarkably, culled from **Protestant** sources. The book is a bombshell.

Philip Blosser, Ph.D.
Professor of Philosophy, Associate Director, Center for Theology,
Lenoir-Rhyne College (Lutheran–ELCA)

While still an evangelical Protestant, I was dismayed to find that the Catholic Church could consistently serve up a devastating "one-two punch" of Biblical and patristic evidence in support of her doctrines. In this study, Butler, Dahlgren, and Hess have shown definitively that the papacy is no exception.

David Palm, Trinity Theological Seminary (Baptist) Graduate

Decades ago, T.S. Eliot declared, "In my beginning is my end."
In scholarly, professional and ecumenically sensitive manner, our authors examine the scriptural basis for the Petrine office, that ministry which Pope Paul VI frankly admitted was *the* major stumbling block to the reunion of all Christians. But like the Pontiff, these men also regard it as *the* essential basis for any true unity

grounded in the saving plan and will of Christ for His Church.

Like Eliot returning to the sources, they help all – those in full communion with the See of Rome and those who are not — to rediscover the scriptural foundations of the papacy. For this service, they deserve an open hearing – and a grateful one.

Rev. Peter M.J. Stravinskas, Ph.D., S.T.D.
Editor, *The Catholic Answer*

Some people call ours the post-Christian era. The people of the world are seriously divided. The scandal of particularity plagues the Christian Church with centuries old arguments for division.

But the readers of this Scriptural handbook will gain certain knowledge that Christ's authority over the Church is supreme and it continues to this day. He appointed leaders for the Church beginning with the Apostle Peter.

Christians will find unity and direction only as they obey the leaders Christ appoints through the leading of the Holy Spirit in the Holy Catholic Church. The historical sources quoted in the handbook give important evidence of that fact.

Rev. Kent W. Kinney
Associate Pastor, First Presbyterian Church, Lake Forest, IL

Jesus, Peter and the Keys is an excellent resource for discussion of this most important theological issue. Its starting point is a detailed examination of the Scriptural evidence, with careful grammatical analysis, exposition of the vocabulary and historical background. The authors gathered an enormous amount of data from widely diverse sources: Messianic and Orthodox Jews; protestant Reformers Martin Luther and John Calvin and Counter-reformers like Cardinal Cajetan; Protestant and Catholic Scripture scholars; classical and recent scholarship. After gathering rich information, the authors push the data to the logical conclusions about the role of the Papacy. The information is invaluable and the conclusions inevitable. Buy this book!

Fr. Mitchell C. Pacwa, S.J., Ph.D.
Professor of Sacred Scripture, University of Dallas
Institute of Religious and Pastoral Studies

Visit your local bookstore for other great titles from:
QUEENSHIP PUBLISHING